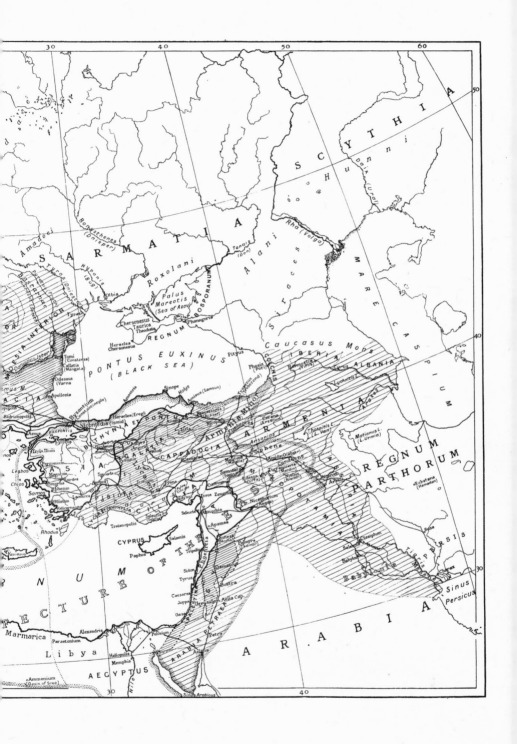

IMPERIAL ROME

NILSSON

IMPERIAL ROME

I. MEN AND EVENTS
II. THE EMPIRE AND ITS INHABITANTS

TRANSLATED FROM THE SWEDISH OF

MARTIN P. NILSSON

PROFESSOR OF CLASSICAL ARCHAEOLOGY AND ANCIENT HISTORY
IN THE UNIVERSITY OF LUND
AUTHOR OF "PRIMITIVE TIME-RECKONING,"
"A HISTORY OF THE GREEK RELIGION," ETC.

BY

G. C. RICHARDS, D.D.

FELLOW OF ORIEL COLLEGE, OXFORD

ARES   PUBLISHERS   INC.
CHICAGO   MCMLXXIV

Unchanged Reprint of the Edition:
London, 1926.
ARES   PUBLISHERS   INC.
150 E. Huron Street
Chicago, Illinois 60611
Printed in the United States of America
International Standard Book Number:
0-89005-054-6
Library of Congress Catalog Card Number:
74-82060

PREFACE

THE fall of the Roman Empire is the greatest tragedy in the history of the world. Before and since that catastrophe, empires have been destroyed and peoples wiped out; but the Roman Empire contained the only highly-developed civilisation embracing different peoples, before our own, which deserves to be called a world-civilisation. This vanished along with the Empire, and for many centuries humanity was thrown back into a far more primitive stage of spiritual and material, political and economic life. Other periods in the history of the world have been chiefly remarkable for the phenomena of development and progress; but it is only in the Roman Empire, on a large scale, that we can follow and study their opposite—a. decline—the forces that bring about retrogression in all phases of the life of states and individuals, the dissolution of civilisation and the community. Herein lies the unique interest and value of this period of history.

The cause of the fall of the Roman Empire has long been debated as an attractive and fascinating problem. Formerly it used to be simply accounted for by the racial movements which overthrew the Empire; but the Germanic hordes were not such swarms of devastating locusts, as they are popularly represented. If the Empire had not been rotten internally, it would not have been destroyed by the storms from without. It is this internal process of decay and dissolution which really explains the decline and fall of the ancient world-civilisation and the world-wide Empire of Rome.

We are without a popular and comprehensive survey of the Roman imperial period and its problems in their full extent; but the process of investigation, assisted by finds of inscriptions and papyri, has been so thorough and far-reaching that an attempt can now be made to trace the main lines of development in their various aspects from beginning to end.

An examination of the internal condition of the Empire from the social, economic, and cultural points of view has been my chief object. But it was necessary, to attain a true perspective, that this should be preceded by a survey of events, and a description of the Roman world power as a civilising force. The final catastrophe is delineated against this really brilliant background. In a further volume, which I hope will be published in England at a later date, I have dealt with the administration of the Empire and its Finance, with its Social order, with its Educational systems, and with the clash of the Pagan and Christian religions.

In the autumn of 1915 I examined the domestic history of the imperial period in a course of University lectures. Even at that time it was impossible to anticipate that the events of the next few months and years would so vividly illuminate its problems, and make them so astonishingly realistic. I neither can nor will deny that the experiences of the war and the history of those critical days have left their impress on my book. For the historical events which one observes as a contemporary, strike the imagination with a force and realism far removed from those which can be studied only in books and documents, however realistically one endeavours to visualise the life of antiquity, and lead to a far more concrete conception of similar problems in a past age.

I have endeavoured to give a broad survey of the Social Life of the Roman imperial age in all its aspects. In this age of specialism so comprehensive a task should rightly be distributed among half a dozen authors. As well as the historian, the archaeologist, the philologist, the philosopher, the economist, the student of religions and the theologian should each have his say. This plan is often followed in large and comprehensive historical works, but the result is that the common point of view is sacrificed. Each contributor pipes a tune of his own, and harmony is a secondary affair. I do not fail to recognise the risk entailed in a method directly opposed to this: it is not in the power of man to multiply his special qualifications as required. That I have ventured on this method, is due to my conviction that a complete picture must be given from a single point of view, and I have been confirmed in my opinion by the approbation and active support I have received from friends and colleagues.

With Professor Herman Nilsson Ehle, whose fame as one of the leading authorities on genetics is established, I have repeatedly discussed the main thesis and the details of one of the most difficult chapters, namely, that which deals with the problem of population.

MARTIN P. NILSSON.

CONTENTS

LIST OF ILLUSTRATIONS

CHRONOLOGICAL TABLE

B.C.

63. Sept. 22. C. Octavius (Octavianus Augustus) born.
44. March 15. C. Julius Caesar murdered.
43. Spring. The war round Mutina.
  Oct.–Nov. The Second Triumvirate.
42. Autumn. Battle of Philippi.
40. Feb. Fall of Perusia.
  Late summer. The Treaty of Brundisium.
37. The Treaty of Tarentum.
36. Sextus Pompeius conquered. Fall of Lepidus.
31. Sept. 2. Battle of Actium.
30. Aug. 1. Alexandria taken by Octavian.
27. Jan. 13. Legal constitution of the Empire.
20. The Parthians restore the standards and captives.
12. Death of M. Agrippa.
 9. Death of Drusus.
 2. Death of Lucius Caesar.

A.D.

4. Death of Gaius Caesar.
6–9. The rising in Pannonia.
9. The Battle in the Teutoburg Forest.
14. Aug. 19. Death of Augustus.
14–37. TIBERIUS.
19. Death of Germanicus.
31. Fall of Sejanus.
37–41. CALIGULA.
41–54. CLAUDIUS.
43–47. Conquest of Britain.
54–68. NERO.
59. Death of Agrippina.
62. Death of Afranius Burrus.
68–9. GALBA.
69. VITELLIUS : OTHO.
69–79. VESPASIAN.
70. Destruction of Jerusalem.
79–81. TITUS.
79. Eruption of Vesuvius. Pompeii and other cities destroyed.
81–96. DOMITIAN.
96–8. NERVA.
98–117. TRAJAN.
101–2, 105–6. Conquest of Dacia.
117–38. HADRIAN.
132–4. Insurrection of Bar-Kochba.
138–61. ANTONINUS PIUS.
161–80. MARCUS AURELIUS.

A.D.

161–9. LUCIUS VERUS.

162–6. War with the Parthians.

167–75.⎫
177–80.⎭ War with the Marcomanni, etc.

175. Insurrection of Avidius Cassius.

180–93. COMMODUS.

193. PERTINAX.
Didius Julianus.

193–211. SEPTIMIUS SEVERUS.

194. Pescennius Niger overcome.

197. Clodius Albinus overcome.

199. The province of Mesopotamia conquered.

202. City organisation introduced into Egypt.

211–17. CARACALLA.

212. Roman citizenship granted to all free inhabitants of the Empire.

217–18. MACRINUS.

218–22. HELIOGABALUS.

222–35. ALEXANDER SEVERUS.

226. The new Persian Empire (The Sassanids) set up.

235–38. MAXIMINUS THRAX.

238. GORDIANUS I. and II.
Balbinus and Pupienus.

238–44. GORDIANUS III.

244–49. PHILIPPUS ARABS.

249–51. DECIUS.

251–3. TREBONIANUS GALLUS.

253. AEMILIANUS.

253–7. VALERIANUS.

253–68. GALLIENUS.

256–8.⎫
262–7.⎭ Raids of the Goths.

258–68. Postumus Emperor in Gaul.

268–70. CLAUDIUS GOTHICUS.

270–75. AURELIAN.

272. Palmyra captured.

274. Gaul reunited with the Empire.

275–6. TACITUS.

276–82. PROBUS.

282–3. CARUS.

283. NUMERIANUS.

283–5. CARINUS.

284–305. DIOCLETIAN.

285–305. Maximian.

285. The Bagaudae subdued.

286–93. Carausius.

293. Constantius Chlorus and Galerius Caesars

A.D.
296.   Britain reunited to the Empire.
296–7. War with Persia.
301.   Publication of the tariff.
303.   Beginning of persecution of the Christians.
305–6. CONSTANTIUS CHLORUS.
305–11. GALERIUS.
306–37. CONSTANTINE THE GREAT.
306–12. Maxentius.
307–23. Licinius.
310.   Death of Maximian.
312.   Battle of Ponte Molle.
        Edict of Milan (toleration).
313.   Death of Diocletian.
        Maximinus Daja conquered and killed.
323.   CONSTANTINE (sole ruler).
325.   Council of Nicaea.
330.   Foundation of Constantinople.
337–40. Constantine II.
337–61. CONSTANTIUS.
337–50. Constans.
350–53. Magnentius.
350–54. Gallus Caesar.
355.   Athanasius condemned and exiled.
        Julian appointed Caesar.
357.   Victory over the Alamanni at Strasburg.
360–63. JULIAN.

West.	*East.*
A.D.	A.D.
364–75. VALENTINIAN I.	364–78. VALENS.
	365–6. PROCOPIUS.
375–83. GRATIAN.	378. Battle of Adrianople.
	379–95. THEODOSIUS I.
	381. Council of Constantinople. Arianism condemned. Settlement of dispute about the See of Constantinople.
383–92. VALENTINIAN II.	
383–8. Maximus.	
387. Valentinian II. driven out by Maximus.	
388. Valentinian II. restored as ruler in Gaul.	
392–4. EUGENIUS (Arbogars).	
395–423. HONORIUS.	395–408. ARCADIUS.
	395–7. Alaric's raid in Greece.

A.D.	West.	A.D.	East.
397.	Gildo's revolt.	400.	Rising against the Goths in Constantinople.
401–2.	Alaric's first march into Italy. Radagais' attack on Italy.		
406.	Germanic tribes cross the Rhine and settle in the Empire.		
408.	Fall of Stilicho.	408–50.	THEODOSIUS II.
410.	Rome taken by Alaric.		
412.	Visigoths in Gaul.		
413.	Burgundians settle in Palatinate.		
425–55.	VALENTINIAN III.		
429.	Vandals cross to Africa.		
		431.	Council of Ephesus. Nestorius deposed.
432.	Boniface arrives in Italy.		
433.	Aëtius returns.		
446.	Britain given up.		
		450–57.	MARCIAN.
451.	Battle of Châlons.		
453.	Death of Attila.		
454.	Aëtius killed.		
455.	Rome plundered by Genseric.		
455–6.	AVITUS.		
457–61.	MAJORIAN.	457–74.	LEO I.
461–5.	SEVERUS.		
467–72.	ANTHEMIUS.		
		471.	Aspar overthrown.
472.	Death of Ricimer.		
473–4.	GLYCERIUS.		
473–80.	JULIUS NEPOS.		
474.	Rising of Orestes.	474.	LEO II.
474–6.	ROMULUS AUGUSTULUS.	474–91.	ZENO.
476.	Aug. 23. Odoacer King of Italy.		
480.	Death of Julius Nepos.		
486.	Syagrius in Gaul overpowered, and killed by the Franks under Clovis.		

NOTE.—HS is the Roman symbol for the ordinary unit-coin, the sestertius or sesterce ; thus HS1000=1000 sestertii or sesterces. Quite often, in later times regularly, they reckoned in denarii (1 denarius or denare=4 sesterces), but for the sake of uniformity all amounts will be expressed in sesterces.

BOOK I
MEN AND EVENTS

IMPERIAL ROME

I

THE JULIO-CLAUDIAN HOUSE

THE act of tyrannicide that took place on March 15, 44 B.C., was a sensational one. Caesar had been a tyrant : of that there was no doubt. He had assumed the Roman title of Dictator, but he had exercised his power in the spirit of the Hellenistic kings. Like them he had caused his head to be stamped on the coinage of the Empire, and he had caused a Roman month and a Roman tribe to be called after his name, an honour which Greek cities paid to the Kings of Egypt and Syria. He had reduced the Senate to impotence, and when it laid at his feet the honours it had decreed him, he had no mind to relinquish the seat in which he proudly sat in front of the temple of Venus, from whom he claimed to be descended. Rumour asserted that he intended to humiliate Rome, the conqueror of the world, and to remove the capital of the empire to the East—nay, that he even desired to adopt the same title as the Kings of the East.

Among the murderers were Stoics. They had read in their books that when a tyrant fell, the liberated people would come forth with joy to welcome their liberators. What actually happened was very different. A paralysing terror fell upon the population of Rome. The streets were deserted. People shut themselves up and barricaded their houses. The tyrannicides took refuge in the Capitol, where the Romans had once defended themselves against the Gauls. No one knew what was to be done. The murderers had acted without

3   B 2

caring for, or thinking of, the consequences. The consul, Marcus Antonius, one of Caesar's closest intimates and co-adjutors, was one of those who shut themselves up, for he feared for his own life. The only man who could do anything was the Dictator's master of the horse, Lepidus, who com-manded a legion in the neighbourhood of Rome, and he lacked decision to seize the opportunity.

Only after two days did it become obvious that the murderers and the Senatorial party had no plans and were completely at a loss. Antonius ventured out. The Senate determined that the murderers should go unpunished, and that the acts of the Dictator should be ratified: not merely those which he had executed in his lifetime, but also those decisions for the future found in the papers he had left behind. These, together with Caesar's property, were seized by Antonius, who now occupied a strong position, and made use of the funeral of the Dictator to strike terror into the Senatorial party. He exhibited Caesar's blood-stained toga, pierced by daggers, and publicly declaimed his will, which provided for large gifts to the Roman populace. The people were stirred up to a state of frenzy, and attempted to storm the houses of the murderers. When this was prevented, crowds gathered in the Forum, erected a mighty pyre, and burnt on the spot the mortal remains of the Dictator. After this the murderers did not venture to remain in Rome, and made their escape. But Antonius had still to proceed with caution, for he had no army at his disposal, and only cold steel could decide the issue.

In the meantime a disturbing factor in the gamble for power came into prominence. In his will, Caesar had made Gaius Octavius, a youth of eighteen, the son of his sister's daughter, his chief heir and had adopted him. The news of his elevation reached Octavius at Apollonia in Illyria, where he was pursuing his studies. A family council dissuaded him from asserting his right to Caesar's name and inheritance; for a claim to Caesar's property and name would have carried with it a claim to be his political heir. Antonius had laid hands on both the personal and the political inheritance of Caesar, and had no idea of relinquishing them. The claim could only be made good by the sword, and what reliance could a youth of eighteen place upon that ? He did not belong to a distinguished family, but merely to the local gentry of the country town of Velitrae, and his father had been the first of the family to attain Senatorial rank.

But the youth soon came to a decision, and when he had made it, his family supported him. He adopted the designation Gaius Julius Caesar Octavianus, the last name being in memory of his actual father. Friends and relatives realised their property in order that he might have the means to pay Caesar's donations to the Roman populace, and to stage magnificent games in memory of his adopted father. During the games a comet appeared in the sky—the Julian star. This was taken as a sign by the people that Caesar had mounted to the heavenly place, and it shone before Octavian in his path. The name of Caesar had a magical power. The veterans gathered round the young Caesar and protested their devotion to him. The lad now became not merely an object of derision and mockery to Antonius, but so dangerous, that he felt it necessary to summon the Macedonian legions to Italy.

Civil war was imminent. Octavian and Antonius vied with each other in enlisting Caesar's veterans who had acquired land and dwellings in Italy : the one by his old renown, the other by the attraction of his name, which showed itself to be at least as alluring a factor as the former. Nor was gold spared. Two legions promptly deserted Antonius, who, in order to strengthen his position, had caused the people to cancel the appointment of Decimus Brutus, one of Caesar's murderers, as governor of Cisalpine Gaul and to assign to himself Caesar's former provinces. Thus open war broke out. Antonius besieged Decimus Brutus in Mutina (Modena). Relying on the military strength of Octavian, which was united to that of the two Consuls, the Senate vigorously intervened. Antonius was defeated, and had to retreat with his army to southern Gaul, where Lepidus already was with another army.

It was a strange triangular contest. Caesar's supporters had split into two parties. The one had joined the Senatorial party which had protected Caesar's murderers and was led by Cicero with a zeal and resolution he had never shown before, and had assisted it to vanquish the other. The alliance was unnatural, and when the victory was won, the Senate seemed inclined to shelve its ally. Octavian saw through these designs and anticipated them. He let Antonius escape and join forces with Lepidus. In defiance of statutory law, he demanded of the Senate the Consulate for himself and a triumph at the age of nineteen, and when this was refused, moved against defenceless Rome. The Senate vainly attempted to resist. He marched into Rome, and on August 19, 43 B.C., was elected Consul by the people. His first action was to avenge the memory of his adopted father, and to set up a special tribunal to judge Caesar's murderers.

One can understand that Caesar's soldiers could not conceive why they should fight with each other. However, the army which the chief of Caesar's murderers, Marcus Brutus and Cassius, had assembled in the East, was so menacing, that Caesar's adherents were compelled to unite and postpone the settlement of their personal rivalries. In spite of the most profound mutual distrust, Octavian and Antonius, along with Lepidus, who brought about the reconciliation, agreed to form a triumvirate in the sight of their soldiers on an island in a river at Bologna. A decree of the people invested the three with unlimited power for five years. Thereupon followed vengeance on Caesar's murderers and the opponents of the triumvirs with Cicero at their head. By proscription they were declared outlaws. Murder became a business. The property of the slain was confiscated, and supplied means for carrying on the war and satisfying the troops.

Octavian began his career with a ruthless policy of self-interest, difficult to credit in a youth of nineteen, and with a pitiless massacre of the leading men of the Senate. His method of procedure cannot be justified. His cold and calculating policy shrank from no measures, however extreme, and he realised that what was now required was money and troops for the campaign which was imminent against Brutus and Cassius, who could draw on the richest provinces of the Empire.

The opposing parties moved to meet each other. The upshot was a battle at Philippi near the Thracian coast, in which the victory was won by Antonius, whose talent for generalship was his strong suit. He defeated the troops of Cassius, and Cassius in despair committed suicide. Octavian was entirely without ability as a general. During the battle he was indisposed and remained in his tent; and when his army was beaten by Brutus, it was only by accident that he escaped capture. Some days later Brutus was also defeated and shared the fate of Cassius.

Antonius had won back his position by the sword, and completely outshone Octavian : the rôle of Lepidus was comparatively insignificant. Antonius went to the East, where Cleopatra hastened to meet him. Octavian returned to Italy, where he was confronted with almost insoluble difficulties. About 170,000 veterans expected to be provided with land and property in Italy. The rights of property were turned upside down, and those who lost land and possessions complained and bewailed their fate. It was now the turn of the middle class to feel the pinch of an unprecedented state of affairs, whereas the troops had to be satisfied at all costs. Antonius' brother, Lucius, and his wife, Fulvia, profited by the opportunity to cause a civil war, in which the best known incident is the siege of Perusia. The victory of Octavian strengthened his hold on Italy, but he was excluded from the sea, which was controlled by Pompeius' son, Sextus, who was a power to reckon with, being in a position to cut off Rome's supply of provisions.

Antonius required fresh troops to undertake a campaign against the Parthians, who were overrunning Syria and penetrating into Asia Minor, and had to return to Italy. Octavian went to meet him. Sextus Pompeius also played a part in the events which ensued, and the inevitable decision by arms seemed imminent. But none of the parties was, as yet, ready for that. Through the mediation of common friends, especially Octavian's clever diplomatist Maecenas, the triumvirs were reconciled at Brundisium, the seal of the reconciliation being the marriage of Antonius and Octavia, the sister of Octavian.

Sextus Pompeius was recognised as master of the sea and the islands of Sicily and Sardinia. But peace between him and the ruler of Italy was impossible for any length of time, and war soon broke out afresh. Antonius, for his part, desired to maintain a counterpoise to his chief rival in the person of Sextus. The tension between the two triumvirs again rose almost to breaking point, but again they were reconciled, this time at Tarentum through the mediation of Octavia, and the triumvirate was prolonged for five more years. Antonius now deserted Sextus Pompeius on condition of receiving troops for the Parthian War. With the help of Lepidus, Octavian began a war against Sextus, and his loyal friend Agrippa brought it to a successful conclusion. Sextus had to fly and retired to Asia Minor, where he endeavoured to found a new empire. This Antonius could not endure, and caused him to be captured and executed. Another and an unexpected turn of fortune came to Octavian. The troops of Lepidus went over to him, and the third triumvir had to content himself with the position of High Pontiff, and retire into private life.

Antonius, too, had his difficulties to overcome. The shameful defeat of Crassus at Carrhae was, as yet, unavenged. The Parthians still retained the Roman captives and standards. The daggers of the murderers had prevented Caesar from renewing the conflict, but in this undertaking, as in much else, Antonius was the Dictator's heir. His officers succeeded in driving the enemy beyond the frontiers of the Empire. Subsequently, he himself, in two campaigns, attempted to strike a decisive blow at the Parthian Empire, but though he demonstrated once again his skill as a general, he failed. Antonius had not succeeded in accomplishing the national task that was incumbent on him, and his reputation suffered in consequence. By the treaty between the triumvirs, Octavian had pledged himself to send a considerable force to help Antonius in the Parthian campaign, but as far as possible he had evaded his obligation, and by so doing had contributed to the preservation of the national foe from defeat. But the defeat of the Parthians would also have been a defeat for Octavian : for if Antonius had triumphed over the worst enemies of the Empire, Octavian's position would not have been worth much.

Antonius' connection with Cleopatra was not merely an amorous entanglement which deprived a statesman of his senses. Egypt was a country rich in money and commodities which Antonius sorely needed for the execution of his plans. Still it was not a province which Rome governed, but a nominally independent kingdom, although virtually subject to Rome. As the husband of the Egyptian queen, Antonius had unlimited control over the resources of her country. But in Alexandria he developed an inclination to govern in the spirit of the Hellenistic kings—a policy which he may have learned from Caesar—and in a manner which was offensive to Roman national sentiments. He appeared in the royal dress of the Ptolemies, caused himself and his wife to be worshipped as gods after the manner of the Ptolemies, and celebrated his triumph over the Parthians in Alexandria. He had put the deepest personal affront on his colleague, when he divorced his sister Octavia and formally married Cleopatra. The Egyptian queen was a clever diplomatist, who aimed at the aggrandisement of her country, and Antonius abetted her desires. She and her children were provided with high-sounding titles and with lands at the expense of the Roman Empire.

Antonius had always been a man of an impulsive and headstrong character, and in the East he failed, apparently, to gauge the psychological effect of his actions on the Roman people. In the long run it was public opinion which decided men which of the two rivals they should support, and settled once and for all the issue of the struggle. Octavian availed himself of his rival's mistakes with all the subtlety of an accomplished intriguer, and Antonius finally came to be regarded as the Oriental enemy of Rome. Even during his last campaign against the Parthians, the inevitable and crucial struggle with Octavian had cast its shadow in advance, and the war against the foes without was interrupted by one against a foe within the Empire. Antonius collected a numerous army and fleet in Western Greece and tried to cross to Italy, but failed. Instead, Octavian and Agrippa took their army and fleet over to Epirus. There Antonius was out-generalled, and was compelled to risk a decisive conflict. So, strangely enough, it came about that the battle which decided the fate of the Roman Empire, reversing all precedents, was fought at sea near Actium (September 2, 31 B.C.). After failing to relieve their land army by a victory at sea, Antonius and Cleopatra only managed to save themselves, together with a third of the fleet, while the remainder were captured or destroyed by the victor. The army of Antonius, seriously demoralised, began to retreat by land, and soon surrendered.

Antonius passed an anxious winter in Alexandria, not knowing what to do, but with a mind seething with fantastic projects. In his misfortune he was deserted by almost everybody, and when Octavian's troops closed on him from east and west, Alexandria alone remained faithful. He attempted to defend himself, but both his land and sea forces deserted to his opponent, and in despair he fell by his own hand. Such was the end of a man of remarkable talents, who, if circumstances had not driven him into perilous courses, might have been a great ruler. The unrest and unlimited possibilities of the age and contact with the strange Greco-Oriental world caused his impulsive nature to lose touch with realities. The cool and calculating policy of his opponent was the antithesis of his own. At the last Cleopatra had failed Antonius and abandoned him. She now hoped to captivate Octavian as she had captivated Caesar and Antonius, and schemed to save Egypt for herself, or at least for her children. But Octavian was not to be snared by woman's cunning or woman's beauty ; he saw danger in her person, and realised the advantages to be gained by sacrificing the Egyptian queen to the wounded national pride of Rome. When Cleopatra became aware of his intentions, she committed suicide. Her son by Caesar and her eldest son by Antonius were captured while attempting to escape, and put to death. They were too dangerous : but both her other children by Antonius, as also the latter's daughters by Octavia, were received into Octavian's family. Later on, the daughter of Cleopatra became Queen of Mauretania, as the wife of King Juba.

The booty obtained and the treasures of Egypt paid the expenses of the war. The country was finally subjected to Rome, not directly, but as the personal property of the Emperor. In that state it continued for centuries, and was a corner-stone of the imperial policy.

About two years after the battle of Actium, Octavian returned to Rome, closed the temple of Janus and celebrated his triumph with the greatest magnificence. The *de facto* commencement of the Empire dates from the battle of Actium which made Octavian sole ruler, but the old order of things remained in force until a decree of the Senate of January 16, 27 B.C., gave him the title of honour by which history knows him—Augustus. Thereby the imperial power received full recognition, and to this we shall return in another context.

AUGUSTUS (27 B.C.–A.D. 14)

After this the ruler was confronted with tasks of a less spectacular but yet momentous character. He had to restore to order and stabilise an empire suffering from the misgovernment of the Republic and the convulsions and financial drain of the civil war : to subdue those nations and tribes within the limits of the Empire which, as yet, had not submitted to Rome, and to round off the frontiers and adapt them for defence. Augustus spent the next decade chiefly in prolonged and extensive tours both in the West and the East, during which he made himself acquainted with many countries, peoples, and their needs. By the help of his generals, especially Agrippa and his two stepsons, Tiberius and Drusus, he subdued the peoples that were to be incorporated in the Empire. The only great reverse he sustained was that which caused him to abandon the conquest of Germany between the Rhine and the Elbe, which he had begun. What Augustus achieved in rectifying the frontiers and organising the administration was of fundamental importance to the future of the Empire. Later we must dwell on these sides of his activity.

Augustus had won the dominion over the Roman Empire as Caesar's heir, and he inherited with the Empire its many problems. It fell to his lot to complete the work which the daggers of the murderers had cut short. His method of executing it differed as much from that of his predecessor as Augustus himself differed in character from his father by adoption ; and during the decisive struggles of his youth with Caesar's spiritual heir—for Antonius was that, though of greatly inferior talents—he was driven by the force of circumstances to rely on and to foster the Roman element in the Empire, which Julius Caesar had rejected as antiquated and rotten. He himself was attracted to this element by his natural inclinations and from the circumstances of his birth in a small Italian town.

Bold and revolutionary genius, of which Caesar is probably the most notable instance known to history, when glorified by the crown of martyrdom, attracts irresistibly the imagination and emotions of posterity. To clear the site and draw up plans for a completely new building is more spectacular than to prop up what exists and mend the cracks. The tedious and laborious task of selecting from the old fabric what will still stand a strain and of welding together old and new structures, appears to be but a half-hearted policy. Posterity sees nothing magnificent in a long life spent on such a task as that.

Posterity has, in consequence, placed Augustus far below Caesar. In glorification of Caesar it has been said that the future proved him to have been right, and that his ideas anticipated the developments which Augustus could not hinder but only postpone. Posterity has regarded the work of Augustus in its growth, its weakness, its shortcomings, and final collapse ; but it has not considered how the plans of the great Dictator would have stood the acid test of actuality, and resisted the march of time. In theory his plans were those of a Hellenistic monarchy : a type of state like that which was introduced by Diocletian. He would have accelerated that blending of the different peoples and social types, which characterised the later Imperial period. The conservatism of Augustus, on the other hand, gave a respite to the old Roman element. Though in the end it almost disappeared in Rome herself, it had time to stamp its impress of civilisation and politics on the Western provinces, which to a great extent were drawn into the circle of ancient civilisation during the first two centuries of the Empire. The Roman element and the Roman order of things had a chance to take root, temporarily at least, instead of being eradicated by a revolutionary change of system. This must be remembered when the two men are arraigned before the tribunal of history.

Every radical revolution ends in a compromise with the old order : for man cannot shed his skin or throw off the traditions of civilisation and the forms of social life like old clothes. Caesar's work must have ended in some form of compromise, just as was the case with the most radical movement known to antiquity, Christianity. A period of doubt and ferment must ensue before revolutionary radicalism realises its limitations, and enters into the inevitable compromise with elements already in existence. The conflict involves much distress and suffering, which are forgotten by posterity—we ourselves have experienced the trials of living in a historic period of transition—whereas the splendour of genius, the high ideals and adventurous undertakings that accompany the transition period and the actors in the drama, are never forgotten. It is a legendary splendour of this kind which surrounds Caesar's laurel-crowned head like an aureole.

His heir did not covet the splendour but pursued a very different course. He certainly built up a new system of state and society, but it was a system raised on the foundations of the old, and of set purpose he attempted to conceal what was new. He compromised from the first, and left it to the future to bring about a blending of the conflicting elements. His work appears all the more clearly as a compromise when one studies the usual processes of settlement after a revolution. In the case of the Empire this did not result from the force of circumstances, but was a conscious and deliberate creation of the will of an individual possessing the ability of a statesman. Thus he gave the word that peace which it was sighing and yearning for, after a century of civil war and revolutions.

Augustus erected his fabric on peace, and thus founded it firmly in the feelings and consciousness of the inhabitants of the Empire. With the deepest conviction and the warmest gratitude they hailed him as the world's saviour and prince of peace. When after a devastating war we find a man silencing the tumult of hatred and passions, and bringing the spirit of peace and justice into the world, we, with recent events fresh in our memory, can fully appreciate why he was honoured and worshipped as more than a man. We must judge Augustus not only by our own conceptions, but also by those of his contemporaries. No ruler of a great and divided empire has ever held his people in the hollow of his hand as he did. His authority was unbounded. He never needed to appeal to the military forces he controlled, but kept them sternly in their place, as the servant and tool of society.

One peculiarity Augustus had, which is said to distinguish great men. He believed in his lucky star. His faith was expressed in a certain inclination to astrology and a naïve credulity in signs and omens. It was of a more popular, or rather a more superstitious character than Caesar's belief in his luck, which took heaven by storm. Apollo, under whose temple on the Actian promontory Augustus won his decisive victory, was his special protecting deity, as Venus had been Caesar's. In other respects there is a striking contrast between the intuitive genius of Caesar and the solid common sense of his heir. Augustus could not improvise and always avoided being taken by surprise. He wrote out and read his speeches to the soldiers, the people, and the Senate. He conducted conversations with important men—nay, even with his wife— with a notebook in his hand. With such a nature he could be neither a revolutionary nor a great tactician. He lacked the power of seizing intuitively and utilising his opportunities on the spur of the moment ; but yet he was a statesman. His shrewdness and clear-headedness, unconfused by emotions, but not inaccessible to them, could visualise the condition of state and society, and choose ways and means with calmness and accuracy. The statesman requires not merely intelligence but also that quality of psychological insight, which is sensitive to and estimates at their true value the trend of opinion among individuals and society as a whole, and this quality Augustus possessed to a high degree. This combination of the psychological with the judicial faculties made him a statesman and empire builder. In spite of his moderation in everything and a mode of life almost affected in its old-fashioned simplicity, he shared the life and feelings of his nation and contemporaries.

Antonius' unsuccessful campaign against the Parthians had not redeemed the reputation of the Roman arms. Public opinion, which is always remarkable for inconsistencies, demanded peace, but, at the same time, called for vengeance on the Parthians, and poets celebrated Augustus as the coming avenger. Augustus succeeded in satisfying popular sentiment without incurring the dangers of a war, which, even if it had resulted in a victory, could not have led to a permanent result. By a clever manipulation of the unrest arising from a disputed succession in the Parthian Empire, he induced King Phraates IV. to surrender the Roman prisoners and standards after they had been in their possession for thirty-four years. Poets celebrated this peaceful victory with as much enthusiasm as they would have greeted a triumph won by arms.

If it is a proof of greatness to surround oneself with wise and loyal helpers, Augustus was one of the greatest of men. Foremost among these was the friend of his youth, Agrippa, who had won his battles both in the East and the West, and with an equal vigour and insight assisted him to organise the Empire. He consolidated the administration of the East, constructed roads, erected buildings for use and ornament, and carried out a geographical survey of the Empire. After Agrippa's premature death, Augustus' two stepsons, Tiberius and Drusus, conducted his wars with ability and success, and at the close of his life Tiberius assisted him in policy and government. His right-hand man in all delicate and psychological matters was Maecenas, a scion of the old Etruscan nobility. Maecenas despised the honour of Senatorial rank ; without it he could move more freely. Under a refined, almost effeminate exterior, he concealed great energy and subtlety. He brought about the agreement with Antonius and Sextus Pompeius, smoothed over the domestic quarrels in the imperial family, and, in the absence of the Emperor, acted as his representative in the administration of Rome and Italy. Maecenas loved luxury and pomp, literature and art. He surrounded himself with the great poets of the day, brought poets and poetry under the patronage of the Emperor, and sought thereby to influence public opinion. Posterity has to thank him for such works as the *Odes* of Horace and the *Aeneid* of Virgil, which would never have been composed had not the two poets been convinced believers in Augustus and his aims.

Augustus towered head and shoulders over his coadjutors, who all willingly subordinated themselves to him. Occasionally one or another retired into seclusion, when their amicable relations with the Emperor were disturbed, but they never cherished any retaliatory designs against him, and when Augustus recalled them, they returned willingly to his side. That such men submitted to his will is the best proof of his greatness and nobility of character.

The opposition was only Platonic. It consisted of an attenuated company, who cherished the memories of past traditions which had vanished for ever. Augustus had deprived them of their best platform by the respect he always showed to the Senate, and the share of power which he granted to it. He appointed Senators, as before, to conduct and manage all important matters ; and they, in practice, demonstrated that the Senate had lost the ability to conduct the affairs of the Empire. The people looked up to him as the man through whom they lived and throve, enjoyed their freedom and property, and as the only being who could aid them and clear up all difficulties. He won their hearts by his good nature and by living like one of themselves. His power was, in fact, firmly rooted in the love and respect of the people.

No one doubted that in reality a monarchy had been instituted, and the clear-sighted realised that it was bound to be lasting. Along with monarchy came the question of the succession. It could not be regularised, since Augustus wrapped the new-born monarchy in republican swaddling-clothes, and, moreover, ancient monarchies either did not comprehend or only had vague ideas of a fixed succession, such as is inseparable from a modern monarchy; otherwise the history of the old royal houses would not have been so filled with accounts of conflicts and murders as it is. If the order introduced by Augustus was to be permanent, it was necessary that there should always be a successor ready, in the event of his sudden demise. The chances of death are incalculable, and Augustus' health was never robust, and at times was precarious. Family affection and popular instinct saw that a successor must be of his own blood and family, but first and foremost it was an imperative necessity that he should be a man who could fill satisfactorily the dignified station to which he would be called.

A family policy, which would secure the continuation of his work, was thus, from the first, one of Augustus' most immediate cares, but in this respect the good fortune, which otherwise attended him, deserted him, and he experienced disappointment after disappointment. His first marriage with Antonius' step-daughter Clodia, and his second with Scribonia, which he entered into in order to ally himself with the party of Sextus Pompeius during the critical period of tension with Antonius, were political matches. By Scribonia he had a daughter, Julia. His third marriage showed that passion still glowed, even under a hard and cold exterior. Tiberius Claudius Nero had taken part in the rebellion stirred up against Octavian in Italy by Antonius' relatives. Octavian fell so violently in love with this man's wife, Livia, that he could not even wait for the birth of her child, but had her divorced from her husband, and took her home to his house, certainly not without the complicity of Nero, who hoped by this means to atone for his participation in the war. The scandal was, however, great. Livia brought with her a four-year-old son, Tiberius, and, soon after, in the house of Augustus, gave birth to a second son by Nero, Drusus. Augustus' hopes of a male heir of his own were not realised. So he married his daughter to his nephew Marcellus, and designated him as his successor. His chief friend and coadjutor, Agrippa, to whom he had once, during a dangerous illness, handed his signet ring, felt himself

C

passed over, and retired to the East, but returned when, a few years after, Marcellus died. Agrippa shared Augustus' power till his death, and was married to Julia, who bore him a number of children. The continuance of the dynasty seemed assured, but Augustus endeavoured to consolidate it still further, after Agrippa's death, by marrying his daughter to his stepson Tiberius. Soon after, Drusus died during his German campaign, leaving behind his wife, a daughter of Antonius and Octavia, and a number of children. When Agrippa's two sons, Gaius and Lucius, reached man's estate, they were marked out as successors to the throne. Tiberius felt himself shelved, and, disgusted at his forced marriage with the frivolous Julia, retired to Rhodes in voluntary exile. And now the Emperor sustained blow upon blow—his daughter's open disgrace and banishment, and the death of two of his grandsons. The third, Agrippa Postumus, had a boorish character not susceptible to educational influences, and could not be seriously reckoned with. Tiberius thus became the Emperor's only hope and support, in spite of the antipathy he felt for his obstinate and reserved character. So he formally adopted Tiberius, who, in his turn, had to adopt Germanicus, the son of Drusus. Thus the wheel of fate had determined the succession in a manner far different from that which the Emperor had desired and hoped. In ancient and modern times Livia has been accused of intrigues and horrible crimes committed on behalf of her sons, but this is certainly untrue. Augustus was not the man to allow, in such matters, any woman to influence his settled intention, and the unlucky destiny of his family lies plain and open before our eyes. Like others, Livia submitted to his will. His last words on his death-bed were addressed to her : " Livia, live in memory of our marriage, and fare well." The day before he had taken leave of his friends with the question, whether they thought he had played his part well in the drama of life.

Those who regard Augustus' life and work as an organised hypocrisy, have fastened on these words. But Augustus did not use them in that sense. It is not unreasonable that a man who carefully considered and pondered over all his actions, should have desired to know, before he was taken away, whether he had succeeded in his task. Augustus' life-work was no hollow sham, but the outcome of deep thinking and sincere conviction. When the contradiction between this and the undeniable excesses of the period of the triumvirate is pointed to, one must remember that he began his career at the age of eighteen. Many others have sowed their wild oats before starting on a political career. Augustus was not a ready-made statesman ; he had to learn his lessons and adjust his experience and view of life, while he was fighting to maintain himself and defend the inheritance of his father by adoption.

TIBERIUS (A.D. 14–37)

When the old Emperor departed this world, full of years and honour, his successor had long been determined. Augustus' adopted son, Tiberius, was practically the only one of his intimate associates who survived, and certainly was the only one to whom there could be no opposition. Tiberius had faithfully stood by his side, had shown marked ability in the conduct of affairs both in war and peace, and was a convinced supporter of Augustus' principles of government. Augustus could leave his work to a worthy successor, and yet he was not quite satisfied, for he foresaw the difficulties that Tiberius' natural disposition would entail.

Tiberius was a man of mature age, being about fifty-six years old. One could expect nothing else of him than that his activity as Emperor would be a continuation of the activity he had shown as the right-hand man of his predecessor. Yet the shadows fall heavily over his reign, and he is remembered as a gloomy misanthropic tyrant. To a large extent this is the fault of our sources of information. Tiberius' reign was a time of peace, and hardly any wars of importance took place. As the ancient historians were not interested in home affairs and administration, they turned to his relations with the Senate and its leading men. A verdict was given in favour of the Senatorial opposition in Tacitus' effective but partisan description of his actions, a description which was spiced by

Suetonius' nasty gossip and completed by the superficial picture drawn by Dion Cassius. Modern critics have directed their attention to Tiberius' good qualities as governor of the Empire, his just and painstaking administration of the provinces, and the ordered economy of his financial policy. In comparison with the benefits conferred on the provinces by his good government, they have considered it an insignificant matter if some few Senators had to smart from his tyranny. They have gone further and exposed the partisan character of the sources, and given a very different picture, in which the conception of the tyrant has disappeared and Tiberius stands out as one of the best and most righteous governors of the Empire. One must not deny that dark clouds gathered round him in his old age, but one must try to understand the man.

To Augustus Tiberius had been a distinguished coadjutor, who with prudence and care executed every task which was delegated to him. It was he who suppressed the Pannonian rising, the greatest peril in the reign of Augustus, and it was he who, after Varus' defeat, maintained the prestige of Rome against the Germans. He was a good servant, but he lacked the spirit which shoulders responsibility with alacrity. He was one of those men who find it difficult to take the initiative and form quick decisions ; but when once they were made, he would carry them out with the inevitability and relentlessness of some great boulder, which, when once set in motion, cannot be checked. But when he no longer had any one to set him tasks and direct his actions, he had to make decisions on his own responsibility, and act on his own initiative. This he did, impelled both by his own strong sense of duty, and by his fidelity to the political legacy of Augustus ; but it was no pleasure to him, and his inclination to procrastinate and put off decisions, even in trifling matters, increased as the years went by.

His position was secure but not easy. The disturbances in the army, which broke out on his accession, were only intended to extort better conditions, not to overthrow the Emperor. A new generation had grown up, which only knew by hearsay of the tumults and miseries of the civil war. It had bowed in deep respect to the authority of Augustus, and had been won over by his good sense and accessible nature. To this generation Tiberius belonged. He had power but no authority, and his nature was, as Augustus had foreseen, his great handicap. The chief traits of his character were a straightforward sense of duty, which he lived up to himself and required of others : a strong consciousness of his own limitations, and a hatred of high-sounding titles and the outward pomp of power, which made him refuse most of the honours which were offered him. On one such occasion a contemporary rightly exclaimed to him, that they were not meant for the individual Tiberius, but for the Roman Emperor. His stoicism was exhibited at the death of his son, Drusus, when, to show that duty should not give place to private sorrow, he took part in the usual routine of business without observing the conventions of mourning.

Augustus had known and understood men and took them as they were : thus he had been able to induce them to follow him. Tiberius pictured to himself men as they ought to be, and by this standard measured himself and others. With such qualities he could lead soldiers, but not a nation. He had few friends, but held fast to those he had. All his experiences of life did not teach him knowledge of men, but only made him more bitter and misanthropic. He despised the Senators, who cringed before him, but yet were incapable of taking their part in the government of the Empire, and intrigued for personal advantages and rank. He conscientiously conceded to the Senate the status that Augustus gave it, but from a feeling of duty, not from conviction. There was a mutual dislike between him and the Senate, and this had its effect on their relations. Of a similar character was his relation to the people. He could not but despise Rome's excitable and frivolous population, and abominated their chief pleasures, the circus and the gladiatorial shows. Seldom and sparingly did he give them himself, and preferred to avoid being present at them. Such a man could never become popular, and his eleven years' absence from Rome in the later part of his reign made him a total stranger to the public. One can understand why the people called out after his death, " Tiberius to the Tiber," and also why Tiberius, who was drawn by his sense of duty from his residence at Capri to the vicinity of the city which was the seat of government, could not induce himself to enter it, though he came close enough to see it.

The trials for high treason are the black spot on Tiberius' government. Tacitus wishes to imply that Tiberius introduced and multiplied them, but this is not true. There was an old law dealing with treason to the majesty of the Roman people, which Augustus applied to the Emperor, who, in his person, embodied the majesty of Rome. If one examines the facts more closely, the conclusion is noteworthy. There is scarcely any record of a case in which a person was accused and condemned for treason alone. The real grounds of accusation were gross and serious crimes. It had become the fashion to accompany every accusation with an accusation of high treason. Usually men stand by one another, but when an individual is in danger of falling, all rush upon him like a pack of wolves on a corpse. Men thought to do a service to the Emperor by defending his dignity, but only succeeded in fastening upon him the personal odium which a condemnation for high treason always involved. Tiberius saw this, and did what he could to check the epidemic. Before Sejanus' overthrow there was only one case in which he sanctioned the death penalty. If, after the shock of that conspiracy and double-dyed perfidy, he dealt out justice with more severity, it is not to be wondered at. In his bitterness he retired ever more within the shell of his lonely contempt for humanity. His last years were a martyrdom both to himself and to others.

The second main accusation against him is the mysterious fate of the imperial family. Like Augustus, Tiberius had to provide for the succession. He had, himself, a son, Drusus, on whom he placed little reliance. At the bidding of Augustus he had adopted his nephew, Germanicus, who was thus designated as his successor. Germanicus had inherited the popularity of his father, Drusus, and at the beginning of the new reign was in command of the army in Germany, where he cut a poor figure during the mutiny. Then he started a war against the free Germans. In spite of his repeated failures Tiberius let him go his own way for two years, but then recalled him, remembering the advice of Augustus—not to squander the valuable forces of the Empire in an extension of frontiers—and sent him on an important mission to the East. There he became involved in a quarrel with Piso, the Governor of Syria, a quarrel which was embittered by a feud between his headstrong wife, Agrippina, and the wife of Piso. When he died soon afterwards at Antioch, malicious rumour stated with confidence that he had been poisoned. Piso was recalled, and anticipated punishment for his criminal defiance of orders by suicide after a notorious trial. Tiberius was loyal to his adopted son, and the latter to Tiberius, though he cannot be acquitted of a rashness, which conflicted in the highest degree with Tiberius' own nature. Tiberius' fault was that, as usual, he had not understood how to judge men, and had placed two people, who were irreconcilable, in positions of close relationship to one other.

Agrippina's senseless and passionate hatred, which saw in Tiberius the author of her husband's death, embittered relations and led to the catastrophe. As long as the aged Livia was alive, she seems to have had a restraining influence, but soon after her death calamities fell on the house, hastened by Tiberius' evil genius, Sejanus. Agrippina and her eldest son were banished and the second imprisoned, for plots against the Emperor. Of their guilt there can be no doubt ; the fall of Sejanus brought no improvement in their condition. Augustus punished his relatives in the same way, but Tiberius exhibited a cold-blooded severity, which justly revolted public opinion.

Lucius Aelius Sejanus, the prefect of the guard, was a man of great ability. He had attracted Tiberius' attention when the Pannonian legions mutinied at the beginning of the reign. Nominally Drusus, the Emperor's son, suppressed the mutiny : in reality it was Sejanus. It was he who collected together the praetorian cohorts and placed them in a single camp at home, from which they were so often to exercise a fatal influence on the destinies of emperors and the Empire. We have no details of his activities, but we do know that he won Tiberius' confidence and became his right-hand man. In Sejanus he thought he had really found a man after his own heart, who would stand by him as Agrippa did by Augustus. But Tiberius did not possess the gift of winning a man and controlling his actions. His own will required a support, and that is the psychological explanation of Sejanus' power over him, after his suspicious mind had become convinced of his ability and fidelity. Sejanus was a man of unlimited ambition. He was not content with being the right hand, he wanted to be the actual head. By a series of crimes he removed those who stood in his way. He seduced Tiberius' daughter-in-law, and poisoned his son. He fostered dissension between the Emperor and the family of Germanicus, while Tiberius noticed nothing, but raised him higher still in favour. Finally, all that was lacking for a formal share in the throne was its symbol, the tribunician power. As usual, Tiberius hesitated long before granting it, and Sejanus could wait no longer, but formed a plot to attain his object more quickly. At the last moment the Emperor was saved by a warning from his sister-in-law Antonia, the mother of Germanicus. How dangerous the situation was, and how firmly had the power of Sejanus been established in the Emperor's absence, is best shown by the fact that Tiberius did not venture to go the short way to work. In the moment of danger his old energy and caution returned once more, and the traitor was overthrown without being able to lift a hand in resistance. The royal favourite was led off to execution amid the curses of those who had recently fawned upon him. A similar sentence was passed on his family and on many who supported him in his enterprise. Not even in this terrible crisis did Tiberius lose his sense of justice. A knight, Marcus Terentius, was accused before the Senate of having been Sejanus' friend. He defended himself boldly with the plea that this was not a crime—the Emperor had been one too, he said—and he had never taken part in anything criminal. He was acquitted and his accusers punished.

This was the great tragedy in the life of Tiberius—his last and most awful disillusionment. In advanced age the ruler of the world found himself alone in the world, with hardly a friend, and his home was desolate. In his retinue at Capri was the last of Germanicus' sons, Caligula. By a greater show of submissiveness he had escaped the fate of his brothers, and had never complained of their ruin. It was said of him, that there never was a better servant or a worse master. Tiberius had no illusions, but also he had no choice. Caligula was destined to be his successor. Seneca, a writer who well knew the secrets of the imperial court, relates that, when Tiberius felt the approach of death, he drew off his signet ring as if to hand it to some one, but put it back again on his finger, and lay long with clenched fist. Finally, he rose to his feet and collapsed in death by the bedside. He realised that there was no one in the Empire who could replace him. He died in harness, a man of duty to the last, seventy-seven years old. Had a kinder fate ordained that he should die twenty years earlier, he would have stood out as one of the best men of the age, and his decease would have been reckoned a great blow to the Empire. The misfortune of his life was, that circumstances did not permit him to remain in a secondary position, for which he was naturally adapted, but elevated him to the first, for which he possessed too little strength of purpose, and too much stereotyped attention to duty. On the whole his reign was a happy time for the Empire. It finally established the constitution Augustus had created for the State, and showed that this could resist the changes of *personnel.*

CALIGULA (A.D. 37–41)

The world breathed more freely when Tiberius died and a young Emperor ascended the throne. The glamour of his father, Germanicus, still rested on Gaius Caesar, usually called Caligula, because as a little boy he frolicked about in his father's camp wearing tiny soldier's boots. He grasped the situation, and began his reign with a marked policy of reaction against the régime of Tiberius, *e.g.* pardons, remissions of taxation, politeness to people and Senate. Even his extravagance made him popular with the Romans. But these halcyon days soon passed away. As soon as he had squandered the sums amassed by the frugal Tiberius, he imposed new taxes, and endeavoured to fill the treasury by confiscation and undisguised extortion. Caligula is usually reckoned as the first example of an imperial maniac, but this is scarcely correct. He had one fixed idea—a consciousness of the might and majesty inherent in his elevated position. He required people to bow to the ground before him and kiss his foot. Like the Egyptian kings he placed his sister Drusilla at his side, and regarded Jupiter as his colleague. This cannot be called madness, but Rome was not yet ripe for these Eastern manners. He did not lack ability, but preferred the society of charioteers and jugglers. He had the gift of facility of speech, and particularly of sarcasm, which was his undoing. The natural termination of such a reign was the murder of the Emperor, but the man who dealt the fatal blow was avenging personal affronts.

CLAUDIUS (A.D. 41–54)

No one of the imperial house was left who could be considered capable of taking over the reins of government. The Senate prepared to do so and gave the guard the watchword " Freedom." During the general confusion after the murder a few praetorians had entered the palace to see what they could steal. They saw two trembling legs protruding from under a curtain. They went behind it and found an old man, who fell on his knees and begged them to spare his life. Then they were struck by the thought : here we have the Emperor ! It was Caligula's uncle, Claudius. In his inoffensive way he was the black sheep of the family. His shuffling gait and shaking head betokened a degenerate body. His relatives were ashamed of him and kept him in seclusion. He consoled himself by compiling the history of Etruria and Carthage in many bulky volumes ; while Emperor he introduced a stillborn reform of spelling. He was not altogether devoid of common-sense and prudence, but through disposition and force of circumstances he had become a pedantic and long-winded bookworm. We have the text of a speech of his on the introduction of the Aedui to the Senate. It is full of confused learning and shows careful composition. What he altogether lacked was will : he could not resist the smell of roast meat or the face of a woman, and always agreed with the last person he talked to.

Claudius in fact was not fit to be Emperor, but the praetorians required a candidate, and the instinctive reverence for the house of Augustus was so great that it silenced objections. The Senate was more critical, but submitted to the choice of the army. Claudius inaugurated the dangerous habit of making a donation to the praetorians on ascending the throne, a practice which taught them how to become emperor-makers. He retained his position by their favour. Yet the reign of Claudius was remarkable for more energy and initiative than any other in the first century. In it was achieved the Empire's one great conquest, Britain. No government showed as great interest and energy in works of general utility. It gave Rome, what it now lacks, a harbour in place of the open and dangerous roadstead of Ostia. It reclaimed large tracts for cultivation by the draining of Lake Fucinus, though the work was only partly successful. It formed an epoch in financial operations and in the matter of the franchise. Claudius' traditionalism made him a strict upholder of the Senate's rights. He had a positive mania for the administration of justice. Though he sometimes made himself ridiculous, it must not be denied that he exercised a good influence by levelling down the inequalities and severities of the laws, and by creating a more rational procedure for business.

How much of all this may be assigned to the credit of the Emperor, each man must judge for himself. He certainly cannot be deprived of all credit ; for in certain matters his own inclinations and ideas are plainly apparent. As little does one know how much is to be attributed to his notorious freedmen, who, acting as his ministers, carried on the administration of the Empire. They were doubtless competent people, who also attended to their own interests, feathered their nests at the expense of the State, and, individually, amassed riches. That the freedmen, whom previous emperors also had made use of to conduct the administration, now became so prominent, was due to Claudius' weakness ; his predecessors had only treated them as their tools. A still more degrading weakness was his overmastering sensuality. Before his elevation to the throne he had been married to Messalina, a lady of high rank, whose name was soon to become a byword. She succeeded, indeed, in living up to the notoriety of her name. Claudius either did not know or did not trouble himself about her unbridled lust, and when in defiance of her feeble-minded husband she went to such lengths as to celebrate publicly her marriage with the young Gaius Silius, Claudius certainly had Silius executed—for the consort of the Empress was a pretender to the throne—but could not prevail on himself to take any further measures against his seductive wife. Eventually the freedmen, who feared for their lives, took the matter into their own hands, and had Messalina put to death. Claudius received the news of her death without making any further inquiry.

When Claudius again found himself in need of a wife, the question was, who should it be ? The only survivor of the imperial house was Germanicus' daughter, Agrippina, and the unlucky idea occurred of avoiding a renewal of family feuds by marrying her to Claudius. Certainly she was his niece, and such a marriage was forbidden and as repulsive to Roman ideas as it is to Christian. The obstacle was overcome by the obsequiousness of the Senate, and scandal had no effect on Claudius. If Messalina had used her position to satisfy her craving for excesses, Agrippina used it to satisfy her lust for power. More victims fell to her ambition than to Messalina's sensuality. By her former marriage to Domitius Ahenobarbus, a son of Augustus' niece, the elder Antonia, she brought him a son, Nero. All her efforts were devoted to securing the throne for him. She enlisted strong support in the Senate, from the people, from the guard, and among the influential freedmen, and induced Claudius to adopt Nero and marry him to his daughter Octavia. A bitter and prolonged struggle then ensued between the adherents of Agrippina and the legitimists, who championed Britannicus, the son of Claudius by Messalina. In spite of Claudius' weakness, his paternal affection made the issue doubtful, and eventually Agrippina brought the struggle to a premature end by having Claudius poisoned. The guard, who were devoted to her, put forward Nero as Emperor, and not a hand was lifted on behalf of the Emperor's son, Britannicus. Thus perished the last of the Claudian line. His talents and good intentions cannot be doubted, but he suffered from that fatal lack of a sense of the dignity befitting his position which disqualified him from being a successful Emperor.

NERO (A.D. 54–68)

Agrippina had no intention that her sixteen-year-old son, when he succeeded, should take the reins of government, but seized them herself. Nero had still to be educated for his imperial task, and Agrippina had appointed as his tutor the most famous philosopher of the day, Seneca, whom she recalled from the banishment to which Messalina had sent him. Seneca is one of the most interesting and characteristic figures of the age, a Stoic philosopher who preached virtue and the simple life, although possessing wealth and power to a greater extent than any of his contemporaries. He was a practical statesman of great attainments, and so obliging to his imperial master, that he placed his pen at his service in order to shield and defend him from the charge of matricide. He occupied no definite official position, but controlled affairs as the Emperor's personal confidant. The praetorian prefect, Afranius Burrus, was a rough soldier, who, however, knew how to adapt himself to the age in which he lived. He had been Agrippina's chief ally in setting Nero on the throne, and after Agrippina's murder—at the head of his officers—he congratulated Nero on having escaped the attempt made on his life.

Agrippina was utterly unscrupulous. Her imperiousness took such a form that only a few months passed before her two assistants found it expedient to remove her from the

government. To win over Nero, they aided and abetted him
in his liaison with a liberated slave-girl, and so as to create
a faction hostile to Agrippina they leaned for support on
the Senate, whose authority was increased. This circumstance left its impress on the early years of Nero's government. It was one of the best the Empire ever had. The
administration was improved, and abuses in provincial
government and tax - collection were punished or suppressed. The Parthians, who had established themselves in
Armenia, were driven out by Corbulo, and eventually the
Armenian king was glad to receive his diadem at the hand
of Nero.

Agrippina was not a woman to be lightly set on one side.
She aided and abetted Britannicus against her own son in a
manner which compelled Nero to have him put out of the way.
In spite of all efforts she never succeeded in regaining her
influence over her son. He was plainly more afraid of her
than of his counsellors. The crisis arrived when Nero became
passionately enamoured of a noble lady, Poppaea Sabina, the
wife of Salvius Otho. Poppaea aimed at a higher position
than that of merely being the Emperor's mistress. Against
her were arrayed not only Nero's mother, who knew that her
influence would be for ever at an end if a woman who realised
the value and advantages of power sat by the Emperor's side,
but also his wife, Octavia, who in the estimation of the nation
and of the guard, had brought him the Empire as her dowry.
Octavia was banished, and some years afterwards, when public
opinion in her favour found expression in a wild disturbance,
was put to death. From his mother Nero endeavoured to
free himself by a pretended disaster. He built a pleasure-
boat, which was designed to sink with her in the bay of Baiae ;
when the attempt failed, he caused a freedman to assassinate
her.

The Roman Empire was too complicated a fabric of
civilisation to be controlled by a youth. It was from sheer
necessity that Nero let his two confidential servants have a
free hand in the government. But as his natural propensities
developed, he was compelled to govern in person in order to

satisfy his dilettantism out of the resources of the imperial power. The decisive turning point was the death of Burrus. Nero seems to have had great respect for this man, who commanded the guard on which depended ultimately the Emperor's weal or woe. Seneca's position was undermined and he withdrew into private life, offering to resign all his riches to Nero in exchange for a reconciliation. The new praetorian prefect, Tigellinus, schemed to strengthen his influence with the Emperor by pandering to his vices, and by denouncing plots against the throne. It was he who concocted a charge of adultery against Octavia ; but in spite of all efforts the action failed, and Nero had formally to divorce her in order to marry Poppaea.

From his earliest youth Nero had aesthetic leanings and a passion for games and competitions. He declaimed his rhetorical exercises and recited his verses in public ; he staged circus games and theatrical performances with the greatest splendour and devised many novelties. He thought himself a great player on the lyre, and loved to appear and give musical performances in the costume of a tragedian, accompanying himself on the lyre. When the astrologers foretold to him that he would be dethroned, he is said to have replied, that then he would live by his art. So greedy of applause was he that he organised a claque. He took sides in the petty intrigues of the professional artistes, and from boon companions of this character submitted to sneers and insults which would certainly have brought others to ruin. His great ambition was to win triumphs on the stage. His first public appearance he reserved for the semi-Greek city of Naples, where he thought he would find a more appreciative audience than in Rome. Most notorious was his journey, undertaken in the last year of his life, in the pursuit of art, to Greece, where, at the world-famous games, which, at his instigation, had been renewed and remodelled, he won an easy victory, obtained a victor's laurels, and also seized the opportunity to plunder the holy shrines of their art treasures. He rewarded the Greeks by giving the province of Achaia freedom from taxation, and returned to Rome riding in

Augustus' triumphal chariot, decked with his Olympian and Pythian wreaths, while tablets proclaiming his victories were carried in the triumphal procession. The Romans must have regarded this frolic as an ignominious parody.

Nero was a prodigal on a grand scale. His administration, after he had got rid of his advisers, was governed by his insatiable need of money. He satisfied this by the usual means and artifices employed by the emperors, *viz.* judicial murders, confiscations and compulsory legacies, and was the first to debase the currency on a large scale. The great fire of Rome still further aggravated the financial stringency, for the Emperor had to support those who were rendered homeless and to contribute towards the rebuilding of the city. He added to the burden, when he used the opportunity to erect a luxurious palace with gardens and artificial lakes. This was his " Golden House," of which well-preserved remains were discovered at the Renaissance. Its scheme of decoration inspired the frescoes of Raphael in the Loggia of the Vatican. Many rumours were current as to the origin of the conflagration. It was asserted that Nero was inspired by the fire to compose a poem, which he recited in sight of the raging flames, and even that he himself had started the fire. Nero made scapegoats of the Christians, who had recently made their existence felt, and caused some of them to be executed to calm the excitement.

During the past century the Romans had learned to endure much, but Nero's challenge to public opinion was too blatant. The old traditions of public decency, which his behaviour completely ignored, had by no means been extinguished, and his extortions were a continual source of annoyance. Shortly before his Greek expedition a serious conspiracy was discovered. Its detection involved many, both guilty and innocent, in destruction, among them being Seneca and his nephew, the poet Lucan. This did not, however, deter others from hatching a fresh conspiracy, which also ended in failure. Nero could disregard public opinion in the capital, so long as the troops were devoted to him. The praetorian guard could always be bribed, but the simple legionaries in the provinces had already begun to ask themselves with wonder what sort of Emperor they had. A comparatively unimportant and apparently hopeless rising supplied the impetus which finally hurled Nero from his throne. Julius Vindex, Governor of Gallia Lugdunensis, rose and took an oath to the Roman Senate and people. Embittered by the weight of taxation a great number of the Gallic tribes joined him. His troops were few, only partially trained and ill armed. He had no prospect of success, unless he could induce other portions of the army to join him. The legions of Upper Germany moved against him and defeated him. But these legions had not fought for Nero, and after the victory they proclaimed their commander, Verginius Rufus, Emperor. But he refused the honour, being a man of humble birth, and realising the dangers and perils involved by acceptance.

Vindex had had more success in his overtures to Galba, the Governor in Spain, a wealthy aristocrat, who, after the murder of Caligula, had been spoken of as a candidate for the throne. Galba was already on bad terms with Nero, and now had himself proclaimed Emperor ; but as long as the German armies would not declare for him his prospects were more than doubtful. In the meantime the unrest of the provinces had infected Rome, and here the decisive events occurred. The praetorian prefect, Sabinus, induced the guard to join Galba, by promising them colossal donations in his name. The Senate sentenced Nero to death in the old Roman fashion by scourging and beheading. Nero only realised that his hour was come, when the cohort on guard marched away from the Palatine to be present at the proclamation of Galba in their barracks. He attempted to escape, but unsuccessfully. All kinds of fantastic schemes came into his head before he decided that the only way out was suicide. Unable to nerve himself to wield the dagger, he availed himself of a freedman's assistance and died with the exclamation, " What an artist dies in me ! " His last request was that his body should not be maltreated but burned. Galba's freedmen, who had just been released from prison, granted him this last boon.

Nero was popular with the mass of the city populace, who

were not directly affected by his misgovernment and had not experienced his meanness. Wherever a pseudo-Nero arose during the next few years, he was sure of finding support. His popularity has been perpetuated, for in novels and on the film he is still the most popular of Roman Emperors. The glare of the great fire and the funeral pyres of the Christians, whom he burnt to illuminate the circus, cast a lurid light upon his personality. His achievements intrigue the mind of a sensation-loving age, which is restrained by its code of morals from indulging in the pleasures of the age of Nero, but revels in seeing them depicted on the screen. It is deplorable that the great public of our day obtains its notions of antiquity from such a man and such an age !

Nero is one of the least interesting of the long line of men who occupied the throne of the Caesars. A sensuality, the development of which was never checked because from early youth he was taught that everything was for his enjoyment : an aesthetic dilettantism, the hollowness of which he never understood because he could not distinguish between the homage due to the Emperor from that paid to the artist, were the leading traits of his character. If he knew any art, it was the art of living ; but that is not the art which should be cultivated by the monarch of a world-empire.

II

THE CIVILIAN EMPERORS

GALBA (A.D. 68–69)

SERVIUS SULPICIUS GALBA entered Rome at the age of seventy-two. He was the first Emperor who did not belong to the house of Augustus, and the last who can have had a personal recollection of the founder of the Empire. Age had blunted his faculty of judgment, and he was completely in the hands of a few intimates of little repute. He was greedy in his own interests and stingy in those of the State. Economy was highly necessary to repair the ruined finances of the State, but highly imprudent for an Emperor who sat so insecurely on his throne. Galba antagonised the praetorians by not paying the sums which Sabinus had promised them in his name. He antagonised the German legions by harsh treatment; for he favoured and rewarded the supporters of Vindex, whom they had defeated. The German legions had also attempted to set up an Emperor of their own, though the attempt came to grief owing to Verginius' refusal. For the moment they reluctantly recognised Galba, but they formed the strongest and most dangerous section of the imperial army, and considered they had a better right to nominate an Emperor than the less important Spanish troops. Their discontent came to a head on the next New Year's Day, when they refused to take the oath of allegiance to Galba, and proclaimed Aulus Vitellius, the commander in Lower Germany, Emperor.

Galba had scarcely any reliable troops with which to confront his rival, since the praetorians were hostile to him. One of his chief supporters had been Salvius Otho, the man who had thrown his wife, Poppaea Sabina, into the arms of

Nero, and after that, had been practically exiled from Rome as Governor of Lusitania. He had worked zealously for Galba in order to get back to Rome, and hoped that Galba would adopt him and make him his successor. In the meantime Galba adopted another, and Otho saw himself disappointed in his hopes of the throne and of the opportunity of paying off the enormous debts which he had contracted by his frivolous and dissolute mode of life. His only chance was a successful rebellion. The praetorians were easily won over ; two subordinate officers and one freedman managed the affair, and thirty-two soldiers proclaimed Otho Emperor in the Forum. They were supported by the whole guard, and Galba was put to death along with his adopted son and counsellors.

OTHO : VITELLIUS (A.D. 69)

Otho began negotiations with Vitellius, whose high birth, rather than his qualities, was the reason for his elevation. Vitellius, preferring a life of quiet and luxury to the risks of the throne, was not disinclined to resign, but the decision did not rest with him but with his troops, who were anxious to reap the harvest they regarded as their due. His generals and soldiers crossed the Alps. Otho's chances depended on whether the Danube army, which sided with him, could arrive in time. His lieutenants succeeded in holding the line of the Po, but Otho, who was by nature nervous and unmilitary, could not endure to delay the decision. He forced on an engagement at Cremona, before the main strength of the Illyrian troops had arrived. The battle was contested with the greatest bitterness, since both armies were fighting for their privileges and their position. Otho's army suffered a defeat, which was scarcely decisive, but Otho displayed the same nervous impatience after the battle as before. He decided the issue by taking his life, against the advice and prayers of his followers. Thereby he robbed his army of its leader, and made it the prey of the German troops. Vitellius was recognised as Emperor in Rome, and the towns of Italy, after an interval of almost a century, began once more to experience the mailed fist of the soldier.

Hitherto the Oriental legions had not made their voice heard, having been engaged in a serious struggle, the rising of the Jews. Augustus' firm friend Herod, called the Great, had put down the last of the Maccabees, and seized the Jewish throne. He was a typical Oriental Sultan, severe and harsh to his subjects, cringing to the Roman authorities, and an executioner to his own family. His forcefulness cannot be denied. He succeeded in keeping the unmanageable people in order, though he incurred the displeasure of the faithful by his fondness for display and Hellenistic customs. After his death the country was divided among his sons, but Archelaos, who received Judaea, proved incompetent and was banished, the country being placed under a Roman procurator. In the meantime other members of the dynasty continued to rule over other districts. The ambitions and mismanagement of these petty princes and the rapacity of the procurators weighed heavily on the country. Religious fanaticism intensified the feeling of unrest. The Romans made far-reaching concessions to Jewish orthodoxy, as, for example, when the legionaries entered Jerusalem they removed the Emperor's portrait from their standards. But the Hellenistic culture which the Romans and their vassal princes promoted, was an abomination to the Jews. The Romans could not understand the Jewish religion, and relations became so strained that an outbreak was inevitable. The country was filled with robberbands, which found a refuge in the mountains ; insecurity became general, and the Roman troops were unable to cope with the situation. Fanatics incessantly fomented rebellion, and zealots for Judaism, working by stealth, stirred up the Messianic hopes of the nation. The air was so loaded with explosives, that a very small spark was required to cause a violent conflagration.

Two years before Nero's death there was a regular battle in the port of Caesarea, where the Roman procurator resided. The energetic Jewish minority demanded control of the town's administration, and when the Governor took the side of the Greek majority, this created indignation among the Jews, who regarded the town as belonging to their own country. The procurator, Gessius Florus, and the leading Jews intrigued against each other till a rising occurred in Jerusalem. Two cohorts moved in to occupy the citadel and restore order, but the party of action had anticipated them, and forced them to retreat. This was the beginning of the war. The Roman garrisons in Judaea were massacred, and the legate of Syria, when he tried to occupy Jerusalem, was driven back. Persecutions of the Jews broke out in the Syrian cities and Alexandria, and in the towns where the Jews were powerful, they took a bloody revenge on their opponents. The government had to intervene vigorously. From Achaia Nero sent one of the foremost men of the Empire, Licinius Mucianus, to be Governor of Syria, while the military command in Judaea was entrusted to a general who had been tried in the British campaigns, Titus Flavius Vespasianus, whose political insignificance made him suitable for a high command. The campaign was carried out thoroughly. Town after town fell into the Romans' hands. Finally, only Jerusalem held out, and there quarrels between the fanatics and the more moderate Jews resulted in an internecine struggle in which more than 12,000 men are said to have perished. At the moment when Vespasian was preparing to besiege the city in earnest, Nero's death and the conflicts ensuing thereon broke off operations for a time.

The Oriental army had seen one corps after another set up an Emperor, and had acquiesced until it thought its own turn had come. The arrogance of the German legions must have been provocative ; but the decision seems to have come from the officers rather than the rank and file. The most respected and important of them was Licinius Mucianus, the Governor of Syria, but he refused the purple and caused the choice to fall on Vespasian, the commander in Judaea. He, too, seems to have accepted the honour only after considerable hesitation. For the time being he remained in Egypt, while Mucianus began his march on Rome. The Danube army, which had been inclined to favour Otho and had only accepted Vitellius under pressure, went over to the side of Vespasian. Vitellius' troops were being reorganised and were still poorly equipped, and during their winter quarters in Italy their discipline had been relaxed, and their numbers reduced by desertions. The headstrong commander of the Pannonian legions, Antonius Primus, broke into Italy without waiting for the Syrian troops. At Cremona he met the enemy forces, and drove them into the town. But just then a reinforcement of six legions arrived, and a bitter struggle began again in the moonlight night, until at sunrise Vitellius' cause was lost. Antonius Primus postponed further action, waiting for his opponents to split up into factions, and the timid Vitellius vainly hoped that this would also happen to the victors. But after negotiations with the prefect of the city, Flavius Sabinus, Vespasian's far less famous brother, he declared himself ready to abdicate. His new praetorian guard, however, who knew that if this course was pursued, they themselves would receive short shrift, refused to allow it. They forced Vitellius to break the agreement, stormed the Capitol, in the course of which the famous temple was burned, and slew Sabinus. These scenes of horror were the last signs of resistance. Next day Antonius Primus marched into Rome and took summary vengeance on Vitellius and his guard.

Vespasian repaired to Rome, and left to his son Titus the chief command of the reinforced troops in Judaea. The siege of Jerusalem began, but in spite of this the internecine conflicts did not cease. The overcrowded city was ravaged by disease and famine, but there was no thought of surrender. The end could be nothing but the total destruction of the city and the temple of Yahweh. The Romans had realised that only by this means could they put an end to the recrudescence of disorders. Finally, when only the upper city and the temple still held out, the temple burst into flames and the citadel was stormed on September 26, A.D. 70. A Roman garrison occupied the ruined city, and the tribute, which every Jew hitherto paid to the temple, was henceforward paid to Jupiter Capitolinus. This was the outward and visible sign of the dethronement of Yahweh.

In the Rhine district two widespread disturbances had broken out. When Vitellius levied soldiers for the struggle

against Vespasian, the Batavians in the islands of the Rhine
delta rose under Julius Civilis, a member of the royal family
of the tribe. He had no intention of helping Vespasian to the
throne, for the insurrection went on after his victory, and
was joined by some Roman troops, who were adherents of
Vitellius. The movement spread far into Gaul, and the un-
conquered Germans also, beyond the frontier, fired by the
prophetess Veleda, rose up in rebellion. The intention was to
sever the connection between Gaul and Rome, and even parts
of the Roman army took an oath to an *imperium Galliarum*.
Confusion was rife among the Roman troops which did not
join the rebellion. The two legionary camps, Castra Vetera
(Xanten) and Mainz, had to surrender. Hatred of Rome led
to barbaric cruelties. In Mainz all the officers were put to
death : the garrison of Castra Vetera, though it had obtained
a promise of immunity from attack, was cut down as it marched
away. Only after the contest for the Empire had been
decided, could the Government send a large force to suppress
the rebellion. By then the Roman soldiers who had joined in
the insurrection were weary of the barbarians, and returned
to their allegiance. In spite of this, various difficulties
cropped up, and the end was a treaty by negotiation in which
even the leader, Civilis, was pardoned.

VESPASIAN (A.D. 69–79)

That weak spot in the monarchical system as laid down by
Augustus, *viz.* lack of a regulated succession to the throne,
had been demonstrated by two years of civil war, a prelude
which was forgotten during a hundred years' peace, though it
was to be remembered in the great tragedy of the next century.
One army corps after another had put forward its candidate
for the throne ; the last comer in the strife, after the others
had exhausted their efforts, was the successful candidate.
Thus by force of circumstances a plain man without lineage
or fame was elevated to the throne—a man who never could
have been thought of as a candidate at the death of Nero.
Happily for the Empire he was a man of exactly the type
that was wanted. Vespasian was born in Reate, a Sabine

hill-town, and was brought up in the country. His family was humble, for his father, as a tax-collector, had acquired the property which opened a Senatorial career to his sons. The ambition of Vespasian was so little developed, that he only reluctantly gave in to his mother's prayer that he would follow a more brilliant profession than had hitherto been the lot of the family. He did not specially distinguish himself, but performed his duties with uniform efficiency. His appearance suited his character—a sturdy, thick-set body and a face in which seriousness was blended with good humour. He was noted for a somewhat rustic and at times cynical wit. He was the most *bourgeois* of all those emperors who ruled Rome during the century which was regarded as its happiest age. He lived without the luxury which marked his predecessors, but appreciated good fare and society.

The tasks which confronted the new Emperor were more than troublesome. The finances had to be re-established after Nero's mismanagement, and the military forces reorganised after the civil war, in which the rivalry of the armies had loosed the bonds of discipline. Most of the German legions were disbanded, and new ones formed in their places. The defences of the Empire against Parthia and Germany were strengthened, and the wedge of country between the Rhine and the Danube was occupied in order to create a better line of communication between the armies stationed on the two rivers. The internal organisation of the Empire was overhauled. Various vassal States were annexed, and some free cities incorporated with the provinces, while Achaia lost its immunity from taxation and once more became a Senatorial province. The last-named measures were dictated by financial needs. Vespasian had to raise money wherever he could get it. He estimated the expenses of the State at Hs.40,000 millions. He carefully controlled the collection of taxes, and exercised a strict oversight over State property ; yet he could not avoid imposing fresh taxes, and considerably increasing the old. There is an anecdote told of him that when he put a tax on public lavatories, his son, Titus, upbraided him for raising revenue from such a source. Vespasian took out a coin, and bidding Titus smell it, uttered the words which became proverbial : " Money has no smell." He was accused of avarice. The Romans had a peculiar custom by which in funeral processions a man appeared wearing the mask of the deceased. A famous actor, who took Vespasian's part at his funeral, being asked jestingly what the funeral expenses amounted to (the actual sum being about ten million sesterces), exclaimed, " Give me a hundred thousand, and throw me into the Tiber." The dead Emperor would have appreciated the joke. He was not avaricious for himself. He returned from the province in which he was proconsul no richer than he went. But sheer necessity made him parsimonious in financial matters, and, no doubt, his upbringing contributed something in this connection.

In spite of everything he contrived to do much building. The Capitol was restored. Nero's golden house was untouched, and in place of a lake in the park he reared the Flavian amphi-theatre, the Colosseum—now the most imposing ruin of imperial days in Rome. The Forum and Temple of Peace were erected after the triumph over the Jews. Necessary and useful buildings had been neglected under Nero, so there was much lost ground to be made up. He gave splendid games, and distributed princely gifts to the performers. He was interested in education : he was the first to establish teachers of rhetoric in Rome with a State salary, and he was liberal to poets and artists.

When Vespasian was seized with his last illness, he ex-claimed with his usual humour, " Ah ! I fancy I am becoming a god." The simple burgess of Reate, whom destiny had placed on the throne of the Caesars, was apotheosised, and he deserved the honour more than many others. As death drew near he rose from his bed. " An Emperor must die standing," he explained, and died supported by the arms of those who stood round. His end was characteristic of the man. He was endowed with the old Roman sense of duty, and that, together with the similar Roman characteristics of stolidity and common sense, qualified him for his position. Blind destiny for once had chosen the right man.

TITUS (A.D. 79-81)

One of Vespasian's merits was his sincerity, and this showed itself in his relations with his eldest son, Titus. The two are a unique example in Roman history of harmonious co-operation between an Emperor and his son. Titus had served his apprenticeship under his father in Britain and Judaea. He had celebrated a triumph over the Jews by his father's side, and was his colleague as censor and as consul seven times. He shared with him the tribunician power and was also his praetorian prefect. In effect it was a joint-rule. In contrast to his father, Titus had been educated at court in the train of Britannicus. He was richly gifted, had political and musical talent, but had also revelled in the luxury and excesses of the age. During the Jewish War he had entered into a notorious relation with the Jewish Princess, Berenice. His succession was awaited with some anxiety, for people were not sure what attitude Titus would adopt when he grasped the reins of power. A few cases of cabinet tyranny during Vespasian's reign had been ascribed to him as their author. But Titus soon showed that their fears were groundless. He sent Berenice away, and it is reported of him that one evening, when he had had no opportunity of befriending anybody, he said to his friends that he had lost a day ! His principles were never put to a prolonged trial, for he died after a reign of only two years. His popularity with the people was largely due to the games with which, on a scale of unexampled magnificence, he inaugurated the Flavian amphitheatre. His short reign was afflicted by great disasters—ravages of the plague, another gigantic fire in Rome, and the eruption of Vesuvius, when the volcano which had been passive for so many centuries that men had forgotten about it, woke up and overwhelmed with ashes the three flourishing towns of Pompeii, Herculaneum, and Stabiae. The Emperor had all too abundant opportunities of showing the liberality which tradition imposed on him in providing the necessary relief.

DOMITIAN (A.D. 81–96)

Vespasian's relations with his second son Domitian, had been very different from those with Titus. Domitian had been in Rome at his father's accession. He only just escaped with his life at the storming of the Capitol, and for a short time played a prominent part in politics as the only member of the imperial family on the spot. When Vespasian returned home, he sternly asserted his paternal authority over his son, consistently putting him in the background, and compelling him to devote himself to study instead of granting him a share of power. Domitian submitted, but with bitterness in his heart. He was burning with a desire for power, the sweets of which he had tasted, and felt himself to be the man fitted to carry on a more consistent policy than the opportunist rule of his father and brother.

This preparation boded ill for the future, when Domitian would take the reins of government. He is represented as one of the imperial tyrants. But his instincts were correct : he had in him the faculty of government, and he took the direction in his own hands. He kept himself free from the influence of favourites and freedmen, who had so often guided the actions of the Emperors. In important and dangerous offices, such as that of praetorian prefect, he made frequent changes in order to minimise the influence of the individual. The administration was strictly centralised, and provincial governors were made to do their duty more effectively than under any other reign with the exception of that of Tiberius. Severity and impartiality were observed in the judicature ; the Emperor put down the *delatores* and prevented partial judgments. But he was also inclined to govern by police methods, and in this way supervised and regulated everything possible. His financial administration was economical and good ; he filled the treasury and succeeded in improving the depreciated currency. He could also satisfy his inclination to the pomp and state which befitted the imperial majesty. He gave splendid games, and instituted the Capitoline festival, at which Greek and Latin poets and authors competed with each other. He took good care of the public libraries, and surrounded himself with poets like Statius and Martial. He was celebrated as the patron of the Muses by Valerius Flaccus and Silius, and entrusted the education of his cousins to the great teacher of the age, Quintilian. From Nero's vanity and meretricious art he was completely free.

It is stated that the favourite reading of Domitian was the memoirs of Tiberius. There is a certain likeness between the two Emperors and their activities, and in the judgment passed on them by posterity ; but the great difference between them was that Tiberius, though filled with a sense of duty, had great difficulty in forcing his will to function, and was always on the look-out for a real friend and helper. Tiberius became a solitary man, but Domitian was one by nature. He was dominated by a craving for power, which jealously reserved to itself every decision and action. This found expression even in his outward appearance. He regularly wore the purple : he only allowed statues of himself to be made of gold and silver : his attendants had to call him " our lord and god." Such a ruler was bound to come into conflict with the Senate, which, in spite of its subservience to the Emperor, jealously retained its privileges. Domitian despised it. He reserved to himself the right of trying Senators, and effectively put an end to the Senate's independence by constituting himself perpetual Censor, which gave him the right to determine its composition. Those who opposed him on principle, following the example of the younger Cato, were severely persecuted. In Senatorial circles this caused a secret and silent bitterness of feeling, of the strength of which Tacitus is our witness. The oppression was the more severely felt, as Domitian's interference was not the result of caprice but a deliberate policy, based on the consciousness of his strength and carried out with undeniable vigour and thoroughness.

Domitian knew he had offended the Senate : he did so with his eyes open. In spite of the splendour of his reign he could never be popular in the way his brother had been. He would do everything himself and therefore relied on no one. Thus he was driven to support himself by means of the army, and bought the devotion of the soldiers by successive increases of pay. On account of this the hitherto stable finances of the Empire fell into disorder, and he was forced to have recourse to those doubtful and odious methods by which Emperors in financial straits were wont to fill their chests. His greed for power grew ever more insatiable, and his government rapidly deteriorated from a just severity towards a despotism.

Domitian lacked all military skill and experience, and could not, therefore, on the battle-field win the respect with which he might have propped up his government. But his campaigns were not so unsuccessful as they were said to have been in later days. During seven years Agricola waged war on the Caledonians and Scots. Domitian recalled him, not from jealousy, but because the losses were great, and the possible gain, the barren highlands of Scotland, insignificant. His victories over the Germans, which were decried and questioned by later writers as zealously as they were celebrated by contemporary poets, have been confirmed by archaeological researches. With his usual systematic energy he proceeded to plan out a defensible barrier against the independent German tribes. More serious were the inroads he had to face on the lower Danube. The Dacians in Transylvania and Eastern Hungary had been so much influenced by civilisation, that they had reached a condition suitable for a united league, and even for the foundation of an Empire, if the right man appeared. In Caesar's time such a king had arisen, but Rome had been freed from the danger, when after his death his kingdom fell to pieces. Now a successor was found in Decebalus, who crossed the Danube and defeated and killed the Governor of Moesia. If the movement spread and affected the kindred population within the limits of the Empire, it would become doubly dangerous. The Emperor took the field himself, but soon returned to Rome and left the conduct of operations to his generals. They fought with very varied success. The praetorian prefect was defeated and fell in the enemy's territory. Though, later, Decebalus was defeated near his capital, Sarmizegethusa, the victory was inconclusive, because the Dacian King induced the Germanic tribes, the Marcomanni and Quadi, to intervene. In this war a whole legion was virtually annihilated. Domitian came to the conclusion that it was better to negotiate than to wage a costly and prolonged war. He granted Decebalus an annual subvention in cash, placed labourers at his disposal, and granted trading concessions. The Emperor's sense of dignity was satisfied when Decebalus' brother received the crown in the Roman camp. Domitian, who in other respects was anything but an opportunist, became one in foreign policy, because he did not understand how to wage war, and had no real grasp of external problems. After the ceremony just mentioned he could regard Decebalus as his vassal; but Decebalus could also regard Rome as a tributary State. Domitian had established a fateful precedent for the future in buying off the barbarians with money. He sacrificed the moral weapon, which in fighting the neighbouring peoples was as important for Rome as the sword, namely, her prestige. The triumph he celebrated after the Dacian War must have been regarded as a disgrace by all who had a clearer view of what should have been the foreign policy of the Empire, and the honour of Roman arms.

A ruler of the calibre of Domitian does not suffer with impunity a failure in campaigns and foreign policy. During the winter after the conclusion of the Dacian War the Governor of Upper Germany rebelled. He was soon overpowered and killed, since the assistance which was promised him by the Germans did not materialise, because the ice on the Rhine broke up. The consequence was a series of trials and executions. Domitian's naturally suspicious temper was not improved by his misfortune; and from his growing conviction that he had to face a secret opposition, trials for treason and denunciations became more numerous than ever before. An uncle and his two cousins, heirs-presumptive to the throne, fell under suspicion and were executed. One of them, Flavius Clemens, along with his wife Domitilla, probably had a leaning towards Christianity. Domitian's tyranny and unbalanced temper had brought him to such a pass that he could be sure of no one and no one was safe from him. It is asserted that he had the walls of his audience chamber faced with marble polished like a mirror, that he might see what went on behind his back. There is a certain tragic element in the fact that the only genuine affection that this man experienced led to his death. He had taken his wife, Domitia, a daughter of the famous general Corbulo, from her former husband during the short period when, after the death of Vitellius, he had played a part in politics. As Empress she became entangled in a liaison with a well-known actor, and Domitian divorced her, but loved her so much that he could not live without her and took her back. When Domitian laid hands on members of his own family, Domitia began to fear for her life, and became the heart and soul of a conspiracy hatched by the two prefects of the guard and some courtiers. Domitian was murdered by his own servants after a reign of fifteen years.

NERVA (A.D. 96–98)

The people were indifferent; the Senate exulted, denounced the memory of the murdered Emperor and pulled down his statues; the guard was angry, but had no candidate ready, for Domitian had extirpated his family. So the Emperor whom Senatorial circles had in readiness, the aged Marcus Cocceius Nerva, was recognised. He was a distinguished lawyer, who, during the previous reigns, had succeeded in steering a safe course through dangerous shoals. The manner in which he succeeded to the throne fixed the policy of his government— reaction against the absolutist tendencies of Domitian, and the restoration of the power of the Senate. But his position was insecure, and he had to sacrifice the murderers of Domitian to the wrath of the praetorians. More wise than Galba, he adopted the foremost general of the Empire, Marcius Ulpius Trajanus, and gave him a share in the government. By this means peace was ensured, but the Emperor himself died after being on the throne barely a year and a half.

TRAJAN (A.D. 98–117)

Trajan was at Cologne when he received the news of his adopted father's death. He was born in the Spanish town of Italica (near Seville). His father had raised himself from the ranks, distinguished himself in the Jewish War, and become consul and proconsul—a good example of the new nobility from the provinces, which filled the vacancies in the Senate. The son was the first Emperor to be supplied by the provinces, a sign of the times, as showing that Italy and the conquered peoples were now on a level. Like his father, Trajan was first and foremost a soldier, the first Roman Emperor who was really a capable general. He maintained order and discipline with severity, favoured merit alone, and took his share of the toils and dangers of a soldier's life. Hence he obtained the unquestioning obedience of his men. His first measure was to apprehend the praetorians who had compelled the execution of Domitian's murderers. He had them punished, and the praetorians in Rome did not venture to protest. They had found their master.

Trajan stayed a year longer on the Rhine, occupied in negotiations with the Germans, organising the troops, strengthening the defences of the frontier, building roads, and founding colonies (Nimwegen and Xanten). In consequence there was peace on this frontier for a century. The danger zone was removed to the middle Danube, where Trajan had to settle the incomplete reckoning with Decebalus and his German allies. In the first campaign, lasting two years, the Roman army invaded Dacia in three columns, won several battles, and took the capital. Decebalus had to surrender arms and engines of war, give up the southern part of the country, and promise to furnish auxiliaries. A stone bridge over the Danube at Turn Severin, and a road cut in the cliff through the Iron Gates, linked the new conquest to the Empire. A few years afterwards war broke out afresh. It ended with the complete victory of the Romans, and Decebalus, while in flight, took his own life. Many Dacians were killed or emigrated ; the whole country became a Roman province and

E

was filled with colonists, Sarmizegethusa receiving the status of a Roman colony.

In internal administration Trajan exhibited the same grandeur as in his wars, which were the only great offensives that imperial history has to boast of. On a grand scale he constructed the alimentary foundations begun by Nerva, the importance of which will be examined when we come to the question of the population of the Empire. He built a new harbour at Ostia, and the greatest and most magnificent of the imperial *fora*, which bears his family name and in which his ashes are deposited under the gigantic and still surviving column, the reliefs of which depict his Dacian wars.

Trajan was a straightforward soldier of simple habits, but not averse to good food and wine and love. His education was comprehensive but not deep or refined, his writings and despatches, some of which may be read in the correspondence of the younger Pliny, are remarkable for a compact and pithy style, which hits the nail exactly on the head. He was remarkable for an acute and shrewd common sense, and was animated by a feeling for justice and humanity with a certain touch of chivalry, which may have been due to his Spanish origin ; for with all their great qualities the Romans were always absolutely devoid of chivalry. This trait can be recognised in his relations with the Senate. Without relinquishing any of the imperial privileges, he treated it with a formal respect which caused that august assembly to confer on him the title of " the best " (*optimus*). Trajan was flattered by a distinction of this kind, for he had the soldier's inclination not to hide his light under a bushel. Colonies, legions, and buildings were named after him so freely, that one of his successors made it the subject of a jest.

Towards the end of his reign he had occasion to revive the never finally settled feud with the Parthians. The *casus belli* was, as usual, interference in the affairs of Armenia by the Parthian King. No Roman Emperor ever won such great successes against the hereditary foe as Trajan—successes which were facilitated by the disunion and confusion in the enemy's country. He conquered Babylon and Ktesiphon, the capital of the Arsacids, and Assyria and Babylonia became Roman provinces. But Trajan learned by experience that in the East it is easier to make conquests than to retain them. While he was penetrating as far as the Persian Gulf (it was asserted that he aspired to prolong his march of conquest to India in the footsteps of Alexander the Great) a dangerous rising occurred in his rear, which his subordinates could not suppress. He made his way back through hostile populations and recovered the most important cities, but all his gains were obviously in jeopardy. A Jewish outbreak, which raged in the south-eastern provinces, had probably a connection with this rising. In the midst of this crisis Trajan fell ill and began a return journey to Rome, but died on the way, in Cilicia.

HADRIAN (A.D. 117–138)

Before his departure, Trajan had appointed his relative, Publius Aelius Hadrianus, governor of Syria and commander of its army. On his death-bed he adopted him, and he was immediately recognised by the troops. The new ruler's first task was the settlement of the Eastern question. He solved it quite simply, by surrendering the conquests of his predecessor, an act of self-denial which Roman pride considered humiliating, but which was certainly well advised. Trajan's active policy had probably overstrained the resources of an Empire, which was no longer young, to the utmost limit of its capacity, and the land of the Euphrates and Tigris could not have been defended against the Parthians without great sacrifices, especially as the population showed itself consistently hostile and averse to the Romans.

Rumour had it that it was not Trajan who performed the act of adoption, but his wife Plotina, after the Emperor's death. We can understand that Trajan hesitated to appoint as his successor a man so completely different from himself, and one on whom he had not previously conferred any of the special official posts, by which the succession was usually distinguished. Hadrian had displayed great efficiency and had been serviceable in various tasks, but his chief recommendation was his relationship to the deceased Emperor.

The troops immediately saluted him as *imperator*, but some of Trajan's chief men, who disliked the change in public policy, and perhaps aspired to the throne themselves, formed a conspiracy, which, however, was detected and suppressed before Hadrian reached Rome. This was not a good beginning for the new Emperor, any more than was the sudden abandonment of the brilliant and forceful policy of his predecessor. The contrast between the two men was obvious and must have been generally felt. Hadrian began his rule by seeking to win popularity in all quarters. To the soldiers and the people of Rome he gave unusually large donations; to the subject populations he granted remission of arrears of taxation to an unprecedented degree, and he guaranteed to the Senate its privileges.

Trajan had directed the energy of the Empire outwards, but all Hadrian's activity was devoted to conserving and organising it internally. He never waged war except in cases of absolute necessity, and these wars aroused but little interest when they took place. On the contrary, he tried by negotiations and presents to exorcise the disturbances which constantly arose on the frontiers. Of these the most memorable was a fresh great rising of the Jews. Hadrian had founded a Roman military colony, Aelia Capitolina, on the ruins of Jerusalem, and had inaugurated the altar of Jupiter with sacrifices on the site of the Temple of Yahweh. He forbade circumcision, probably regarding this as a humane act, just as he forbade castration; but the Jews regarded these measures as a studied affront and a profanation of their religion. They rose and found a leader in Bar Kochba, the son of the Star, whose name suggests Messianic hopes tinged with the astrological superstitions of the day. The war was waged with all the bitterness of which religious fanaticism was capable, and when it ended, the Jews in Palestine were practically extirpated. Since then the Jews have had no native land, but their spirit of nationality, rooted in instinctive race-feeling and dearly cherished religious traditions, has resisted all attacks.

Hadrian was not a soldier, but he understood better than any one the importance of an effective army for the welfare of the Empire. The organisation of the army was one of his principal cares, and writers ascribe to him the initiation of the reforms which were carried out in the following age both in technical details and in organisation. We shall return later to the importance of these measures. He laid great stress on discipline and training, on which he desired to found the efficiency and fidelity of the army. He himself set a good example by sharing in the soldier's fatigues and daily life, and exercised a strict supervision of the troops. In internal administration Hadrian's reign formed an epoch. The Imperial Post was remodelled. He exercised a great influence on judicial administration and jurisprudence, and filled his council, which was the Emperor's supreme court, with prominent jurists, and reorganised the secret police. With untiring zeal he remodelled and recreated in every sphere of government. He had a genius for organisation, which profoundly affected future developments.

At his accession the finances were in a bad way. He himself left a memorandum on this subject in order to justify the necessity for his policy of tranquillity. In spite of the great expenses involved by the change of ruler, he soon succeeded in putting the finances in good order without imposing fresh taxation. He achieved this not merely by reductions in the military budget, but chiefly through his thorough-going reorganisation of the financial administration. Later on in his reign he was able to make a liberal grant to poor Senators, provident institutions, and to certain cities—especially Greek cities—which he loaded with presents. His buildings are countless. In Rome he rebuilt the Pantheon. His chief building, the double Temple of Venus and Roma, the largest in Rome, has been destroyed and much later was rebuilt with additions, part of which afterwards became the church of S. Maria Francesca. Near Tivoli he built his famous villa, still a place of pilgrimage for tourists and a quarry for works of art ; it was a vast undertaking, with annexes of various kinds, surrounded with parks and ornamental waters. He had a deep love for Athens, the city of ancient memories, in which he made a long stay, and held the office of archon. He completed its greatest temple, the Olympieion, which had been standing half finished since the days of the Seleucids, and added a new suburb, the gate of which is still standing, with the inscription : " This is the city of Hadrian, not of Theseus." Corinth received an aqueduct, and many a little town with a historic name rose again from its ruins. Next he turned his attention to Asia Minor, where the process of Hellenisation was making great headway and was deliberately abetted by him with energy. Various cities were founded, bearing his name, of which Adrianople in Eastern Roumelia is one that still retains it. His activities extended to every corner of the Empire, and evoked an increased zeal in the towns, many of which regained some of their old prosperity. On an equally grand scale he provided buildings of public utility, and devoted special attention to the construction of a network of roads.

All this restless and far-reaching activity was based on an intimate knowledge of the Empire, its needs and forms of government, which he had acquired in the course of his service in various posts under Trajan, and, during his reign, by constant journeys in the provinces. No Emperor travelled so much as he, not even Augustus in his early days. His first great journey at the beginning of his reign lasted five years. First he went north to Germany, where he set on foot his army reforms and completed the defences of the frontier ; then to Britain, where he made a rampart against Caledonia (the Scotch Highlands), then through Gaul and Spain to Africa, which he soon had to leave, because events in the East required his presence. By negotiations with the Parthians peace was restored for a long time to come. Then he travelled up the Euphrates and through Asia Minor to the Aegean Sea, the islands of which he visited. Then he visited the countries on the lower Danube, delimited the frontier, and returned to Greece, where he revived many old institutions and was honoured as a benefactor and a god, and was also initiated into the mysteries of Samothrace and Eleusis. By way of Sicily he returned to Rome. Three years later he visited Africa a second time, and in the following year made a fresh

journey to the East and Greece, where he founded Aelia
Capitolina, and again stayed in Athens. In Egypt he lost his
favourite, Antinous, the handsome young Bithynian, who
was drowned in the Nile, voluntarily sacrificing his life, it was
said, to prolong that of the Emperor. Where this accident
happened, Hadrian founded a city, Antinoopolis, and caused
Antinous to be deified. His cult spread all over the East, and
has preserved for us countless representations of the young
man's fair and melancholy features. To us this is the most
inexplicable instance of the deification of men in the imperial
age. The Hellenistic world knew no better way of rewarding
the Emperor for all his benefits.

Hadrian's journeys were an expression not only of a desire
to survey the Empire he governed with his own eyes, but also
of the nervous unrest, which was the chief characteristic of
his wonderfully complex and essentially modern personality.
His work as Emperor was guided by a genuine Roman
energy and sense of duty, but he was not bound by tradition
like the Romans. He was a reformer, who remodelled the
administration and military system on new lines, the consequences of which would be realised only in the future. He
demanded much of himself and also of others. With bared
head and often on foot he travelled through his domain,
taking part in the soldiers' exercises and sharing their food.
He loved the excitements of the chase. There was a good
deal of romanticism in him. He ascended Etna to see the
sunrise from its summit. His love of travelling was that of
the tourist as much as of the Emperor. In his villa at Tivoli
he imitated the notable places he had visited, the Academy
and Lyceum of Athens, the luxurious watering-place, Canopus
by Alexandria, the valley of the Muses,—it even contained
an Inferno. It was the romantic side of Hadrian which
cultivated the old memories and institutions of Greece, and
attempted to restore its cities to new life ; which loved the
archaic art of the age of Pisistratus, and made it the fashion
of the day. But at the same time he was influenced by the
current scepticism of his time and the restless search for a
spiritual anchorage. He was initiated into the old mysteries,

to which the spirit of the age once more gave power over men's minds, but on his death-bed he dictated the jesting lines to his soul :

> " Little tender wandering soul,
>   Body's guest and comrade thou,
> To what bourne, all base and pale,
>   Wilt thou be a'faring now,
> All the merry jest and play
> Thou so lovest put away." [1]

Hadrian had a prodigious memory. He remembered all the men he had ever seen, and all the names he had heard : he retained in his mind every detail of the figures of administration, and never forgot the books he read. He could, simultaneously, write, dictate, and carry on a conversation with friends. He had great literary and artistic interests, and was in touch with the most refined culture of his age. In all the arts he was an amateur, and as is usually the case with amateurs, he was sensitive and vain. It is said to have been dangerous to wound him in these respects. He surrounded himself with scholars and philosophers, disputed with them, and amused himself by puzzling them with knotty questions. He was especially proud of his architectural skill, and is said to have prepared the plan of the Temple of Venus and Roma himself.

His legislation was strongly influenced by the humanitarian ideas of the age. He tried in every way to foster justice, mildness, and liberality, but his intentions were hampered by his irritability and restlessness. He allowed no one to obtain any influence over him, and no one could be sure of his friendship. He soon dropped his assistants. In his relations with the Senate he respected its privileges and rights as strictly as Trajan, but he lacked the latter's broadmindedness, and, since the Senators could never count on him, he forfeited their sympathies, and they did not fail to recognise that his vigorous government and administration put them in the shade. So they grew to hate him, and after his death would fain have annulled his acts, as they did those of Domitian.

The last years of the old Emperor were clouded by such a

---

[1] Translated by Dr. B. W. Henderson.

grievous malady that he sought to take his life, and were embittered by the intrigues for the succession amongst his entourage. This led him to commit acts of severity ; for with regard to the succession he could not stand the interference of outsiders. His nonagenarian brother-in-law, who, when Hadrian was brought very near death by a severe hemorrhage, showed aspirations to the throne, was put out of the way, as was his eighteen-year-old grandson. What induced him to adopt Lucius Ceionius Commodus, we do not know. The descriptions we have of this man cannot be accurate ; for Hadrian would never have wished to make a dissolute cypher his successor. But Commodus died just before Hadrian, and then the Emperor immediately adopted a Senator, sprung from a family in Southern Gaul, Titus Aurelius Antoninus, but in order that Commodus' young son, Lucius Verus, might not be excluded from the succession, Antoninus was obliged to adopt him. At the same time Hadrian caused him to adopt his wife's nephew as well, a youth of eighteen, Marcus Aurelius Antoninus, a member of a Spanish family, which had attained Senatorial rank a century before. However moral and serious the young man may have been, it was certainly not a prophetic instinct of his qualities as a ruler that induced Hadrian to take this step, but rather a romantic interest in a youth who would be not unlike himself, or a mistrust of Lucius Verus, which the future showed to be justified.

Antoninus immediately received a share of the tribunician and pro-consular powers. Thus he became joint-ruler, and, because of Hadrian's illness, the ruler *de facto*.

ANTONINUS PIUS (A.D. 138–161)

When, after some months, Hadrian died, the change of rule was effected in complete calm. Antoninus, called Pius, because he defended the memory of his adopted father against the Senate's vindictiveness, and in spite of all protests carried through his apotheosis, has often been stated to have been the best of the Roman Emperors. His long reign is uneventful and our information is scanty. Quiet reigned everywhere. After Hadrian's great work of reform there was nothing to be done but to let the new order take firm root. Antoninus Pius was the pattern of a good and benevolent father of a family, economical in spite of his great personal wealth, simple and kindly, more fond of agriculture and country life than of the details of government. With the exception of one short visit to the East he never went further afield than Campania, excusing himself on the ground that imperial travels were a costly honour to the provincials. Thanks to his economy he was able to remit taxation. He was liberal with games and donations, and carried out much building. His chief construction was the great Mausoleum Hadriani, which the Popes converted into the fortress of Castel Sant' Angelo. He maintained excellent relations with the Senate, owing to his conscientious and somewhat indolent temperament. His reign of twenty-three years was a happy time, but rather for the Emperor than the Empire. He succeeded in living and dying in the tranquillity he so much loved, but it cannot be denied that the want of energy which he showed in his policy towards the neighbouring peoples, contributed to the storms which burst on his successor.

MARCUS AURELIUS (A.D. 161–180)

In his treatment of his two adopted sons, Antoninus Pius made a very marked distinction. The first place was given to Marcus Aurelius, whom he married to his daughter, Faustina. At his death he designated him as his successor ; but Marcus Aurelius thought it just to take his brother by adoption, Lucius Verus, into co-partnership. A joint-rule had existed before, but in this case a novelty was introduced, which was to have unsuspected consequences and foreshadowed the division of the Empire. Previously, certain Emperors in their old age had raised the heir-apparent to joint-rule in order to ensure the succession ; what happened now was a sharing of the Empire between two rulers of about the same age. But Marcus Aurelius had the advantage. Both to his contemporaries and to posterity he appeared as the real wielder of imperial power. Lucius Verus was a very insignificant person, who devoted his time to feasting and horse-racing.

His greatest merit was that he subordinated himself to his more important colleague without any attempt at rivalry. No credible accounts assert that the harmony between two such different men was ever disturbed.

During his earlier life Marcus Aurelius had been such an example of all that was good that it created uneasiness among his relatives. The old Emperor used to call him " that most veracious man." He devoted himself zealously to the Stoic philosophy, whose principles he not only studied but applied to the facts of life, and adhered to his teachers with an enthusiastic devotion, which he continued to exhibit even after his elevation to the throne. One can understand how a young man, filled with the highest philosophic and moral ideals, grieved when he found that he was destined to be heir to a throne and was faced with the certainty of having to exchange the sphere of thought and the realm of principle for an earthly realm, full of imperfections and opportunism. But he shouldered the burden manfully, and was an ideal son to his foster-father. It was a sense of justice which induced him, perhaps against the interest of the Empire, to share the government with his brother by adoption. Antoninus Pius had won universal respect by his justice ; the justice of Marcus Aurelius was on a higher plane and, perhaps, rather too abstract for an Emperor, but it was appreciated and supported by his government, as is shown by the universal sorrow at his death.

To his justice was added a benevolence which bordered on weakness, if we may trust our authorities. Gossip tells of his wife's breaches of matrimonial fidelity, yet he loved and honoured her, and in his writings thanks her for a happy wedded life. During his last years he elevated his son, Commodus, to a share in power, though he realised his worthlessness. But the instinct for legitimacy was so strong that nothing else was possible ; it was not to be expected that he would disinherit his own flesh and blood. He treated those who took part in the rebellion of Avidius Cassius with an unexampled leniency, but the circumstances and the consequences fully justified him in this course. To the Senate he showed the greatest respect, and never left a sitting until the consul formally dissolved it. In following this policy he trod the path laid down by Hadrian, and built up, even more durably than he, the imperial administration.

Behind all his deference he displayed a tenacious energy, in the way in which, without enthusiasm, but without hesitation, he took up and brought to a successful conclusion the tasks he deemed necessary. He felt no enthusiasm, and could excite no enthusiasm, because he was passing through a life which he regarded as a lower form of existence. At the games he read, received petitions, or signed papers in his box. His face was so immovable that it reflected neither sorrow nor joy ; he was not strong physically, and walked with feeble steps. In the field he usually rode, and therefore is represented on horseback in the famous statue of the Capitol—an equestrian statue being a rarity in antiquity. We can read his *Meditations,* the chief pagan book of edification that has come down to us. These confessions do not stir us with the fascination of freshness or originality ; they are the record of a soul, which has always kept and still keeps control of itself, which, in life's turmoil, longs to see things *sub specie aeternitatis.* Many of them were written in camp on the banks of the Danube. He warns himself against yielding to the temptation of power. " Beware lest thou play the Caesar ! Danger is for ever near at hand. Keep thyself good, pure, serious, justice-loving, affectionate, steadfast in the fulfilment of thy duties." He laments that life is so short and the good endless. " Life is short, and human existence has only one fruit, a blameless temper and acts of public usefulness." His benevolence is a philosophic duty, which he cannot ever fulfil adequately ; he forces himself to see the good in every one, and shuts his eyes to the evil. He will not believe in his wife's frailty and his son's degeneracy. His joyless optimism, which is repelled by the perversity and vanities of the world arises from the philosophic conviction that the world, somehow, is being guided to a rational goal. " The world is a tearing river which carries everything along. What avails against it—the activity of the statesman or the philosopher ? Hope for a Platonic state,

but be content if it only goes a little bit forward ! " Even
the bad has its function in the world plan. It is fitting that
man should love the stumblers, and suffer gladly the ungrateful and hostile. We should be compassionate to the
failings of men, and forgive them instead of being angry and
astonished.

What is human life, he asks—a dream or a shadow, a
strife and a wandering in a foreign land ? One thing alone
can point out the way—philosophy. He plunges deeply into
his own inner nature. " Why distress thyself about external
matters ; only in thyself thou shalt find rest. Think of thyself ! Care for the divine in thyself ! Free thy real self from
all outward appendages ! Know that everything changes and
is perishable ! Only within thee flows the stream of happiness,
which never dries up ! " As a Stoic he believed in providence
and revelations by dreams and prophetic utterances. He
thought that he himself had been assisted in this way. When
the war with the Marcomanni was imminent, he summoned
priests from all sides, filled Rome with strange ceremonies,
and purified the city by all methods so zealously that he had
to postpone the date of his departure to the war. The
Pasquino of antiquity produced an epigram which alludes to
the lavish sacrifices, in which his piety was expressed :

> " To Marcus the white oxen greeting send :
> Win one more fight, and all our lives must end."

It was decreed by the irony of fate that this Emperor
should have, more than any other, to do with the sorrows of
the Empire and the distress of the world. His predecessor
left him an evil legacy of strained relations with the Parthians,
against whom sufficiently strong measures were not taken.
The Parthians annihilated a legion in Armenia and defeated
the Governor of Syria. War had to be conducted on a grand
scale. Marcus Aurelius, who probably hoped that his colleague
would relieve him from the burden of actual military operations,
sent him to Syria. Lucius Verus enjoyed himself in Antioch,
while his generals drove the Parthians over the frontier. The
greatest merit was acquired by Avidius Cassius, who restored

the discipline which, as usual in the East, had become lax, and took Ktesiphon and Mesopotamia. Severe losses, however, were incurred. The war ended with Rome asserting her superiority and apparently slightly advancing her frontier in Northern Mesopotamia. The worst consequence was that the returning troops brought the plague with them into the Empire.

For the Parthian War it had been necessary to move troops from the Danube frontier, and the risk involved by this became evident when a storm gathered over all that part of it contained within the limits of the former Empire of Austria-Hungary. The German tribes were on the move from the Hermunduri in Thuringia to the Suebi by the Morava. Most prominent were the Marcomanni in Bohemia, and the Quadi in Moravia. They were joined by the Iazyges, a Sarmatian tribe occupying the wedge between the Danube and the Theiss which separated the provinces of Pannonia and Dacia. The tribes attempting to cross the frontier were probably being pressed on by unknown movements of peoples in their rear ; it looks as if the Slavs had also taken part. Dacia was ravaged ; other swarms passed through Pannonia over the Alps down into Italy and besieged Aquileia. The terror became great and even the Italian towns had their dilapidated walls rebuilt. It seemed as if an imperial disaster impended. Within the Empire the plague was raging, and of its effects the notes of an Egyptian official give us a glimpse. The villages were deserted and the fields left desolate, while the people sought safety in flight. In Rome the waggons which carried out the corpses were constantly rattling by, and strict measures were taken to secure their burial. The disease had originated in the army, and the troops, concentrated in camps, died like flies. In the midst of this misery, fresh dispositions of troops had to be made, losses of men replaced, and fresh recruits obtained. Slaves and gladiators were drafted into the army. Dalmatian pirates and German free-booters were enlisted, and two new legions were raised in Italy. The Parthian War had already strained the finances of the Empire, but the German outbreak produced a real crisis. The coinage was debased, and in a public auction, which lasted two months, the Emperor sold, in Trajan's Forum, the priceless imperial heirlooms, the accumulation of well-nigh two centuries, vessels of gold and precious stones, jewels, the gold-embroidered silk dresses of the Empress, the pictures and sculptures of famous artists.

Marcus Aurelius himself took command of the military operations, for he had learned by experience that Lucius Verus was incapable. But Verus accompanied him, and on the journey died of an apoplectic stroke. Only after two years' hard fighting and after many defeats and heavy losses did he succeed in driving the enemy out of the Empire and in re-establishing the security of the frontier. But this was not enough ; if there was to be quiet for the future, the foe had to be followed up and crushed in his own country. The first attack was directed against the Quadi, in a campaign which ignored for the moment the most dangerous opponents, the Marcomanni in Bohemia and the Sarmatians on the Hungarian plains. The Quadi were forced to surrender deserters and prisoners, their cattle and horses. Meanwhile the Marcomanni, harrying and plundering, swept over Rhaetia and Noricum. The Roman army overtook them at a moment when, loaded with booty, they were halting on islands in the Danube near Ratisbon. They were surrounded, defeated, and had to leave their booty behind them. Roman rule produced fresh conflicts and severe punishments. Masses of Germans were given homes inside the devastated Empire. Finally, the Sarmatians were beaten, the passes of the Carpathians blocked, and Roman divisions penetrated into Eastern Galicia. The Emperor was able to conceive the plan of adding two new provinces to the Empire, Sarmatia and Marcomannia.

Just then came the news that the victor over the Parthians, Avidius Cassius, to whom had been entrusted, in full confidence, the command in Syria and Eastern affairs, was in revolt. A premature rumour of the death of Marcus Aurelius had induced him to have himself proclaimed Emperor. He was a Syrian himself, and had much support from his fellow-countrymen and the Eastern troops. But when the rumour proved baseless he was soon deserted by his supporters and put to death. Marcus Aurelius was obliged to go to the East and leave the German War ; so the Sarmatians got off easily. On his return to Rome he celebrated a well-earned triumph over the Germans and Sarmatians, and soon afterwards raised his young son, Commodus, to a share in the government.

The tribes of the Danube were, however, far from pacified. A few years afterwards the Emperor, accompanied by his son, had to take the field again. The Marcomanni and Quadi were reconquered, and their country occupied by Roman garrisons. During the settlement Marcus Aurelius died in camp at Vindobona (Vienna). His son, who longed to return to Rome, soon withdrew the garrisons, remitted the tribute, and contented himself with levying recruits for his army. Thus he sacrificed all that had been won. A genuine doubt as to how far the recent conquests could be defended cannot be attributed to him. The last thirteen years' war must have dissipated all illusions as to a lasting peace between the Germans and the Roman Empire. The most peace-loving of the Caesars had been driven by the force of circumstances into a policy of aggression in Germany. It is possible that the Empire was no longer strong enough to complete it, but it was the only solution if its domination was to last in the future. In reality the policy of Trajan was more correct than that of Hadrian. The complete conquest and pacification of the Germans would not have entailed so much bloodshed and devastation as did the Civil Wars of the next century. It would at least have been worth while to make the attempt. Rome had her civilising mission to fulfil, but she was, and could only continue to exist as, a conquering State.

III

THE MILITARY EMPERORS

COMMODUS (A.D. 180–193)

A MOUNTAIN of disaster had been heaped by destiny on the royal philosopher, but the greatest tragedy of his life was his son. When for the first time for several generations a father was succeeded by his own son on the throne, the contrast between the two was seen to be extraordinary. It is quite intelligible that many should have thought it impossible that Commodus could be his father's son, and rumour would have it that his mother bore him in adultery with a gladiator. Commodus was dull-witted and absolutely devoid of intelligent interests, cruel and addicted to Oriental superstitions. He was completely in the hands of those who surrounded him, but at the same time he was cowardly and abandoned his favourites out of distrust, or to save his own skin. His greatest pride was his physical strength. He liked to appear as a fighter and gladiator, and to slay opponents who could not defend themselves. He sought all his society in the ring, and had himself represented and worshipped as Hercules with the club and the lion's skin. Like Hercules, too, he was immoderate in other pleasures, and had made himself comfortable with a well-furnished harem.

He quickly dismissed his father's counsellors and assistants. A conspiracy, in which some prominent men and his own sister, Lucilla, widow of Lucius Verus, took part, afforded an excuse for a massacre of Senators and vigorous revival of the *delatores*. The Senate was terrorised. A prefect of the guard, Perennis, managed the government, till some officers, who felt themselves threatened, roused the Emperor's suspicions against him. Perennis was succeeded by a freedman, Cleander, who, in true slave fashion, offered everything for sale, bartered offices and seats in the Senate, and in one year appointed twenty-five consuls. By chance a famine occurred in Rome. The soldiers were ordered out against the mob, and fared but poorly in the narrow streets, where tiles and stones were rained on them from the houses. The Emperor only allayed the tumult by sacrificing his favourite to the irritated populace. Such a Government, in which the Emperor and his favourites vied with each other in depleting the treasury, was bound to make the financial situation even worse. It is clear that judicial murders and confiscations were, as usual, resorted to in order to raise money. To such a government, constitution and tradition were mere empty words. No one cared about the Senate and its rights ; it had nothing to do but to flatter the Emperor.

If an attempt be made to divide the imperial age into periods, the violent contrast between Marcus Aurelius and his son suggests a natural dividing line. Commodus himself was anything but a warrior, but may claim to have inaugurated that which distinguishes the coming century, the power of the army. A Government like his had only one support, the sword. The guard was overwhelmed with money and favours, and was blindly devoted to the Emperor who taught it to manage the Empire and finances as it pleased. Throughout the length and breadth of the Empire affairs were allowed to follow their own course. The frontier armies with difficulty kept the enemy back, and luckily for Commodus, serious attacks were not forthcoming. But in the interior, distress and misgovernment upset all order. Italy was infested by bands of robbers : in Gaul marauders broke open the prisons, conquered towns, and, in unconcealed alliance with the oppressed population of the country, waged open war on the Emperor's generals.

At last power turned Commodus' head and he caused himself to be represented as a god on the coinage. His end, like that of Domitian, was brought about by a conspiracy at court. He had put away his wife, and lived with Marcia, a Christian woman, who did not think herself too good to be the Emperor's concubine. When she also and several of his courtiers fell under his suspicions, they determined to anticipate him, and caused a wrestler, with whom he was wont to practise, to strangle him. This happened on New Year's Eve. The next day the Emperor had intended to assume the consulship in gladiatorial costume.

PERTINAX (A.D. 193)

The conspirators offered the crown to an old Senator, Pertinax, son of a freedman and timber-merchant. He had shown efficiency in a series of high posts, and acquired a large private fortune. As before, in similar situations, the Senate took advantage of the accession to regain its influence and satisfy its vengeance on the murdered Emperor. But the praetorians were in a dangerous mood. When Pertinax presented himself to them, he did not venture to announce the murder, but gave out that Commodus had died a natural death. His first task was to scrape up money to repair the finances and pay the donations, which, according to custom, were promised to the guard at the beginning of a new reign. He ruthlessly auctioned Commodus' valuables and harem, and, besides, took sensible measures in the administration of finance. He soon succeeded in paying half the presents promised, but the praetorians would not be pacified. They understood that under the new régime they would not be allowed the same licence as under Commodus'. After barely three months a mob of praetorians rushed into the palace, murdered Pertinax, cut off his head, and carried it on a spear through the city.

When this happened, Pertinax's father-in-law, Sulpicianus, was in the camp in order to calm the troops. He immediately announced himself as a candidate for the throne, but another rich Senator, Didius Julianus, hurried to the camp and made his offer before the gates. One bid against the other, till Julian made the highest bid. In his excitement, and blinded by the glitter of the imperial dignity, he little thought how he was to pay the amount, or how he could defend his throne. The people of Rome were weary of the arrogance of the

praetorians ; they were sorry for Pertinax, and wished for
Pescennius Niger, the distinguished Governor of Syria, as
Emperor. But the decision lay with the legions, who had no
more intention now than they had at Nero's death of letting
the guard in Rome decide the question of the succession.

Three claimants put themselves forward, Pescennius Niger,
Septimius Severus, Governor of Pannonia, and Clodius Albinus,
Governor of Britain. Septimius Severus had an advantage
over the others. He commanded the strongest and most
redoubtable army in the Empire, and had the shortest way to
go to reach Italy. He adopted as an additional name that of
Pertinax, and moved on Rome as his avenger. There was
scarcely any resistance. Didius Julianus was quite helpless,
was deposed by the Senate and put to death, and Septimius
Severus was recognised. The praetorians received the punishment they richly deserved. This achievement is closely
connected with the important reforms in the army system
introduced by Septimius Severus, which will be described in
their proper place.

SEPTIMIUS SEVERUS (A.D. 193–211)

The most difficult task remained, the settlement with the
two other claimants. For the time being he left Clodius
Albinus alone, adopted him, recognised him as Caesar, and
committed Britain, Gaul, and Spain to his keeping, but placed
at his side a financial procurator to circumscribe his freedom
of action. He himself went eastwards to meet his most
dangerous opponent, who had already made every preparation
for the war. Pescennius Niger had possessed himself of the
key to Asia, Byzantium. Septimius Severus isolated the town,
passed over into Asia Minor, routed the troops of Niger and
forced them to retreat. Another victory on the historic ground
of Issus, where Alexander the Great overcame Darius, decided
the conflict. Niger attempted to fly to the Parthians, but
was overtaken and killed. Rivalry between the Greek towns
of Asia had broken out in their partisanship for one or the
other claimant. The conquered were severely punished.
The walls of Byzantium, which only fell after a three years'

siege, were demolished, and the city was reduced to the status of a village under the government of Perinthos.

Meanwhile Clodius Albinus had remained passive. He could not seriously have had any confidence in sharing power with Septimius Severus ; possibly he expected the latter to be defeated by Pescennius Niger, and that then, reinforced by the remains of Severus' troops, he would succeed in overcoming Niger. In the meantime he adopted the title of Augustus, and won considerable support in Senatorial circles, who rightly feared Septimius Severus. A conflict between the two was inevitable.

At Lugdunum (Lyons) the Illyrian legions faced those of Britain and Germany. After a severe struggle, in which the issue was doubtful, Severus, after a narrow escape from death, won the victory. Clodius Albinus was killed. Lugdunum was plundered and burned and never regained its old importance.

Almost immediately the Emperor turned again to the East, where the Parthians, probably instigated by the partisans of the vanquished, were creating disturbances. His successes were not very inferior to those of Trajan. The Parthian capital, Ktesiphon, was again taken and plundered. Northern Mesopotamia became a Roman province. The triumphal arch of Severus, still standing in the Forum at Rome, bears witness to his victories.

Severus was an African and did not fail to exhibit the ferocity of temper and vindictiveness for which Africans were notorious. We have seen an example of how he treated conquered antagonists. Then it was the turn of the Senate. After the defeat of Clodius Albinus, the Senators who fell in the battle were refused burial. When he got hold of the correspondence of his fallen rival, he did not burn it like Caesar, but, on the strength of it, sixty-four Senators were accused of high treason and twenty-nine condemned to death. The convictions were followed by colossal confiscations, by means of which he was enabled to pay the expenses of the war, reward the soldiers with large increases of pay, and amass a tremendous fortune. For the goods seized were added to the

Emperor's private property, and their revenues are said to have exceeded the revenues of the provinces and those of the old domains put together. Naturally this colossal sum became, in the end, crown property.

With the accession of Septimius Severus the State was considerably affected by the provincialism and militarism which had, for a short time, come into prominence with Avidius Cassius. The army was increased by the formation of three new legions, and the soldiers rewarded with money, social rights, and privileges. The old Italian guard had been dissolved, and now it was the soldiers from the provinces who played the part of masters. One of the newly formed legions was garrisoned at Albano near Rome, a sign of the rise of military domination, and Italy's loss of her privileges. The Senators were more and more excluded from important posts. The Senate was studiously ignored, and had little to do except signify its assent to the will of the ruler. The bureaucracy was militarised, the offices in large measure being occupied by officers and under-officers who had served their time. The jurists also played a great part. From this time forward the great jurists appear as praetorian prefects, but the hearing of cases was withdrawn from the publicity which was the rule in earlier days, and transferred to the privacy of the imperial palace.

It was said that Africans were superstitious. Septimius Severus certainly believed firmly in astrology. It is reported that he looked for a wife with a royal horoscope, and found her in Julia Domna, who belonged to the family of the ruling high priests of Emesa, the city of the Syrian Sun-god. She and her family were destined to play an important rôle in the history of the Empire. She herself was an energetic and cultivated woman, who collected authors and philosophers round her, and also opened wide the doors of Oriental influence.

By his wife, Septimius Severus had two sons. The eldest was called Bassianus, after his maternal grandfather, the high-priest of the Sun-god at Emesa. Septimius, who had the upstart's desire to exalt his pedigree and at first called himself Pertinax, subsequently adopted himself into the glorious

family of Marcus Aurelius Antoninus. Therefore he reha-
bilitated the memory of his brother, Commodus, and punished
his murderers, and renamed his eldest son with the honoured
appellation, Marcus Aurelius Antoninus. In history the son
is known by the nickname, Caracalla, from the Gaulish
soldier's cloak, which he generally wore. He was raised to
the rank of Augustus during the contest with Clodius Albinus.
The younger brother, Geta, was made Augustus just before
his father's death. The incessant quarrels between the
brothers were the sorrow of the old Emperor's life. It is said,
that in order to withdraw them from life in Rome and find a
diversion for them, he took them with him to his last campaign
in Britain, which was being troubled by the Highland tribes.
There he died at Eboracum (York).

CARACALLA (A.D. 211–217)

Caracalla and Geta jointly assumed the government.
This state of things was impracticable. As children they had
quarrelled over playthings, as grown-up men they quarrelled
over power. Their mother sought in vain to mediate between
them ; court and army were divided into two hostile parties.
Everything depended on the question, which of them would
overreach the other ? Geta had himself carefully guarded ;
but one day his brother invited him to attend a conference
with their mother in order to try and settle the dispute. Geta
came, and Caracalla also, but the latter had secretly brought
with him several centurions who rushed in and flung themselves on Geta. He fled to his mother's arms, and there he
was killed. Caracalla gave out publicly that the deed was
committed in self-defence, but his guilty conscience showed
itself in the presents he made to soldiers and people, and his
attempt to mollify the Senate by the recall of banished
Senators. He persecuted the memory of his brother with the
bitterest hatred, overthrowing statues of him and erasing his
name from inscriptions.

Caracalla aped Alexander the Great, but only succeeded in
caricaturing him. Misanthropy, wickedness, and dissolute-
ness are apparent in his features : he was no man's friend.

He persecuted the Senate like his father before him, and many prominent men, including his praetorian prefect, the great jurist, Papinian, became his victims. By inclination and disposition he was a soldier in the ordinary meaning of the word, but he lacked both the qualities of a leader, and the power of attaching the soldiers to him and taming their wills, which his father had. He could only make himself popular by paying them extravagantly and by sharing as a comrade in their life and pursuits, their work and fare. Thus, to some extent, he became popular, as is testified by his statuettes, used for domestic cult, which are more numerous than those of any other Emperor except Trajan. Caracalla also waged many wars, though few of great importance. He relinquished the government at Rome to his mother. He was a great builder. The Thermae of Caracalla are the largest in Rome, and were adorned with a magnificence hitherto unknown. He fought with the Germans, first on the Rhine, afterwards on the Danube : he also followed the dangerous precedent of purchasing peace with gold. Then he turned his attention to the East where there were threatenings of a Parthian war, and to Egypt. It is said that, irritated by the malicious wits of Alexandria, he instigated a massacre in the city. Alexandria was plundered and a great part of the population killed, but the reasons for such a proceeding were probably of a more serious nature. He returned to Syria and marched against the Parthians. On the march he was murdered at the instigation of his prefect of the guard, Macrinus, who had fears for his own life. Julia Domna died or committed suicide soon afterwards.

Macrinus, the first Emperor who belonged to the equestrian order, was not popular in the army, for he was suspected of the murder of Caracalla in spite of his efforts to conceal the truth. In Emesa there was living Julia Domna's sister, Julia Maesa, with her two daughters, Soaemias and Mamaea, each with a son of her own. The eldest, Soaemias' son, a youth of fourteen, was high-priest of the Sun-god, Elagabal, in Emesa. Probably his scheming grandmother formed the idea of putting this youth on the Roman throne, and it is significant of the power of the dynastic idea, even when, as in this case, the succession went through the female line, that the soldiers immediately accepted him. Officially he, too, was called Marcus Aurelius Antoninus ; usually he bears the name of his god, which the Greeks by a popular etymology changed to Heliogabalus.

HELIOGABALUS (A.D. 218–222)

What is told us of this boy, from sources which certainly do not err on the side of squeamishness, is a record of vice and scandalous depravity. While the Emperor wallowed in filth and perversions of all kinds, incited by the voluptuousness of the Oriental religion, whose priest he regarded himself first and foremost, his grandmother carried on the government, received a statue in the Senate's house of assembly, and was actually present at its meetings. Female rule had, at last, made its entry into Rome. Of Heliogabalus there is further to be related that he appeared wearing the symbol of royalty, the diadem, and demanded adoration; that he brought his deity to Rome in the shape of a black stone; celebrated a magnificent marriage between the Sun-god of Emesa and Astarte of Carthage, and caused the venerable Roman office of Pontifex Maximus to be supplanted by the Syrian high-priesthood. But this proceeding was not so eccentric as it is usually made out. Within a few decades the worship of the Sun was the official religion of the Empire, but the outward forms employed by Heliogabalus were at first too exaggerated and unfamiliar for the Romans.

Heliogabalus' behaviour and the economic disorders it inevitably entailed became, finally, too much even for the soldiers, who forced him to adopt his cousin, Mamaea's son, Alexander Severus, and when he attempted to put him out of the way, he and his mother were killed in a military rising. He was then eighteen years of age.

ALEXANDER SEVERUS (A.D. 222–235)

The new Emperor was thirteen and a half, a docile lad, who zealously devoted himself to his studies, and completely

lacked his cousin's precociousness.   A regency—a thing unique
in the history of the Caesars—became necessary.   His mother,
Mamaea, took the leading place though she avoided the offensive
form which, under Heliogabalus, practically made his mother
a member of the Senate.   And now again, as was the case
at every change of ruler which did not have a soldier as its
author, the Senate regained some of its influence.   The
Emperor had to rely on it, as he had not the control of the
troops.   A council of regency was appointed consisting of
sixteen Senators, augmented to seventy in dealing with more
important questions.

Alexander Severus' reign was the age of the great jurists.
The foremost of them, Ulpian, was praetorian prefect, but the
unmilitary and pedantic jurist was not popular with the
soldiers.   They mutinied, and he only escaped through the
Emperor intervening personally to protect him.   He could
not avert riots, in which for three days in succession the
Roman population and the soldiers fought a battle in the
streets.   Finally he was killed in a fresh rising of the soldiers,
and Alexander did not venture to punish the authors of the
crime.   The historian, Dio Cassius, had called down on himself the wrath of the soldiers by maintaining discipline while
Governor of Pannonia.   The guard demanded his death ;
Alexander made him consul, but advised him not to stay in
Rome during his consulate.   Frequent insurrections took
place.   They were certainly unimportant, and the pretenders
were soon rendered harmless, but they were portents of the
increasing lack of discipline in the army and of the impending
break-up of the Empire.

Alexander Severus' misfortune was his weakness of will.
That he was, throughout his life, in his mother's leading
strings, and took her about with him wherever he went,
lessened still more the respect for a monarch who was governed
by a woman.   In other respects he was an interested, extremely
well-meaning and sincerely right-thinking ruler.   Modesty was
not a virtue which distinguished the Caesars, but Alexander
rejected the name Antoninus, and the title Magnus.   He himself lived simply and economically, and did his best to abolish

abuses, to govern justly, to regulate the finances, to diminish the pressure of taxation, and to check luxury and support the destitute. The task was exceedingly difficult, and Alexander's weakness and lack of system and authority thwarted his good intentions. Significant of his character was his attitude towards the religious systems which were then contending for the control of the world. He had a vain hope that he could combine and reconcile them. Every morning he performed devotions in his private chapel, in which he had erected statues of the best of the deified emperors, the wonder-worker Apollonius of Tyana, Christ, Abraham, and Orpheus. To the Jews and Christians he showed favour. It is significant, too, that he had a greater knowledge of Greek than of Latin.

In happier days Alexander Severus might perhaps have become a second Antoninus Pius, but unfortunately he lived in an evil age. During his reign an event occurred, which was to prove fatal to Rome, in the neighbouring State in the East, with which Rome had fought for so many centuries. The Arsacids were overthrown by the Sassanids. In place of the Parthian Empire, always liable to disorder and often on the point of disruption, arose the powerfully organised and governed neo-Persian Empire. The first ruler of the Sassanid house, Ardeshir, demonstrated the renewed vigour of his realm by declaring war on Rome. The Syrian legions, as usual weak and undisciplined, fled before the shock, and the enemy penetrated far into the Empire. A great war was imminent, and after extensive preparations Alexander himself took the field. The Roman army advanced in three columns against the enemy. Defeats, mutinies, and the climate weakened its strength. Though the Persians were driven back and Alexander could celebrate a triumph, the feeling that the result was anything but satisfactory was widespread.

In the North, too, the enemy was knocking at the gates of the Empire. The Germans broke through the Rhine frontier, where no important war had been waged for two centuries, and penetrated deep into Gaul, harrying and plundering as they went. Other tribes crossed the Danube. The Emperor, with Mamaea, took the field again, but he retained only the shreds of his authority. In a rising of soldiers at Mainz he and his mother with him were killed.

MAXIMINUS THRAX (A.D. 235–238)

In the author of the mutiny, Maximinus, called the Thracian from his birthplace, the soldiers had found an Emperor to their taste, a man whose bodily stature and feats of strength became legendary. His wife's bracelet is said to have fitted his thumb ; his appetite and thirst were as fabulous as his strength. He had made his way up from the ranks, and won over the soldiers by the respect which his strength, simple soldier-like justice, and severity inspired. After the rule of Eastern monarchs, a barbarian of the North had succeeded to the throne. The parents of Maximinus were the one an Alan, the other a Goth. To a man of this kind the Senate meant nothing. He was the first Emperor who did not cause the Senate to confirm his position, and he designated his son as successor without even consulting it. He was also the first Emperor who never entered Rome during his reign.

His immediate task was to drive the Germans back, and in this he seems to have succeeded, both on the Rhine and the Danube. But the uneasiness in Italy was great. Would the country be once more given over to the tender mercies of the soldiers ? The people shared the disgust of the Senate, when Maximinus confiscated for the army the money which had been appropriated to the requirements of the civilian population of Rome. Then followed disturbances among the peasants of Africa, caused by the burden of excessive taxation. The aged proconsul, Gordian, and his son were proclaimed Emperors, and the usual sequence of events followed. Every rebellion that occurred in these times was accompanied with the proclamation of an Emperor. It was dangerous to refuse, for not only did the favoured individual risk his life at the hands of the excited mobs, but he was ever after suspected by the actual Emperor as a pretender. Thus many, however small their prospects of success, chose the purple in preference to the dangers of refusing, and were proclaimed Emperors unwillingly, like the two Gordians. The latter were soon defeated by the Governor of Numidia ; the son fell in battle and the father hanged himself. But the Senate had taken their part, and the attempt, by reason of the feeling in Italy, had not been without some prospect of success.

For the last time the Senate played a real part in politics. They appointed two Emperors, Pupienus and Balbinus, who really were only presidents of a committee of twenty Senators who conducted the government and the defence of Italy. But the country was seething with unrest, and the Senate thought it advisable to proclaim Gordian's young grandson as Caesar. Maximinus moved over the Alps down into Italy, but was detained before the important commercial town of Aquileia, which refused to submit to him. His attempts to storm the town were unsuccessful, and his fury was vented on his officers, while the rank and file became disaffected because of the lack of supplies, and turned against their hero. The mutiny originated with the legion which garrisoned Albano, and had left their wives and children behind them there. Maximinus and his son were slain in the street of the camp. But if the Senate thought it had won, it was mistaken. When it tried to restrain the soldiers, they retaliated by slaying Pupienus and Balbinus, and so the Empire once more had a minor of fourteen as Emperor, Gordian III.

GORDIAN III : PHILIP : DECIUS (A.D. 238–251)

His earlier years, during which others governed in his stead, are practically unknown to us. When after some years he married, he appointed his father-in-law, Timesitheus, as praetorian prefect, and he was the real ruler. Goths, Alans, and Sarmatians broke into the Balkan Peninsula, and the Persians into Syria. The Emperor and his father-in-law took the field, and on the way to the East, hunted down hordes of barbarians. The Persian king, Sapor, was defeated, but unhappily for Gordian, Timesitheus died, and his new praetorian prefect, Philip the Arabian, with the help of the army, demanded and obtained a share of power. Soon afterwards Gordian was killed in a mutiny, and Philip was proclaimed Emperor.

Philip was the son of an Arab sheik, or rather robber-captain, in the land east of the Jordan. It is of interest to know that he was favourably disposed to the Christians (who asserted later that he even secretly embraced their religion), and that it fell to his lot to celebrate the millenary jubilee of Rome, which was commemorated with great pomp and magnificent games. According to the traditional chronology, the city had been founded in 752 B.C. The jubilee looked like an irony of fate, for never had the ancient Empire been so hard pressed. It was creaking in every joint. The Goths had crossed the Danube in swarms, and devastated the Balkan cities far and wide, and rival Emperors were set up in various localities, one of them being Decius, the commander of the Danube army. In fighting with him at Verona, Philip lost the battle and his life.

Decius was the first of the series of Illyrian Emperors, who finally settled accounts with Rome's enemies and restored order—men of great vigour, but plain soldiers without culture or traditions. Decius handed over the conduct of affairs to an old Senator, Valerian, bestowing on him the antiquated title of censor. A notable event in his reign was the first systematic persecution of the Christians. He himself fought the Goths, but he was not successful as a general, and he is said to have been betrayed by his subordinate commanders, who made a secret understanding with the enemy in order to promote their own interests : Decius is the only Roman Emperor who fell in battle against the enemy, while dozens fell at the hands of their own soldiers. After two short-lived Emperors, Trebonianus Gallus and Aemilianus, Valerian was unanimously elected. He was an old man and immediately gave a share of power to his son, Gallienus.

VALERIAN : GALLIENUS (A.D. 253–268)

His reign, unusually long under the conditions of the time, was the blackest period of the Empire, which was, to all intents and purposes, broken up into independent sections. The Persians and Germans ravaged far and wide ; the coinage was debased almost to worthlessness. The Alamannians and

Franks crossed the Rhine, poured over Gaul and penetrated into Spain. The Roman possessions on the right bank of the Rhine, the *agri Decumates*, were lost. The Alamannians broke through Rhaetia into Italy, but were defeated at Milan. The Goths and their neighbours conquered Dacia, and overran the Balkan Peninsula. In the harbours on the north coast of the Black Sea they seized merchant ships, plundered the Roman towns on the south coast, and after acquiring a taste for Viking voyages, ravaged Greece and the coasts of Asia Minor. Other swarms crossed the Bosphorus, destroyed the cities of Bithynia, whose ruins for a century afterwards were a mute witness to their progress, and pressed on into the interior of Asia Minor. The plundering raid of the Heruli into Greece is famous, when the old historic cities were burned, and the historian Dexippos inflicted a defeat on one of their bands outside the walls of Athens.

It is uncertain if there was any connection between the Germanic inroads and the simultaneous attacks of the Persians. While Gallienus was fighting on the Rhine, Valerian took the field against the Persians, who had seized Armenia, overwhelming the Roman provinces, and massacring the population of Antioch. Failures in the field and the ravages of the plague induced Valerian to open negotiations with Sapor, the Persian King. At a personal interview he was treacherously taken prisoner. This event made a tremendous sensation. The Roman Empire had indeed sunk low, when its Emperor languished and died a prisoner in the enemy's hands. The demoralised Roman troops were overthrown by the Persians, who penetrated into Asia Minor, conquered Tarsus, besieged Caesarea, the capital of Cappadocia, and harried the coasts of the Aegean Sea with cavalry raids.

Out in an oasis of the Syrian desert lay Palmyra. The city had become a centre of Oriental traffic and provided convoys over the dangerous desert roads. It had only nominally submitted to Rome, since, in the interests of its trading position, it wished to stand well with both Empires. Its ruler, Odenathus, now realised that a decision must be made. He was inclined to prefer an alliance with the distant

Romans to one with the fanatical and arrogant young Persian Empire. So he sought an understanding with the Romans, and, supported by fragments of the Roman army, threw himself on Sapor as he was returning loaded with booty and preparing to cross the Euphrates. Other Roman forces closed on him from the North. The unexpected attack caused Sapor to leave booty and baggage behind and retreat over the Euphrates. Odenathus followed him into his own country, and there inflicted on him a severe defeat. Thus Syria was saved. Gallienus could celebrate a triumph, and formally appointed Odenathus his chief commander in the East, though his status was actually that of an independent ruler in alliance with the Empire.

While Valerian marched against the Parthians, Gallienus remained on the Rhine to face the Germans. Suddenly he was called away by the insurrection of a general in Pannonia, and left the conduct of the war against the Germans to his young son and to Postumus, the Governor of Gaul. He succeeded in overthrowing his rival in Pannonia, but meanwhile Postumus was proclaimed Emperor and, after killing Gallienus' son, ruled over Gaul, to which Britain and Spain were united, at least in name. The schism in the Empire was so real, and each portion was so fully occupied with its own enemies, that Postumus did not think of extending his claims further than over the Western provinces. These were, in fact, practically divided from the rest of the Empire, though there was no question as yet of a regular breach of its unity. Postumus imitated Roman institutions, creating a Senate, and issuing coinage in the name of Eternal Rome. His capital was Trèves. He reigned longer than most military Emperors, and Gallienus was not able to suppress him, but in the end he shared the usual fate of Emperors. His successors were masters of Gaul for some years longer. These Gallic Emperors succeeded to some extent in their chief task, that of holding back the Germans.

Meanwhile, in Africa disturbances took place. The wild independent tribes on the southern frontier rose *en masse*, with more co-operation than usual, and ravaged the country, until their king was taken captive. Finally, one of Gallienus' chief generals rose against him, but was beaten and besieged in Milan. At this crisis, however, a conspiracy was hatched against him by his generals in the camp. Gallienus was decoyed out by a false alarm, and received his death-wound from an arrow.

Gallienus is accused of slackness and want of energy, and during his last year is said to have become a slave to luxury and voluptuousness. But our sources of information are unjust to him. It can have been no ordinary man, who, at such a time, occupied the throne for fifteen years, and during the ten years after his father was taken prisoner, overthrew eighteen usurpers. His personal courage cannot be doubted, and he devoted as much attention to the army as any of his predecessors had done, introducing reforms in military tactics and a system of promotion suitable to the age. Even in Rome he regularly wore uniform, and it was he who excluded Senators from army commands. But obviously he himself was no general, and he lacked the toughness and the military bearing, which were regarded as distinguishing marks of a soldier during the supremacy of the Illyrians. Moreover, Gallienus belonged to one of the great Senatorial families, and had not worked his way up from the ranks. He retained an out-of-date liking for a refined and luxurious mode of life which the Illyrians regarded as a sign of weakness. He was the last Roman Emperor who really occupied himself with intellectual pursuits. He was a friend of the famous Neoplatonist Plotinus, the greatest philosophic genius of the imperial age, and at one time contemplated helping him to translate his philosophic ideals into practice by founding a city of philosophers in Campania. He had himself elected archon at Athens, like Hadrian, was a successful speaker, and wrote *vers d'occasion*. He was a gifted and ingenious man, but was devoid of that untiring energy by which the Illyrian Emperors succeeded in restoring the unity of the Empire. He had also to face not only the first great onset of the Germanic invasions, hitherto with difficulty held in check, and from now onwards a constant and increasing menace, but also the first great attack of the most vigorous of the Kings of the new Persian Empire, Sapor I., and a most serious mutiny of his own soldiery. It is certain that Gallienus did not deserve the ill repute which was cast upon his memory, but this treatment had now become the usual reward of the fallen Emperors.

CLAUDIUS : AURELIAN (A.D. 268–275)

His successor was the chief of the conspiring generals, Claudius, who, as a tribute to his victories over the Goths, earned the appellation of Gothicus. Tradition praises him in contrast to Gallienus as one of the best and most just of the Emperors. During his short reign he had only time for a war with the Goths. He recognised Palmyra, and let Gaul alone. First he repulsed the Alamannians, who had broken through the Brenner Pass, by a victory at Lago di Garda. Then he marched into the Balkan Peninsula, to meet a fresh great attack of Goths and other East German peoples. They came, it is said, 320,000 strong, with their wives and children, herds and waggons. This was no longer a mere plundering raid, but an attempt at settlement within the Empire. On the Dniester a fleet of 1200 ships was fitted out, and other hordes sailed southwards in these through the Bosphorus. One army besieged Thessalonica, another went further afield and ravaged Greece and Asia Minor as far as Pamphylia and Cyprus. Claudius threw himself between the two hosts. The one which moved from Thessalonica northwards was overcome by his general, Aurelian. With the main army there was a bloody battle at Naïssus (Nish in Serbia). The pursuit was more calamitous to the Goths than the battle itself. Famine in the devastated land and pestilence completed their destruction. Only a fraction escaped, while others settled as colonists in the Empire.

Soon afterwards Claudius Gothicus fell a victim to the plague and was succeeded by his chief general, Aurelian, the son of a small farmer near Sirmium. Aurelian began by driving back fresh German hordes. Then he decided to abandon Dacia, and its inhabitants were transferred to the near side of the Danube. Since the time of Gallienus all

Dacia, with the exception of a few strongholds, had been in the enemy's hands ; yet it was significant that one of the Empire's strongest rulers acquiesced in the first great loss of territory the Empire had sustained. Another sign of the times was the encircling of the city of Rome itself by strong walls ten miles long. The Alamannians and other tribes had overrun the plains of the Po, inflicting a distinct reverse on the army of Aurelian, and had crossed the Apennines. Warned by the proximity of this terrible danger the Romans proceeded to fortify the capital, which, since the days of Hannibal, had not seen an enemy. Eternal Rome was no longer defended against the Germans by its army on the frontiers, but required in addition the protection that walls could give. These walls, which in places are still standing, were only completed by Probus. But for the moment the barbarians divided their forces into plundering raids and were thus once more conquered.

Now was the opportunity once again to restore the unity of the Empire. Odenathus had vigorously maintained the independence of Palmyra, and overcome two Roman usurpers. Just before Gallienus' death, he was put out of the way by his own people. His widow, Zenobia, seized the government for her young son. She was an energetic woman of refined tastes who retained the philosopher, Longinus, as her chief adviser. She succeeded in acquiring Egypt by overthrowing an usurper against whom Claudius Gothicus had not time to take the field. Even Aurelian at the beginning of his reign recognised her dominion, which embraced the greater part of the East ; for in addition to Syria and Egypt, part of Asia Minor was subject to her. Under a vigorous Emperor this division of the Empire could not long be borne. Aurelian secured Egypt and marched into Asia Minor. Antioch fell without resistance, and only at Emesa was a great battle fought. Aurelian gained the day, and determined to attack Palmyra itself, which believed itself secure in the remoteness of its desert fastness. The city was beleaguered, and after Zenobia had been captured while attempting flight, surrendered. It was treated leniently : Zenobia was sent to Italy and there ended her days in peace, only her advisers being executed. But the city could not put up with an inferior position, and when the Roman army marched away, rose in rebellion. In hot haste Aurelian returned, and inflicted severe punishment. The city was again taken and plundered, and its inhabitants put to death. The greatness of Palmyra was over, and its fate was sealed by a change in the trade-routes. The desert sand covered the city which once ruled over the whole nearer East : its ruins, to this day, are more imposing than those of any other cities of the Roman age.

The recovery of Gaul was an easier task. After Posthumus' death there was a succession of rulers under whom the rival Empire went to pieces. The last, Tetricus, was in such a plight that he found his worst enemies among his own followers. In the final struggle Tetricus is said to have revealed the plan of campaign to Aurelian, and during the battle went over to him. Thus the unity of the Empire was restored, and Aurelian celebrated a brilliant triumph. He planned a renewal of the war with the Persians, but while on the march was murdered by some rebellious officers near Byzantium. A clerk, who was afraid of punishment, had made them believe that the Emperor was thinking of condemning them to death.

Aurelian is celebrated as the restorer of the Empire (*restitutor orbis*), and he should not be deprived of the credit for this, even if it was not due to his own vigour alone, but was also partly the result of the efforts of his predecessors. His reign lasted so long that his achievements were considerable at home as well as abroad. They were remarkable because of the great changes in the form of government and the great increase in the Emperor's personal power. Like all the Illyrian Emperors he had the simple habits of a soldier, but when he made a State appearance, he wore the diadem and the gold-embroidered and jewel-decked robes of an Eastern potentate. He was addressed as " lord and god." The monarchy had become absolute. The financial stringency was eased because the tribute from the provinces flowed in again, and the booty of the Palmyrene War provided its share : but it was a slight and only temporary relief. Aurelian endeavoured in vain to improve the currency, but only succeeded thereby in causing a great riot in Rome, instigated, it is said, by the dishonest officials of the mint. He provided liberally for the provisioning of Rome, and tried to relieve distressed agriculturalists.

In the battle of Emesa there was a divine apparition which gave fresh courage and discipline to the troops of Aurelian, who were on the point of giving way. When the Emperor entered the Temple of the Sun-god at Emesa, he recognised the god who had helped him to conquer Zenobia. The same god, whom, half a century before, Heligobalus had attempted to make the supreme god of the Empire, now received a grand temple in Rome, and his priests superseded the old and venerable Roman college of pontiffs. Under Aurelian Sun-worship became the official religion ; he was its zealous devotee, and his mother is said to have been priestess of the Sun-god in the Moesian town where he was born. Thus Aurelian, in addition to his other innovations, was the founder of a new State religion in accordance with the ideas of the time.

TACITUS : PROBUS (A.D. 275–282)

When the treachery to which Aurelian fell a victim was discovered, the army was ashamed, and determined to refer the choice of a ruler to the Senate. It was no wonder that the Senate hesitated. Finally, it nominated the aged and respected Senator, Tacitus. Tacitus himself realised that a younger man was needed, but the Senate wished to regain its old supremacy. This supremacy was secured for a short time only, for after a few months Tacitus was murdered by the soldiers. In his place came Aurelian's chief lieutenant, Probus, the commander in the East. Probus treated the Senate with great respect, and allowed them to retain the rights which Augustus had granted them. His short reign was spent in constant struggles with the Germans and with pretenders. It is suggestive of the state of the Empire, that a body of captive Franks, who had been planted on the Black Sea, having seized some merchant vessels, harried the coasts of the Aegean, then sailed along the Mediterranean—plundering Syracuse and Carthage on the way—through the Straits of Gibraltar, and finally succeeded in reaching the mouth of the

Rhine. Nowhere did the peoples of the towns think of offering any resistance to this band of robbers, though they could not have been very numerous. When the enemy gave Probus a respite he caused the soldiers to execute works of general utility, to build bridges, make aqueducts, and plant vineyards. This peaceful work was his undoing, for the soldiers he commanded were not like those of Augustus. In a struggle with a new pretender, Carus, he was killed by his own people. Carus renewed the war with Persia, once more conquered Ktesiphon, and prepared to move further into the Persian Empire. Then he fell a victim to a military conspiracy, though, according to another account, he was killed by lightning in his tent. He had given a share of his power to his two sons, Carinus and Numerian; the latter had accompanied him on the Persian campaign, and now led the army back. As he was suffering from a malady of the eyes he was carried in a closed litter. When they arrived at Nikomedia near the Bosphorus, some one thought he detected the smell of a corpse; the curtains were drawn and the Emperor's dead body was discovered. The suspicion fell upon the praetorian prefect, Aper, who was accused of having murdered the Emperor. The election of a new Emperor was demanded, no one considering that there was one already in the person of Carinus. The council of chief officers selected Diocletian, who, when he appeared before the army, unsheathed his sword, raised it to the sun, and swore that he was innocent of the murder of Numerian, and had not aimed at the crown. Then he turned to the praetorian prefect, who stood behind him, and exclaimed : "This man was the murderer," and ran him through with his sword. A Gallic prophetess is said to have foretold that the crown would be his, after he had slain a wild boar (*aper*). The soldiers applauded this summary execution. Carinus, who is described as a debauchee, but not lacking in courage, had still to be dealt with. He collected his forces to battle, and met Diocletian at Margus (Morava in Serbia). The victory had almost been his, when an offended subordinate seized the occasion to deal him a death-blow. Thus Diocletian became sole and undisputed ruler.

IV

REORGANISATION AND THE CONFLICT OF RELIGIONS

DIOCLETIAN (A.D. 284-305)

GAIUS VALERIUS DIOCLETIANUS was a Dalmatian. His birth is as obscure as that of most of the Emperors of this period. His father is said to have been a freedman, who originally bore the Greek name Diokles, which he latinised that it might sound more imposing. He had not held any high command, but had been consul, and under Numerian was appointed commander of the Emperor's bodyguard. His trustworthiness was thus known, and his efficiency must have been widely recognised, as the generals were united in their choice of him as Emperor. He is said to have been under forty at the time, but this statement is disputed.

Diocletian resembled Augustus in this respect, that he was not primarily a soldier, but devoted himself to the organisation of the State. Certainly, like the other Emperors, he had raised himself by a military career, but having done so, he generally left the conduct of his wars to others. A year after his accession he appointed a somewhat younger brother-in-arms, Maximian, as Caesar, and soon afterwards made him his partner and co-regent with the title Augustus. Maximian was typical of the soldiery of the day, an Illyrian of low birth, a brave and capable soldier, but no more. For the interior organisation of the Empire he had neither interest nor knowledge, but completely subordinated himself to Diocletian, who knew how to bind to himself his rude and unbridled nature.

Maximian was allotted the West and took up his residence

in Trèves. Gaul was vexed, not only by the usual German inroads but also by grievous internal disturbances. The ferment among the oppressed peasants had already, at times, broken out in open insurrection, but now it took on greater proportions than ever. The peasants were joined by the nomadic shepherds from the great pasture lands, and the German forced settlers, who had not forgotten the use of their weapons. The insurgents, who were called Bagaudae, put two so-called emperors at their head, harried and plundered the farms, and burnt the towns. The whole of North and North-eastern Gaul was already desolate, and all social order dissolved. When Maximian arrived with sufficient troops he quickly succeeded in restoring internal quiet—though the social abuses continued—and in keeping back the German marauders ; but more trouble was caused by piracy. The Franks had moved down the Rhine to the sea, and in alliance with the Saxons had built ships and were plundering the rich coasts of Gaul. The command against the pirates was entrusted to a German in the Roman service, who understood sea warfare, Carausius. He built a fleet at Boulogne, and instead of driving away the pirates, he let them go out on their raids, and met them when they returned loaded with booty. Thus he obtained the means wherewith to purchase his soldiers' devotion. When Maximian found out his treachery and condemned him to death he hoisted sail and repaired to Britain, where the troops saluted him as Augustus. Thus came the notable episode in which England, for the first time, played the part assigned to her by nature, that of a sea power. For the present Carausius had to be recognised as ruler, and was left in undisturbed possession of Britain.

Possibly it was this failure which determined Diocletian to subdivide the imperial power still further. Two men were not sufficient to wage all the wars in which the Empire was involved. Diocletian adopted Galerius, Maximian adopted Constantius Chlorus. Both were, as Caesars, to be lieutenants of their Augusti, and in course of time to succeed them. Constantius was an Illyrian, but of a good family which included Claudius Gothicus in its pedigree. He had a respect

for culture and humanity, was loyal in disposition, and famous
for his mild government and humane fiscal policy. His first
task was to subdue Carausius. He began by depriving him
of his bridgehead on the Continent, without which, then, as
later, Britain could not maintain her supremacy at sea. First
he took Boulogne, Carausius' *point d'appui* on the Gallic side
of the Channel, and the larger part of the fleet fell into his
hands. Then he suppressed the Franks, and punished the
crews of Carausius' fleet. As soon as he had built a flotilla
on which to cross over, he was in a position to strike at
Britain. Under cover of a thick fog he landed his troops on
the south coast. The victory was easy, for Carausius, who
was undoubtedly a striking and vigorous personality, had
previously been murdered by his praetorian prefect. Britain
was now reunited to the Empire. Constantine showed great
leniency to the population (which in fact was innocent of what
had happened), and after this often resided at Eboracum
(York).

His other headquarters were at Trèves, a convenient centre
from which to hold in check the constant inroads of the
Germans. The frontier was strengthened by the building of
a series of forts. After a great victory at Langres he took the
offensive and invaded the Alamannian country. At the same
time Galerius fought the Germans on the Danube and succeeded in inflicting on them a severe but only temporary
defeat.

Diocletian had reserved the East to himself. Like the
other Emperors he travelled constantly, and when not doing
so he resided at Nikomedia near the Bosphorus, which he
adorned with splendid buildings. His chief military expedition was directed against Egypt, where the ever-restless
population of Alexandria had risen and proclaimed a rival
Emperor. The city offered an obstinate resistance, and when
it fell, was sacked by the soldiers amid horrible scenes of
devastation and massacre. But when the penalty had been
paid, Diocletian sought to propitiate its impoverished inhabitants by granting them for the future a plentiful supply of
corn.

The never-ending struggle with Persia remained quiescent during the early years of Diocletian. The Persians had, however, seized Armenia, where, since the Sassanids overthrew the Parthian power, a branch of the Arsacids had been ruling. The heir to the throne, Tiridates, had taken refuge with the Romans and distinguished himself in the Roman service. With the consent of Diocletian he returned to his native country and was greeted as a liberator; for the religious oppression of the disciples of the Avesta pressed hard upon the inhabitants. When a young and ambitious King, Narses, ascended the Persian throne, he turned against Armenia and drove out Tiridates. The Romans had to intervene, and Galerius, who had completed the campaign on the Danube, assumed the chief command. He committed the same mistake as Crassus, being involved in a battle on the plain not far from Carrhae, where the superior numbers of the Persian cavalry could be utilised, and lost all his army, barely escaping with his life. Diocletian came with reinforcements, and when Galerius met him, the Emperor compelled his Caesar, clad in the purple, to run alongside his chariot for a full Roman mile without vouchsafing a single word. But he did not supersede him, but gave him another chance, and this time he atoned for his fault. The army was led against Armenia through the mountains where the Persian cavalry could not deploy. On a suitable occasion Galerius himself reconnoitred the Persian camp, and surprised it the next morning with success. Narses fled, wounded, and abandoned his army, war-chest, and harem. The battle was so decisive in its effects that the great King himself began negotiations, and conceded a rectification of the frontier advantageous to Rome, by which the upper Tigris valley came under Roman sway. After this peace actually prevailed for half a century.

Diocletian's reign was a period of success in warfare and was also remarkable in internal administration. In our sketch of the constitutional history we shall constantly have to refer to his reforms. It was he who converted the Emperor into a despot, far removed above his subjects, and raised to the dignity of a god. He was aware of the dangers involved by the consequent isolation of the Emperor, and expressed regret at the necessity for it, and it is clear how weighty must have been the reasons which induced him, of all men, to adopt this change. It is incredible that the reason could merely have been his personal love of power and pomp ; from these failings he was completely free. He attempted to regulate the succession in a manner which would provide the Empire with the most efficient rulers. He reorganised the army and the provinces, bureaucracy and taxation. He attempted to restore the currency and sound economic conditions. In every branch of the administration and in its minutest details his influence was felt, and beneficial reforms inaugurated.

It has been said that Diocletian's work, like that of Augustus, was a restoration, which looked back to the past. That is scarcely correct. Diocletian built on the foundations already laid, and developed institutions already in existence, but he was without a scrap of enthusiasm for the past, and only retained what he regarded as suitable to the time and to his purpose. He cannot perhaps be numbered among the world's greatest men, but he had a genius for organisation and he had an enthusiasm for systematising, though he may perhaps have over-estimated the value of a system. His great mistake was his regulation of the succession : in other respects his system stood the test. Moreover, he had to deal with a people who, from the oppression and experience of centuries, had learned to acquiesce in systematisation from above.

There was an iron will latent in that tall lean figure. The influence he exercised over his coadjutors—self-willed and headstrong men, who had grown up to manhood during the licensed orgy of the military despotism—was wonderful. Never was discord or division heard of among them ; they submitted without a question to the great man. In spite of intense personal resentment which future events revealed clearly, Maximian made no attempt at resistance when Diocletian called on him to resign the purple. No one who has ever read of it can forget that incident, when the Caesar, Galerius, clad in the purple, had to run like a slave alongside of his Emperor's chariot. Diocletian was quietly confident that the quick-tempered and ambitious man, who, whenever he read his title " Caesar," exclaimed, " How long shall I be only Caesar ? " would never turn against him. He knew he could always rely on his loyalty and ability, and sent him back immediately against the enemy at the head of an army. Diocletian, like Napoleon, was a ruler of men : to us he scarcely seems a good judge of men, but that is due to the great gulf between the spirit of that age and of our own.

Diocletian was not in the least hard and suspicious by nature. He abolished the secret police, and exhibited remarkable leniency on his accession, when he did not take vengeance on his defeated rivals, and even allowed Carinus' officials to retain their posts. Like all systematic men he judged resistance to his system as being on a very different plane to resistance against his person, and to those who revolted against the State he was irreconcilable. This explains his severe treatment of unfortunate Alexandria, and the measures he took against the Manichaeans, who were persecuted with the severest penalties—death by burning, penal servitude in mines, and complete confiscation of property. Manichaeism had spread, especially in Africa, and had been the cause of disturbances. Besides, its Persian origin and the Persian connections of the sect rendered it suspect.

This dominating tendency in the character of Diocletian— his only passion—must be remembered in any examination of his motives for the persecutions of the Christians, on account of which he was for long given a place among the number of imperial tyrants. The historical sources of our information are extremely biassed. The heathen authors, who described the persecutions, have been deliberately mutilated in this matter, and the imperial edicts have been suppressed. The only explicit account is the treatise on the death of the persecutors by the Christian father, Lactantius. It was certainly written by a contemporary, who lived in Diocletian's capital, but objectivity and veracity are naturally the last things one would look for in it. Lactantius states as the cause of the outbreak of persecution, that an important sacrificial rite, with its attendant inspection of the entrails of the victim, by which the future was read, was disturbed by the Christians present, who, by making the sign of the Cross, drove away the spirits. In that form the account is, of course, incorrect. Diocletian had had Christians about him for eighteen years, and previously they had often been present at his sacrifices. Nor can one shift the blame to Diocletian's superstitious beliefs or to an increase of pagan piety. His superstition was limited to the fatalism peculiar to the disposition of a ruler like himself, with a tinge of the current ideas and cult usages of the age. The real instigator of the catastrophe is said to have been Galerius, whom the Christians rightly hated far more than Diocletian. His repeated and vehement warnings are said to have impelled Diocletian to let loose the persecutions. But Diocletian was not the type of man to yield to warnings if he did not approve of the reason. Another account infers that the Emperor had been influenced by an oracle of Apollo of Didymae, but that cannot have been more than the official excuse for initiating the persecution.

The persecution of Diocletian was the only attempt on a grand scale by the heathen State to suppress Christianity. All the earlier persecutions had either been accidental or of short duration, like those ordered by Maximian, Decius, and Valerian. For half a century the Church had had peace and complete security. This was the period of the great spread of Christianity, as was obvious to all. Great and stately basilicas rose in the cities. Conversions to Christianity of individuals in the higher and highest circles of society were numerous. There were Christian officials, officers, and governors of provinces, and the court itself was full of Christians. The Government respected their religious scruples, and they, on their part, respected the pagan forms of State life. For eighteen years Diocletian had let everything go on in the old way. He was lenient and well disposed to the Christians around him. There is something mysterious in the outbreak of persecution, for the change in Diocletian's attitude cannot be ascribed to a sudden whim or the instigation of others. When he had formed his resolution, he put it into effect with his usual systematic and implacable energy.

The general persecution had one precursor, or two, if we reckon the bloody suppression of the semi-Christian Manichaeans. As early as A.D. 297 a sifting out of the Christians among the officers and in the army took place. Sacrificing to the Emperor, from which Christians had hitherto had a dispensation, was made obligatory for men in official positions. This was a point which the adherents of Christianity could not concede, and those who steadfastly adhered to their faith had to resign. Six years later, on February 3, A.D. 303, the praetorian prefect, with his followers, presented himself at the church of Nikomedia, had the doors broken open, the sacred books burned, the sacred vessels plundered, and, finally, levelled the building to the ground. On the following day an imperial edict was issued, which gave orders to destroy the churches and burn the sacred books, and prohibited all meetings of the Christians. Then their civic rights were curtailed ; they might not hold offices and posts of honour ; they might, without regard to their social position, be subjected to torture after trial ; men of low rank lost their franchise and Christian slaves might not be liberated. Christianity was to be confined to the lowest strata of the population, which were not eligible either for administrative posts or the army. According to the evidence of Christian writers themselves, Diocletian at first, on principle, avoided bloodshed.

Confident in their strength and embittered at their degradation, the Christians brought the catastrophe on themselves. The first martyr was a distinguished Christian, who, with scornful words, tore down the imperial proclamation. Soon after its publication, twice in a fortnight, a conflagration broke out in the quarter of the imperial palace inhabited by Diocletian himself. It was no wonder that the Christians were suspected of having caused the fire. An inquiry was held with the usual accompaniment of torture. Many Christian court officials and members of the congregation of Nikomedia were put to death. The next event reported was an insurrection of the Christians of Antioch and of Melitene in Cappadocia. These were attempts which were doomed to failure from the start. Resistance led to the adoption of stronger measures. A second edict ordered the imprisonment of the leaders of congregations ; a third prescribed that if they sacrificed they should be released, but if they refused they should be forced to do so by every possible means ; a fourth finally extended this alternative to all Christians.

Diocletian began by purging the army and officialdom of the Christian element. After an interval of some years he went on to deprive Christians of their right of assembly and to stigmatise them with other marks of social inferiority, and in the end was driven by force of circumstances to employ still more drastic measures. The whole sequence of events points to his gradually having arrived at the conviction that Christianity was incompatible with the organisation of the State, as he conceived it. The Christians' readiness to make concessions in matters of form and to submit with a good grace in many cases in which they came up against officialdom, had long concealed the irreconcilable opposition in principle which actually existed between the claims of Christianity and those of the State. It was no accident that Diocletian began with the army ; there the conflict of principle first became acute. An intense Christian faith might lead to a refusal to bear arms. When Diocletian once realised the source of danger he attacked it with his customary energy.

There is no time here to narrate the story of the persecutions in detail, or to try to distinguish those scenes of horror which actually took place, and are numerous enough, from those which were invented to add lustre to the martyrs. The result was that the great persecution strengthened the Church, and prepared it to undertake a more important rôle. It was in the East that the worst instances of persecution occurred. That was due, not merely to Diocletian's merciless energy and Galerius' pagan zeal, but also to the fact that here the Christians were more numerous and, therefore, more powerful and dangerous than in other parts of the Empire. In Africa it was chiefly a question of the giving up (*traditio*) of the sacred books. In the West, where the Christians were least numerous, Constantius Chlorus contented himself with pulling down churches and forbidding meetings ; here the Christians were not persecuted and were even permitted to remain at court. His milder temper seems to have restrained him from actual persecution. The Christians who, in him, honoured the father of the man who enabled Christianity to triumph, gave out that he himself was attached to Christianity.

Soon after the publication of the first edict Diocletian repaired to Rome, which he had scarcely visited before. His wish was to celebrate a triumph at Rome for all his victories and, simultaneously, though somewhat prematurely, the twentieth anniversary of his accession. He constructed in Rome the grand Thermae, which bear his name, and made a great donation to the populace, but did not feel at home in the city of ancient memories and historic institutions. The games he gave were inconsiderable, and when complaint was made about them he replied, that profusion must be limited in the presence of the Censor. He would not even remain at Rome to inaugurate his consulship, but left the city on one of the last days of the year. During the journey he fell ill, and at the end of the following year his malady became so much worse that it was thought he would die. Not until the spring did he appear again in public, and was then so much broken in health that he was hardly recognised. The malady must have caused him to take the decision he now put in force ; for the supposition that Galerius compelled him to resign in his favour is contradicted by everything else that we know of the relations between the two men. Diocletian felt that he no longer retained the vigour which a ruling Emperor required, and drew the obvious conclusion. On a hill outside Nikomedia he laid down the purple in the presence of the representatives of the army and appointed Galerius Augustus, and his nephew Maximinus Daja and Severus, Caesars. At the same time Maximian, loyal to his friend to the last, also abdicated at Milan, and in his stead Constantius Chlorus became Augustus. The travelling carriage stood ready, and carried the ex-Emperor back to his birthplace, which he revisited after a life distinguished by greater successes and achievements than that of most men. At Spalato he built a palace, the plan of which is reminiscent of the camp in which he spent the greatest part of his life. There he spent the evening of his days in digging and planting his garden with his own hands. Maximian settled in Lucania.

GALERIUS (A.D. 305–311)

It is said that Diocletian's choice of Caesars was a surprise. Maximian had a son, Maxentius, and Constantius Chlorus had by a concubine, Helena, a son thirty years old, named Constantine, whose competence had already attracted attention. It had been expected that their natural right of inheritance would be recognised by the conferring on them of the title of Caesar. Galerius attempted to retain Constantine at his court, but eventually had to allow him to return at his father's express desire. Constantine accompanied his father to Britain, where a war was in progress. Soon afterwards Constantius Chlorus died at Eboracum (York). His army, which was devoted to him and his son, followed the usual procedure, and proclaimed Constantine *imperator*. This was a breach of Diocletian's order of succession, according to which the right of appointment was vested in Galerius, the senior, but it was made legitimate by Galerius recognising Constantine as Caesar. Constantine was content for the moment with what he had obtained, but in his heart had no respect for Diocletian's arrangements.

Maxentius, the other Emperor's son, who was passed over, also had aspirations, but he was too unimportant to be able to enforce respect for himself. Then chance came to his assistance. He was living as a private citizen in Rome. In the capital the feeling was universal that the Eternal City had been humiliated. Diocletian had treated it with scant respect. He had diminished the number of praetorians, and his government entirely ignored the Senate. Discontent was rife among all classes of society. Then came information that Galerius intended to apply to Rome the provincial system of taxation. This was the spark which caused the conflagration. A mob of praetorians proclaimed Maxentius Caesar. Galerius could not permit this, and sent his own Caesar, Severus, against Rome ; but when Maximian returned to public life and interfered, Severus was deserted by his soldiers and perished. Galerius had to take the field against Maxentius in person, but suffered the same experience, since the fidelity of his army was not to be depended on. On the other hand the praetorians, who had not forgotten their old spirit of licence, would not submit to the strict discipline of Maximian. The latter probably wanted to play the chief part and supersede his son. In all these difficulties the one expedient that presented itself was to appeal to old Diocletian. He refused to reassume the purple, but was induced to take part in a conference at Carnuntum. His will was once again decisive. Maxentius was excluded from the succession, the vacancy being filled by an Illyrian general, Licinius, who was immediately elevated to the rank of Augustus. Maximian was induced to return to private life, but his restless spirit could not dispense with power. He tried to form connections with Constantine, who had improved his position by victories over the Germans, after which he had the prisoners torn to pieces by wild animals in the amphitheatre of Trèves. Maximian married his daughter Fausta to him, and confirmed the title of Augustus, which he had adopted. But Maximian was frustrated in his hopes of playing a part in politics with the assistance of Constantine. Constantine accepted his help, but reserved to himself all power and control of policy. After an unsuccessful attempt to overthrow his son and to negotiate with Galerius, Maximian went to Gaul and declared himself Emperor once more. His own followers, however, delivered him up to Constantine, who for the sake of appearances pardoned him, but soon drove him to suicide.

In Rome Maxentius had adopted the title of Augustus, and Maximinus Daja, Galerius' Caesar, did the same in the East. Galerius was a brave soldier and a determined man, but he was not capable of exacting respect and obedience from his colleagues. He was a faithful follower of Diocletian's system, but he had not the personal strength and authority that alone could maintain it. He continued the persecution of the Christians. It is uncertain what induced him, by an edict of April 30, A.D. 311, the tenor of which too plainly shows his antipathy to Christianity, to grant the Christians free exercise of their religion, on condition that they did not attack the existing order, and to release the prisoners. Possibly this decree was dictated by the general political situation, for the Christians were a factor to reckon with in disputes about the throne. Possibly the approach of death inclined him to leniency. He died a few days afterwards, eaten by worms, as the Christians triumphantly asserted. Once more the Empire had four rulers only, but all hostile to each other, and all calling themselves Augustus.

For the moment Constantine maintained a neutral or rather a friendly attitude towards Maxentius. He had not actively opposed the senior Emperor, Galerius, who was entangled in difficulties and unable to maintain his authority. But with his death the situation altered. There was tension between Licinius and Maximinus Daja. Constantine and Licinius came to an arrangement that each should pursue his own ends, and Licinius married Constantine's half-sister, Constantia. It was easy for Constantine to find an excuse for war. Maxentius was exercising a tyranny in Rome to satisfy his army, and was not keeping it in check. In Africa an insurrection broke out, which was suppressed with the greatest severity. Maxentius on his side represented Constantine as his father's murderer. He had a respectable army, but Constantine's initiative and strategic skill more than counterbalanced his numerical inferiority. His campaign is one of the most notable in military history, and has been compared to Napoleon's first Italian campaign. Constantine was over the Alps before Maxentius had heard of or could hinder his advance. At Turin he won the first victory over his opponent's mail-clad cavalry, who were massacred with clubs. Then he marched against Verona, and besieged it. A bloody battle in the night decided the issue ; a relieving army was defeated, and Verona fell. Maxentius had allowed his forces to be beaten in detail. When Constantine advanced on Rome Maxentius moved out from the protecting walls, and opposed him at Saxa Rubra immediately north of Rome with the Tiber at his back. This was his undoing, for when Constantine was victorious, the beaten masses streamed back to the city over the only bridge, the Milvian (Ponte Molle), which has given its name to the battle. It broke under the weight; Maxentius and part of his army were drowned in the river, the praetorians were cut down on the spot, and this was the end of the famous guard. Constantine was greeted as a liberator, and the Senate erected a triumphal arch to him, because by the grace of God he had vanquished the tyrant.

From Rome he repaired to Milan for an interview with Licinius. To this interview the aged Diocletian was also invited, but it was small wonder that he stayed away, for he had no influence over the new men. Soon afterwards he died, and it was rumoured that he had taken his life for fear of the new rulers. In Milan was issued the famous edict of toleration which officially recognised Christianity and the Christians, and reinstated them in their former position. Maximinus Daja was a zealous pagan. It is true he had not cancelled Galerius' edict of toleration, and had liberated the Christian prisoners, but he deliberately contrived that persecutions should again be set on foot by the authorities of the cities with his support. He honoured the cities which adhered to paganism, and had recourse to propaganda, distributing polemical and contumelious pamphlets against Christianity, and tried to revive paganism by creating a pagan hierarchy. In the provinces men of distinction were made chief priests, to organise the pagan priesthood and to further the struggle against Christianity. His Christian subjects turned longing eyes to the West. He did not, however, venture to omit to publish the edict of Milan, for his opponents were too strong for him. But in the winter, when Constantine had retired to Gaul, Maximinus Daja thought he had a freer hand and moved on Byzantium, which surrendered to him. Licinius was surprised, and could only raise a very inferior army. Feeling his superiority Maximinus refused to negotiate and risked an appeal to arms, but lost the day, and had to take refuge in Asia Minor. Thither Licinius followed him, and issued a new edict of toleration from Nikomedia to win over the Christians to his side. Maximinus was forced to do likewise, and also promulgated an edict of toleration. The fact that the two rivals vied for their favour demonstrates the importance of the Christians. Plainly Maximinus' policy of hostility to them reacted unfavourably on his destiny. Soon afterwards he suddenly and opportunely died. Licinius became sole master in the East, as Constantine was in the West ; but Licinius controlled that part of the Empire, the East, which was psychologically and economically of greatest importance, and in addition he held Illyria, the most important recruiting centre.

Constantine made an attempt to secure a better balance of power. He proposed to form a kind of buffer-state under another Caesar. When this project came to nothing, open war followed, in which Constantine won two victories. But plainly they were not so decisive that he could think of suppressing Licinius altogether. An agreement was concluded, which gave Constantine a far stronger position. Licinius contented himself with the East and the eastern half of the Balkan Peninsula. Constantine knew how to wait till he could deal a decisive blow. For six years they ruled side by side with an ever-growing mutual distrust, which was illustrated by Licinius' treatment of the Christians. The man who had overcome Maximinus Daja by displaying a policy of friendliness to the Christians, now began to play fast and loose with them. They were only allowed to meet in the open air ; women and men were not to take part in the same meetings, and women were only to be instructed in their religion by women. Christian officers were degraded. In some instances he took measures against bishops and churches. Yet he did not venture to cancel the edict of toleration, and only succeeded in embittering the Christians and undermining his own position. The policy was not wise, but it is not difficult to understand.

It is doubtful what were the immediate causes of the final conflict. It was in any case a necessity, which could only be postponed, not averted. The Goths made an inroad into Licinius' part of the Empire, possibly at Constantine's instigation. Constantine moved against them, and defeated them, an act of interference which was too much for Licinius. War was now inevitable. Constantine took the command of the land army, and sent his son, Crispus, with the fleet, to Asia Minor to take Licinius in the rear. But the latter sent a large fleet against Crispus, and hurriedly crossed the Bosphorus with a powerful army. In the battle of Adrianople Constantine's strategic genius and personal bravery secured the victory. Licinius threw himself into Byzantium. When Crispus was reinforced, he succeeded in completely defeating the fleet of Licinius, who, so as to avoid being shut up in Byzantium, fled into Asia Minor, but soon found that further resistance was impossible. His wife, Constantine's sister Constantia, acted as mediator. Licinius retired into private life, and settled at Thessalonica. Constantine kept his word with him, as he had done with Maximian. The year after he was put to death on the grounds of an attempted rising, it was said.

CONSTANTINE (SOLE RULER A.D. 323–337)

Constantine was now sole ruler of the Empire. The later years of his rule were peaceful, apart from the usual wars with Germans, which, however, were comparatively unimportant. The great event was the creation of a new capital. For a century the Emperors had lived, for the most part, in the field and moved from place to place, where circumstances demanded their presence. Diocletian and his colleagues, whose reigns were long, had residential cities, where they often stayed and in which they showed special interest — Diocletian in Nikomedia, Maximian in Milan, and Constantius Chlorus in Trèves. Constantine chose old Byzantium, which he renamed after himself. The choice showed the far-sightedness of genius. Like Nikomedia it lay between, and not too distant from, the two most important danger zones on the Euphrates and the Middle Danube. But its geographical position on the great waterway through the Bosphorus, and flanking the landway from Asia to Europe, was far more important, and provided the suitable conditions for the growth of a great city. Its strategical importance and key-position had often been apparent in the civil wars.

Constantine was sole ruler. When he chose a residence for himself, the city became the capital of the whole Empire, and he intentionally emphasised this by putting Constantinople on an equality with Rome. It was called New Rome. The privileges and institutions of Rome were imitated, a Senate created, and great quantities of corn distributed and games instituted for the populace. Constantine's decrees are full of references to wonderful omens and dreams. The foundation took place on November 4, A.D. 326, with a performance of Christian and pagan ceremonies, which were to emphasise the importance of the act and to ensure the city for ever of a permanent existence. By liberal promises and privileges all classes were enticed to it, and the city soon contained a numerous population, which in licence and unmanageableness was destined to rival Rome herself. Once more, and to a greater extent than before, the old cities of antiquity were robbed of their famous art treasures. The Olympian Zeus of Pheidias, the Samian Hera, the Athena of Lindos and thousands of other statues decorated the new city. Old temples were pulled down and furnished building materials, especially columns of valuable marbles. The new Imperial city was adorned with the plunder of lesser cities with a historic past, a proceeding significant of an age which could not itself create the material culture and splendour with which it loved to surround itself, but was reduced to plunder the creations and works of art of a greater age.

The foundation of Constantinople was the crown of Constantine's life-work. Proclaimed as Emperor in the furthest West, in Britain, he had with each success moved further East. He died in Nikomedia while making preparations for a war against Persia, and was buried in Constantinople. For four centuries an internecine contest between East and West had gone on within the Empire. The spiritual and economic superiority of the East seemed to assure it of victory, but this had constantly been wrested out of its hands by the still unexhausted national vigour of the West. Augustus had endeavoured by his policy to ensure the domination of the West for the future. This policy had, on the whole, succeeded, in spite of the infiltration of Oriental religion and social ideas, and the domination of the Illyrians had once more emphasised the physical superiority of the West. What Constantine did, was, with the support of the military strength of the West, to hand over the political and spiritual supremacy to the East. He enlisted more and more Germans in the army, and to a greater degree than any one else contributed to the predominance of German mercenaries in the Empire.

On the other hand it was he, the ruler of the least Christian of the four quarters of the Empire—*i.e.* the most western— who brought about the final victory of Christianity. In the East, where the Christians formed a very important section, perhaps even the majority of the population, the persecutions had raged with greatest violence. Maximinus Daja con- tinued to suppress the Christians even after Galerius had ceased to persecute, and Licinius, who soon overcame Daja, was heart and soul a pagan, though for opportunist reasons he consented to the Milan edict of toleration. When the rivalry between him and Constantine increased, he could not refrain from petty annoyances of the Christians. Circum- stances ordained that from the moment when the ambition of winning the dominion over the whole Empire took hold of Constantine, the Christians were to be his support. His power in the West was certainly based on his faithful army, which had forced on him the imperial dignity, and in successive battles had become more formidable and more attached to his person. By espousing the cause of the Christians, who, in those parts of the Empire which were not under his rule, formed a numerous but persecuted and downtrodden minority, he paved the way for his plans. The Christians saw in him the man of God, and the liberator of the oppressed Church.

A similar tendency appears in his treatment of Roman law. While ruler of the West he broke down its strict forms, and sought an approximation to the still unforgotten popular law of the East. There was no reason for such a policy, if he was not thereby preparing to subdue the East. When he won the final victory he transferred his residence from the scene of his youthful triumphs to the last conquered Greek half of the Empire, although he had, himself, but an imperfect mastery of the Greek language.

Constantine did not act upon an ideal programme, and in this respect differed totally from his predecessor. Diocletian has very few counterparts in Roman history : Sulla is the only one on a great scale. The basis of Constantine's action was the will to power. The ambition that guided all his actions was plain and simple. He wanted to win the East. Unlike the Illyrians, he understood that militarism and bureaucracy were not enough. He realised how powerful a lever politics were in diplomacy and party conflicts, even if they were conducted on religious grounds. He put himself forward as a liberator of the oppressed but most energetic and most highly organised section of the population.

There has been much controversy over Constantine's religious convictions, or want of them. If the truth be told, he cannot have been much superior to the common run of his contemporaries. He was like them in believing in omens, magic, and dreams. He reverenced the God of the Christians as the most powerful of all gods, and placed himself under His protection. He supported the organisation which Christianity had created, and by granting privileges and public recognition to its priesthood put it on an equality with the organised pagan religions which were recognised by the State. He legislated in the spirit which Christianity represented and which was supported by the current religious and humanitarian ideas of the age, as when he abolished the old penalties for celibacy, forbade frivolous divorce, and abolished the gladiatorial games. In the end he was so completely obsessed by these ideas, that in his old age he delivered regular sermons to the court. But, on the other hand, he would not put himself unreservedly in the hands of the Christians, but aimed at controlling them also. This was not to be achieved by the usual methods ; for the Church could not, without being unfaithful to itself, recognise any other ruler of itself than God. But by cleverly making use of the Church's divisions he managed to control it by a profession of Christian humility, and by placing the secular power at its disposal, he made himself, in effect, its master. He originated the Byzantine combination of Caesar and Pope.

It cannot be denied that Constantine retained a good deal of respect for the heathen gods. Some years after the victory over Maxentius he placed figures of heathen gods on his coinage, and only at the approach of death caused representations of the standard (*labarum*) with the Cross to be struck. When he forbade the inspection of the entrails of victims for the purpose of prophesying the future, he excepted the chief pagan rituals, and he himself employed soothsayers. In this connection Christianity had no substitute to offer. He forbade the sacrifice of animals, that being the part of heathen cult which caused the greatest offence to Christians, and was repellent even to many pious pagans. He closed temples that were scenes of licentious worship, but he decreed that no one should suffer for his heathen beliefs. He allowed the pagan priesthoods to continue their ritual and to receive State support, and permitted the town of Hispellum to build a temple to his family. In the conflict of religions his attitude was that of benevolent neutrality towards Christianity. Thus he induced the Christians to think that they needed him, while the pagans saw in him a protector against Christian aggression; for heathenism had no organisation that made it capable of resistance on its own account.

This attitude has exposed Constantine to charges of hypocrisy, but the accusation is not a fair one. Nor is it right to accuse him of guile, merely because his prudence was superior to that of other men. He possessed in a high degree the power of waiting patiently till the time was ripe for interference, and then he would intervene with firmness and decision. Those who were surprised by him, blamed his bad character. He was benevolent and trustful, relying on the power of his personality over men. He treated conquered opponents leniently, unless they were likely to become dangerous, as in the cases of Maximian and Licinius. Trading on his good nature, his officials were inclined to abuse their trusts, but Constantine had a genuine desire to prevent this, and when he caught them red-handed he was severe and

implacable in punishment. His quickness of temper sometimes caused the innocent to suffer with the guilty, and gave
to his domineering will, which brooked no resistance, the stamp
of despotism. Of some questionable actions he cannot be
acquitted. He executed his eldest son, Crispus, and his wife,
Fausta ; but we do not know the whole truth about these
tragic events.

The same qualities made him one of Rome's greatest
generals. His campaigns were carefully prepared, and carried
out with surprising rapidity. He usually fought with numeri-
cally inferior forces, but was never defeated. His soldiers
were steadfastly attached to him, relying on his good fortune,
and his personal bravery won their devotion. Generally he
fought at the head of his men.

Less attractive were his financial methods. He was liberal
and lavished gifts freely ; he delighted in pomp, and was
extravagant in his court and his building schemes without
considering what the state of the treasury permitted. During
the latter part of his reign, when the building of Constantinople called for extraordinary expenses, there was a bitter
outcry at the intolerable taxation. But on the other hand
he also discovered in an inspired moment a simple means by
which he once more succeeded in putting a sound coinage into
permanent circulation.

In internal government he continued the work of Diocletian.
Often, at this distance of time, we cannot distinguish between
their respective achievements, but must treat and speak of
the constitution of Diocletian and Constantine as a unity
affecting the whole later Empire. But these men started from
diametrically opposed standpoints. Diocletian raised the
Emperor to a superhuman position, and organised the court
and the bureaucracy, because he thought the interest of the
State required it, whereas Constantine found in all this an
expression of his sense of power. To him the diadem and
robes of State, the adulation of troops of chamberlains and
eunuchs were a necessary expression of his personal conception
of the ruler's position ; he not only was addressed by others,
but called himself *dominus*, lord. He took a keen interest

in the precedence of ranks, and created titular as well as functional offices.

His was a wonderfully composite nature, in which dark shadows were pierced with flashes of genuine greatness. This is often the case with genius, which never proceeds on conventional lines. Constantine perceived and understood the tendencies of his age better than most ; his chief quality was intuition, not a reasoning sagacity such as Diocletian possessed. Because he understood his age and believed in his strength, he could direct and anticipate developments. Many of his actions seemed amazing to his contemporaries, especially the encouragement he gave to Christianity ; but the future has justified him. He was the most gifted of the Roman Caesars, and deserved to be called the Great, even if this does not include the gratitude of the Church to him who gave her the victory.

The ever-recurring problem of the succession was not solved by Constantine. His conception of power was incompatible with Diocletian's idea of the imperial authority. The career which had been rendered easy for him by the fact that he was the son of an Emperor, and his own personal views, made him an adherent of hereditary right as the lawful principle. But the necessity of dividing the Empire geographically was clear, even to him. It looks as if he regarded it as legitimate to stretch the hereditary principle so far, that all the adult male members of his house should have a share in the inheritance ; otherwise his arrangements are incomprehensible. He had three sons, of whom Constantine received Gaul with Britain and Spain ; Constantius, the East ; Constans, Italy with Illyria and Africa. A half-brother had left two sons, of whom the one, Dalmatius, received the borderland adjoining the Goths on the Lower Danube, the other, Hanniballianus, got Pontus with the title of " King of Kings," which points to rivalry with the great King of Persia. These two were plainly intended to bear the brunt of the fighting against the external foes of the Empire. Constantine's arrangement was upset immediately after his death. The army refused to recognise any other Emperors than Constantine's sons. A mutiny broke out, in which all his more distant male kin were killed with the exception of two minors, Gallus and Julian, sons of another half-brother. The instigator was Constantius, the only one of the sons who appeared at the funeral. The three brothers then proceeded to divide the Empire.

CONSTANTINE II : CONSTANS : CONSTANTIUS (A.D. 337–361)

The system of several Emperors, whether nominated according to the scheme of Diocletian, or direct heirs as in this instance, was intended to avert usurpation. In effect it only resulted in a contest between them for precedence. Only a few years elapsed before the eldest brother, Constantine, attacked the youngest, Constans, but lost the battle and his life. Constans annexed his provinces, for the other brother, Constantius, was engaged in a war with the Persians. With alternate success and failures this detained him for several years, till the news came that his brother had fallen a victim to a rebellion. A German general, Magnentius, had caused himself to be proclaimed Emperor and had had Constans, who had fled, put to death. Then Constantius delegated the conduct of the Persian War to his generals, and started for Gaul. Meanwhile the Danube army had not recognised the usurper, but had chosen an Emperor of its own, Vetranio, one of Constantine's veteran generals. He seems to have accepted the position in order to save the situation for his master. For when Constantius arrived he divested himself of the purple, and received, not only pardon, but a princely reward. When Magnentius failed to induce Constantius to recognise his position he invaded Pannonia and was beaten at Mursa, in what was said to have been the bloodiest battle of the century. He succeeded in escaping with part of his army, but after his defeat his followers deserted him, and within two years he committed suicide at Lugudunum.

Constantius was a poor edition of his father. He cannot be denied a certain degree of courage, prudence, and a desire to govern justly ; but he was pedantic and small-minded, suspicious and reserved. His most notable characteristic was an almost ludicrous notion of the imperial dignity. His

theory of court etiquette caused him to isolate himself from
the world, so that he hardly knew anything of the way in
which his officials governed. So as not to disturb his dignity
he never altered a feature and made himself rigid and immo-
bile. At his Roman triumph he sat as motionless as a Buddha
in his chariot. If he thought that his dignity had suffered,
he was irreconcilable, and his small-mindedness made him
irritable. Hence his government was unpopular. His great
misfortune was his Christian faith. He became involved
in the great struggle over Arianism, of which he was a warm
supporter, and risked losing his carefully guarded position as
lord of the Church and bishop of bishops. By his attempts
to bring about unity in the Church, he only earned the bitter
hatred of the orthodox. He only achieved his victory over
Athanasius by force, and the victory was more apparent than
real. His brother, Constans, and the usurper, Magnentius,
exploited his Arian creed to his political disadvantage.

Constantius regarded himself as Emperor under the special
protection of Heaven, and his successes against his opponents
only strengthened him in this belief; but on the other hand,
after the massacre of his kindred at his accession he felt himself
branded as a fratricide like Cain, and regarded his childlessness as the punishment of God. To settle the succession
was an urgent necessity, which he could not avoid in spite of
his suspicious dislike of parting with any portion of his power.
His brothers had left no sons behind them, and there remained
of Constantius Chlorus' family only Gallus and Julian. They
were well brought up, but when they became young men,
Constantius sent them to an estate in Cappadocia, where,
for six years, they lived in complete isolation, exercising themselves in religious asceticism and pious works. Of the outer
world and the duties of a ruler, to which they were destined
by their birth, they were kept in entire ignorance. This was
a poor preparation for a Caesar. When Constantius took the
field against Magnentius, he was obliged to delegate the imperial
power in the East, and sent the elder brother, Gallus, as Caesar
to Antioch. Gallus, as the result of his upbringing, was a
zealous Christian, but possessed neither moral nor traditional

standards to guide him in the exercise of his power. Under the fatal influence of his wife, a sister of Constantius, who is described as a veritable fury, he became a mere tyrant, and, moreover, committed many acts of violence and folly, which rendered his position untenable. He first resisted Constantius's envoys by violence and murder, but was not able to evade acceptance of a friendly invitation to the imperial court at Milan, for a refusal would have implied usurpation. Double-faced as ever, Constantius had adopted an attitude of friendliness towards him while he was still in the East. But as he journeyed westwards this diminished, and at Poetovio (Pettau in Styria) he was deprived of the title of Caesar, and was tried and executed at Pola. He no doubt deserved his fate, but Constantius's methods were liable to excite suspicion of his honest intentions in the future.

When Gallus, the elder brother by six years, became Caesar, Julian was released from his isolation. He was nearly involved in the fall of Gallus, and was summoned to Milan for an inquiry, but was saved by the Empress Eusebia, who seems to have sought consolation for her childlessness by devoting her energies to protecting the strange young man. Constantius's distrust was, however, not completely allayed, and he sent Julian to a place where he was out of the way, Athens. The city was thinly populated, but was a resort of students and professors, as well as a place of banishment for statesmen. Julian retired with joy to a city where he could read and study to his heart's content. The few months he spent in Athens were ever afterwards a happy memory to him. Many have felt as he did. In the turmoil of practical life there often is felt a longing for the past— those happy youthful days spent in the midst of congenial companions and pursuits.

Meanwhile events on the Rhine frontier took a threatening turn. Court intrigues and the suspicions of Constantius incited a general of German birth to set himself up as an usurper. He was skilfully got out of the way, but Gaul was left defenceless in the enemy's hands. The frontier fortresses fell, and the territory on the left bank of the Rhine was overrun by the Germans. A great campaign was necessary, and it was dangerous to entrust such an important command to a general who was not a member of the imperial family. So Eusebia succeeded in inducing Constantius to send Julian as Caesar to Gaul. Julian received the news of his elevation with despair, regarding it as a death in the purple, and deeply mistrusting his own capacities. What did he, the pupil of rhetoricians and philosophers, understand of the arts of government and campaigning ? Constantius, always distrustful, tried to tie his hands. It was true that the inexperienced prince needed helpers and counsellors, but he was surrounded by envious intriguers. Probably there was no precise delimitation of his authority in relation to the other high imperial officials, and this was a further cause of disagreements and bitterness.

He, first of all, had to undergo military training. To this he devoted himself with the same conscientiousness and zeal which he had shown in his philosophic studies, and events soon demonstrated that in military competence he was no degenerate representative of his uncle, Constantine. He succeeded in saving Augustodunum (Autun) from a surprise by the Alamannians, and followed this up by a successful offensive which took him to the Rhine, and won back Cologne. The situation was, however, critical, because his troops were too few. Julian's representations were so effective that Constantius sent reinforcements under one of his most trusted generals, but the latter tried to conduct operations on his own account and was soundly beaten. The Alamannians then attacked Julian with a force three times as large as his own ; but by this time, having gained confidence in his own powers and the allegiance of his troops, he engaged them and won a brilliant victory at Strasburg. The Alamannian host was annihilated, and one of their kings taken prisoner and sent as a captive to the Emperor.

In spite of, or perhaps in consequence of, this brilliant success, Constantius could not bring himself to support his Caesar effectively. Money was scarce, and the praetorian prefect in Gaul, with the consent of the Emperor, desired to impose an extra tax in spite of the prevalent distress due to the already excessive taxation. Julian had realised that financial straits and the weight of taxation were largely due to the fact that the amounts levied stuck to the fingers of the officials instead of reaching their destination, and offered to improve matters, if he was allowed to undertake the collection of taxes in Gallia Belgica, dispensing with the usual officials. The offer was so advantageous, that Constantius, in spite of the resistance of the officials, consented. Julian was successful. His just financial policy reinvigorated Gaul, while a victory over the Franks restored the importation of corn from Britain which had been interrupted by piracy. He forced the Alamannians to supply wood and iron for the rebuilding of the destroyed cities and fortresses on the Rhine, and he put an end to the raids of roaming hordes of Germans by organising flying columns.

While Constantius was engaged in repelling the tribes on the Middle Danube, the Persians declared war. After a year's hard fighting the Emperor resolved to take the field in person with reinforcements from the West. He ordered Julian to hand over the flower of his army, to be selected by the Emperor's own commissioners. Undoubtedly Constantius required and had the right to take over the troops, but many Germans had been recruited on condition of not having to serve over the Alps. The soldiers were discontented at the prospect of having to march and fight under the burning sun of the East ; and the conclusion was obvious, that Constantius with his usual distrust feared that Julian was becoming too strong and was plotting to weaken and remove him like Gallus. Julian loyally did what he could to induce his troops to obey orders. When the imperial commissary wished to collect the contingents at Paris, where Julian resided, the latter warned him that the discontent of the troops would end in a violent outbreak, if they were all assembled in one place. The warning was neglected, and what Julian had feared took place. The soldiers refused to march and proclaimed Julian as their Augustus. This honour Julian refused. He must have known Constantius sufficiently well to be aware that, as events had turned out, he could only choose between death and the purple. But his loyalty was not of the kind which shrank from consequences. In the end a dream induced him to accept the election, but by far-reaching concessions he sought to induce Constantius to recognise it.

Constantius was then in Asia in order to prosecute the war against Persia. He refused Julian's overtures, and when the latter saw that his efforts at peaceful reconciliation were vain, he began the civil war. Fortunately Constantius died at an opportune moment on his way back. Julian, the sole heir to the throne, was recognised without opposition throughout the Empire ; entered Constantinople amid universal rejoicings, and celebrated Constantius's funeral rites with great solemnities.

JULIAN (A.D. 360–363)

Once more the Empire had a popular Emperor. The man who regarded philosophy and rhetoric as life's ideal, had won his popularity among the barbaric troops in Gaul. They loved him, because he led them to victory in person, and though he wore the purple, associated as a man with men. The pupil of the philosophers neglected his personal appearance. Contrary to the fashion of the day he let his beard grow, boasted that it harboured lice, dressed himself meanly, and in the middle of winter refused to occupy a warmed room. He put into practice the theories of asceticism, which was emphasised by the current philosophy of the day, with its doctrine of the soul's captivity in a sinful body. The soldiers admired a general who, with unfailing courage, shared their own privations, whereas the educated could only see in him an Emperor who was induced by foolish fixed ideas to degrade his imperial dignity. But Julian's great failing was his lack of tact. In his youth, from motives of prudence, he had learned to conceal his opinions, but he never learned to control his momentary fancies and impulses. It is typical of him that, when at a meeting of the Senate he heard that his beloved teacher, Maximus, had arrived, he immediately started up, rushed out into the street, kissed him on the lips, and presented him to the assembled fathers with an improvised panegyric. He buried Constantius with all the pomp and manifestations of sorrow that befitted an Emperor and a relative, but could not resist recounting a list of his sins in his address. His nervously restless movements, twitching shoulders and gesticulating hands, his speech, in which one word tumbled over another, his thoughts constantly leaping from subject to subject, provoked derision. He never harboured suspicion, and was high-minded enough to answer personal affronts with a shrug of the shoulders. An age which was notorious for private and personal feuds, regarded him with contempt. Hence he was at first received with exuberant rejoicing, and soon afterwards with derision and ridicule. He was not thick-skinned enough to be able to ignore public opinion entirely, and his philosophic pride and self-esteem were deeply wounded by the malice of perverted human nature. He hated litigation and violence, the expedients to which others in a similar position might have resorted : but he was a scholar, so he took his pen and wrote a pamphlet in which he compared his own unkempt appearance with the effeminate and empty life of the great city of Antioch, in which he had taken up his residence for a time. His real meaning, which the Antiochenes can have appreciated as little as the Emperor's personal appearance, may be read between the lines of this treatise.

At court and in administrative matters Julian's simplicity brought about a much-needed reform. When the court-barber presented himself in his magnificent robe of office to cut his hair, he broke out in wrathful expressions, and on learning of the high wages he received dismissed him, together with a great company of chamber attendants, cooks and officials, whose maintenance cost vast sums. Of the highly organised secret police very few were left, and still fewer of the imperial secretaries. Julian sympathised with the sufferings of the people, and realised the corruption prevalent among the treasury officials. He set up a special tribunal to try the blackest sheep of the late Government. He sought to distribute the burden of taxation more equitably, and insisted on unbiassed judgments being made in actions between individuals and the Treasury. Eunuchs and other court officials, who had surrounded his predecessor with an impenetrable camarilla, were dismissed, and Julian made himself easily accessible to his subjects. Though he abolished government by favourites he did not hesitate to give his confidence to competent men. But his tendency to mysticism caused him to be the dupe of charlatans and rhetoricians, soothsayers, and magicians, and as a literary man he was not unsusceptible to flattery. His restless nature often led him to take hasty decisions, and not infrequently, after a night's reflection, he altered sentences which he had pronounced the day before. He was the first genuine Greek to occupy the throne. He conversed in Greek instead of Latin, and, at the beginning of his reign, caused it to be used in the deliberations of the council. At night he devoted himself to writing, and used to compile lengthy treatises in the space of a couple of nights. They were not very original, but were usually diffuse, and often confused, expressions of the pagan theories current in that age. He was too much of a *littérateur* to be an Emperor.

As an historical personage Julian has been named the Apostate. His mother was a zealous Christian. He always preserved a grateful remembrance of the man who had brought him up and grounded in him those ideals of morality for which he was famous. As a lad he had studied grammar and rhetoric. He spent his youth on a remote Cappadocian estate, which was a sort of prison to him. The training in Christian piety, to which he and his brother were subjected, was passively absorbed by Gallus without any effect on his natural propensity to vice, but Julian, with his independent disposition, actively revolted against it. He read his Bible, but after his own fashion. He showed in his writings that he knew it well. He had at his fingers' ends the whole arsenal of weapons which the enemies of Christianity have always loved to draw from the Bible, and he was quick to note the wide departures from the Gospel and primitive Christianity made by the Church of his day. The contradictions between the sacred writings of the Christians, and between these and the demands of reason and morality, which the Christians glossed over in their doctrine of the necessity for faith and belief, were keenly realised by him. The unedifying spectacle presented by the contemporary Church, the frantic theological battles, the ambitions and intrigues of the hierarchy, the violent acts of the Christian mob against those who differed from them, confirmed his doubts of Christianity. He himself had shuddered at the viciousness and deceits of his cousin, the most Christian Constantius, so long as his fate lay in his hands. At the age of nineteen years he had escaped from what was practically banishment, and devoted himself to rhetorical studies in Nikomedia. There he also became acquainted with the philosophic theories of the day. He absorbed the idealism of Neoplatonism, in which he discovered a theory of a more ideal and philosophic character, and also its mystical side which took a firm hold on his mind. He was not repelled by the allegories which sought to reinstate the pagan myths by explaining away their meaning, nor by the casuistry of the philosophers which reserved a place in their system for magic and soothsaying; for his natural temperament drew him in that direction. He believed in dreams, looked for omens, and his writings are replete with the wisdom of pagan theology.

When he heard that Maximus, to our conception a mere charlatan who had devoted himself to the occult sides of Neoplatonism, had opened a school in Ephesus, he hurried to him. He discarded the faith of his youth so openly, that his brother wrote to him in warning. Julian took the warnings to heart, for he knew that his life was at stake, particularly if it was brought to the ears of the suspicious Constantius that his cousin was occupying himself with magic. So, outwardly at least, he conformed again to Christianity. But paganism certainly did not regard one who paid lip service to the God of the Christians as lost. When, on the death of Gallus, he was summoned to court, his studies were brought to a sudden end except during his short stay in Athens, where he was initiated into the mysteries of Eleusis. In Gaul he had to exchange the study for the tent and battlefield, and could only return to his beloved books during the short hours of the night; for he was ascetic to the extent of allowing himself the minimum of sleep.

After he had assumed the dignity of Augustus, every reason which had hitherto prevented him from openly declaring his adhesion to paganism, had gone, and when he became undisputed ruler, he took measures to combat Christianity and to revive paganism. He was sure of his army. The soldiers feasted without scruple on the flesh of his numerous sacrifices ; took his money, and in gratitude scattered a few grains of incense on the altar beside him. Very few were afflicted by scruples afterwards and returned the money. The officials were equally pliable, and when their numbers had to be considerably diminished, it was the Christians whose services were dispensed with first of all. So far all went easily, but Christianity had a stronger resistance to offer, and paganism was weak and decadent. Maximinus Daja, by creating a pagan hierarchy, had already compelled it to fight for its existence. Julian followed up his idea. As *pontifex maximus* he assumed the right to nominate a sort of pagan metropolitan in all the provinces. These appointed and supervised the heathen bishops of each city, and subordinate to them were hosts of priests and priestesses, servants of the cults and temples. As an indispensable condition for these priests real piety was required, pure and blameless living, and no suspicion of any Christian taint in their families. Julian said that compassion for the poor and care for the dead had brought to Christianity the bulk of its adherents. Therefore he instructed the priests to perform works of charity towards all, without distinction of creed. A sign of their piety and that of the faithful should be a willingness to sacrifice part of their worldly possessions. Julian also supported the cause with State assistance. The Christians were furious at this obvious competition, and accused him of imitation, but they could console themselves with the reflection that in a system of piety and charity dictated by a temporal power there was no spiritual driving force. But Julian had correctly diagnosed the policy by which the Church had acquired its greatest hold over the masses.

In the internal dissensions of the Church he observed strict neutrality, and gave equal rights to all sects, as well as to Judaism—all the banished sectaries being recalled. If he flattered himself that he was weakening the Church by furthering its internal factions, he was mistaken. On one point all Christians were united—in their hatred of paganism. Julian was too wise and humane to adopt methods of persecution. He left churches and priests at peace, but he brought heathen propaganda to bear upon the Christians, openly showed his favour to cities which exhibited heathen zeal, and when a few riots and other violent acts took place against Christians, he did not punish them too severely. He ordered the closed temples to be reopened, those which had been destroyed to be rebuilt, and the confiscated temple property to be restored. This seemed to him to be an ordinary act of justice, but much of it had got into private hands and to the owners it seemed a very unfair proceeding. It must have been a satisfaction to him to forbid the bishops to use the imperial post, a privilege which they abused in their frequent journeys to synods, while, at the same time, he limited its use and misuse in other ways.

In his positive measures against Christianity he took a literal view of Christian doctrine. The Bible forbade the taking up of the sword : therefore Christians could not be soldiers. It was the duty of the Emperor to sacrifice to the gods : consequently Christians could not serve at a court which was plagued with demons. They declared the pagan myths to be immoral : therefore they had no right to occupy themselves with intellectual pursuits based on Homer and the poets. There was an inconsistency involved in explaining writings which they rejected. The Christians could stick to Matthew and Luke, and leave Greek literature alone. He went even further and forbade Christian youths to enjoy heathen instruction, and learn the arts of dialectic and rhetoric, which they applied as weapons against their teachers. Their intellectual education was to be confined to their religion. The logic of this cannot be denied, but life is never consistent. The Christians raged and complained. They were no longer poor fishermen and slaves, but were participants in the culture of their age. They felt the danger of being cut off from intellectual pursuits, the value of which they certainly denied in theory, but which, in practice, they needed to defend their faith and their status in society.

From Antioch Julian moved against the Persians. He projected a campaign on a large scale, the details and plans of which are obscure. He attacked the enemy on two sides, from Mesopotamia and in Armenia. He refused an offer of peace, and marched up to the walls of Ktesiphon. There he burned the fleet which had carried him down the Euphrates and through the canals to the Tigris, and after encountering many difficulties and privations marched northwards on to the east bank of the Tigris, where he probably intended to join the second army. His force was surrounded by the enemy, and in an unimportant skirmish, to which he hurried without taking time to put on his armour, he was wounded in the side by a spear. He was carried to his tent, gave directions as to the disposal of his property, and conversed with some philosophers in his suite on the immortality of the soul and the blessedness of the other world, till his strength failed him. At midnight he passed away peacefully. The Christians rejoiced, asserting that the hand of God had struck down the Apostate. Even the heathen thought that the enemy were too distant for a Persian spear to have been able to wound the Emperor.

JOVIAN (A.D. 363–364)

On his death-bed Julian refused to appoint a successor. It was impossible for him : events must take their course. So the army proceeded to the election of an Emperor in the middle of the enemy's country. Julian's praetorian prefect and faithful friend from the Gallic days, Salustius, refused on the score of age. The choice fell on Jovian, a good-humoured man of so little note that a story was current that his selection was due to a pure accident. The first thing the new Emperor had to do was to disentangle the army from its difficult situation, but he did not venture to take it over the Tigris, and allowed himself to be detained by negotiations. When the situation was critical the Persian King offered peace, and Jovian accepted the proposal, though the terms involved the loss of Diocletian's conquests, together with the important frontier fortresses, notably Nisibis, against the walls of which the Persian attacks had so often been broken. The city wanted to defend itself at its own risk, but Jovian ordered the inhabitants to evacuate it.

Jovian's greatest merit was a faithful adherence to the Nicene Creed. He promised Athanasius victory over the Arians, and the heathen expected a persecution. But one day, while on a march, he was unexpectedly found dead in his tent. Again the officers proceeded to the election of an Emperor, and this time appointed one of themselves, a well-tried warrior named Valentinian.

Julian was not a great man nor a great genius. His weaknesses and idiosyncrasies were many, but his good qualities, perhaps, outweighed them. He was one of the most genuine representatives of expiring paganism. Under him it fought its last fight. For though his successor for a time tolerated paganism, it was hopelessly bankrupt. The paganism which Julian mobilised for the last battle was much more like its opponent than like the old type of paganism, which, in its true character, lingered on only among the down-trodden and ignorant country people. It imitated Christianity because it was its spiritual relation. Which of the two conquered really meant less than the embittered opponents supposed. Both introduced new heavens and a new earth. A merciful death called Julian away after a reign of a year and a half. He was spared many broken illusions, and the Empire was saved from calamitous civil wars. He escaped being driven by the logic of events into the position of an ordinary persecutor. He had but made a beginning, and that was as much as his nature was capable of achieving. Whether his modifications of the court and bureaucracy would have stood a lengthier test it is difficult to judge, but it is to be regretted that his humaner system of financial administration did not have time to be really tried. If it had stood the proof, Julian would have been worthy to be praised as the Empire's greatest benefactor. That he was a sincerely well-meaning ruler, free from deceit and the influence of favourites, is praise, and praise indeed, for that age.

V

THE FALL OF THE EMPIRE AND THE GREAT MIGRATIONS

CHRISTIANITY had overthrown paganism and now the Church proceeded to gain control over the State itself. The constant attacks and infiltration of the Germanic race were being converted into national migrations, by means of which, in compact bodies, they secured for themselves dwelling-places within the Empire while preserving their independence. The two halves of the Empire were so impotent, that they seldom could co-operate, but each looked after itself, and soon reached a state of mutual antagonism and hostility. In the Western Roman Empire the power of the State began to break up. The Emperor became a puppet in the hands of the master of the army, usually a German, until such time as the latter had had enough of him, and cast the doll on the scrap-heap.

VALENTINIAN : VALENS (A.D. 364-378)

When Valentinian was elected Emperor, the army at once demanded that he should appoint a colleague ; so firmly rooted had the idea of the necessity for a division of the Empire become, although since Constantine's victory over Licinius it had, with brief interruption, had only one ruler. Valentinian named his brother, Valens, Augustus, and committed to his charge the East and Eastern Thrace. Valens lacked both physical and mental qualifications, and in military service had risen no higher than to be a member of a picked corps, but he willingly subordinated himself to his more important brother, and this was fortunate for the Empire. Valentinian repaired to Gaul, where he had his hands full in repelling an invasion of the Alamannians. An offensive into their country resulted in heavy losses without any corresponding success. He attempted to bar the frontiers with a line of forts, but before they were finished new swarms poured in. Then he attempted to make a league with the Burgundians, the neighbours of the Alamannians, in order to crush them ; but when a strong Burgundian army appeared in the Palatinate, demanding the help he had promised, he was, with good reason, alarmed at the forces he had put in motion, and refused to keep his word. The unbridled character and divisions of the Germans made it impossible to enter into any permanent relation with them, while the faithlessness of the Romans still further embittered them. The Emperors often found no better means of getting rid of dangerous German princes than by the employment of hired assassins. Pledges and promises were not taken very seriously by either side. A band of Saxons, who, on certain conditions, had been granted permission to depart freely, were surprised and massacred. Against the barbarian enemy any method was regarded as permissible, and this was bound to bring bitter vengeance.

Valentinian's bright complexion, fair hair and blue eyes betrayed his German blood. The army was filled more and more with Germans, either free Germans from the further bank, or from those living in the Empire. It was an exception for a Roman to rise to a high military post, and from this time onwards, purely German names begin to dominate the history of Rome. For internal administration the German Varangians had neither intellect nor capacity, and in that sphere the Roman officials went on with their venal robbery. Valentinian, indeed, issued a series of regulations intended to prevent abuses, to introduce stricter control, and to relieve the oppression of the people, but he was not equal to the Herculean task of cleansing the Augean stable of the corrupt bureaucracy. He was, and remained, on the whole a Germanic child of nature, with a good deal of dullness, a blind confidence in his friends, and occasionally exhibiting terrible outbursts of temper. His life was terminated by a stroke, brought on by over-excitement during an interview with envoys from the Quadi.

His contemporaries praised his justice, but he was chiefly remarkable for exhibitions of senseless and childish rage, when he was not obeyed or discovered that he had been cheated.

Africa was being ruined by its governor, Romanus, who kept back the pay of the army, so that the troops in desperation plundered the province. The desert tribes were allowed to prosecute their robberies with impunity. The inhabitants of Leptis, in despair, begged protection from Romanus, which should have been his obvious duty. He used the opportunity to impose an absolutely ruinous war-tax—a contribution of 4000 camels—as a pretext for extracting a bribe. As this could not be paid he remained inactive, and allowed the desert tribes to ravage freely. When Valentinian ascended the throne, the inhabitants plucked up courage to send a delegation to the Emperor. But Romanus had previously put himself in communication with his relative the chancellor (*magister officiorum*), Remigius, offering him a share of the booty, and the latter knew how to represent the matter in a favourable light to the Emperor. But when a fresh inroad occurred, Valentinian sent a special commissioner to Africa to investigate. He saw how matters stood, but Romanus succeeded in implicating him in his double dealing, so that he did not dare to reveal the truth, and the accusation was declared to be groundless. In wrath the Emperor ordered the head of the deputation to be executed, and the leading spokesmen to have their tongues cut out.

Romanus' infamies appear to have exceeded all bounds, so that in time they attracted universal attention. From the Emperor they were concealed, and might perhaps, like much else, have remained so, had not one of those family murders, so common among the African tribes, taken place in one of the Mauretanian vassal principalities. The murdered man had enjoyed the favour of Romanus, and when the murderer did not succeed in winning the Emperor's ear, he was forced to attempt to save himself by a successful revolt. He got great support, particularly from the persecuted Donatists who hated the Government, and many of the people, in desperation, joined him. The position of the Emperor and Church in Africa was in jeopardy, entirely owing to their own mistakes and crimes. Valentinian had a brilliant general, Theodosius, who had recently won back Britain, where similar conditions prevailed, for the Empire. There the Highland tribes had taken advantage of the weakening of the garrison and the unrest after the death of Julian for an invasion, and the oppressed population had helped them. Theodosius was sent to Africa, and restored discipline with barbaric severity; his usual punishments were to cut off men's hands and burn them alive. He waged the war with more than usual treachery, and succeeded in suppressing the insurrection. But the deeds of the court camarilla could no longer be concealed. The chancellor and the commissioner committed suicide, but Romanus, the most guilty of them all, succeeded in saving himself. Probably he was not without responsibility for the execution of Theodosius soon after the death of Valentinian.

Meanwhile Valens was experiencing trouble in the Eastern half of the Empire. His influence was small, for he had been elevated to the throne straight from the ranks of the guard. A collateral relative of Julian, one Procopius, having managed to win over some divisions of the Goths, who were in Constantinople on their way to the East, seized the city and was proclaimed Emperor. Other troops joined him, and Valens was so desperate that he thought of relinquishing the purple, but the high officials round him dissuaded him from this step. Procopius wasted the winter in collecting money and provisions instead of aiming at a quick decision. When, in the following year, a decisive battle took place he was deserted by his troops and killed. Owing to the fact that Gothic troops had supported Procopius, Valens had an excuse to renew the war with the Goths, who, on the Lower Danube, were neighbours of his territory. He had also inherited a war with the Persians which dragged on indecisively for several years accompanied by intrigues at the Armenian court, till it was interrupted by a catastrophe on the northern frontier.

In the middle of the century Christianity had obtained a footing among the Goths. Ulfilas, who translated the Bible into

Gothic, was consecrated their bishop in A.D. 371. The Goths had adopted the Arian creed, which at this time was favoured by the Emperor, but they cared but little for theological dogmas. The new religion had resulted in schisms which eventually caused the Christian party to ask the Emperor for protection against their pagan fellow-countrymen.

Then the Goths were struck by a terrible blow from the East. The Huns had appeared. The shock had many indirect effects and gave an impulse to the migration of the Germans. The outlandish appearance of the Huns created, both among the Germans and Romans, the same terror mingled with superstitious awe, which the vanguard of the Germans, the Cimbri and the Teutones, had once aroused among the Romans, and contemporary accounts make this intelligible. The Huns were Mongols, small and squat, extremely ugly and dirty. Their ugliness was increased by tattooed stripes on their beardless faces. They wore their clothes of linen or skins till they dropped from their bodies. They had few needs, and in their agility and cunning were like wild animals. They had the primitive dislike of the wild creature for entering under a roof, and a room seemed to them a prison. They took their women and children with them in waggons : they ate lean raw meat and wild herbs, and even slept on their little, shaggy, but agile horses. They seemed to be glued to them, and their phenomenal proficiency as horsemen was one of the reasons for their successes.

First they conquered the Alans. The East Goths who attempted resistance were beaten, and their King Ermanrik, who was a hundred years old, is said to have committed suicide in despair. Then it was the turn of the West Goths. Some of these escaped into the mountains of Transylvania ; another section, 200,000 strong, together with some East Goths, asked to be admitted into the Roman Empire. Valens made no objection, but it was a serious matter to receive such a mass of men as auxiliary troops ; he would let the Goths settle as tillers of the soil : there was sufficient room for them. If this was to be carried out, the Goths had to be disarmed ; but they had also to be supported, as they brought no provisions with them. The peculations of the officials, who, during the past years of comparative peace had been accustomed to a profitable traffic with the Goths, brought about a catastrophe. In order to feather their own nest the officials distributed corn so parsimoniously that the Goths were on the verge of starvation, while at the same time, in return for bribes, they were allowed to retain their arms. The officials do not seem to have been troubled with the thought that these might be turned upon them in revenge. They must indeed have been blind not to foresee that a rising would be the consequence of such shabby treatment. One day the Gothic captains were invited to a meal with the Roman commissioner. The most distinguished of them, Fritigern, was, as leader of the Christian section, on good terms with the Romans. Suddenly the bodyguard of the Goths was surprised and cut down. Fritigern retired, ostensibly to pacify the tumult, but actually to summon his countrymen to arms.

The Goths harried the country far and wide, though they were unable to capture the fortified towns. Even so they could hardly maintain themselves, for all provisions had been consumed or removed. German settlers, and occasionally bodies of soldiers, joined the Gothic bands. Valens hurried to the scene from Asia, and Gratian, who succeeded his father, Valentinian, sent help from the West. His generals drove the Goths back to the Dobrudja, after a great but indecisive battle, but the Goths rallied again and carried devastation up to the walls of Constantinople. Reinforcements were required, but Gratian was held up by an inroad of the Alamannians. He warned Valens to wait till they could attack the Goths with their united forces. The open contempt which the population of Constantinople showed to Valens and some unimportant successes, tempted him to offer battle to the Goths at Adrianople. The formation he adopted was not successful. His left wing was isolated by a violent cavalry attack, and the whole Roman army was rolled up and annihilated. The Emperor was missing. Later a fugitive reported that, grievously wounded, he had taken refuge in a house which the Goths burnt over his head.

The young and weak Gratian probably regarded the Eastern half of the Empire as lost ; in any case it needed an Emperor. Of the Roman generals the only one who had any successes to his credit was Theodosius, a son of the Theodosius who had fought in Britain and Africa. In him Gratian believed that he had found the right man, and he was not mistaken. Theodosius was one of the more imposing productions of this gloomy age. He was appointed Augustus, and his share of the Empire augmented by the addition of Moesia. Gratian lent him troops, for the army of the East was quite demoralised. In the long run the Goths ruined themselves. They lived by plundering, and the more they plundered, the less there remained to take. Quarrels divided and diseases decimated them. Theodosius succeeded in pushing them back, but once more they overwhelmed the hitherto spared region of Epirus and Greece. Finally they had to be granted dwellings within the Empire and corn, so that they should not have to maintain themselves by plundering. The Gothic troops in the imperial service were more esteemed and better treated than the Romans. So the disturbances were quieted for the moment, but a great nation, restless and undisciplined, was now planted within the Empire itself.

The population of the Empire endured the devastations of the barbarians with Christian submission, but contended bitterly in theological disputes and in the interest of bishops. Valentinian was a good Christian and an adherent of orthodoxy, but he was too simple to be interested in theological debates and ecclesiastical quarrels. He cancelled Julian's edicts, confiscated the temple property once more—but this time for the State—and showed a certain measure of toleration to heathenism. He permitted heathen cults, with the exception of midnight celebrations and bloody sacrifices, and allowed the official priests of heathenism to retain their positions. He rejected all attempts to remove Auxentius, the Arian Bishop of Milan. He defended the rights of the State against the Church, prohibited city counsellors from evading their burdens by assuming clerical orders, and tried to prevent by legislation the clergy from inducing Christians to assign their property by will to the Church, for fear of damnation. The privileges of the clergy and the possessions of the Church were making too great an inroad on the State's sources of revenue. On the other hand he legislated in true Christian spirit, decreeing suspension of work on Sundays, and granting pardons at Eastertide.

The task before Valens was more difficult. He was an Arian, and the Church in the East was irreconcilably divided into hostile factions. Following the example of Constantius, he tried to bring about a unification of the Church. After Julian's reign his Arianism had been forgotten, and he was extolled as the supporter of the Christian faith. But Valens did not venture to take decisive measures against the pillars of orthodoxy, and the effort he made was a failure. Subsequently the Church condemned him as a tyrant, not only because of his heretical opinions, but because he attempted to oppose monasticism. Disgust of the world, the attraction of asceticism, an exaggerated and almost fanatical wave of pietism had, both in Egypt and Syria, impelled thousands and thousands to go out into the desert. There they collected in hermit colonies or convents, but when their spiritual brethren and ecclesiastical leaders were threatened, they poured back in crowds into the towns, and fought for them with their reputation for special sanctity and their stout cudgels. With their help Athanasius had terrorised Alexandria, driven out his opponents, and inflicted more than one defeat on the Emperor. The West, however, had little sympathy for the movement. Valens considered that the monks were neglecting their civil duties, and ordered that those who had evaded their obligations to the State should be brought back. This interference with the holy men aroused great exasperation, for it was directed against one of the strongest weapons of the Church, which was soon to acquire further merit by a crusade against the remnants of paganism.

The dispute over the See of Rome is typical. During Constantius' reign, Bishop Liberius had been deposed by a synod at Milan. A new bishop was chosen, but was only recognised by a section of the congregation. When, a few

K

years afterwards, Liberius was pardoned, the other bishop, Felix, was expelled by the Roman populace, in spite of the Emperor's order that both should be recognised as bishops in Rome. Fortunately Felix soon died, and Liberius was wise enough to admit his supporters into his communion. But the lesson had been learned that force could be applied successfully in the settlement of Church disputes, and as the Emperor seldom visited Rome, the bishop had become the foremost man in the city. In the conflict over Arianism, the orthodox in the East had appealed to him for help, and he had attempted to assert his authority in the East. The West was fairly free from the infection. The Bishop of Rome appeared in the trappings of an external pomp and state which surpassed those of the imperial officials. The revenues of the See were so great that one of the richest members of the Senate, the heathen Praetextatus, declared that if he was made Bishop of Rome he would become a Christian. A large part of the revenues was applied in almsgiving and charity, and, in consequence, the bishop's adherents included all the poor and the idlers of the city.

After Liberius' death his supporters hastened to elect Ursinus as bishop in a church on the other side of the Tiber. The opposition party chose Damasus, who was a great preacher and a special favourite of the female sex, although there were unpleasant stories afloat concerning his morals. Which election was canonically valid, it is hard to say. Damasus settled the matter. Led by jockeys from the circus, his party seized the bridges over the Tiber, and after three days' street-fighting got possession of his rival's church. The prefect of the city was unable to restore order, and had to take to flight. When the conflict was over, he had no alternative but to banish the vanquished, and Valentinian consented to this step for the sake of peace. Some captive priests were liberated by Ursinus' supporters, and taken to Santa Maria Maggiore. Damasus then collected his bodyguard, who tore a hole in the roof, forced the doors, and massacred 160 men and women in the church.

It was no wonder that Ursinus' partisans were embittered,

and that they were fired with the courage of fanaticism. They gathered in the streets and squares, and chanted in unison the text : " Fear not those who kill the body and cannot kill the soul." They cried out in the churches that the Emperor should call a synod and eject the murderer from the chair of St. Peter. The disorder could not be quietened. Eventually Valentinian allowed Ursinus to return ; but as he, naturally, feared still further disorders, he appointed an impartial prefect of the city, the heathen Praetextatus. Ursinus was rapturously received by his followers as a martyr. But when he seized a church Damasus drove him out with much bloodshed. Praetextatus restored order, and succeeded in confirming the banishment of Ursinus, whose supporters were deprived of their church, but continued to hold services at the graves of the martyrs outside the city, as the Christians had done during the first persecutions. This, too, was forbidden, and Damasus broke up their meetings with the usual violent scenes. Even eighteen years after the death of Ursinus his supporters maintained a separate sect. But the bishop had conquered, and was well on the way to becoming Pope.

GRATIAN : VALENTINIAN II. (A.D. 375–392)

During a serious illness Valentinian had appointed Gratian, his eight-year-old son, Augustus. At the age of sixteen Gratian, on his father's death, became Emperor. As was usual with an heir to the throne, he had had a good bringing up, but had been kept secluded from the world. In his early years his tutor, the professor and poet, Ausonius, conducted the government. Above all Gratian had learned to be a good Christian, who prayed, fulfilled the moral law, and was in every way orthodox. He abandoned the traditional claim of the Emperor to be the head of the pagan State religion, and was the first Emperor who did not bear the title *pontifex maximus*. He withdrew State support from heathen worship, and deprived its priests of their privileges. If any gift was made to temples, it was confiscated to the treasury. The Senate was largely pagan in sympathy. In its meeting-house was a statue of

Victory, once taken as loot from Tarentum, and an altar, which was the Palladium of heathenism. Constantius had removed it, but it had been brought back and was still standing, till Gratian again moved it, and the Senate's prayers did not induce him to alter his decision. In other respects Gratian was an unimportant person. He loved hunting, and favoured the Germans in the army to such an extent that the Roman troops became seriously discontented. In Britain, Maximus, a general, was proclaimed Emperor. When Gratian went to Gaul he was deserted by his troops, and was treacherously slain on the road to Italy by one of Maximus' generals.

At Valentinian's death the army desired a more vigorous ruler than young Gratian, and wanted to proclaim a colleague, but a German general succeeded in defeating the project by producing Valentinian's wife, Justina, and her second son Valentinian, a boy of four. The child was proclaimed Emperor, and assigned Italy and Africa, but Gratian governed in his name. At the latter's death Valentinian II. was twelve. He could do nothing but recognise the usurpation, and Theodosius did likewise. Maximus was a competent man, and tried to establish his power by zeal for orthodoxy. Priscillian had founded in Spain a sect which followed some of the tenets of the Manichaean heresy. A strict asceticism brought it into vogue, and the practice of secret rites at divine service rendered it dangerously attractive. Maximus in this connection had an opportunity of proving his orthodoxy. Priscillian and some of his supporters were executed, some of them being forced by torture to declare themselves guilty of witchcraft. Whatever may be said in justification of the sentence, this, the first persecution of heretics by death and torture for conscience' sake, was a peculiar ordering of fate, inasmuch as it occurred in Spain, where it was to be followed by so many other similar scenes. However, it is only fair to add that many bishops and others disapproved of the proceedings.

Young Valentinian was a good Christian also. Soon after his accession the Senate repeated its request for the restoration of the statue of Victory. One of its chief members, and the leading literary man of the day, named Symmachus, stated its case in a composition, which not only cleverly put forward a justification, but also was full of real conviction. Even the Christian members of the imperial council were over-persuaded, but in spite of this Valentinian refused. Ambrosius' reply depended for its effect, not on force of argument or formal excellence, but on the threat of excommunication.

Meanwhile tension arose between the imperial court and Ambrosius. This remarkable man, the first prince of the Church in the West on a grand scale, and the first who forced an Emperor to go to Canossa, was an experienced agitator. On the death of Auxentius, the Arian Bishop of Milan, the usual riots had followed in connection with the election. When, as Governor of Liguria and Aemilia, Ambrosius appeared in the square to pacify the mob, some one cried out, " Let Ambrosius be bishop ! " The crowd agreed. Ambrosius accepted the election, was baptised and consecrated bishop. He showed such capacity, that the civil government must have regretted it had lost such a force. He was the zealous champion of orthodoxy, and his chief ambition was to extirpate Arianism in the West. He sought to extend the power of the Church, and exercised a decisive influence on Gratian. His influence on Valentinian II. would have been as great, if the Emperor's mother had not chanced to be an Arian, and if also the Gothic body-guard had not supported Arianism. The Emperor made the modest request that a church outside the walls should be conceded to the Arians, but Ambrosius refused ; he would leave no place for heresy. When the Emperor summoned him before the Council, Ambrosius appeared with an excited Christian mob at his back, and promised to pacify it only on condition that his churches were not interfered with.

The Emperor was rebuffed, but replied by a law, which allowed toleration to the Arians and threatened with death any one who stirred up the people. Ambrosius took occasion to proclaim that he would sacrifice his life with joy for the orthodox faith, and the Emperor dared do nothing. The congregations occupied the churches both by night and by day in order to prevent Arian intrusion, passing the time in singing hymns, which were now introduced into public worship. and in Bible readings. Valentinian now demanded a church inside the city for the Arians. Ambrosius delivered sermons to the congregation to maintain their zeal at boiling-point. He appealed to the weapons of the spirit, and could well do so, for he had behind him the fanatical mob. The Emperor's weakness made even his own supporters doubtful. He got the church, but his own officers advised him to attend Ambrosius' mass. "If Ambrosius orders it," he replied bitterly, "you are ready to hand me over, bound, to him." The victory rested with the Church, and Ambrosius ventured to declare that the bishop had not to answer to the Emperor, but the Emperor to the churches, in matters of faith.

Maximus now aimed at securing the reward of his orthodoxy. He wrote to Valentinian and warned him to desist from his heresy and persecution of the faithful, and also to the Bishop of Rome setting forth his services to the Catholic Church. As Valentinian would not cancel the edict of toleration towards Arianism, Maximus declared himself wounded in his most sacred feelings and compelled to overthrow the heretical Emperor. Italy went over to him, and Valentinian and his mother with difficulty found a ship and escaped to Thessalonica, where Theodosius resided. Theodosius found himself placed in an awkward position. On the one hand was his orthodoxy and the power of Maximus, on the other his feelings for the dynasty. He owed his throne to Valentinian's brother, and Maximus was only an usurper, though circumstances had necessitated the recognition of his position. Valentinian was the first man to save his throne by a mass—for he returned to the orthodox faith on the death of his mother—and Theodosius, not the last to be impressed by a handsome woman, promptly married Valentinian's young sister, Galla. Maximus was defeated in two battles and killed, and Valentinian was restored to his throne, which he now only held by Theodosius' favour. He took up his residence in Gaul, while, for the present, Theodosius resided in Milan, probably hoping, eventually, to appropriate the central part of the Empire for one of his two sons.

THEODOSIUS (A.D. 379-395)

Theodosius' portion of the Empire was the chief seat of Arianism ; but Theodosius was far more energetic than Valentinian, who was hardly grown up, and Arianism was more tolerant than orthodoxy and so did not possess the same power of resistance. One of the first acts of Theodosius' government was a law which declared the Christian doctrine in the form in which St. Peter taught it, and the bishops, Damasus in Rome and Peter in Alexandria, men of apostolic sanctity, practised it, to be the only correct and permissible doctrine in the Empire. Now for the first time it was called " Catholic " in the sense in which we use the word. This was the first of a long series of laws directed against Arianism, and was vigorously put into force. The Arian Bishop of Constantinople had to choose between deposition and conversion, and the orthodox Gregory of Nazianzus, who was only supported by a small minority, was introduced by force into the church of Santa Sophia. A synod was summoned at Constantinople, which declared the Nicene Creed to be the only correct faith, and condemned all heretics. Arian bishops were everywhere deposed and deprived of their churches, and every service that did not follow the Nicene ritual was stigmatised as criminal, and even meetings in private houses were forbidden. Theodosius succeeded in extirpating Arianism, and thus earned the title of the Great. But on the other hand, he was not blind to the Church's misuse of its power, and sought to restrain it. Notwithstanding his piety he was a true representative of the combination of Caesar and Pope in one person. He rejected the attempt of the Bishop of Rome and Ambrosius to extend the authority of Rome over the Eastern Church by interfering in disputes connected with the See of Constantinople, and vetoed the proposal of a general Council at Rome. He maintained the ecclesiastical independence of the two halves of the Empire, and this paved the way for the division of the Church.

Theodosius went to Canossa, but it is doubtful if he would have done so had it been only on a question of authority and not in connection with offences against humanity and morals. The Emperor himself held strict views on the sanctity of the matrimonial tie and required the same of his subjects. In accordance with Christian doctrine he forbade marriage between cousins, and between pagans and Christians : he decreed loss of position and property to a widow who married again, and severely punished unnatural vices, though in some other respects he relaxed the severity of the laws. During his first two years he hardly allowed a single death sentence to be carried out. But he had in a high degree a failing, common to the age—lack of self-control. In spite of being a Spaniard, he was liable to outbreaks of wrath as senseless as those of a German. It was characteristic of him that he determined that a death-sentence should not be carried out till after the lapse of a month; but his clemency was equally capricious. At Antioch, the people, in despair at the burden of taxation, overthrew and mutilated the statues of the Emperor. A terrible punishment was expected, and as many as were able left the city and hid themselves. But when the bishop of the city went to the Emperor, and humbly begged for pardon, he remitted all punishment. On another occasion it happened that an officer of high rank was killed by the mob at Thessalonica. As a punishment Theodosius ordered the soldiers to fall on the multitude assembled in the circus who were expecting no harm, and 7000 were massacred. Soon afterwards he went to Milan, and Ambrosius had occasion to put into practice his theories of the Emperor's subordination to Church discipline, particularly as he knew that Theodosius was penitent. It certainly was not such a dramatic incident as when the bishop at the church porch refused admittance to the blood-guilty Emperor. But he denied him the privilege of communion till he had done penance, and Theodosius submitted, conscious that he had grievously sinned.

Paganism was also suppressed in the West. Apostasy from Christianity was punished by loss of the right to execute and receive testamentary dispositions. For the present incense and visits to temples were permitted. Paganism as a matter of conviction persisted, and even in Theodosius' service pagans occupied high posts. Paganism was difficult to attack when it did not express itself in acts, and there was still a certain degree of liberty of action inasmuch as people were not driven to church by force. But Theodosius did what he could to uproot the outward and visible signs of pagan piety, and thus to suppress paganism. He forbade private sacrifices of every kind everywhere, even within the home, on pain of outlawry, and the authorities of the cities were made responsible for the strict prohibition of pagan worship. The troops were made available for securing obedience to these ordinances, and the crusades of the bishops and fanatical monks dealt even more vigorously with the relics of paganism. The latter regarded it a work of special merit, well pleasing to God, to destroy temples and idols, Jewish synagogues and sectarian churches, with tumult and murder, and the civil power supported them. An order that monks should not leave their abodes in the desert very soon had to be cancelled.

But paganism was not yet completely dead. There were pagans among the German soldiers and officers. One of them, Arbogast, was a man of such importance that Theodosius placed him by the side of Valentinian when he restored him, and gave him the charge of Gaul and the western provinces. Valentinian was a weak young man, pious and inclined to asceticism. He had willingly followed his mother's guidance, but the strict guardianship of the German wounded his feelings. Arbogast even ventured to recommend a fresh petition of the Senate for the re-erection of the statue of Victory. On this point the Emperor asserted his authority; but when the Germans invaded Italy and an embassy led by Ambrosius asked for help, matters became strained. Arbogast opposed a war in Italy, probably in the interest of Theodosius, who wanted to withhold from Valentinian the central portion of the Empire. For the same reason the latter desired actively to uphold his claim to the old territory. Violent scenes took place in the imperial council, in one of which, during an outbreak of uncontrollable passion, Arbogast knocked down an opponent. It was no wonder that Valentinian handed a letter

of dismissal to Arbogast. Arbogast tore it in pieces, exclaim-
ing with scorn that Valentinian had not given him his office
and could not take it away from him. The miserable young
Emperor was helpless, and a few days later was found hanging,
dead, in his room. Many regarded Arbogast as the murderer,
but it is just as likely that Valentinian in a fit of nervousness
and depression took his own life.

It was an unwritten law that a German born outside the
Empire could not become Emperor. At first it looked as if
Arbogast aimed at ruling the West in the name of Theodosius,
whose commission he had. But it was thought that his
hands were stained with the blood of the dynasty, and when
Theodosius overthrew his heathen praetorian prefect, Tatian,
Arbogast deemed it advisable to set up an Emperor of his
own making. Eugenius was a rhetorician and one of the most
highly educated men of his age. Even the Germans valued
rhetoric, and in the chancellery it was necessary to have
stylists who were masters of the literary language, now very
different from the vulgar tongue. So Eugenius became a
minister, the confidant of Arbogast, and finally his Emperor.
Eugenius permitted the re-erection of the Victory in the Senate
house. When Ambrosius threatened excommunication,
paganism raised its head once more. Flavian, the praetorian
prefect, one of the highly cultivated pagans who had previously
been in Theodosius' service, openly practised soothsaying,
and Arbogast had an image of Hercules, which the Germans
no doubt imagined was Thor, carried at the head of the
army.

At first it seemed as if the new usurper, like Maximus,
would be able to make a settlement with Theodosius, for
the latter did not shine as a general, and realised and feared
Arbogast's military competence. But the blatant display
of pagan tendencies made it his Christian duty to avenge the
death of his brother-in-law. When Theodosius' army
debouched from the Julian Alps, Arbogast met it at the mouth
of the Wippach valley. Theodosius in vain strove to break
through, and the situation seemed lost, when it was saved by
treason and a miracle. The division which Arbogast had sent

to take Theodosius in the rear, went over to him by night, and the next day the terrible " bora," which sweeps down from the Karstberg mountains, so violently as to derail railway trains, wrested the victory out of the hands of Arbogast's troops. Theodosius marched into Milan, restored Christianity, and for the last time united the whole Roman Empire under one ruler. Four and a half months after the victory he died.

HONORIUS : ARCADIUS (A.D. 395–423)

Theodosius left two sons, both already created Augustus : Arcadius, aged eighteen, who was left behind in Constantinople, and Honorius, aged eight. Both were the most inefficient and unimportant rulers the Empire ever had, and resided exclusively in their courts. Both died in possession of the throne, a sign of the victory of the dynastic principle. In the Western Empire the principle perished in the general ruin, but in the East it survived, and dominated the Byzantine epoch. On his death-bed Theodosius made the master of the army, the Vandal Stilicho, Honorius' guardian ; Arcadius was assisted by his praetorian prefect, a Gaul named Rufinus. Stilicho aimed at the dominion in the East as well, but had not the capacity for bold intervention, and also was faced by the difficulty that he could not be present, in person, at both courts at once. Owing to him and his rivals in Constantinople, the two halves of the Empire drifted into the position of two mutually hostile States. In Western Illyria the West Goths under Alaric were domiciled, and in the winter, after the death of Theodosius, they emerged on a plundering raid. Stilicho marched after them but effected nothing, and had to obey Arcadius' command to evacuate the country and hand over his troops which belonged to the East. These Goths were commanded by Gainas, who, at Stilicho's instigation, induced his soldiers to murder Rufinus, when he was reviewing a parade of troops in Constantinople, in attendance on the Emperor.

Arcadius was quite incapable of standing by himself, so the government fell into the hands of a eunuch and former chamberlain, Eutropius, who finally received the highest honour of the Empire, the Consulate. It must be admitted that he was a competent man. At first he maintained friendly relations with Stilicho, and when Alaric ravaged Greece, took Athens and carried away its inhabitants as slaves, burnt Corinth and even plundered the valleys of Arcadia, Stilicho was summoned to the rescue. But this time also he effected nothing, and the Goths settled in Epirus. Then Eutropius adopted another policy in appointing Alaric master of the army in Illyria. This meant that the Goths received provisions, arms, and money from the Emperor at Constantinople, and occupied the position of a buffer State between the Eastern and West Roman Emperors.

Over Africa the two realms were on the point of going to war. Since the later years of Theodosius the governor of the province, Gildo, had established himself as an independent ruler. This was extremely dangerous for Rome, which depended on Africa for her corn supply. The capital was put on such short commons that great riots broke out in the city. Stilicho had to depose Gildo, but the latter appealed to the senior Augustus in Constantinople, who took him under his protection. Stilicho adopted the plan of resuscitating the Senate and causing it to proclaim Gildo a public enemy. He succeeded in overcoming him, for Africa was too far distant to obtain practical support from Constantinople.

Certain Goths, whom Theodosius had allowed to settle in Phrygia, became weary of cultivating the soil and sought relaxation in the usual plundering raids. This led to the fall of Eutropius. The commander of the imperial troops, the Goth, Gainas, plotted for his removal and was assisted by court intrigues. The Germans took the leading places in both realms ; and the native Romans, who had to take a back seat, grew to hate them more and more. Unhappily, the hatred could be translated into a theological formula, the easiest expression the age could conceive for all divisions and antipathies. The Goths were Arian heretics. When Gainas and his people came to Constantinople, there arose violent uproar and tumult, and after the greater part of the army had left the city, the remaining Goths were surprised and slain, some of them being burnt in the Arian church. Gainas, when he marched on Constantinople, found the gates closed, so he began to plunder Thrace, and schemed to return home over the Danube. There he encountered the Huns and met his death. Anti-Germanism had triumphed, but the defence of the Empire was correspondingly weakened. The Romans could not endure the hardships and discipline of military service, but were quite prepared to fight in the streets in spontaneous and excited expressions of popular hatred against those with whom they disagreed.

As a consequence of the changed circumstances, the tribute to Alaric and his Goths was cancelled. In the Balkan Peninsula, so often plundered, there was nothing more to be got, so Alaric turned on Italy. The march was the migration of a whole people. The women and children were transported in waggons. The court took refuge within the strong walls of Milan, and Stilicho drained the frontiers of troops as far as Britain to repulse the invaders. A pagan under-officer proposed that the waggon train of the Goths should be surprised on Easter Day, when they had scruples against fighting. The Romans captured it, and Alaric undertook to withdraw if the prisoners were given back. In spite of this he tried to march into Gaul, was surrounded, but succeeded in fighting through and getting back to Illyria with a decimated following. But the terror had been so great that the court removed to Ravenna, which was protected by extensive marshes.

An ecclesiastical dispute had broken out again in Constantinople. The brilliant preacher, John Chrysostom, had been made bishop. He had as advanced ideas as Ambrosius regarding the majesty of his office and of the Church, but his temperament was ascetic, more idealistic and less practical. He neither knew how nor had the will to steer among the hidden rocks of court intrigue. Thus he made the Empress, who at first was his admirer, his special enemy. As usual, appeal was made to the Bishop of Rome, who requested that the questions at issue should be laid before a council summoned from both parts of the Empire. When the Emperor at Constantinople, without considering the Pope, deposed and exiled John and persecuted his supporters, Stilicho schemed

to use the occasion for finally executing his designs on the
Eastern Empire. But he was hindered by a fresh German
attack. Radagais crossed the Danube and broke into Italy
with a great host composed of various tribes, chiefly Goths
and Alamannians, according to the lowest contemporary
estimate, 200,000 strong. When part of this army besieged
Florence, Stilicho succeeded in relieving the town and surrounding the Germans at Fiesole. Most of them had to surrender
unconditionally. Only a minority were taken into the army,
and the rest were sold ; and it is said that the price of a slave
went down to a *solidus*. The two remaining armies were
induced to return over the Alps.

When the tide of invasion was stemmed in Italy, it flowed
over the Rhine frontier from which Stilicho had removed the
garrisons. Vandals, Suebi, Burgundians and Alans overran
Gaul as far as the Pyrenees, while pirates plundered the coasts.
The Emperor could give no assistance. Britain severed its
connection with the Empire and tried, on its own account, to
ward off the Saxons. A rival Emperor seized Gaul. Vandals,
Alans, and Suebi penetrated into Spain.

Meanwhile Alaric had, at Stilicho's suggestion, made a
raid into the East Roman territory. He achieved but little,
for Stilicho was hindered from coming to his assistance, but
Alaric claimed an extravagant compensation for the failure
of the expedition. The country was drained dry, the treasury
was empty, and money was only to be found in the hands of
rich Senators. In spite of vehement opposition in the Senate,
a capital levy was enforced. Just then Arcadius died, leaving
as his successor a minor, Theodosius II. Again Stilicho cast
envious eyes eastwards, but was resisted by his Emperor,
who wanted Gaul to be reconquered. The consequent ill-
feeling was utilised by the anti-German party, which also
existed in the Western Empire. By cleverly making use of
the discontent of the troops, their leader, Olympius, succeeded
in overthrowing Stilicho's supporters and Stilicho himself.
The Emperor caused his guardian for many years to be
executed, his adherents to be tortured and killed, and their
property confiscated. The Roman soldiers took their revenge

for the privileges enjoyed by the Germans by murdering their wives and children.

Alaric had made his terms with Stilicho. He now had to deal with other men, and considerably lowered his demands, which were rejected owing to the strong nationalism of the new Government. In consequence Alaric moved into Italy, and reinforced by the German soldiers whose families had been murdered, marched straight on Rome. The city was cut off from supplies, suffered terribly from hunger and disease, and had to ransom itself with unheard-of sums. The Goths could not live by plundering for any length of time, so Alaric strove for a settlement similar to that which he had made with the Eastern Empire. His ambition was to procure the office of master of the imperial forces and to obtain lands and provisions for his people. When Honorius, holding out in inaccessible Ravenna, was defiant, Alaric set up an Emperor of his own, Attalus, the prefect of the city. Both for the Goths and for Rome it was a vital necessity to seize corn-growing Africa, but the attempts failed. Then Alaric abandoned his Emperor, and Honorius ordered the restoration of the provision of corn. A relative and personal enemy of Alaric who had taken service with Honorius, now seized an opportunity to fall on some of his countrymen. The Emperor, who detested the oppression of the Goths, connived at the deed. Alaric in fury moved on Rome again. The city was taken and sacked by strangers for the first time since the Celtic invasion nearly 800 years before. But the Goths could not live in Rome. They moved southwards, enticed by the lure of the riches of Africa, but they did not even succeed in crossing over to Sicily. Then Alaric turned northwards and died while on the march. It is said that the Goths diverted a river at Cosenza, buried their dead prince, together with much treasure, in its bed, and then let the water flow back over the grave, that it might never be discovered and violated. Alaric's brother-in-law, Athaulf, took over the command, and led the Goths out of devastated Italy into Gaul, where he entered the service of an usurper, who had risen against Honorius. His successor, Valia, concluded an agreement with Honorius which eliminated the Gallic usurpers. The West Goths received the south-west part of the country between Toulouse and the sea, entered into the Emperor's service, and evicted the peoples who had migrated there before— Vandals, Alans, and Suebi. The Emperor did not succeed in driving the Vandals out of Southern Spain. In the north he had to concede territory to the Burgundians on the Rhine by Mainz. All his life Honorius had been a puppet in the hands of his courtiers, and the possessors of power varied according to circumstances and intrigues. But his person constituted a rallying-point for the realm thanks to the theory of legitimacy, and what that meant was evident when Honorius died after a reign of twenty-eight years without leaving any heirs.

VALENTINIAN III. (A.D. 425–455)

The court party made a high official, John, Emperor, but he was not recognised outside Italy. In Africa, which had often previously taken up an independent attitude, the governor, Boniface, resisted John, and the Eastern Emperor, Theodosius II., seized the opportunity to extend his influence in the West. Honorius' sister, Galla Placidia, with her young son, little Valentinian III., had taken refuge with him. Theodosius transported them with an army over to Italy, and the West had once more a minor as Emperor with a woman as guardian. Boniface, who supported the new Emperor, found himself compelled to face an adversary at court. This was the Roman Aëtius, whose strength depended on his good relations with the dreaded Huns. The court summoned Boniface to Italy to deprive him of the basis of his power, and Boniface refused to go. The consequence was war between the Emperor and his viceroy. After the fashion of the age both engaged the help of bodies of Germans, but this was fatal. Africa was Rome's granary, and had already appeared to Alaric as the promised land. Africa was also the home of the Donatist sect. In spite of the prohibitions of Gratian this heresy had spread, and the imperial persecutions only made the Donatists welcome any other authority with enthusiasm. Previously they had supported native risings ; now the partisans of ecclesiastical separatism prepared the ground for the complete severance of Africa from the Empire. Under Geiserik, the Vandals, with a body of Alans, crossed over from Spain to Mauretania, and soon occupied the greater part of imperial Africa. The rôles were now reversed : for Geiserik was a zealous Arian and persecuted the orthodox. Valentinian III. could not do otherwise than recognise Geiserik's possessions, and soon Carthage, the capital, fell into his hands.

The defeated Boniface had repaired to court, where he was welcomed, because Aëtius' rule was felt to be so oppressive that a counterpoise was needed. He was appointed master of the army, in place of Aëtius. It was customary at that time for powerful men to surround themselves with a bodyguard of their own. Aëtius had no intention of yielding weakly. A regular war began between him and Boniface. After the latter had died from wounds received in a skirmish, Aëtius had to retire to his good friends the Huns, and by their intervention was again received into the Emperor's favour, was reappointed master of the army, and continued to rule with undeniable vigour and skill. With the help of the Huns he maintained the Emperor's authority over the German peoples who had settled in Gaul, waged war with the West Goths and Franks, who had spread over the northern part of the land, and defeated the Burgundians, who soon afterwards were crushed by the Huns, and only after the lapse of several decades regained strength and secured settlements on the Rhone. A complete subjugation of the country was at present no longer feasible. Britain had to be given up, as the Emperor could give no assistance against the Highland tribes. Then the Britons invited the help of the Angles and Saxons. They came and took possession of the country. Part of the expelled British population migrated to Brittany, and supplied that peninsula with its name and Celtic population.

The mightiest prince of that age was Attila, one of those outstanding men like Tamerlane or Genghiz-Khan, who for a moment succeeded in keeping together the restless nomad-tribes

L

and giving them occupation, maintaining them by wide-spread raids and forays. He had united the various Hunnish tribes throughout Asia and Europe, in Hungary and South Russia, and had subjected the Germanic peoples right up to the Rhine. The East Roman Empire was repeatedly harried, and had to ransom itself with a tribute which was constantly increased. With the West Roman Empire he maintained friendly relations, and the Emperor's sister, Honoria, promised him her hand. As she, however, was married to a Roman, Attila demanded not only the princess but half the kingdom. This demand could not be entertained, so Attila invaded Gaul with frightful devastations, and this danger united the Romans and Germans. Aëtius took the field against his former friend at the head of the Roman army and the Germanic tribes who dwelt within the Empire. Attila was accompanied by Germanic tribes under his sway, East Goths and Gepidae. The armies met on the Catalaunian Plain near Troyes, and fought with so much bitterness, that legend related that the shades of the fallen continued to fight in the air for three nights over the battle-field. The heaviest loss fell on the West Goths, whose king was killed. The conflict was not decisive, but Attila's invasion was checked. He retired over the Rhine, and in the following year invaded Italy. Without meeting any resistance he ravaged the north and threatened Rome. The city could rely on no defence but in the efficiency of prayer. Pope Leo, accompanied by the noblest Romans, went out to meet the King of the Huns, and prevailed on him to spare the city. Another reason, perhaps, for his clemency was the report that troops sent by the East Roman Emperor to the help of the realm were approaching. Attila in the following year meditated vengeance on the Eastern Empire, but death forestalled him. Under his sons, his kingdom broke up as quickly as it had been formed, and the subject German peoples were liberated. The East Goths settled in Pannonia as the allies of the East Roman Emperor, from whom, as a reward for their services, they were to receive pay and provisions, and the usual disturbances did not fail to follow.

Aëtius was the most powerful man in the Western Empire.
Consequently he had many jealous enemies, and Valentinian
III., who found his domination oppressive, was induced to
overthrow and execute him. But this step was to prove his
undoing, since he had no longer any trustworthy supporters,
and the following year he was murdered in Rome by the
adherents of Aëtius. The Senator, Maximus, became Emperor,
and forced the Emperor's widow, Eudoxia, to marry him. But
Eudoxia planned vengeance. Valentinian III. had been
constrained to recognise the authority of Geiserik in Africa,
where a great attack supported by an East Roman fleet had
failed. Geiserik had organised his military resources with
skill and built a great fleet, with which he harried the coasts
far and wide. Eudoxia turned to him, and Geiserik, who
felt himself no longer bound by the treaty with Valentinian,
eagerly seized his opportunity. His army landed and took
and plundered Rome. Maximus found death in flight, and
Eudoxia went off to Africa with Geiserik.

When this happened, Maximus' master of the troops,
Avitus, was in Gaul. With the support of the West Goths
he was proclaimed Emperor. Both parties had their interests
to preserve. The West Goths moved into Spain, overcame
the Suebi, and occupied a great part of the peninsula. Avitus
went to Rome with a West Gothic army and obtained recognition of himself as Emperor. But the real master of the
Empire was no longer the Emperor but the master of the army.
The Suevian, Ricimer, grandson, through his mother, of the
West Gothic King, Valia, was then at the head of the troops.
He rose against Avitus, defeated him, and forced him to resign.
A humane method of making fallen Emperors harmless had
been invented, and Avitus was consecrated a bishop. With the
help of Leo, the East Roman Emperor, Majorianus was raised to
the West Roman throne. He too was soon removed by Ricimer,
who proclaimed a new Emperor, Severus. When Severus died
soon after, Ricimer did not appoint a new Emperor, but
managed the government himself, leaving the nominal imperial
authority to the East Roman Emperor, Leo. After a time Leo
sent Anthemius as Emperor to Rome and married him to

Ricimer's daughter to confirm his position. Geiserik's ceaseless Viking raids forced the two empires to co-operate in despatching a great expedition against the Vandals. Sardinia and Tripoli were conquered, but the fleet was defeated before Carthage, and Geiserik's power was not crushed.

THEODOSIUS II. (A.D. 408–450)

The East Roman Empire had had more repose. It had quivered before the first shock of the racial emigration, but later the hordes had gone westwards, and left the Eastern Empire comparatively at peace. So in spite of all difficulties the Emperor in Constantinople had managed to maintain his authority. It was fortunate that during these years the Persian Empire was weakened by internal dissension, and also had not escaped some of the effects of the migrations, since the Huns made at least one inroad into Armenia. Theodosius II.'s long reign is most notable for the first great collection of imperial edicts, the *codex Theodosianus*, (a forerunner of Justinian's great collection and an invaluable source for the domestic history of the Empire,) and also for the beginning of the Nestorian dispute. Nestorius, patriarch of Constantinople, was deposed, his doctrines condemned, and his supporters persecuted, but Nestorianism spread widely in Syria and Egypt. Religious antagonism estranged these provinces from the Empire, and prepared the way for the Arab conquests. Theodosius II. was succeeded by two competent Emperors, Marcian and Leo.

MARCIAN : LEO I. : LEO II. (A.D. 450–474)

Under Leo, the Goth, Aspar, occupied the same position in Constantinople as the masters of the troops in the West Roman Empire. He succeeded in having his son appointed as his successor, but the people would not hear of an Arian Emperor. Aspar was overthrown by a popular rising, and his rival, the Isaurian Zeno, who was married to a daughter of Leo, placed his son, Leo II., on the throne. Leo took his father as colleague, and when he died Zeno became sole ruler. Aspar's fall produced, as a consequence, a rising among his fellow-countrymen, the East Goths, but after a few years the old amicable relations were restored.

The tottering West Roman Empire was hastening to its final doom. Anthemius, whom Leo had appointed Emperor, quarrelled with Ricimer, was besieged in Rome, and killed. Soon after, Ricimer died, together with the new Emperor, Olybrius, whom he had set up. A nephew of Ricimer, Gundobad, took up the rôle of king-maker, and set up Glycerius. Leo again interfered, and put forward a candidate called Julius Nepos. This man deposed Glycerius, but eventually had, himself, to retire to Dalmatia. A noble Roman called Orestes rose against him, and set his young son, Romulus, surnamed Augustulus, on the throne, and governed in his name, with the assistance of the German soldiery. Since in the other provinces of the Empire German bands had acquired land and fixed abodes, the Germans in Italy could not understand why they should be worse off, and put forward a claim for similar advantages. When this was refused them, they seized them by force, and proclaimed their leader, Odoacer, king on August 23, A.D. 476. Orestes was vanquished and killed, Romulus returned to his estate in Campania, and peacefully ended his days there. The Germans appropriated a third of the soil of Italy.

This was the end of the West Roman Empire, if one does not take into account the outlying portions. There was one more Emperor, Nepos, who ruled in Dalmatia for four years, and there was still a Roman governor, Syagrius, in Northern Gaul, who retained his position for ten years, till he was overpowered and killed by the Franks under King Clovis.

To us the fall of the Roman Empire is a landmark in history, though at the time it aroused very little notice. It occurred as the natural result of a long process of dissolution. It had long been of little importance who sat on the throne of the Caesars : the Emperor had sunk to be an unimportant figurehead, alongside of the holders of the real power. But an Emperor was essential, for, legally, power issued from him, and even in the days of the breaking up of the Empire traditionary forms were still retained. These were, with all the force of tradition, rooted in the minds of both Romans and Germans, and they were the only safeguard against complete chaos. When there was no Emperor in Italy the imperial dignity reverted to the Emperor in Constantinople. This was now the case. Odoacer sought confirmation for his acts from the Emperor Zeno, and exercised the imperial power in his name. But his power was limited to Italy. The Germans in the provinces felt themselves entirely independent of a mere tribesman. The kingdom of Odoacer was therefore the sign of the dissolution of the West Roman Empire. Even Theodoric announced himself as the plenipotentiary of the East Roman Emperor, and, after a march against Constantinople, extorted a commission to attack Odoacer. He ruled over his East Goths as king, but over Romans as the representative of the Roman Emperor at Constantinople. Three hundred years were to elapse before racial differences disappeared, before tradition had entirely lost its hold and the Emperor at Constantinople had become so alien that the imperial crown could be placed on the head of a German. Then, too, it meant something very different to what it had in the days of the Caesars.

The Romans had brought their fate on themselves. They would not bear arms for the State and subject themselves to the discipline and privations of military service. They had a greater aversion to this than to fighting and bloodshed. They fought heroically against enemies of the Faith within, and met the persecution of the State with an equally heroic exhibition of endurance, but they encountered external enemies with Christian submission. Sometimes the old Roman pride rose like a ghost from the grave, but it was handicapped, for the national party was usually also the pagan party. Occasionally it happened that the spirit of nationalism coincided with the hatred of the masses and the Church for heretical foreigners. Movements of nationalism and anti-Germanism were foredoomed to fail in a world where might was decisive. Only Germans could, and would, fight in wars, and they were indispensable. Rome sacrificed her Empire of this world, and created an Empire of the other world.

Under the ruins of the State the Church was consolidated. The dissolution of the Western Empire took away the opportunity of continuing the subjection of the secular power which Ambrosius so successfully began. Instead it had to deal with undisciplined and divided Germans, and it did, in truth, make a beginning of its great work of disciplining them. The Roman Empire of the other world succeeded in taming their stubborn wills, and Rome dominated them for a thousand years, till the decisive shock to the new Roman organisation was dealt by the man who taught humanity the true freedom of a Christian.

The Roman imperial idea lingered on and was reintroduced into practical politics by the Pope. When he placed the crown on the head of Charlemagne, the influence of the new Roman Emperor was felt over all those countries which were not Greek, Catholic, or Mohammedan. After the death of Charlemagne the new Empire was divided into independent States, but the imperial idea and its claim to universality did not lose its hold over men's minds. In theory " One Pope, one Emperor " was the watchword ; in practical politics efforts were limited to retaining Rome and Italy under the power of the Roman Emperor. It was a belated repetition of the process which was interrupted when Augustus, after the defeat in the Teutoburg Forest, pusillanimously gave up the Romanisation of the Germans. The Germanic State which remained, after the Germans in the old Roman provinces were scattered among the native populations, endeavoured with all its might to preserve a connection with Italy. This fruitless endeavour was the fundamental misfortune of Germany. Its strength was wasted in fighting for Italy and against the Pope, in whose eyes the universal power of the Emperor was by no means so desirable as his own. In the pursuit after the chimera of Empire and the lure of Italy, the State organisation and national consolidation of Germany went to pieces. The Western States, which confined themselves to the practical requirements of the age, far outdistanced it.

The Byzantine Empire was the real heir of the later Roman Empire. There, the state organisation created by Constantine withstood all trials with an astonishing tenacity, but also with a terrifying sterility. But Byzantium retained much of the old civilisation which was trampled underfoot by the barbarians in the West. Like its civilising work in the preservation of the heritage of antiquity, its historical stand against the later movements of peoples, Slavs and Arabs, is usually estimated far too low. Constantly hard pressed and surrounded on all sides, it stood like a bulwark against the onset of the East for nearly a thousand years more. That is as long a period as elapsed between the dawn of history in the Rome of the Kings and the fall of the West Roman Empire.

BOOK II

THE EMPIRE AND ITS INHABITANTS

I

THE EMPIRE

(i) THE FRONTIERS

THE first European civilisation that attained to an advanced stage of development—that of the Greeks—spread far and wide over the Mediterranean basin, but was almost entirely confined to its coasts. The Greeks were a seafaring people, whose surplus population constantly needed new dwelling-places, and whose merchants required new openings for trade in foreign countries. Hence we find Greek colonies adhering to the countries round the Mediterranean and the Black Sea like the fringes on a garment, wherever stronger peoples, such as the Carthaginians, Etruscans, and Latins, did not repel the Greek colonist by force. But the Greek merchant and his wares were always gladly received. Greek civilisation seldom penetrated far into the country, except in Sicily—more than half of which was Hellenised—in Etruria, whose art is entirely an offshoot of archaic Greek, and northwards from Marseilles up the valley of the Rhone. The Greek colonies on the coast were, even in the most favourable circumstances, in a difficult position, and were often further weakened by domestic quarrels which paralysed their own strength, and by lack of support from home ; for the mother-country was never in a condition strong enough to support them adequately in their struggle for existence. The Greek colonies could only exist and maintain their independence so long as the peoples of the interior were weak and undeveloped ; but when these peoples united their forces, they were inevitably directed against the colonists. The Greek colonies lost their independence, and the population was absorbed into the surrounding native races. This was what happened in Sicily and Southern Italy, which nevertheless was called Magna Graecia, while in Gaul the Gallo-Greek civilisation was driven out and replaced by the Roman. The Greek colonies went under, but they had contributed largely to the expansion and development of civilisation all round the Mediterranean basin.

In contrast to the Greeks, the Romans were a rural people, and this was their special characteristic till the fall of their Empire. Their sphere of influence spread very slowly at first, but afterwards with great rapidity; and only when they had old Italy, the peninsula south of the Rubicon, securely in their hands, did they reach out over the sea. The attempt of the powerful nobility to appropriate the conquered lands confiscated to the Roman State, which plays so great a part in the ancient history of Rome, must not obscure the essential fact that in the early days of the Republic every extension of Rome's sphere of influence created new homes for Roman and Latin farmers. Italy was covered with a network of colonies which, in contrast to the Greek, were inland colonies, which obeyed and were supported by, the mother-city. In them the expanding Roman people found dwelling-places and maintenance, and they strengthened Rome's power. Not until after the conquest of Central Italy in the war with the Samnites and Etruscans, which was completed in 290 B.C., did Rome become a really great state. One of Rome's oldest historians says that the Samnite War first gave the Romans a taste for wealth. After the war with Pyrrhus, which soon followed, the Greek colonies of Southern Italy were brought under Rome's sway.

The Roman farmers might well be satisfied with their conquests, for there was land enough for them in Italy; but the capitalist and commercial interests, which now grew up in Rome, were not. On the other side of the Straits of Messina they saw the shore of fruitful Sicily, and Roman trade must have felt itself confined by the power and trade of Carthage which was dominant in the Western Mediterranean. Rome was at a turning-point in her history. Was she to be an Italian or a World power? That the importance of the decision was keenly appreciated, is shown by the unusual hesitation exhibited by the Senate, when the question of interference in the affairs of Sicily arose. For the western angle of Sicily was Carthaginian, and an attack on Sicily was bound to lead to a conflict with Carthage. Rome made her decision and involved herself once and for all in world-politics. It was soon apparent that she had interests to watch over in the complex of Hellenistic States fringing the eastern coasts of the Mediterranean.

It was not with conscious purpose that Rome trod the path of world-conquest—had it been so, much suffering would have been spared the world—but her conquests followed one another owing to circumstances over which she had no control : necessity threw them into Rome's lap. As the result of the three Punic Wars she succeeded to the Empire of Carthage. By the first she obtained Sicily and the adjacent islands, including Sardinia and Corsica—for so the Romans construed the peace treaty, when Carthage was in difficulties ; by the second she gained southern and eastern Spain ; while in the third, Carthage itself and the surrounding country, the province of Africa (approximately the modern Tunis), succumbed to her armed forces. Behind this was the principality of Numidia, which, so long as Carthage existed, was instigated by Roman intriguers to hamper and thwart her, and was not converted into a Roman province until the time of Julius Caesar. The connection by land between Italy and Spain was brought about only at the end of the second century B.C., when the French Mediterranean coast was made a Roman province.

In the East, Rome entered as a disturbing factor into the equipoise of Hellenistic states, which consisted of the three great powers, Macedonia, Syria, and Egypt, and various smaller states, the most important of which were the Pergamene kingdom in Asia Minor, the commercial republic of Rhodes, and the federated states of Greece proper. In the political gamble for power among these states, each in turn sought an ally in Rome ; but Rome ruthlessly followed her own aims by imposing herself as arbitrator and supreme judge, especially by manipulating the balance of power to her own advantage, and gradually reducing the Hellenistic states to impotence.

Rome's foreign policy was consistently hostile to the great Hellenistic powers, particularly to Macedonia, as being nearest to her and possessed of the most vigorous spirit of nationalism. She favoured the minor states, but did not scruple to give them scanty reward for their trouble, when she had no further use for them. Thus, for example, with calculated selfishness she nipped in the bud the prosperity of Rhodes. Certain states were actually in a status approximating to that of Roman vassals, and it seemed but a natural and logical consequence when some of them were bequeathed to Rome by their rulers, *e.g.* Pergamum by Attalos III., Bithynia by Nikomedes, Cyrene by Ptolemy Apion, and even Egypt by Ptolemy Alexander II., though this particular legacy was regarded by the Senate as being of such doubtful value, and the genuineness of the will so disputable, that it was declined.

The states which did not voluntarily merge themselves in the Roman Empire, were, nevertheless, bound hand and foot. In Greece the parties within the states were divided by their attitude to Rome, and Rome ruled through the party of her friends. When the people rebelled against the brutally selfish tyranny, and the heavy yoke which galled their necks, the punishment was inexorable and merciless. But Rome soon discovered that it was impossible to govern through the agency of partisans for any length of time, and had to take the countries over directly as provinces. This happened in Greece, and also in Macedonia, when Rome, after conquering Perseus, the last Macedonian king, sought to render it harmless by dividing it into four republics, which were not to have anything in common, and whose subjects were forbidden even to trade with each other or intermarry. This was a typical example of Rome's policy of ruling by division, but the future was to demonstrate the limitations of this system. States which are bound hand and foot by a foreign power, so that they are unable to take a single step independently, cannot stand alone : the mentor must formally take them in hand.

In addition to the political, there were other interests which compelled Rome to procure provinces—not commercial ones, for Rome had always been an importing, not an exporting state, but purely capitalistic. She, in common with other states of antiquity, was not in the habit of directly levying customs, taxes, and imposts. The collection was farmed out to the highest bidder. This system was very convenient for the State, which merely got a lump sum in cash and avoided the necessity of maintaining an elaborate official system for the levying of taxes and customs ; but it led to the most grievous oppression of the subjects, since the tax-farmers, by every means, lawful and unlawful, secured their own interests. Great companies were formed with huge capital and shoals of employees for the farming of the State revenues, and by the end of the Republic they had obtained a dominant position in the economic and political life of Rome. Moreover, there was an opening for loans on a large scale, for which the Greek cities were the chief customers. The Roman creditors let nothing slip through their fingers, as many cities found to their cost. The Roman capitalists developed into a special class, the Equestrian Order, whose influence in the State during the last century of the Republic is well known. To these men a new province meant a new country to exploit, new taxes and customs to farm, and new customers for loans. They were deeply interested in the extension of the Roman Empire, and owing to their great political influence they could influence foreign policy in the direction they desired. The machinations of the capitalists were blatantly visible at the time when the Pergamene kingdom became a Roman province, and they always exerted a strong impulse to conquest in the rich Oriental lands.

In the East, Pompeius was the great conqueror. He incorporated the kingdom of Mithridates and what was left of the Seleucid Empire, Syria, in the Roman Empire, and set up, in addition, a bevy of vassal States.

The last conquest of the Republic was Gaul. It was the result of the initiative of one man, Caesar. What his motives were, can only be the subject of conjecture. It is certain that the campaigns in Gaul gave Caesar an opportunity to organise and devote to himself the army which he needed as a decisive factor in the contest for power : but he may also have said to himself that Gaul was a country which was worth conquering, not merely for its potential wealth, but as a necessary link between Italy and Spain.

Of the old civilised countries, only Egypt remained an independent State, but one only in name. It had, in fact, for long been a client State of Rome, and first Caesar and afterwards Marcus Antonius had resided in Alexandria as the unlawful or lawful husband of its queen. After Octavian's victory at Actium it fell like a ripe fruit into his lap, but acquired a special status, which will be described later.

The Roman Republic was not a pioneer of civilisation. In all directions it laid its hand on countries of a more ancient civilisation which fell a prey to it owing to their political inferiority or from some inherent weakness. This is true of the Carthaginian possessions in Africa and Spain, and of the Hellenistic and Greek States in the East. It is also true of Gaul, which by way of Marseilles had received a strong tincture of Greek civilisation. The Mediterranean civilisation was unequally distributed, and apparently in the West had not penetrated further than the coasts. The Roman State which inherited this civilisation also became an unequally divided realm. The countries which passed from the Republic to the Empire formed an heterogeneous medley, difficult to assimilate, and divided by racial animosities. Only in the west, south, and, to some extent, in the east, had it natural frontiers, *viz.* the ocean and the desert. In the mountainous tracts between the Syrian desert and the Black Sea it was encircled by a fringe of vassal States ; Armenia was a constant bone of contention between Rome and Persia.

Less satisfactory was the long European land frontier in the north. In Thrace and Macedonia Rome controlled little more than the coast-line, the Illyrico-Dalmatian coast of the Adriatic being open and exposed to the independent tribes in the north of the Balkan Peninsula. At the northern extremity of the Adriatic, Rome controlled no more than a strip of coast. The Alpine tribes were independent, and, on the western frontier of Italy, drove in a wedge between Italy and Gaul which reached almost down to the sea. Even within the borders of the Empire there were untamed and barbaric tribes. In Italy itself some of the Ligurians in their mountain fastnesses had preserved their independence. North-west Spain was unsubdued ; Algeria and Morocco (Mauretania) were nominally Roman vassal States, but far behindhand in civilisation.

A Government conscious of the need of solidifying its power —and that was the *raison d'être* of the Empire—was, therefore, confronted with a heavy task. It was necessary that the unsubdued tracts within the Empire should be assimilated and that the frontier should be both natural and easily defensible, and, above all, that it should protect the heart and centre of the whole, Italy. That could only be done by pushing forward the northern frontier, even at the risk of including within that frontier barbarous tribes and territories whose allegiance was doubtful and precarious. For the conquests now made were not lands of an old civilisation, but peoples and tribes in the lowest stage of barbarism. The conquests were, from a precautionary point of view, necessary, but they made the problem of civilisation within the Empire more difficult. Its next great task was to eliminate these nests of barbarism from the map by spreading civilisation over them.

Augustus prided himself on being a peace-making Emperor, and, by promoting peace, he established the imperial rule ; but he grappled vigorously from the first with the unavoidable task of pacifying the independent tribes within the Empire. He spent much of the earlier portion of his reign in lengthy journeys to settle matters in the provinces which had been neglected during the civil war. One of his first journeys was to Gaul and Spain. In the latter province he stayed over two years (27–24 B.C.). The Asturians and Cantabrians, who had preserved their independence in the north-western mountains, were subdued. They rose again, and their final submission was only brought about in 19 B.C. by the Emperor's faithful coadjutor and right-hand man, Agrippa. In the Forum of Augustus at Rome a golden statue was erected to him " because, owing to his favour and constant care, the province Baetica (Southern Spain) had been pacified."

M

Above Monaco, on the old Roman road which went westwards, half-way up the Riviera mountain range, still stands the massive masonry of the monument, now called La Turbie, commemorating the victory over the Alpine peoples, which the Roman people and Senate raised to Augustus. The inscription, of which only a few unimportant fragments remain, enumerated fifty tribes. Any one who has seen the Alpine valleys and mountains, and knows what a mountain-war means, can understand the difficulty of the task. But it was necessary. Southeast of Mt. Blanc were the Salassi. They controlled the route over the Great St. Bernard, and also the Little St. Bernard, which was still more important for communication with Gaul. For fear of their dangerous neighbours, the farmers at the foot of the Alps sometimes did not even venture to harvest their fields. An occasional punitive expedition was soon forgotten.

Even during his stay in Spain Augustus intervened and finished the business thoroughly. Almost the whole tribe was captured and sold into slavery, and their name disappeared from history (25 B.C.). A colony of praetorians was planted on their territory to keep the country in subjection. Its centre was called Augusta Praetoria (Aosta), where, even to-day, almost the whole of the ancient walls of the town, laid out in a square like a military camp, a triumphal arch to Augustus, and the arch of a bridge, preserve the memory of the importance of the town in Roman days. No doubt the ferocity of the Salassi rendered such drastic measures necessary ; but, whenever possible, Augustus employed gentler methods. The Cottian Alps are named after Marcus Julius Cottius, whose father, king Donnus, submitted to the Romans. The son ruled as a Roman citizen and prefect over the same tribes which his father had ruled as King, and built in honour of his master, Augustus, a triumphal arch at Susa at the foot of Mt. Cenis. The people were rewarded with Latin rights, as were some of the Ligurians, who were now for the first time completely subjected to Rome.

Thus the wedge of disturbers of the peace, which had interposed between Italy and Gaul and severed Rome from her Western provinces, was subdued, and the roads to the West were increased in number and rendered secure. After the inhabitants of the country north of the Po, which, at the period of transition from Republic to Empire, was clearly the freshest and most vigorous district of Italy, had received the citizenship in 49 B.C., the territory of Roman citizens extended as far as the foot of the Alps.

But it was not enough to subdue the people of the Alpine valleys, for through the passes wild hordes, greedy for plunder, could at any time descend into the plains of Italy. In spite of the physical and climatic difficulties it was necessary to form a kind of buffer state to Italy, which could break or ward off attacks. In the middle of the Alpine country lay the Rhaeti, who controlled the St. Gothard Pass, and whose territory stretched from the Brenner Pass to the Lake of Como, and northwards as far as the Lake of Constance. North of them were the Vindelici, whose northern boundary was the Danube. East of the Brenner was Noricum, rich in iron, which corresponds approximately to Carinthia, Styria, and Austria south of the Danube. Noricum, which was only cut off from the Adriatic by a narrow strip of Roman territory, was conquered in 16 B.C. and, in the following year, a methodical concentric attack was planned against the Rhaeti and Vindelici. The plan of campaign was carried out by the Emperor's two stepsons. Tiberius entered the country from the west, beat the Vindelici by the Lake of Constance, and reached the sources of the Danube. Drusus entered by the far more difficult route over the Brenner from the south and completed the subjection. Thus the frontier was advanced to the Danube, and Italy was protected. As a capital, Augusta Vindelicorum (Augsburg) was founded; and Augusta Rauracorum, the predecessor of Basel, the most eastern colony of Gaul, received increased importance, after the frontier-land in the East was added to the Empire. Southern Noricum with its fruitful valleys was quickly latinised, and soon almost counted as part of Italy; its flourishing and important mineral industry contributed greatly to this end; but in the northern parts of the new district—wild, mountainous and thinly populated—the extension and development of civilisation went on but slowly.

As in the West, so in the East, Italy was only connected
with her transpontine provinces by a narrow strip of territory.
Wars against Illyrian pirates had on various occasions brought
the east coast of the Adriatic under Roman domination, but
her power did not reach far into the interior. Illyria was an
unimportant and neglected province, which had to look after
itself. The journey to the East was usually made over the
narrow straits of Otranto. Then, as now, the country was
cut up and divided by mountains which rendered all communications difficult ; then, as now, it was inhabited by a
vigorous and warlike people, backward in civilisation. On
one occasion a tribe had raided North-Eastern Italy, conquered
Trieste, and besieged the highly important commercial
centre, Aquileia. During the civil war another had inflicted
two serious defeats on Roman armies, and a legion had even
suffered the disgrace of losing its eagle to the barbarians.
This was the reason why Augustus intervened here, even before
he settled accounts with Antonius. On the Save a Roman
point d'appui was established, and Dalmatia, which was
then regarded as stretching considerably farther inland than
now, was constituted a province. North of Dalmatia and
east of Noricum dwelt the powerful Pannonians, in what is
now the south-west part of modern Hungary. The circle was
completed by their inclusion in the Empire, this step being
taken immediately after the subjection of Noricum. Here,
too, the Danube afforded a natural boundary to the
north.

Further east, in the Balkan Peninsula, the territories which
had previously formed part of the Macedonian Empire and
were now in Rome's possession, lay open to attack from less
civilised tribes. So, by means of tactful interference in her
domestic quarrels, Thrace was brought into the position of a
vassal State under a trustworthy king, Rhoemetalces. Further
north dwelt the Getae or Daci, who during the civil war had
combined into a single power which inspired even the Romans
with respect ; but, as usual among semi-barbarian peoples,
the kingdom broke up after the death of the king, so that the
Romans had an easier task, though a German nation, the

Bastarnae, took part in the war. The war against the Getae was one of the earliest waged by Augustus, owing to the fact that they had promised support to Antonius. The brave grandson of the famous triumvir, Crassus, defeated and subdued them between 29 and 27 B.C. Naturally the country was not immediately pacified, but the frontier was pushed forward to the Danube, individual Roman commanders crossing its lower course and penetrating to the Dniester.

The exposed Greek cities on the north coast of the Black Sea found it profitable and expedient to come to an agreement with Rome.

By these military undertakings, which occupied the first part of Augustus' long reign, the danger spots on the imperial map were wiped out, the Western and Eastern provinces were linked up with Italy by land, and a natural northern frontier created, *viz.* the two greatest central-European rivers, the Rhine and the Danube. In actual area Augustus increased the extent of the Roman Empire more than any other of her rulers. But the value of conquests depends not so much on the extent of territory gained as on the character of the people that inhabit it. The price was high. Extensive, thinly peopled provinces, which cost more than they brought in, and tribes on a low level of culture had been annexed to the Empire. Experience was to teach that effective occupation meant more than the mere conquest of a people, and the reduction of their country to the status of a province. It still required hard struggles to retain the conquered districts in a condition of permanent obedience, and still harder was the task of permeating them with Roman civilisation.

The northern frontier was the Empire's bulwark against the barbarians. It was far flung and could be shortened if the Rhine frontier was pushed eastwards over Central Europe. Such an advance would be over a purely German country, while the Romans had hitherto only encountered scattered bands of Germans, who roved about in the lands of other tribes. Here was the danger-spot of the Roman Empire, the point where, after the lapse of a few centuries, the tide of migration was to break the dykes and flood the Empire. It calls, therefore,

for more detailed attention than the other successfully achieved
attempts to round off the Roman territory.

The Romans had first become acquainted with the Germans
by the panic caused by the Cimbri and Teutons at the end of
the second century B.C. The unrest among the German tribes,
of which their wanderings are a proof, did not then come to
an end. The pretext for Caesar's interference in Gaul was
the determination of the Helvetii, who had entered Switzerland,
to leave their own land and seek new settlements in Western
Gaul. Their reason is unknown, but they were joined by
another well-known Celtic tribe, the Boii. This tribe had
previously dwelt in Bohemia, and given the country its name,
in the Latin form of Boiohaemum. Sometime after 63 B.C.
the Boii were expelled by the Getae, who—as mentioned
above—had just had an accession of strength, probably in
alliance with German tribes. In the Balkan Peninsula we
have already found a German tribe, the Bastarnae, acting in
concert with the Getae. By Strabo the land is called " the
wilderness of the Boii," but in the period before the birth of
Christ it was occupied by another German tribe, the
Marcomanni. The former territory of the Helvetii in South
Germany was occupied by Germans, chiefly Suebi, who reached
the Upper Rhine. The important and permanent result of
these migrations was that South Germany, which was
previously Celtic, along with the adjoining parts of Austria,
obtained a German population.

The further penetration of the Germans into Gaul was
aided by disputes between the Gaulish tribes. Ariovistus and
his German bands were invited to help the Sequani against
the Aedui, the allies of Rome, who were beaten and invited
Rome's help. Ariovistus and his people settled in the region
of the Sequani in Alsace. After Caesar had forced the Helvetii
to desist from their plan and remain in Switzerland, he took
up the fight with Ariovistus, who was defeated and forced to
recross the Rhine. But we may conjecture that some of the
Germans remained in Gaul. The Treveri, after whom the city of
Trèves is named, were proud of their German blood, and archaeological researches seem to show that theirs was no empty boast.

It was, then, a determined German attack on Gaul which Caesar stemmed. Nor was it the only one. Twice did Caesar, by reason of German raids in Gaul, cross the Rhine as a demonstration to the Germans of the power of Rome. It may be conjectured that they were too unsophisticated to find the demonstration very imposing, and more vigorous measures were required. Caesar had made the Rhine the Roman frontier, but, even so, Rome obtained no lasting peace with the Germans. A German tribe, the Ubii, which was allied to Rome, was transferred by Agrippa from its earlier settlements on the right bank between the Sieg and the Lahn to the left bank at Cologne. In 16 B.C. the fifth legion under Marcus Lollius suffered a disgraceful defeat at the hands of the Sugambri and lost its eagle.

We do not know much about the military organisation of Gaul in this period. The legions were quartered in the interior, which they had to keep in subjection, while on the Rhine there were probably minor garrisons at Novaesium (Neuss opposite Düsseldorf), immediately north of Coblenz, and probably at Mainz. Augustus (who was summoned to the Rhine by Lollius' defeat and resided in Gaul for several years, shortly after he had succeeded in subjecting the country between the Alps and the Danube) formed a plan of terminating the ever-recurring threat of danger on the frontier, by pacifying the Germans, as he had already succeeded in pacifying so many turbulent peoples. By including Germany in the Empire another important advantage would be secured, the shortening of the long northern frontier. The plan would be executed by a concentric movement similar to that which had been applied so successfully against the Rhaeti and Vindelici ; it would start simultaneously from Gaul and from Noricum.

The command of the western army of operations was entrusted to Drusus. Archaeological researches have revealed to us how extensive and methodical the preparations were. The garrisons of Gaul were moved to the Rhine, which became the base of operations. Two camps, each intended for two legions, were founded at Castra Vetera (Xanten) not far from the Dutch frontier, and at Mainz, facing the valleys of the Lippe and Main, the natural ways for invading the heart of Germany. These camps were only furnished with ramparts of earth, and were thus only intended to be provisional, In addition, a line of forts was built along the Rhine from Nimwegen in Holland to Strasburg. A part of the preparations was also, probably, the canal dug by Drusus between the Rhine and the North Sea, since communications by sea along the North Sea coast and up the German rivers played a great part, not only in military operations but also in trade. Drusus opened the campaign in 12 B.C., and subdued the Batavian and Frisian tribes on the coast of the North Sea. This proved a permanent gain, and a number of Batavi served as cavalry in the Roman army, a detachment of them forming the Emperor's personal bodyguard.

During the following years Drusus entered Germany, building fortified camps on his lines of communications, and in 9 B.C. reached the Elbe ; but he died on the way back in consequence of a fall from his horse. Tiberius took over the command from his brother, but after two years was summoned back to Rome, and soon after retired, temporarily, from public life in consequence of disagreements with his stepfather.

After Agrippa's sons by Julia had died and Tiberius had become heir to the throne and had been reconciled to Augustus, he took over the command in Germany once more, and in the two campaigns of A.D. 4 and 5 penetrated so far that the country between the Rhine and the Elbe was looked on as subdued and almost as a Roman province. Roads were built up the Lippe valley, a bridge thrown across the Rhine, and an altar erected in the old country of the Ubii as the religious centre for the new province, just as the altar at Lugudunum was the centre of the Gallic provinces.

Among the Marcomanni in Bohemia and Moravia a more solidly compact State had been founded by a German prince who had lived in Rome, Maroboduus, who, no doubt, acquired there a knowledge, not merely of Roman civilisation but also of Roman state organisation. His authority seemed to the Romans to be too great, and the subjugation of Germany was now to be completed by operations starting from the south. Tiberius assembled the troops for the campaign at Carnuntum, on the Danube immediately below Vienna, the chief military centre of Pannonia. But a great insurrection broke out in Illyria and Pannonia in A.D. 6. Rome's power was not yet securely founded in the newly conquered provinces, and the old spirit of independence still glowed and fretted under enforced obedience. It was only to be expected that it would one day break out in open flame. The conscription for the German campaign probably caused the outbreak, which proved to be a very serious affair. It required three years and fifteen legions, more than half the military strength of Rome, and all Tiberius' stubbornness, prudence, and energy, to make the insurgents yield. One result of the difficulties and expenses incurred was the imposition of two new taxes on succession and property, which Augustus felt compelled to introduce in these years.

Happily for the Empire the Germans were tranquil during these difficult years, or else a catastrophe might easily have occurred which would have swept away Augustus' conquests. In Germany the commander was Publius Quintilius Varus, previously Governor of Syria. It is said that he tried to introduce Roman law and jurisdiction into the country. One who knows the sharp antagonism between German and Roman law extending over a thousand years, can judge what that would mean to a people who regarded their legal traditions as not merely the work of man but as sanctioned by religion and long-established custom. It is not unlikely, also, that Varus did not understand how to distinguish sufficiently the national characteristics of the Germans from those of his previous subjects, the submissive Syrians, a race born to slavery, according to an ancient proverb. Nor was much required to make the fire blaze up. The rising took the shape of one of those far-reaching secret conspiracies, the ramifications of which half-civilised peoples are such adepts at hiding. That it took this shape among the Germans was not surprising, since they attached the greatest importance in keeping faith with one another. The leader was the Cheruscan prince Arminius, who had been in Roman service and acquired equestrian rank. The catastrophe was as shattering and sudden as a flash of lightning. The unsuspecting Varus was surprised on the march, and his three legions totally destroyed in the Teutoburg forest (A.D. 9). Tiberius had to return to Germany to restore the power and credit of Rome. This he accomplished, but his subsequent campaign was not primarily intended to regain the country between the Rhine and the Elbe. Its sole object was to give the Germans such a lesson that the Rhine frontier would be at peace.

The story of the Emperor in his declining years, beating his head against a wall, and crying, "Varus, Varus, give me back my legions," demonstrates the gravity of the situation and its effect on future events. The loss was very serious, especially in relation to the small stock of recruiting material. Rather more than a tenth of the imperial army had been annihilated. But there can be no doubt that Augustus, had he called out all the resources of the Empire and strained them to the uttermost, as Trajan did later, might have won back what was lost, and made Western Germany a Roman and a Romanised province. Later on it was too late ; the Germans had grown too strong. But Augustus did not suspect what influence the unmanageable nation east of the Rhine was to have on the history of the world. To him the German war was nothing but a frontier war, a pacification of troublesome neighbours, and a strategic improvement of the frontier. He gave it up without a thought for the future, when it appeared to cost more than it was worth. The Rhine-Danube line was not a bad boundary.

This was one of those fateful moments, when the flood of history has stood still on the watershed and hesitated for an instant in which direction to flow. One must not under-estimate the Roman influence during the time when the country between the Rhine and the Elbe was almost a Roman province, and when Roman armies had permanent camps and passed the winter amongst the Germans. At Haltern, four miles from the Rhine up the Lippe, are remains of a permanent camp for two legions, twice rebuilt ; a landing-place with a fort and a magazine on the banks of the river. Outside the gates of the camp a civil community had begun to spring up. No doubt the Romans might, though with great exertions, have won back and occupied Germany up to the Elbe. These lands were the very heart and core of the German race, with a population that had taken root and established permanent dwelling-places ; from it proceeded the Germanic Empires which decided the future course of world history, the Frankish and the German. The migrating East Germans founded states which, after a short existence of meteoric brilliance, fell to pieces, the peoples themselves being absorbed by their Roman subjects. What course would the history of Europe have taken had Romanisation extended to the Elbe, and the larger and more permanently settled half of the Germanic tribes become a Romance nation ? That bisection of Europe into a Romance and a Germanic region, both about equal in strength, which determined, once and for all, the future history of Europe, would have been transformed into an overwhelming pre-dominance of the Romance element. Racial antagonism has contributed its fatal legacy in the events of recent years, and even now does not seem to be moribund. It is also a matter for reflection that the boundary between the Church of Rome and Protestantism in the West follows to a great extent the old Roman imperial frontier, the Rhine-Danube line.

The Rhine now became the frontier against the Germans, though, for the sake of security, some garrisons were left on its right bank. These too were removed, when Claudius took up Augustus' old plan of conquering Britain. This is a typical example of the way in which one conquest involves another, The connections between the Celtic tribes in Gaul and Britain were real and vital. The Gallic aspiration for independence had strong support in a free Britain. The Gallic priesthood, the Druids, who were the standard-bearers of the national religion and Celtic national feeling and who, therefore, were severely suppressed by Tiberius, had their chief centre and their schools in Britain. It became desirable to dam up these sources of Gallic unrest at the fountain head. By slow degrees the conquest of Britain was successfully achieved. The island was defended against the barren and impenetrable country of the north with its pugnacious and turbulent tribes; for Hadrian built a frontier wall on a line from the Solway Firth in the west, to Newcastle in the east, and Antoninus Pius removed it to a still narrower neck of land roughly corresponding to the line from Glasgow to Edinburgh.

In the contests for the throne after Nero's death, the Rhine army played a prominent part. There occurred, as an additional factor, the extensive rising of Civilis under Batavian leadership. When Vespasian was raised to power and restored order, he grappled with the German problem. The frontier was considered inconvenient. Between the Upper Danube and the Middle Rhine was interposed a wedge, which caused great inconvenience to the lines of communication between the legions in Rhaetia or Pannonia and those in Germany. Here, by rectification of the frontier, an important advantage might be gained at a comparatively small cost. Vespasian conquered the country corresponding to the modern Baden and part of Swabia, and built roads through it ; it was named the Tithe lands (*Agri Decumates*) and became the domicile of a very mixed population. According to Tacitus it was occupied by the most volatile of the adventurous Gauls. Domitian completed his father's work, and added to it the fruitful country round the lower Main. He also laid the foundations of the great frontier defence against independent Germany, the *Limes*.

Rome's aspirations were now satisfied. She had obtained reasonably defensible frontiers, and was deeply occupied with the problem of how best to weld together and assimilate the far-reaching conquered countries and their semi-civilised populations. She only made one great conquest later, that of Dacia, which, approximately, included Eastern Hungary, Transylvania and Roumania. Among the Dacians north of the Danube, as was previously mentioned (p. 46), a vigorous and united kingdom had been formed. Domitian had concluded a disgraceful peace with its King, Decebalus. There was a real danger of a compact Dacian Empire arising, which Trajan decided to forestall by occupying the country. It was replanted with Roman colonists ; but it should be remembered that when the modern Roumanian draws attention to his Roman origin, he forgets that the majority of those colonists came from the East. Dacia was conquered by the Goths about A.D. 250, and abandoned by the Emperor Aurelian in A.D. 271. The present inhabitants of these districts, the Roumanians, probably do not descend from the colonists of Trajan, but may be presumed to have come into the country later from the south.

(ii) THE PROVINCES

The Roman State, when it had passed from the stage of being a moribund Republic to the rule of an Emperor, was a motley collection of countries and peoples. It stretched from the burning deserts of the south to the mist-covered and ice-bound tracts of the North Sea and as far as the Scottish Highlands; from the mountains of Armenia and the river Euphrates in the East to the Atlantic Ocean in the West. Within its limits were found races and individuals of every description, from the primitive barbarism of the savage to the most refined aesthetic and philosophical cultivation that antiquity had to offer. That the Greek civilisation with an Oriental tinge, which is usually designated as the Hellenistic, eventually triumphed over all other types, must not deceive us into forgetting the existence of essential differences in culture standards between the various provinces, and the equally essential distinction between civilisation and its absence within the Empire. Posidonius describes for us the mode of life of the Ligurians. "They inhabit a poor and wretched country; hard work and poverty make their life miserable and hard. Some fell trees in the thick forests; the peasants break stones, for the ground is so stony that you cannot take up a turf without coming upon a stone. Yet all their diligence realises only a scanty harvest. Constant labour and insufficient nourishment make their bodies sinewy and lean. The women share the lot of the men. It occasionally happens that a woman gives birth to a child in the fields, covers it over with leaves, and immediately returns to work so as not to lose the daily wage. The produce of the chase partly compensates for the lack of corn. They clamber in the mountains like goats. Some live exclusively on flesh and wild herbs ; for corn and vines cannot grow on the high lands. On the coast a little acid wine is produced, which tastes like tar ; the national drink is beer. They live in wretched huts of wood and reeds, but usually in natural caves. Their whole life is primitive and simple. The women are as strong and crafty as men, the men are like wild animals." This description was penned in the last age of the Republic, and during the Empire things altered for the better in this case ; but as the picture is drawn from Italy itself, one can imagine what things were like in the outskirts of the Empire among the semi-conquered peoples.

Every province had its peculiar character, and, if it was at all civilised, its peculiar level of culture. For everywhere the provinces brought their traditions with them into the Empire, and obstinately clung to them even under the powerful protection of Roman arms. One cannot understand the Roman Empire and the special difficulties which confronted the imperial régime, when it was a question of rational government and administration, without knowing something of the peculiarities of each of the provinces of the Empire.

First of all, the bisection of the Empire, which was of fundamental importance for the future, must be emphasised. The Roman Empire was bilingual ; the two "civilised" languages were Latin and Greek, the numerous other different languages being overshadowed and confined to the ordinary speech of the lower classes of the populations. The Romans had received Greek civilisation in its Hellenistic form, and under its influence had fashioned the Latin tongue into a cultural language on a level with Greek through their great writers and orators like Ennius, Plautus, Catullus, and Cicero. With the supremacy of Greek civilisation it followed that Rome had to recognise the position of the Greek language ; it could not be pushed aside, as was done with the local speech of half-civilised or entirely uncivilised peoples. As far as our knowledge goes back—*i.e.* by the beginning of the second century B.C.—a Greek translation drawn up in the secretariat of the Senate was added to the Senatorial Decrees which concerned the countries in which the Greek language predominated, and the same procedure was applied to all edicts of the Roman authorities which concerned those countries. The Senate's Greek has its peculiar idiom, and its correctness is often doubtful. In the first place a fixed terminology had to be devised for Roman authorities and institutions. Similarly the diplomatic correspondence with the East was conducted in Greek ; the Emperors had not only a Latin but also a Greek secretarial department.

This preferential treatment of Greek continued after the Greek States of the East had come under Roman authority, and owing to the predominance of Greek civilisation, and the great extension of the Greek language, nothing else had been possible, though the Romans in their own sphere—that is in the Western part of the Empire—certainly displayed little indulgence to Greek language and civilisation. Sicily and Magna Graecia were latinised, and the half-Greek civilisation of Gaul was supplanted by the Latin. The Northern Balkan Peninsula, after its conquest under Augustus, was also latinised. In the Hellenistic States of Egypt, Syria, and Asia Minor, Greek had, since the time of Alexander, been the language of administration and of the educated, and had also penetrated deep into the national life. Here there was no alternative but to let this continue, and every educated Roman, and many others besides, possessed a knowledge of Greek, or at least could make himself understood in it. Only the army spoke Latin everywhere. In comparison with modern conditions, it was a great convenience in the ancient civilised world to have to reckon with only two languages, or possibly, in certain special conditions, with some local dialect besides.

Thus the sphere of Roman rule is divided into two halves, the one Western and Latin, the other Eastern and Greek, or rather, Greco-Oriental. The partition depended on language and also on civilisation, for the Romans had impressed their own national character on the Greek civilisation which they took over and handed on to the West, while the Greek culture during the Hellenistic period became more and more orientalised, and its centre of gravity was removed further East. In respect of civilisation the Greek-speaking half of the Empire preserved its position, and again took the lead, after the great period of Latin literature in the last century of the Republic and the first of the Empire had spent itself.

Still more dominant was the Eastern half of the Empire in the sphere of economics and industry. Its importance is apparent from the fact that the great decisions in the civil wars took place on battle-fields in Greece—Pharsalus, Philippi, Actium. When Caesar crossed the Rubicon, and Pompeius left Italy, not for his province of Spain, but for Greece, Caesar is reported to have said that he would first march against the army without a general, and then against the general without an army. But Pompeius knew what he' was doing. Caesar himself said that for war three things were necessary, money, money, and again money : and money was easy to find in the East. For the same reason Brutus and Cassius went to the Eastern half of the Empire when they had to settle matters with the triumvirs. We know of the terrible exactions by which they obtained money for the war ; and when the triumvirs, or rather Antonius—for Octavianus was defeated— conquered at Philippi and the two divided the Empire between them, the partition was unequal. The very superior position of Antonius at the time is shown by the fact that he received the Eastern half as his share.

Caesar is said to have discussed plans for removing the capital of the Empire to the East, and called to mind the legend according to which the Romans sprang from Troy. This scheme is consistent with Caesar's radical temperament, his theories being connected with Hellenistic rather than with Roman traditions. If Augustus ever had similar thoughts, they can only have been momentary ; his whole policy tended towards the opposite direction—the preservation of the old Roman national traditions. That the removal of the capital to the East was no mere dream, but a dangerous reality, can still be read between the lines of the third ode of Horace's third book, which protests vigorously against this humiliation of Rome.

Here, as elsewhere, Caesar's genius anticipated the trend of future developments. Under the Empire the centre of gravity was constantly being shifted eastwards. With the exception of Gaul, the West had completely receded into the background, and even that country of vigorous economical and cultural prosperity sank into insignificance in comparison with the East. The political importance and influence of the East became greater in proportion as, under the Empire, the national Roman element died out and was submerged in the flood of Oriental ideas on religion, life, and manners, and while Rome was sinking from her old position of mistress of the world to that of a mere capital city. The triumph of the East was complete when Constantine transformed Byzantium into Constantinople. It became the second capital, the new Rome, equipped with all the prerogatives of Rome, and rivalling her in splendour and population.

The bisection of the Empire, which is not only apparent in language but also in civilisation, was a grave danger to its unity. National sentiment, which is based on common race and language, worked but feebly and unconsciously in the motley collection of peoples within the Roman Empire ; the distinction between the Latin and Greek halves was, if all the circumstances are considered, sufficiently great to cause a cleavage in the Empire. Then, too, the turbulent period of the civil war foreshadowed what would happen in the fullness of time. Antonius and Octavianus partitioned the Empire, and Antonius ruled in his portion in the spirit of the Oriental, while Octavianus, in his, established his position as *princeps* on the basis of Roman traditions.

When Diocletian found that even his vigour was not equal to all the functions devolving upon the commander of the army and the civil administrator, and had placed a colleague by his side, the Empire was naturally divided into its two halves, and Diocletian retained for himself the more important half, the Eastern. Constantine indeed, and some of his successors, were Emperors of the whole Empire, but for administrative purposes the partition continued in force. On the accession of Valentinian it was definitely recognised, and under the sons

N

of Theodosius it became so clear cut that we speak of *two* Empires, a West-Roman and an East-Roman. The East regained its independence when Rome's national vigour and special qualities disappeared. The Greco-Oriental element was more tenacious ; the Greek Empire in Constantinople outlived by almost a thousand years the fall of Rome and the West-Roman Empire.

*   *   *   *   *

In the last and most admirable part of his Roman history Theodor Mommsen based the history of the Empire on the history of its provinces. It has been rightly observed, that this method has not permitted the common element in the development and unity of the Empire to be emphasised sufficiently, but it is significant of the position of the provinces within the Empire, that its history could be written in this way. It is also the case, and perhaps more notably so, with that which seems to us to be essentially an affair of the whole Empire, *viz.* foreign policy and war. All Rome's wars were really only frontier-wars. Thus, for example, a war with Persia affected Gaul only indirectly. It might become necessary to remove troops from Gaul, or levy soldiers and taxes for the war there, but otherwise it was of no great importance to Gaul what happened on the Eastern frontier. There were some advantages, but also some weaknesses in this lack of internal cohesion.

It is not our intention to deal here with the course of external events, but to give a rapid survey of the internal conditions and individual characteristics of the provinces. We will begin with the Greek half of the Empire, and, within this, with the motherland of Greek civilisation.

GREECE

It was a peculiar ordering of destiny that when, after the destruction of Corinth in 146 B.C., Greece fell to Rome, the new province was named after the race whose name Homer applies as the common designation of the whole Greek people, Achaia. The reason of this was that the chief part in the war was played by the Achaean League. But the province included only the least important half of the country. The Romans always showed great respect for the celebrated old cities, which had made so notable a contribution to history and civilisation. Athens and Sparta were free cities and allies of Rome, and remained outside the provincial administration, together with the old religious centres of Delphi and Elis (Olympia), where the Olympic games never ceased to be held with pomp and splendour. But the games had lost their former national importance. Only the interest in sport maintained them, as being the occasion for the most famous races and athletic performances. In addition, a few other less important cities remained nominally free. The Romans founded some new colonies in the province. Caesar rebuilt the ruins of Corinth and established in it discharged Roman soldiers as citizens, and Augustus made Patrai a Roman colony. These Roman colonists in Greece fared as the Greeks had done in Italy, *i.e.* they were rapidly merged in the native population. It is expressly stated of Corinth that it was graecised.

The Republic had always mistrusted the federated States, which, in the final struggle against Rome, had been the champions of independence, so they were dissolved or limited in powers. This, for example, was the fate of the venerable Delphic Amphictyony. But, as time passed, the impotence and unimportance of Greece became increasingly obvious. The old leagues were regarded as harmless historical antiquities and received a new lease of life. Augustus was interested in them, and reorganised the Delphic Amphictyony, incorporating in it Nikopolis, a city which, in memory of the decisive victory at Actium, he had founded on the point opposite the entrance of the Ambracian Gulf. Important games, rivalling those of Olympia, were celebrated there every fourth year in memory of the victory.

This was the only novelty to be introduced among the shadowy historical traditions of ancient Greece. A kind of glamour hung over the country, and the spirit of Philhellenism secured for it the interest and patronage of the emperors. When Nero visited the country he solemnly declared Greece free at the Isthmian Games, but he also plundered it of its masterpieces of art more thoroughly than any of his predecessors. Similar assurances had often been made during the internecine conflicts of the Hellenistic States, but whereas then they had only been a factor in the conflict of rival interests and politics, now the granting of a free status secured real advantages in relation to the Roman administration. The grant was rescinded by the practically minded Vespasian, who had to correct the mistakes of Nero's misgovernment. The greatest Philhellene, however, was the Emperor Hadrian. He was elected archon at Athens and Delphi, and adorned Athens with palatial buildings.

Greece became a country for tourists and devotees of antiquity. In the second century A.D. Pausanias wrote his description of Greece, which has proved invaluable for us and is, to a certain extent, an ancient Baedeker. It is noticeable that he omits to mention any occurrence which dates from the period after Rome's occupation of the country. From the decadence of their own day men looked back to the brilliant past. The cities preserved their old memories, and had a weakness for stamping copies of famous works of art on their coins. The old constitutions were preserved and archaised. In Athens archons held office, and the venerable Areopagus was restored to power and dignity. Sparta certainly no longer had kings, but the Ephors and the Gerousia still functioned, and the Lycurgan system of training was restored. Following the traditions of a past era the Spartan lads had to prove their fortitude by being scourged at the altar of Artemis Orthia. But it is significant of the age, that what previously was a part, if a barbaric part, of religion and training, was now a sensational spectacle not far above the level of a common combat of gladiators. Around the altar was erected a theatre, so that a better view could be obtained of the scourgings, the endurance of the lads, and the sanguinary scenes. Athens was at the time the chief University city of the world. The old schools of philosophy continued and were active. Marcus Aurelius made appropriations from the imperial treasury to provide the stipends of the professors.

At Athens also there was a development of student life and a rivalry between the competing schools, which vividly recalls the conditions in the older European Universities. Here the Emperor Julian himself spent the happiest time of his life, as student years often are.

Otherwise, everywhere and uniformly, old Greece was sinking into decay. Trade passed it by; the harbours of Piraeus and Delos were deserted: only Corinth retained, thanks to its favourable situation, a trade worth mentioning. Nero began to make a canal through the Isthmus, and Patrai had a thriving industry. The population of the country dwindled; even in the middle of the second century B.C., according to Polybius, childless marriages were common and the population was diminishing, though not from the effects of either war or plague. At the beginning of the Empire Plutarch says that the population was diminishing all over the Empire, but most of all in Greece, where the whole country could not supply the 3000 hoplites which little Megara alone had once sent to fight the Persians. When Cicero's friend, Sulpicius, sailed along the Saronic Gulf and saw Aegina, Piraeus, Megara, and Corinth, he thought to himself : " We men are sorry when one man dies, and lo ! here in one place are the corpses of many cities ! " Pausanias relates of one small town after another, that at the time of writing it was in ruins. Of the towns of the league of Eleutherolaconians, which, under Augustus, numbered twenty-four, six had disappeared.

This same phenomenon appears in all the civilised countries of the Empire, but most markedly in Greece. No doubt Plutarch's statement refers only to the free population, and the proportion between it and the slaves certainly changed to the disadvantage of the freemen, but this cannot outweigh the actual diminution of the population. During the Hellenistic period there had been devastating social struggles arising from questions of land tenure in the Greek free states. The popular demand had been for the writing off of mortgages and a fresh division of the soil, so that every citizen got an equal share. The result was that the proletariat became as poor as before, and still more dependent ; for during all disturbances there was an opportunity for individuals to amass large properties. Greece had great magnates, like the Spartan, Gaius Julius Eurykles, in the time of Augustus, and Herodes Atticus, a man of letters and multi-millionaire in the second century A.D. Such men might display their liberality towards the city-dwellers, but the countryside was desolate. During the time of Athens' greatness Euboea had been its granary. Dio Chrysostom, one of the most interesting authors of the earlier Empire, who flourished under the Flavians and Trajan, refers us to a town in Euboea at this time. The palaestrae had been ploughed up, the statues of Herakles and many other gods and heroes were covered by corn. Any day sheep might be seen in the agora grazing around the council-house and the old public buildings. The plough-land just outside the city gate was lying fallow and shamefully neglected. Two-thirds of the territory was untilled by reason of indifference and lack of labour. A citizen promises that if any one will till his land, he will not only let him have it without rent, but gladly pay him money into the bargain.

Greece was worn out. It had been bled to exhaustion by its task of hellenising the world. That Greek culture was continually becoming more strongly orientalised was largely due to the fact that it was no longer carried on by Greeks. Few of the men who made a name under the Empire were Greeks like Plutarch ; most of them were Greek-speaking natives of Asia Minor like Dio, or Orientals like Lucian. The Greek language was the language of the East, but the Greek national character had been swallowed up by the native.

Only in the north-west did the Greeks expand beyond their ancient limits. Epirus was a Greek country. In the past Epirus had never recovered from the terrible vengeance for their defeat by Pyrrhus, with which the Romans visited the country after the battle of Pydna. Seventy cities are said to have been destroyed, and 150,000 men sold into slavery. In Macedonia and Thrace, then as now, the Greeks lived on the coasts. The Macedonians themselves were a backward Greek race, inhabiting a country that is more fruitful than Greece. That their national vigour under the Empire was greater than in Greece, is shown by the larger levies raised from them for military service. Still more was Thrace a recruiting ground. The Thracians never showed any aptitude for a more advanced culture, but were warlike and brave. As a result of the great Celtic migration at the beginning of the third century B.C., they had become tinged with a Celtic element. Under Roman organisation and Roman commanders, the Thracians, like the Celts in Galatia, made good soldiers.

At the point where the waterway from the Black Sea to the Mediterranean crosses the landway from Europe to Asia, stood Byzantium, destined to attain to still greater splendour, whose inhabitants, so long as they were protected from the constant inroads of the Thracians, could flourish undisturbed. Hadrian built an aqueduct, which was repaired by Valens, and still supplies Stamboul with water. At the end of the second century A.D. the city was prosperous by reason of the fertility of the soil, the rich fisheries, and the tolls of the Bosphorus, and was well fortified. At one time Septimius Severus desired to punish the rebellious city with destruction (p. 68); but its natural advantages could not be suppressed, and Byzantium grew up again, and after little more than a century was fit to become the second capital of the Empire.

The most distant outposts of the Empire were the Greek colonies on the north coast of the Black Sea. They had lost much of their old consequence as the chief corn-exporting territories, but were still important as commercial harbours for the products of South Russia. They had always been hard pressed by the native tribes, especially the Scythians, and the pressure had increased in the turbulent Hellenistic age. Rome, however, protected them with her powerful arm. Tyra on the Dniester was even made a part of the province of Moesia. The cities of the Crimea were under a vassal-prince, the only one who retained his position, when all other vassal principalities were abolished. This distant outpost needed greater independence than the usual provincial administration permitted, but there was a detachment of Roman soldiers quartered there.

More dangerous enemies than the Scythians were the German tribes which pressed south-eastwards. About 190 B.C. the Bastarnae ravaged Olbia (near Kherson). At the beginning of the second century A.D. the Goths formed their kingdom in South Russia, and after conquering Tyra and Olbia in A.D. 235, used these harbours as a base for their Viking raids, plundering the coasts as far as Asia Minor and Greece.

ASIA MINOR

From very early days Asia Minor had been a rich and prosperous country, with a numerous Greek population on its western coast. It formed the core of the Pergamene kingdom; to it belonged the great commercial cities, Miletus, Ephesus, Smyrna, of which, in imperial times, Ephesus took the lead. It was the provincial capital with the archives and treasury, and was adorned with splendid buildings, a theatre, aqueduct, and harbour. The alluvial deposits of the rivers have destroyed Ephesus and Miletus, as they threatened to destroy Smyrna. Together with Ephesus, Pergamum, the former capital of the Attalids, was " Asia's other eye."

In the interior Asia Minor had a more mixed population than any other country. Since time immemorial it had been subject to migrations. From linguistic records we can distinguish various tribes, which seem to have been indigenous, Lydians, Carians, and Lyeians. Aryan immigrations had brought there Phrygians and Bithynians, and, in historical times, Galatians. These tribes preserved, partially at least, their nationality. The bulk of the inscriptions in Phrygian date from imperial times. The father of the Church, Jerome, who visited both Galatia and Gaul in the fourth century, says that the same language, with corruptions, was spoken in Ancyra as in Trèves. But hellenisation went on incessantly. At the same period the orator Themistios compliments the city on its zeal for education. Cappadocia, whose inhabitants spoke Greek as badly as the Flemings speak French, supplied the later school of sophists with two or three famous orators and teachers, and gave the Greek Church three of its greatest writers and preachers.

No country is so full of ruins and inscriptions as Asia Minor. One ruined site succeeds another, mute witnesses of bygone prosperity and splendour, all the more striking in view of the present poverty and decay. The absence of civilisation in later times must often have saved the ruins. In various places in the interior, temples, town walls, gates and theatres still stand upright. Large areas are found strewn with gravestones and sarcophagi. The inscriptions create for us again the life of the towns with its vanities and petty disputes, which after the lapse of 2000 years seem extraordinarily vapid. Punctiliousness in regard to honour and precedence gave occasion for numerous quarrels between cities, which the Romans had to settle in spite of their contempt for " the follies of the Asiatics " ; and citizens in the towns squandered their treasure to win popularity and fame.

After the transient episode of Athenian supremacy, the western shore of Asia Minor regained its position as one of the principal districts inhabited by Greeks. Its cities again occupied their natural position as outlets for the products of the interior. The harbours were the terminals for the great trade routes from within. The coastal fringe, too, by its fertility contributed to their wealth. After the ravages and exactions of the civil war the country soon recovered under the peace of the Empire. The highlands of the interior, with its great climatic variations and steppe-like soil, were very different, but even there flourishing towns and vigorous industries existed. The great herds of sheep, which fed on the high plateaux, supplied raw material for the textile industries in Galatia and Miletus, and Smyrna carpets have a long tradition behind them. Laodicea was famous for its linen factories. Asia was called the province of five hundred cities, and the taxes from these cities were one of the most important sources of revenue. From them came most of the Greeks who made a contribution to the civilisation and history of the imperial age. If the Seljuks and the Turks had not supervened, Asia Minor would have remained a Greek country.

But here also there were wild and barbarous areas. The wild mountainous region of the south in Pisidia, Pamphylia,

and Western Cilicia, afforded loopholes and corners for independent tribes and bands of robbers.   There the pirates, whom
Pompeius reduced to order, had their quarters.   Augustus
took vigorous measures against brigandage and founded military posts to keep the country in order.   When the Empire
went to pieces in the third century, brigandage revived ; it
had only been suppressed, not rooted out.   The Isaurians are
notorious in Byzantine history, and attempts were made to
isolate them and render them harmless by putting a military
cordon round their territory.

SYRIA

Like Asia Minor, Syria never experienced such prosperity
as during the imperial age.   The contrast between the enterprise, the prolonged and widespread prosperity that then prevailed, and the decay of the present day is very remarkable.
The land was cultivated more intensively and extensively than
ever before or after.   The Hauran, the volcanic country east
of the Upper Jordan, is still a corn-growing country, but was
much more so in the past, as its many ruined cities testify.
Certain tracts, like the narrow coast-strip and the neighbourhood of Damascus, are still well cultivated with fields and
gardens.   Originally the olive plantations must have extended
far to the east of Emesa, where now the desert prevails.
Throughout the whole of North Syria there have been discovered, in the desert, hewn blocks of stone, which once
served as oil-presses.   Cisterns cut out of the rock show what
great care was taken to conserve the rain-water.   Stone
heaps gathered from fields now deserted, abandoned terracings
which once retained the soil, and ruined aqueducts are found
in the Hauran and far out in the desert towards Palmyra.
Under present conditions the march of a whole army through
the desert, like that which Aurelian undertook against
Palmyra, would be impossible.   Even the independent
Bedouins of the desert were drawn into the magic circle of
civilisation, and were constrained to live a settled life on the
edge of the desert.   It is said that in the fourth century all
Syria abounded in corn, wine, and oil.

Although it was intensively cultivated in antiquity, yet the wealth of Syria did not depend solely on agriculture and nursery-gardening. Syria was the chief industrial country of the Empire, exporting goods on a large scale. In contrast with Asia Minor and Egypt, industry was not confined to working up the native products of the land, but raw materials were imported, *e.g.* silk from China, iron from India, copper from Asia Minor ; and the finished articles were exported. With industry was combined an active trade. Unlike the Egyptian, the Syrian was not content with manufacturing commodities and letting any one who would, buy and fetch them. Merchants worked hand in hand with industry to obtain wider markets and new fields for trade. This is the fundamental condition for a vigorous expansion of industry and commerce, and the Syrian was the only citizen of the Empire to realise this to the full. He was the Empire's chief merchant, and we meet traces of his enterprise in every province.

Syria was the chief clearing house of the important Oriental trade. It is significant that in Diocletian's tariff of maximum prices the Oriental wares preponderate. The caravan routes from Mesopotamia, Persia, and the heart of Asia debouch in Syria. On this trade depended the prosperity of Palmyra and the Nabataean kingdom, with its capital at Petra, in the desert south of Judaea, on the route to the Red Sea. It encircled Palestine on the east and stretched from the Red Sea to Damascus. When, under Trajan, the country became a Roman province, the capital was moved to Bostra in the well-cultivated country east of the Jordan, where the roads from the Red Sea, the Persian Gulf, and Damascus met. To-day the ruins of these once prosperous cities, rising out of the lonely desert, make a profound impression. Petra, and still more Palmyra, are famous ; the ruined cities of the Hauran, Bostra, Gerasa, Kanatha and others are dumb witnesses of past prosperity and present decay of the Roman genius for organisation and the penetrating power of ancient civilisation. Great colonnades, temples, and theatres still stand silent and mysterious in this desert land. This applies to the districts on the edge of the desert ; still more must it have applied to Syria proper. Apamea on the Orontes, which is now deserted, had, under the proconsul Quirinus, 170,000 free inhabitants. The country up to the bend of the Orontes, a stretch of ten miles, teems with ruins ; here more than a hundred towns, great or small, once flourished. A few miles from the mouth of the Orontes was the capital, Antioch, one of the ancient world's three greatest cities—at one time surpassed only by Rome and Alexandria—and even by our standards it was a great city with almost half a million inhabitants. We hear of the fickleness and unreliability of the inhabitants, their street-Arab buffooneries, their licentious festivals, the pleasure park of Daphne, the magnificent buildings, the main street, almost four miles in length, flanked with arcades on both sides and lit up at night—the only instance of street-lighting which is mentioned in ancient history. To-day Antioch is a shabby little town with a few thousand inhabitants dwelling among the ruins. The seaport was Seleucia, but in spite of many exertions, a really good harbour could not be made on the rocky coast. The early Phoenician towns further south, Tyre, Sidon, Byblos and others, flourished as of old, and were famous for purple dyeing, the weaving of silk and linen, glass and metal industries, the products of which were exported all over the Empire. The preparation of perfumes and ointments was another important industry. It was officially recognised that Syria was the most important province of the Empire, for its governor took precedence of all others.

It is often stated that Syria had less influence on spiritual culture. This is not strictly correct, even if one only has in view the Greco-Roman civilisation. The Seleucids had covered the country with Greek colonies, and encouraged the cities and their self-governing institutions. Thus the land was outwardly hellenised. The spirit of resistance was only found among the Jews, when Antiochus Epiphanes tried to hasten hellenisation by violent methods. In spite of the attempts made by Herod and his family, this spirit could not be quelled, but led to the great Jewish rebellion and the subsequent punishment of people and country by the imperial Government.

Hadrian made Jerusalem a Roman colony under the name Aelia Capitolina, and in it Jupiter Optimus Maximus was worshipped instead of Yahweh. With this exception the Roman colonies were very few in number. Beirut was famous for its school of jurisprudence, which could boast of some of the most famous jurists of the Empire, notably Ulpian and Papinian. Syria produced few poets but many philosophers, notably Posidonius of Apamea, and Numenius the pioneer of Neoplatonism, also from Apamea, and Lucian, the wittiest journalist of antiquity. In the fourth century Antioch possessed a famous school of rhetoric of which we know something from its most celebrated member, Libanius. John Chrysostom, the greatest orator of the Greek Church, was his pupil, and both were natives of Antioch.

In the spiritual development of the Empire, Syria had greater importance as a giver than as a receiver. The orientalisation of culture proceeded from Syria and was spread by Syrian slaves, Syrian merchants and Syrian wares, to the most distant provinces of the Empire. Under a veneer of Hellenism the old ideas and the old religion lived on. Of their power, even before the days of Julia Domna and Heliogabalus, the temple at Heliopolis, Baalbek, the most imposing ruins of the Roman age that survive, bears witness. It was begun by Antoninus Pius.

EGYPT

Egypt in all respects occupied a special position. The assimilation of this country was an important event in the internal history of the Empire. It was the Emperor's personal property. He governed it as the successor of the Pharaohs, and built temples in the old style, was represented in art as a Pharaoh, and was acclaimed as immortal in his titles. The Senate and Senators were rigorously excluded from the country. Legally Egypt was a country without cities, with the sole exceptions of Alexandria and Ptolemais in Upper Egypt, and therefore had no self-government. In contrast with all other provinces it had no provincial diet. The country was divided into districts, each with its centre and its special

worship as in the days of the Pharaohs. The Egyptians
were excluded from the management of their own country,
and could not even acquire Roman citizenship. Secondary
offices which were not held by Romans, were reserved for
Greeks, and Greek was the administrative language, though
in the army, as usual, Latin prevailed.

Egypt was essentially an agricultural country, with a
highly developed natural economy. There were public corn
depôts, to which corn could be delivered ; the owner had only
to write out a cheque for so many bushels, as long as his
deposit lasted. The Ptolemies had been masters in the
art of exacting taxes and levies in kind, and the Emperors
followed their example. Egypt was the granary of Rome,
whose population subsisted largely on Egyptian corn, and it
was one of the problems of Empire to keep the population
of Rome satisfied and in a good temper. The country was
jealously guarded by the Emperor ; and was, moreover, one
of his best taxable areas. During the height of Ptolemaic
prosperity Egypt produced annually about three millions
sterling in revenue and 1,625,000 bushels of wheat. At the
time of its decline, mismanagement had reduced the revenue to
about £1,150,000. What it brought in under the Romans
we do not know, but Egypt supplied a third of the corn required
for Rome, *viz.* 4,785,000 bushels, and this was certainly not
all tax-corn, but partly obtained from the imperial domains
or by purchase.

The one great city of the country—for Ptolemais cannot
be compared with it—was Alexandria, the second city of the
Empire, an emporium of commerce and industry. " In
Alexandria there is abundance of riches and luxury, but no
one is without occupation. One is a glass-blower, one a
papyrus-worker, another a linen-weaver. The only god is
money," says an ancient author. From this statement we
can gather what were the staple industries of Alexandria.
The export trade seems, to a great extent, to have been in
the hands of Italian merchants and shipowners, who from
an early period owned factories in Alexandria. A great part
of the trade of the East from India, Arabia Felix, and Ethiopia

passed through the city, and increased its importance and wealth.

Alexandria gave its name to a period of Greek literature and culture, which we, by a less specialised name, usually call the Hellenistic. Art, apart from caricature, and philosophy did not thrive at the court of the Ptolemies, but philology and poetry were well represented. Greek culture in Egypt was as in a hot-house, dependent on the favour and liberality of the rulers. Owing to the misgovernment and the lack of interest shown by the later Ptolemies, it languished away, and in Roman times Alexandria had lost its leading position. Though the treasures of the library, which accidentally perished by fire when Caesar was besieged there, had been replaced, the academy now contained only mediocre scholars, and no spiritual leaders. Rome, during the earlier Empire, was the centre of culture for Greece as well as for Italy. The native and national element came to the front. This gave pagan religion its peculiar mixture of fanciful speculations, and, what was still more demoralising, tainted it with crude witchcraft and magic. From this circumstance also, Egyptian Christianity derived a peculiar fanaticism. It was in Alexandria that the Athenian, Clement, surnamed Alexandrinus, worked; and there Origen was born. These two men effected the union of Greek science and philosophy with Christianity. The actual founder of Neoplatonism, Ammonius Sakkas, was an Alexandrian, and Plotinus, who developed it, was also born in Egypt. In Italian decorative art there was, in the Augustan age, a veritable mania for Egyptian paintings and mosaics, a fashion stimulated by the incorporation of the country in the Roman Empire.

Materially, socially and spiritually, Egypt ranked with the most important provinces. Thanks to papyrus-finds our knowledge of it is fairly extensive, even of the petty details of daily life and the machinery of administration. But we must not forget that it was a country of strong individuality, and that its individuality took a long time to eradicate.

AFRICA

Africa consisted of three provinces, which were on a very different level of culture. First came the territory impressed with an old civilisation—the former Empire of Carthage. The restored Carthage was the largest city after Rome in the Latin half of the Empire. Secondly, Numidia, created a province by Caesar. Here culture had taken firm root and been vigorously propagated by king Massinissa, the great opponent of Carthage and ally of Rome. These two provinces embraced modern Tunis and Eastern Algeria. But the third, Mauretania, with the exception of a few small Roman colonies and cities, was one of the areas of barbarism. The fact that the great land road westward from Carthage did not extend to Tangier, and that the traveller had to find his way along the Riff coast by sea, implicitly discloses the character of the Mauretanian hinterland.

In the province of Africa there was an old culture, the Punic, on which the Romans could build. Punic social organisation and Punic language lingered on in the imperial times. Side by side with the Punic, the Greek tongue was widely spoken, but it was not officially recognised in this part of the Western Empire. Latin was introduced as the official language and spread steadily, though even in the fourth century we find that a bishop, who was ignorant of the native language of the country, was not readily elected. But, by the time of the Arab conquest, Punic had disappeared. If the Arabs had not appeared, Northern Africa would have been a Romance country. The other language of the country, Berber, still survives. To this day, no such success in civilising the unmanageable Berber tribes has been achieved as in the Roman age. These tribesmen wrote their language with an alphabet derived from the Punic, and this is still used in certain localities. One can follow the process by which the Berber tribes were organised under native princes, and their villages gradually converted into towns, and so, automatically, brought into the orbit of civilisation.

Africa, confining the name to the fully-civilised province,

and the fruitful Medjerda valley in Tunis in particular, rivalled Egypt in fertility. It supplied the second third of the corn required to provision Rome. We are told by an old author that Africa had abundance of corn but was not so well provided with oil and wine. Nevertheless Caesar could order a single city, Leptis Parva, to deliver 220,000 gallons of oil to Rome. Its prosperity in Roman times, to which the widespread ruins bear witness, is in striking contrast to its comparative desolation in the present day. If one rides from the Lesser Syrtis to the frontier of Algeria and then northwards to the southern source of the Medjerda, in a journey of three weeks one finds only about eight Arab villages, but no day passes but one comes on ancient ruins—a farm, a village, a town, or at least a grave or a cistern. Here, where now there is a total absence of cultivation, one may visit the ancient city Thysdrus, whose amphitheatre is nearly as large as the Colosseum at Rome ! In a side valley of the Medjerda there are the ruins of six towns, only a few kilometres distant from each other. The population must have been as dense as in a modern industrial district. Further south, where water was more scarce, the towns were further apart, but between them were many villages and farms. The great ruined cities are too numerous to mention, such as Thugga, Tebessa, the camp-city Lambaesis, and Timgad, the African Pompeii, which slept under the protecting shroud of the desert sand, until the spade of the archaeologists restored it to the light of day. The encroachment of the desert on the cultivated land and the retrogression of civilisation have been successful agents in the preservation of the ruins. There are as many triumphal arches in Africa as in the whole of the rest of the Roman world, including Italy. The inscriptions of Africa are over 20,000 in number, whereas Britain, for instance, only supplies 1500.

All this prosperity depended on revenue from the soil. There were certain tracts of land which, in those days, were valued at nearly two shillings per square yard. The soil is still the same, but the water supply is deficient. The Romans were experts in the art of conserving every available drop of spring and rain water. Naturally the cisterns were many

o

and large—in the cisterns of Carthage a whole Arab village is now housed. The water of the brooks that only flowed in winter was conducted into reservoirs, and distributed over the fields in nicely calculated quantities. The great archaeological investigation of the ancient system of aqueducts, which the French have set on foot, has an immediately practical aim, *viz.* to trace the work of the Romans and to restore their irrigation works, since, in many cases, the old plant can be easily repaired. Nowhere is the contrast between the prosperity of ancient civilisation and the decay under Islam so startling as in Africa.

During the period of prosperity there were many grievous latent abuses, probably inherited from the Carthaginian days of plantation economy. Africa was the promised land of the great proprietors. Nero executed six magnates and confiscated their property, which, it is said, constituted a sixth part of the whole area of the province of Africa ! Most of the ruins and sites do not date from a period earlier than that of Hadrian. In the person of Septimius Severus an African came to the throne and inaugurated the age of greatest prosperity. Later on disturbances broke out, owing to peasant risings against their masters, and in consequence, country farms were often fortified. In the south, the landowners had to defend themselves against the raids of nomadic desert tribes. Industry was comparatively unimportant ; we only hear of wool and leather articles.

The Africans were not popular in Rome. This was due not merely to the old instinctive hatred of Carthage but to the violence of the native African temper, which, perhaps, owed something to a strain of untameable Berber blood. Life on a country estate must have resembled in many respects that of a modern country squire. This is epigrammatically expressed in the well-known inscription of the town of Timgad : " To hunt, to bathe, to gamble and to laugh—that is life." To this must be added the pleasures and thrills of horse-racing, which was, if possible, more ardently pursued here than elsewhere. A characteristic feature is supplied by the numerous magical inscriptions which seem to have been intended to

" dope " a race-horse by witchcraft. They show a definite tendency towards a belief in crude superstition and an inclination to the black art. Even Apuleius, the best known African author, came near to getting into trouble through an accusation of witchcraft.

Like many other African authors, Apuleius had experienced some difficulty in learning Latin. This, perhaps, is one explanation of the contorted and artificial style which is a characteristic of so-called African Latinity, but it may have been due to the archaising tendency of the age. Rhetoric was highly esteemed ; Fronto and his associates acquired a name in Roman literature, which they dominated in the second century when Africa was most prosperous. True greatness came with the Christian authors, who struck deeper echoing notes in the heart of the people, especially Tertullian, in his enthusiasm and shrewdness a genuine African, and Augustine, the greatest of all the fathers of the Church. It has been justly observed that Africa created Western Latin Christianity.

SPAIN

It is worth remarking how the provinces in the Western half of the Empire come successively into prominence and then decline. The second century was Africa's period, the first had been that of Spain. Many of the best-known men of the first century were Spaniards, the poet Martial, the educator Quintilian, the rhetorician Seneca, his son the philosopher Seneca, Nero's minister, and his grandson the poet Lucan. The first provincials who ascended the throne of Rome were Spaniards, Trajan and Hadrian. In the third century barbarian Illyria provided Rome with emperors.

In Spain, latinisation was not impeded by an old-established cultural language as in Africa, and yet there was a certain primitive cultured stratum to build on. The progress was more thorough and prolonged in the eastern and southern portions of the country, which came under Roman rule as far back as the second Punic War. Under Augustus there were fifty Spanish cities with full franchise and the same number

with Latin rights : Vespasian introduced Latin organisation
into all the cities which were still without it. In the second
century there were but few tribes still lacking civil organisation.
It is significant that the southern part, Baetica, enjoyed the
same privileges as Italy, *viz.* freedom from conscription
for military service. Civilisation was of course unevenly
distributed. Other parts of the country furnished many
recruits, and up in the north, where Rome's power was first
extended by Augustus, there still lingers on the strange
Basque language, probably a relic of the language of the original
population, Iberians or Ligurians. Celts had migrated into
Spain, and blended with Iberians into the Celtiberians.

Spain's chief wealth was in its minerals, which had already
attracted the Carthaginians to the country—gold in the north-
west and south, silver in plenty in Baetica and near Carthagena,
copper in the Sierra Morena, and lead and iron near Cordova.
Tin was certainly not found in the country, but was imported
by way of Cadiz. The output of precious metals seems to have
fallen off under the Empire when most of the gold came from
Dacia, but for other metals Spain was still the chief source.
There grew up a metal industry, and Toledo was famous
for its iron manufactories. Our chief knowledge of mining
in imperial times is derived from Spain. In comparison,
agriculture and other industries were less important, though
trade with Rome was active. Monte Testaccio in Rome is a
big heap of broken sherds of pottery in which imported wares
had been packed. The trade-marks show that most of them
came from certain towns in Southern Spain. Some corn was
exported to Italy and a certain amount of oil. Flax was
cultivated and worked up in bulk, and esparto grass served
for rope and coarse materials. The Spanish breed of sheep
was famous in antiquity : in earlier times wool was worked
up in the country, later it was exported. The fisheries were
important. Spain's chief city was Gades (Cadiz), concerning
which we find in Augustus' census that no town in the Empire,
with the exception of Padua, could boast so many great
fortunes, and among its inhabitants were 500 men of equestrian
rank. Gades was an ancient mercantile city, which, owing to

its position near the Straits of Gibraltar, was a clearing house for all the trade between the Atlantic and the Mediterranean lands.

The decline of Spain, already alluded to, is peculiar. Under Marcus Aurelius it is said that the country was exhausted. This probably referred to the decline of mining, since other branches of trade had not the same importance. The national character has not altered in the course of centuries. The same stubborn guerilla warfare, the same capacity for standing sieges are noticeable both in the wars of the Romans and of Napoleon I. in Spain. The same *grandezza* distinguished the old Iberians as the modern Spaniards.

GAUL

But Gaul was the chief of the Western provinces. Its conquest counterbalanced, to some extent, the great swing to the East, which the Roman power underwent by the incorporation of the Hellenistic kingdoms.

In Gaul, also, the Romans had an older civilisation to build upon, whose vigour has been under-estimated, because it has been labelled with an archaeological nomenclature (the La Tené period) and thus ranked with the other prehistoric periods, which cannot compare with it in importance. Its first culture-centre was the flourishing Greek commercial city of Massilia, which controlled the greater part of the French Mediterranean coast, and whose influence is especially notable for the wide distribution of its coinage as well as the Greek alphabet along the great trade-route up the Rhone, which was joined by the amber route from Germany and the tin route from Britain. As was the case everywhere in the Western part of the Empire, Greek influence after the Roman conquest was supplanted by the Latin, but nowhere had it struck such deep roots as in Gaul. The fate of Massilia is of some interest in view of future events. This city, which for centuries had been Rome's most reliable and valuable ally, desired to preserve its neutrality during the Civil Wars, and closed its gates against Caesar. It was taken, had to surrender shipping and money, and lost the greater part of its territory, which was divided among recently founded Roman colonies. Its trade fell off, and it was soon surpassed in importance by Narbo (Narbonne) and Arelate (Arles).

Previously the Gallic provinces had included " toga-clad Gaul " (*Gallia togata*)—the plain of the Po—whose inhabitants since the later days of the Republic, when they had obtained Roman citizenship, wore the Roman dress and were counted as being on an equality with the Italians. Among the Gallic provinces of modern France there were considerable distinctions, still marked by linguistic differences (*langue d'oc* and *d'oui*). The Mediterranean coast, called after the Gaulish costume, Breeches-Gaul (*Gallia bracata*), had, at the beginning of the Empire, been for some time a Roman province and included the former territory of Massilia. Caesar founded here a series of citizen-colonies and established other places with Latin rights. At the close of Augustus' reign the province (hence *Provence*) was completely latinised, the older country districts obtaining city-organisation, and those inhabitants who had the franchise were put on a level with the Italians, could enter the Senate, and hold public office under the Empire.

In the rest of the country—the " long-haired Gaul " (*Gallia comata*)—which had been conquered by Caesar, circumstances were different. It was divided into three provinces (*tres Galliae*), between which a distinction of race persisted, the after-effects of which have not been obliterated even to-day. In the south-west was Aquitania, chiefly peopled by Iberians : the central province from the Rhone and the Saone to Brittany and Normandy, named Lugdunensis, had the purest Celtic population ; the northern, Belgica, had a strong German element. The conquest of Gaul, which was prepared by a peaceful economic penetration, had been facilitated by internal rivalries and feuds between the Gallic tribes. The country had been controlled by a powerful nobility, a system which, as usual, led to constant feuds. The tribal constitution continued, but the lesser tribes, which previously stood in the relation of clients to the greater ones, disappear in the Roman age. In contrast with *Gallia bracata* and the rest of the Empire, city-organisation was not introduced into *Gallia comata,* and the inhabitants could not aspire to full citizen rights, and could not occupy a seat in the Senate. The country was divided into not more than sixty-four tribal districts, whose extent was thus considerably greater than the territory usually attached to an ancient city. Grenoble and Geneva, for example, were legally villages belonging to Vienna. The variations between them depended chiefly on the extent of the districts, whose officials and institutions resembled those of cities, but there were also local peculiarities in the recruiting for the army and levying of taxes. Every district had several centres of population which might be described as cities, and one " capital." The tenacity of the tribal organisation is shown in the fact that the name of the tribe has often been retained in that of the city. Lutetia Parisiorum becomes Paris; Mediolanum Santonum, Saintes; Durocortorum Remorum, Rheims; Augusta Treverorum, Trèves. The organisation of Gaul, which Augustus carried out in person during a stay of several years in the country, is a striking instance of the sound practical political sense of the Romans. Far from despising the old organisation of the newly-conquered country, they made it the foundation of the new social fabric, and thus secured the conquest for all time to come.

At first there was only one city in the three Gauls with full Roman franchise, Lugudunum (Lyons). It was not a Celtic city, but had been founded by Italians, who, during the civil war, had been driven out of Vienne. Owing to its advantageous situation at the confluence of the Rhone and the navigable Saone, it quickly shot up into importance and became the centre of Gallic trade. The road system of the whole country met there ; it was the seat of administration, where the provincial diet assembled, and there stood the Gallic altar, which, dedicated to the cult of the Emperor, was the religious centre of the three provinces. Further north Trèves prospered, but it did not surpass Lyons, until, after Diocletian's re-organisation of the country, it became the capital of the most Western division of the Empire.

The old national spirit was directed and controlled by the Celtic priesthood, the Druids, a close priestly caste with special training colleges. It was regarded with antipathy by the Romans, who were accustomed to consider religion merely as an appendage to the state and politics, and looked askance at the gloomy and mysterious character of Druidism. Gaulish monuments which still remain, depict extraordinary gods— gods, for example, with stags' horns or three heads—which are in striking contrast to the plastic forms of ancient Roman deities. Druidism contained a real menace to Rome, and Tiberius severely suppressed it, but it found a refuge in Britain which was still independent.

The three Gauls had under the Empire a mixed culture in which the native elements were strongly represented. Latin was introduced officially, but Celtic lived on as the language of the country. Even in Lyons sermons were delivered in Celtic in the second century ; while as late as the third century it was permissible, in certain official documents, to use alternative languages to Greek and Latin, *e.g.* Celtic and Punic. The Gaulish measure of length, *leuga* (*lieue*, league), replaced the Roman mile on milestones. There sprang up a feeling of Gallic independence, which found expression in the rising of Julius Civilis, in the ten years of independence during the confusion in the middle of the third century, and in a certain spirit of rivalry between Gaul and Italy in the time of the West-Roman Empire.

Then, as now, Gaul was a prosperous and rich country. During the Cimbrian War a consul had, so it is stated, carried off from the Temple of Apollo at Toulouse accumulated treasures to the unheard-of value of considerably over £35,000,000. Augustus' notorious chief-collector, Licinus, is said to have taken the Emperor into a room full of gold and silver, in order to convince him that the Gauls could pay the taxes of which they complained. The wealth was principally due to the fruitfulness of the land. In the south vineyards and olive groves flourished, and had to be restricted by decree to protect the Italian market ; further in the interior corn was grown. Flax was extensively cultivated and supported a thriving industry. The Northern Vosges, now almost exclusively covered with forests, were in Roman, and perhaps

pre-Roman times, plough-land and pasturage with villages
and farmhouses. To this day in the midst of the forest are
found remains of dwellings and gravestones. In the early
Empire Italy was surpassed by Gaul in the manufacture of
the finer sorts of pottery (*terra sigillata*). Trade was in a
flourishing condition. The cities that succeeded to the
position of Massilia—Lyons and Arles—have already been
mentioned. In the north Trèves developed into an important
trading city, whose wealthy merchants built fine villas, raised
sepulchral monuments on the banks of the Moselle, and depicted
in sculpture their luxurious private life, their trade-caravans,
and their shipping on the Moselle.

Trèves is the only city north of the Alps where Roman
ruins occur on a great scale—the Porta Nigra, the Basilica,
the Emperor's palace (which is really thermae)—not inferior to
those of Rome. The city was justly called the Rome of the
North. The wealth of Gaul and the diffusion of culture
resulted in splendid buildings, especially in the south, which
are not inferior to those of Italy as memorials of the Roman
age. Striking examples are still to be seen, *e.g.* the Theatre
of Orange, the Amphitheatre of Arles, the Temple of Nîmes,
and the great aqueduct, the Pont du Gard, which in three
tiers spans a river-valley, the city gates of Autun, and the
triumphal arch at Saintes.

From the very beginning of the imperial age the old province
of the south occupied a conspicuous position in the intellectual
life of the Empire. When Massilia had lost its place as a
trading town, like Athens and Rhodes, it continued its traditions as a University town, where Romans came in search
of higher education. Not a few Gallic names are to be found
in the history of literature. In the later imperial age the rest
of Gaul acquired an importance of its own when the schools
of rhetoric flourished, and here, longer than elsewhere, the
classic age of Latin was maintained in the floods of eloquence,
which were poured out in festal speeches in honour of the
majesty of successive Emperors. More interesting than these
empty displays of rhetoric are the poems of Ausonius, though
his poetry is neither original nor profound. They introduce

us to the life of Gaul in the fourth century, and describe the smiling banks of the Moselle, or his colleagues in the rhetorical school and the University of Bordeaux.

BRITAIN

The conquest of Britain was a direct consequence of the conquest of Gaul. The country was more distant, and had not attained to the same degree of civilisation as Gaul. As the foundations were slighter, so also the Roman superstructure was smaller, and the country cost the Empire more than it brought in. Of the four legions which accomplished its subjection, three had to remain. The distinction which is found between Gaul and Roman Germany, which had to be policed by strong garrisons, recurs also in Britain. The legionary camps were stationed in the north and west, at Eboracum (York), Deva (Chester), and Isca Silurum (Caerleon upon Usk), and were thus directed against the tribes of the north and Wales, with whom incessant warfare had to be waged. Here the administration was military, but in the south and east it was civil, and there country houses and towns are found, of which Silchester (Calleva Atrebatum) is the best known example. But the towns were few and not very important. The country was divided into districts like Gaul, but they were smaller and have left no traces in the names of towns. Under the later Empire the export of corn from Britain to Gaul was considerable. The results of Roman civilisation were swept away by the Anglo-Saxon and Scandinavian invasions, but the roots of that civilisation went deeper than is supposed. Welsh is full of Latin loan-words, even substantives and verbs, which were introduced in Roman times, and yet the Welsh were the people who received the smallest impression of Roman culture.

GERMANY

The Roman province of Germany became a mere fragment. Between A.D. 82 and 90 two provinces, Upper and Lower Germany, were formed. The boundary between them was the Vinxtbach, which still separates the dioceses of Cologne and Trèves. But in reality these two provinces were nothing but a militarised zone over against independent Germany, occupied by the Empire's strongest garrison, eight legions, whereas no more than six were on the Danube frontier. The population was a mixture of Celts and Germans, a circumstance which makes it very difficult for modern research to decide what is genuinely German in the relics of native civilisation and religion. The dominant civilising factor was the Roman military system which will be described later. The cities, of which Cologne was the most important, developed out of legionary camps. This definitely Roman character is in direct contrast to the civilisation in Gaul, which has a marked national peculiarity. There were no troops stationed in Gaul to make the romanisation stronger.

DANUBIAN PROVINCES

In the latter half of the second century A.D. the danger zone of the Empire shifted to the Danube frontier, where Marcus Aurelius had to undertake severe campaigns with the Marcomanni, Quadi and Iazyges. In the middle of the next century the Goths appeared in the same quarter and knocked at the gates of the Empire. Even during Trajan's war with the Dacians, the Danube frontier had become of greater military importance than the Rhine frontier, requiring ten legions as compared with four on the Rhine, and that number had to be raised to twelve during the war with the Marcomanni. Rhaetia had only one city of importance, Augusta Vindelicorum (Augsburg), which was granted full citizenship by Hadrian. Vindobona (Vienna) in Pannonia was a legionary camp, like the more important Carnuntum, somewhat lower down the Danube. A high degree of culture was developed only in the Alpine valleys of Noricum which looked towards Italy. Emona (Laibach) was actually incorporated in Italy. The same was the case with the province south of Pannonia, Illyria. Certainly iron mines were discovered in Bosnia, and Salona was a commercial town ; but the inhabitants, protected by their mountains, preserved their vigorous national character barely touched by Roman culture. This was to have fatal results for the Empire in the third century. The principal portion of the Imperial army was in these regions and was recruited from these peoples. The Illyrian army succeeded the German in the rôle of emperor-maker, and in the third century the Emperors themselves were Illyrians. Descendants of these people probably still inhabit that region, *viz.* the Albanians. Their unmanageableness and ferocity are well known ; but they have given the Turkish Empire some of its leading generals and statesmen, as they gave the Romans those vigorous Emperors who drove back the barbarians, and, for a time, welded the Empire together. But neither then, any more than now, can these people be said to have attained to an advanced stage of civilisation.

The province on the right bank of the Lower Danube was called Moesia. Here in the Balkan Peninsula one would have expected to find a strong Greek influence, but such was not the case. The Greeks always kept to the coast-lands and in those early days the savagery and poverty of the native population hindered the extension of culture northwards. The country was romanised instead. The linguistic dividing line between Latin and Greek went as far south as Uskub and Stobi. Had not the Slavonic immigrations taken place, the Northern Balkan Peninsula would have had a Romance population. There are still to be found in Northern Greece some hundred thousand Koutzo-Vlachs, who speak a Roumanian dialect. These are a remnant of this Roman population, the greater part of which was pressed northwards and is to be found in modern Roumania.

(iii) COMMUNICATIONS

There are two principal factors which weld together the modern State system, if we eliminate historic tradition, the binding force of which can scarcely be over-estimated. One is national consciousness, which is based on a common language and the special type of national culture closely combined with it. This conception of a national state has so entered into the consciousness of our time, that a state like Austria, which included different nationalities, was felt to be an anomaly. The other is the economic unity of the state. The state forms a closed economic sphere, which is, of course, usually in close relations with other and similar spheres, but its interests are opposed to them. This attitude against the foreigner is most plainly expressed by a customs-frontier. Customs are a means of promoting the economic interests of a particular state, whether it is agricultural, industrial, or commercial. In fact the pressure exercised by foreign states tends to unite the state and weld it together.

Both these factors were absent in the Roman Empire. In it were found hundreds of different nations and languages ; it was a typical conquering state and heir to the old Oriental idea of World monarchy. Economic interests did not play the same part as in modern states, and this was largely due to the all-embracing character of the Empire. Economic pressure and competition from abroad did not exist. The customs-frontiers within the Empire were more important than those against the outside world. Exports were insignificant, and imports could, in case of need, be dispensed with. Imports from foreign countries consisted chiefly of articles of luxury, which had little meaning for the great masses of the people. The Roman Empire was, in all essentials, economically independent, and for that very reason did not exhibit those complexities of economic interests, which tend to unify a modern state, whose interests conflict with, and are in opposition to, those of other states.

The underlying bond of unity was the common Hellenistic-Roman culture, which, in spite of the two cultural languages, was, to all intents and purposes, one, and developed uniformly. Of this culture the citizens in the Roman Empire felt themselves to be members, and prided themselves in their superiority to the barbaric peoples that surrounded the Empire. There were also barbarians within the Empire, whose admission into its culture was a vital question. Otherwise the Roman Empire was, like every conquering State, held together by the army and the administrative system, whose threads all met in Rome and whose head was the Emperor.

The army and the administration, then, were the strands which bound the Empire together; but their effectiveness depended on communications; and on communications depended also the movement of trade and the ebb and flow of population within the Empire, the importance of which cannot be over-estimated. The different nations were intermingled, or at least were in close contact with each other, and learned to understand each other as being participators in the same culture and subjects of the same Emperor.

Rome's power was a Mediterranean power, a ring of countries round the great sea. In this it had, to some extent, a resemblance to another Empire on a smaller scale, that of Athens, which embraced the islands in, and the coasts around, the Aegean. The Athenian Empire had been a typical sea power, whose strength and cohesion were dependent on its fleet. The Greeks were born seafarers, as their achievements in colonisation round the whole Mediterranean bear witness. The Romans, on the contrary, were born landsmen and only under force of circumstances ventured on the sea. At a crisis they improvised a fleet, and when the danger was over, quickly laid it up. This they did after the first Punic War; Pompey did the same in 67 B.C., when, in the middle of Rome's victories, the Asiatic pirates carried off unmolested her corn ships within sight of Ostia and made alliances with Mithridates in the East and Sertorius in Spain; so did Augustus in the decisive struggle with Antony.

In the early years of the Empire steps were taken to restore the safety of the seas. Hitherto no firm stand had been made against piracy, except when it actually threatened the populace of Rome with starvation. The merchants had accepted it as one of the inevitable risks of their calling. But a little consideration showed how important the security of the sea was for trade and communications. Augustus, therefore, commissioned permanent squadrons and constructed naval harbours. There were two, at Misenum north of Naples, and at Ravenna. The great value of the trade with the East necessitated squadrons stationed at Alexandria and Seleucia, the harbour of Antioch. A fleet in the Black Sea and the

English Channel were required because all communications with the north coast of the Black Sea and with Britain had to go by sea ; and one may conjecture that these fleets were occupied in transport services. The same applies to the flotillas on the Rhine and Danube.

The measures that were taken were, however, far from adequate. Augustus tried to extirpate piracy in the Red Sea and the Indian Ocean, in the interests of the trade with India. But this was only a beginning : as yet the Empire maintained no fleet on the Red Sea, and for the voyage over the Indian Ocean trading-ships were wont to take archers on board to defend themselves against pirates. The safety of the sea left much to be desired ; and for a long time the pirates continued their depredations on the Black Sea and off the Belgian coast. This indifference to maritime security was a legacy which the Empire inherited from the Republic, and in spite of superior insight into the problem it was never completely solved.

A reason for this is to be found in the contempt in which service in the navy was held. The crews were usually recruited from liberated slaves and men without citizenship, and no distinction was made between rowers and marines. The period of service was six years longer than in the army, *viz.* twenty-six years. In rank and pay the crews of the fleet had the worst position. It is significant that freedmen were repeatedly appointed admirals, even of the main fleet at Misenum.

Trade by sea had no higher position. The Greeks were the seafarers of antiquity. After they had explored the Mediterranean and adjacent seas, prolonged and daring voyages became common ; the daring of their performances can best be gauged, if one compares the open boats with, at most, fifty rowers, described by Homer, and the really large merchant ships that were built in the Hellenistic period. The Roman period was really one of retrogression. The great ships disappeared from the battle-fleet, being too unwieldy for propulsion by oars, while no improvement was made in the art of sailing. The largest vessel of which we have a description, named the *Isis* and built to transport corn from Alexandria to Ostia, was of 1575 tons, and had only one mast. A great vessel built under Caligula to convey an obelisk from Egypt to Rome was immediately scrapped by filling it with stones and sinking it in the harbour of Ostia, to serve as the foundation for a lighthouse.

And yet seaborne trade was very important for the ancient world. On it, for instance, depended the imports of corn, which gave the multitudes of Rome the food on which they subsisted. A walk through the ruins of Ostia, the port of Rome, with its depôts and meeting-rooms for guilds of merchants and seamen from all corners of the Empire and workmen of every kind, furnishes us with a very different aspect of antiquity from that of the peaceful thriving country-town of Pompeii. But seafaring did not develop with the Empire's growth and organisation, and this was a grievous mistake.

Nothing gives us a more vivid picture of the dilatoriness and difficulties connected with a sea voyage in antiquity, than the description in the Acts of the Apostles of St. Paul's journey from Palestine to Rome—a narrative which sets forth the dry facts without comment. From Caesarea St. Paul voyaged along the coast of Asia and under the lee of Cyprus to Myra in Lycia, where he found a ship which had gone so far out of its way on the voyage from Alexandria to Italy. In this he went on very slowly, in the face of contrary winds, and when he finally got to Crete the storms of autumn had begun, so that it was proposed to winter in the island. But while the captain was looking for a safe harbour in which to lie up, the ship was surprised by a storm and driven before the wind. After a hazardous voyage it went ashore at Malta, and the shipwrecked passengers had to wait three months before they could continue the journey in another ship which had wintered at Malta.

This account describes the rule, not the exception. Seafaring chiefly consisted in coasting : few mariners ventured out on to the open sea. The sailor of the present day feels safer out in the open sea ; proximity to, rather than distance from coasts and shoals constitutes his chief danger. The mariners of those days, on the contrary, dreaded to lose sight of land. On the advent of rough weather they hurried to make for the best harbour available and anchored till the wind permitted sailing. At the approach of autumn with its storms, seafaring came to an end, and was only renewed at the beginning of spring. If one was on a journey like St. Paul, one hibernated in some harbour. In 43 B.C. the Roman Governor of Spain had no opportunity of sending despatches to Rome before the following April, and thus all communications between Rome and the province were interrupted for a whole winter.

This was an ignominious state of things, and it is unnecessary to adduce modern comparisons, which would be misleading. We have only to think of what the Vikings accomplished at sea, though their general level of culture and technical skill was greatly inferior to that of the Romans— of their bold voyages and their confident sailing on seas which were of greater extent, more perilous and more treacherous than the Mediterranean. It is true that the ancients had no means of taking their bearings on the open sea when the clouds hid the stars : they had neither compass nor clock, but the Vikings were similarly handicapped. The deficiency was important, but does not explain everything. The real reason was that the Romans had not the slightest trace of the sea-faring spirit that loves the sea, defies dangers, and therefore learns how to overcome them.

It is no wonder that sea voyages were detested by the ancients. They were looked on as a necessary evil, which was inseparable from perils and risks. When Virgil had to travel to Greece and cross from Brindisi to Durazzo, a voyage of twenty-four hours on the most frequented route of the ancient world, Horace wrote a farewell poem to him, in which a sea journey is represented as something unnatural, a calamity that brought all evil into the world. Regular sailings were non-existent. A man who wished to travel to a certain place, had to journey to a seaport and wait there till some vessel chanced to be sailing whither he wanted to go. He took any chance that offered, whether the vessel was good or bad—

P

and it was generally bad—and all comforts on shipboard were non-existent. Juvenal speaks of the wife of a Roman Senator, who ran away with a gladiator : what seemed to him the strangest thing in the case was that she could endure sea-sickness and the smell of bilgewater. " But what is there that a woman in love will not endure ? "

But the imperial age did make some improvement in the provision of harbours, and light-houses were erected as beacons for sailors. These were copied from the Greeks ; the famous Pharos, outside the great harbour of Alexandria, being the pattern. But the greatest undertaking, one on which modern Italy has not even yet ventured, was the creation of a harbour for Rome at the mouth of the Tiber, for Rome was the capital of the world, and the importation of corn for the Roman population was the Emperor's chief concern. Claudius laid out a great basin of 172 acres, and Trajan added a new one of 78 acres in extent. Another important harbour, whose long quays, built on arches, and silted up basins still remain, was Puteoli (Pozzuoli), where St. Paul landed on his way to Rome.

The inland waterways had an importance for heavy transport which must not be under-estimated. There is an unique monument on the family tomb of a merchant at Neumagen near Trèves, which depicts a vessel loaded with wine-casks on the Moselle. The importance of river-transport is best attested by the guilds of shipmasters, who have left numerous inscriptions, especially by the side of lakes and rivers, in Northern Italy and Gaul, also in Spain, Switzerland, by the Rhine and Danube and their tributaries. Under Notre Dame in Paris has been found one of the most important memorials of the Gaulish religion, erected by the shipmasters' guild of Paris, which was responsible for the river traffic on the Seine. Not much was done to supplement the important inland waterways. The canal which Drusus dug from the Rhine through the Zuider Zee to the North Sea served a definite military purpose—the German War. An undertaking of more importance was the reconstruction of Darius' old canal between the Nile and the Bitter Lakes, by means of which a waterway was created between the Mediterranean and the Red Sea.

The imperial age, then, cannot boast of its seafaring and seamanship. From its geographical situation, with a great central sea which divided or united the provinces according to the development or neglect of seafaring, the Empire seemed compelled by force of circumstances to increase and cultivate connections by sea with all its might. The more they were developed, the more saving would there have been in time and in the cost of transport, and the stronger would have been the links between the provinces and the whole Empire. But to achieve this end nothing, or very little, was done. One of the outstanding failings of the age is brought into relief in this connection—the absence of the inventive faculty and enterprise. People relied on the state-organisation as the remedy for all abuses and defects, so that necessity lost its chief incentive to stimulate invention. There were no technical improvements in seamanship under the Empire, therefore it deteriorated and abdicated its vital task. Without development it could not adjust itself to the requirements of the Empire in its struggle to achieve a real unity. This failure is, in part responsible for the final catastrophe.

The elder Cato once expressed bitter regret at having gone on board a vessel, when he might have travelled by land. The Roman who was to travel from Gades or Asia Minor to Rome, seems to have taken the saying to heart, and preferred to travel by land whenever possible. The network of roads was highly developed, since the Roman felt at home on land. But for the circulation of traffic on a larger scale and for heavy transport over long distances, land roads are not suitable, and they are costly to maintain. Trade and communications suffered grievous damage from the lack of shipping conveniences. The Roman road system was everywhere interrupted by the sea or forced to follow circuitous routes. But the network of roads was as important for the Roman Empire as railways are for a modern State. They were the arteries which vivified the members of the Empire. By road the legions marched from the Euphrates to the Rhine : by road the Emperor's messages and commands were transmitted to the most distant provinces, and reports and information poured into Rome. The roads served also for the merchants' carriages and beasts of burden, for the migration of peoples and for the journeys of individual citizens. In contrast with the connections by sea, the roads had old Roman traditions behind them and were maintained with true Roman energy and purposefulness.

" All roads lead to Rome." In Italy the distance from Rome was given on the milestones, not from the ideal centre, the *miliarium aureum* which was in the Forum, but from the city gates. In the provinces distances were reckoned from the nearest important city, *e.g.* from Lyons in Gaul, Carthage in Africa, and Ephesus in Asia Minor.

Italy's system of roads had been built up under the Republic, but during its last turbulent years, it had fallen into decay, and even on the important *via Flaminia* all the bridges but two were broken down. It was one of Augustus' first and most urgent tasks to restore and repair them. The first great Roman road was always the most famous, the *via Appia*, the queen of roads. Like all later Roman roads, it was named, after its builder Appius Claudius, censor in 312 B.C. It ran in a straight line southwards over the Pontine marshes, on an embankment sixteen miles in length. In its contempt for inequalities of ground, in its plain military object—it was built during the Samnite War, when it was necessary for Rome to send her troops quickly south—it was typical of all future roads. It was continued to Brindisi, the port of embarkation for Durazzo on the east coast of the Adriatic. There the *via Egnatia* succeeded to it, leading straight across the mountains of Illyria to Macedonia, having been constructed soon after that country became a Roman province. It continued along the coast of Thrace to Constantinople, and was the great artery of communication with the East, which had a road system connecting with it on the other side of the Bosphorus.

At Capua the *via Popillia* branched off from the *via Appia*, and went on to the Straits of Messina : by way of Sicily, Africa was reached by a sea voyage of only twenty-four hours. The censor who gave the *via Flaminia* its name was in office in 220 B.C. Shortly before that date the Po Valley had been conquered, and immediately a road was constructed from Rome north-eastwards to Rimini, where the country of the Celts began. Soon after the Hannibalic wars, in 187 B.C., it was prolonged by the *via Aemilia*, the most important road in the country south of the Po, which gives this district its present name, Emilia. This went north-west to Piacenza, and was continued to Milan, the chief city of the plain of the Po. Another road ran from Rimini along the coast to Aquileia, the predecessor of Trieste as the chief mart on the north of the Adriatic. Thence roads went northwards to the Danube and eastwards through the Balkan Peninsula. The *via Aurelia*, which ran north-west from Rome, was of later date; like the present Riviera railway, it ran in close proximity to the coast. Its object was to shorten the route as much as possible round the Gulf of Lyons to the South of France and Spain. Its continuation in these countries was called *via Domitia*, taking its name from its builder, Domitius—who, in 120 B.C., made the South of France a Roman province—and terminated at Carthagena.

In Italy little was left for the Empire to do but to add smaller branch roads and to maintain them adequately. But in the provinces the Republic had left most of the work still to be done, with the exception of a few very important arteries constructed primarily for military purposes. With those exceptions the provincials had to be satisfied with the old bridle-paths and tracks, which did not fulfil the Roman requirements of communication by land. In the further development of these, Augustus was the great pioneer.

In Spain he continued the *via Domitia* through the southern province of Baetica, past Cordova and Seville to Cadiz and the Straits of Gibraltar, on the other side of which the road-system of Morocco began, which was apparently divided from the system of the rest of Africa by a break at the Riff coast. The main line of the latter was a coast road from what is, approximately, the present western frontier of Algeria to Egypt. In Gaul, Augustus' faithful assistant, Agrippa, traced the road system with a sure hand. The centre was

Lyons, from which radiated roads to the mouth of the Rhône, Bordeaux, Saintes, Brittany, the Channel, Trèves, Cologne, and Switzerland. These radials were linked up by a great number of cross-roads, so that all the more important places were in easy communication with each other.

The subjugation of the independent tribes in the Western Alps had been necessary to secure the communication between Gaul and Italy. It was quickly followed by the construction of roads over the Alps, and additional Alpine roads were rendered necessary by the submission of the country north of the mountains as far as the Danube. In Roman times there were as many as sixteen routes over the Alps, but not all of them were available for wheeled traffic. The connection with Gaul was especially provided for by a road built by Augustus from Turin over the Mont Genèvre south of Mt. Cenis (which was not used for traffic in antiquity), and by another over the Little St. Bernard ; the road over the Great St. Bernard was only made available for wheeled traffic later, in the first century A.D.

The oldest road through the Eastern Alps was constructed by Drusus in connection with the conquest of Rhaetia. It ascended the valley of the Adige and went down to the Inn— the Brenner railway follows the same route—but went round the Brenner Pass, which was only made traversable at a later date. To the north it was prolonged to Augsburg and the frontier. From the great commercial city of Aquileia started two important roads, one, northwards, through the Julian Alps, and one in a more easterly direction by way of Emona (Laibach) to Carnuntum and Vienna. Probably the Alps were never again so accessible for traffic and so well provided with roads until far on in the nineteenth century.

Branch roads in the northern provinces were chiefly regulated by military needs—the movement of armies along the far-reaching frontier. The chief of these was the road along the south bank of the Danube from Bavaria to the Dobrudja.

The roads to the Balkan Peninsula naturally started from Aquileia. The most important route followed the valleys of the Save or Drave to the Danube, and continued *via* Nish, Sophia, and Adrianople to Constantinople ; another ran southwards along the coast of Dalmatia.

The roads were more or less numerous according to the density of the population and the degree of their civilisation, as is the case to-day with railways. Thus they were numerous and in close proximity to each other in the intensively cultivated province of Africa and in the rich commercial and industrial country of Asia Minor. But then, as now, the considerations which had decisive weight in the making of roads were military and strategic. It was due to these that the comparatively backward Britain had a well-developed system of roads : for in it were stationed no less than three legions to defend the province against the hill-tribes. The roads in England are unusually well preserved and are still serviceable for long distances. They usually bear old Anglo-Saxon names. Watling Street runs from the Straits of Dover by way of London north-westwards and is continued north to the Firth of Clyde. Ermine Street goes by Lincoln and York (Eboracum) through the eastern half of the country and is continued by Dere Street as far as the Firth of Forth. There are also various cross-roads, generally running in a direction from south-west to north-east. London was already the great road-centre.

Specially well investigated and illuminating is the Rhine frontier, whose military importance was obvious. Its road system, therefore, deserves a more thorough attention as an example of the Roman policy of building strategic roads. The nearest great town, a centre in the Gaulish system, was Trèves. From it roads radiate to the various towns and camps on the Rhine, Neuss (Novaesium) opposite Düsseldorf, Cologne, Bonn, Andernach, Mainz and Worms, and these places are connected by a road along the Rhine. At the legionary camp of Mainz the same plan was followed. From it radiated the roads up the Main, through Hesse-Darmstadt to Swabia, and southwards to Baden, and on the left bank of the Rhine to Strassburg, which was itself a road-centre. The conquest of the *Agri Decumates* was due to the need of communications. For this wedge, which intervened between the Danube and the Middle Rhine, made all communications between the legions on the Rhine and the Danube army in Rhaetia and Pannonia take a long détour through Switzerland. When Vespasian brought the country under Roman rule, he achieved his purpose mainly by road-building. In A.D. 74 a road was made from the legionary camp at Strassburg over the Rhine to Offenburg, which at Rottweil, near the source of the Neckar, joined a road coming from the legionary camp at Vindonissa (Windisch) in Switzerland at the confluence of the Aar and the Reuss, a place which, however, lost its military importance when the *Agri Decumates* became a Roman district. Somewhat later a more northerly road was built from Mainz along the Rhine to Bruchsal, thence through the Neckar hill country to Cannstatt and Faimingen on the Danube ; at Cannstatt it joined a road which came from Strassburg by way of Rastatt. It was completed by Domitian.

This is typical of the Roman method of making a conquered country accessible. Similar methods were followed in Dacia after Trajan's conquest. In modern times the same method is applied to new colonies, which are opened up and made accessible to trade and civilisation by the construction of railways. A road or a railway not only supplies military and commercial requirements, but also promotes general security : for the road, when made, has to be protected. Order and culture radiate from it in the newly-conquered district. During the actual process of conquest and the military operations entailed, it is necessary, at least provisionally, to make lines of communication where such do not exist. This was one of the chief undertakings attendant on the first attempt by the Romans to conquer Germany between the Rhine and the Elbe. Lanes were cut in the primeval forest, through which the legions could pass ; a general built *pontes longi*, that is, roads supported on fascines and logs, through the bogs. If Germany had continued to be a Roman province, these provisional military tracks would have been converted into real traffic roads, and on them Roman civilisation would have been introduced into the land.

In Asia Minor and Syria, as has already been observed, the conditions were quite different. These provinces had long been civilised and possessed old roads, so that the necessity for strategic roads was felt only on the frontiers ; hence further construction was neglected in the civilised parts, and the inhabitants continued to make the best of the old tracks. In Asia Minor the road-system is rather hard to follow, owing to the fact that the traditional roads of antiquity were never systematically laid out ; but generally speaking they all led down to the great commercial towns on the west coast. In these countries also the road system was peculiar in that it did not, as elsewhere, terminate at the frontier of the Roman Empire. Only in these provinces did the Empire border on foreign States in an advanced state of civilisation and already carrying on a trade of their own, *viz.* Armenia, Persia, and Arabia. The old Persian Empire had been in this respect a forerunner of the Roman. Cyrus and Darius had constructed the so-called " Royal Road," which, from Susa, led through Babylonia and the interior of Asia Minor down to the coast at Ephesus, and had provided it with halting-places for traders.

Through the mountains of Armenia a few roads led eastwards. A road ran from Trapezus southwards along the Upper Euphrates to Syria. The easiest route to Babylonia and the Far East crossed the bend of the Euphrates, where the river comes nearest to the north-eastern corner of the Mediterranean. Here two roads ran to Antioch, the river being crossed at Zeugma by a bridge of boats. In the later years of the Empire the most important trade route to the East was further south, through the desert, by way of Palmyra. This development was undoubtedly due to measures taken by the Emperors, especially by Trajan, to extend Roman dominion and civilisation over the desert. When the country east and south of Palestine—the Nabataean kingdom—was annexed by Rome, and a protective frontier erected against the roving Bedouins of the desert, naturally a system of roads was constructed. From the north-east end of the Red Sea a road led to the important commercial city of Petra, south of the Dead

Sea, and thence northwards. At Bostra, the capital of Transjordania, it bifurcated, one road leading to Damascus and another through the desert to Palmyra. Another somewhat more westerly road connected other flourishing towns east of the Jordan like Gerasa, and Palestine was linked up with Egypt by a coast road through Gaza.

From the north-east end of the Red Sea went a caravan road southwards to Leuke Kome, half-way to Mecca. This region, too, was subject to Rome. Opposite this place, on the western side of the Red Sea, was Berenice, through which a road, provided with wells and guard-houses, ran to Koptos on the Nile. The necessity for sailing on the Red Sea was avoided as much as possible owing to the stifling heat, the frequent calms and the dangers from coral reefs in stormy weather. The trade in this region consisted of spices, frankincense, and other articles of luxury, which repaid the heavy cost of transport. Even in Egypt the Nile did not suffice for the Romans, but a road was constructed alongside of it down to the first cataract at Assouan.

These are the main features of the Roman Empire's system of roads described, with the utmost possible brevity. It covered and bound together the Empire with its meshes. It was invaluable for the army and for administration, but still more for trade and communications. In new and backward provinces it exercised a civilising power, which one can see clearly illustrated in the American habit of opening up a new country to civilisation by building a railway through it.

Such excellent and comprehensive facilities for traffic were not to be found again in Europe till the nineteenth century, and in present-day Mohammedan countries there is nothing which presents so striking a contrast between what exists now and what existed then, under the sceptre of the Emperors, as a comparison of the road-systems. In Morocco, and to a great extent in Turkey also, in spite of signs of improvement, the state of things is the same as it was in Algeria and Tunis at the time of their conquest by the French, *viz.* a few short stretches of road in a country once covered by a thick-meshed network. When in 1850 General St. Arnaud marched through the pass of Kanga in the Atlas mountains, he thought he was the first man who had traversed a defile apparently so impassable for traffic ; but an inscription cut in the cliff informed him that a division of the 3rd Legion built a road there in A.D. 145. A cursory glance at the chief routes on the road-map is calculated to evoke respect for the Roman Empire as a civilising force.

The respect is increased, if one knows how Roman roads were constructed. The description which follows indicates the usual method. The earth was first of all dug away, and a layer of stones placed at the bottom of the cavity. Next came a bedding of concrete—broken stones laid in mortar of lime—and on that a fresh layer of finer concrete, broken tiles mixed with lime or mud mixed with sand. Finally, on the top was placed the actual driving surface, which on roads much used by traffic consisted of stone-slabs, and elsewhere of small stones and gravel. A Roman road was really a wall with a driving-surface on the top. But this description is far from being universally applicable. The Roman engineers adapted themselves to circumstances—the available material and the weight which the road was destined to carry. We find instances of roads that consist of stone slabs laid on only one concrete bed, and others which have only a driving surface of smaller stones laid on a lower bed of larger stones. In swampy localities the road was strengthened by piles. On both sides it was bordered by large stones which gave it solidity. The driving surface was convex, and, at least in the neighbourhood of towns, had sidewalks on both sides. The breadth was less than what we are accustomed to. The *via Appia* varies from 14½ feet to 19½ feet in width. There were still broader roads, but most of them were narrower. When the work was specially difficult, as in mountainous country, the breadth was reduced to 5½ feet, so that only one vehicle could pass at a time. Mountain roads were built with much steeper gradients than now, because a great part of the traffic was carried on the backs of animals and not in wheeled transport.

A stretch of a Roman road is more like a railway than our winding country roads. The sections of them still in use in England are appreciated by motorists, for their straightness and gentle curves permit of greater speeds being safely attained than is possible on more modern roads whose vagaries betray their origin from bridle-paths. By preference the Romans built on the crest of ridges, for they especially feared the deleterious effect of water on the surface. Such methods of laying out of roads required heavy labour, the cutting through of hill-tops, cuttings in cliffs, dams over marshy spots, supporting-walls in mountainous country, viaducts over valleys and bridges over rivers. The cutting away of rocks was a difficult task for the old road builders owing to their scanty and primitive tools. There are, however, some cuttings on a large scale, the best known being Trajan's road cut in the cliffs on the south bank of the Danube at the Iron Gates. In places tunnels are found like that constructed by Vespasian in the Apennines at Furlo to improve the *via Flaminia*, and Naples and Puteoli are connected by two tunnels through Posilipo, 750 yards in length. As an instance of great sub-structures may be mentioned the *via Appia* in the valley of Aricia, a supporting wall of peperino blocks 35 feet in height and over 300 feet in length. But most impressive of all are the bridges. Some Roman bridges are still doing duty to-day ; many more have collapsed through negligence or catastrophes of nature. Here a picture gives a better idea than a description. The bridge over the rushing Nar at Narni in Umbria was built by Augustus, when he restored the *via Flaminia*. It is 170 yards in length, is elevated to a height of 105 feet above the surface of the water, and the span of the middle arch measures 105 feet. Still greater are the dimensions of the imposing bridge of Alcantara over the Tagus, built by C. Julius Lacer at the expense of the towns of Lusitania in A.D. 106, and still in use.

It is obvious that Roman roads were expensive. On this point we have only one piece of definite information. A road between Beneventum and Aeclanum, restored by Hadrian, cost 100,000 sesterces, *i.e.* about £1000 per Roman mile, which is a little less than an English mile, and the value of money was much greater then than now. In Italy the cost of building and upkeep of the roads fell on the State treasury, which was

administered by the Senate ; but the treasury was never equal
to the demands on it, and continually lost in importance. At
the very beginning of his rule Augustus had to take some
effective measures. He induced generals who had earned a
triumph to build roads instead of giving exhibition games. The
upkeep of the chief roads passed under the control of the
Emperor. Landowners, also, in the neighbourhood had to
contribute, and their obligations in this connection are often
referred to in legal enactments. For example, of the cost of
the road restored by Hadrian mentioned above, we know that
the Emperor found two-thirds of the amount and the landowners one-third. In the provinces the cost of upkeep of the
roads was defrayed by both provinces and towns ; an instance
of this is found in the case of the great bridge over the Tagus.
By-roads were constructed entirely by the towns. But for
military roads it was necessary to have recourse to the labour
of the soldiers, which was utilised in a manner inconceivable
to us. Numberless roads, especially in the frontier provinces,
were constructed and maintained by the army, to whose labours
numerous inscriptions bear witness. The upkeep of roads and
the construction of new ones was an important governmental
function, which had previously been taken in hand by the
censor ; but this office disappeared with the close of the
Republic. In Italy itself the Emperors appointed special
curators of roads, who had a large staff under them. Soon the
roads seem to have been divided up into sections, so that each
curator got one of the great principal roads under his charge.
In the provinces, it depended on special circumstances as to
whether the governors, the communal authorities, or the
military had to look after the roads. The actual maintenance
was performed by detached posts under the command of
subordinate officers.

The roads of the Roman Empire are the greatest and most
enduring memorial of the activity displayed by the Emperors
in guarding civilisation and the Empire, though they may not
catch the eye so obviously as another sort of constructive work,
the aqueducts. With these structures, only the bridges can
vie in magnificence. To get a correct idea of the amount of

work put into the roads, one must picture to oneself these thousands and thousands of miles of solidly constructed roads, which linked up all the provinces and cities from the Scottish Highlands to Assouan, from the Atlantic to the Syrian desert. It was fully realised that they were a great work. Agrippa exhibited in Rome a map of the imperial road system, to the planning of which he had himself contributed more than any one else. A copy of a later travelling-map, and some extant descriptions of roads provide us with information about their ramifications and chief centres. Local archaeologists have a profitable and comprehensive task in rediscovering the traces of old roads in their neighbourhoods.

Strangely enough contemporaries were more conscious of the importance of the work than later ages. In a speech of the Antonine Age, Aristides describes how one could travel all over the Empire. One need fear neither the Cilician gates nor the sandy roads of Arabia. The Romans, he said, have surveyed the whole world, bridged rivers, cut roads in the sides of mountains. They have opened all gates, and given everybody the opportunity of seeing everything with his own eyes. They have linked together the nations of the world into one great family. Roads were the chief means to this end.

The Roman roads seem to have been built for eternity, and wherever they are still used they have defied the ravages of time. With the decline of the ancient world, cities and civilisation perished, the need of communications diminished, and long journeys ceased. The roads became deserted and fell into decay save in isolated cases where local traffic between some town and its neighbours served to keep a section in repair. Nothing indicates better the extraordinary downfall of civilisation and intercourse than the collapse of the Roman road-system. The roads were covered with earth or were used as quarries, and bridle paths came once more into favour. Later generations looked on these roads as the work of gnomes or giants. The Devil's Causeway or the Maiden Way are names applied to them in England. In Serbia a legend referring to a Roman road, relates that it was made for a princess, so that she might have no need to touch the ground with her feet.

(iv) FOREIGN COUNTRIES

Like every empire that has grown up round a sea, as, for instance, the Baltic Empire of Sweden in the seventeenth century, or the Empire of Athens, the Roman Empire suffered from disproportionate length of frontiers. Only in the west was it rendered secure by the ocean. In the south and to some extent in the east it abutted on the desert. There was no great danger to be feared in the south, though deserts are not quite unpeopled, and the greedy roving desert tribes had to be held back from the civilised country. But in the east there was one great power which was a neighbour to the Roman Empire, namely, Persia, and further north lay Armenia, where Persians and Romans continually competed for domination. Of greatest extent and most dangerous was the northern frontier in Europe, from the mouth of the Rhine to that of the Danube. The two rivers, indeed, formed a natural frontier and provided some degree of protection, but they did not present an insuperable obstacle to attacks and raids. Here the Roman Empire had not an organised State as a neighbour, with whom frontier relations could be settled by agreement, but semi-barbarous tribes, which acted independently. Thus a vigilant watch on the frontiers was absolutely essential.

In the later days of the Empire the frontiers were moved forward over the rivers by the Flavian conquest of the *Agri Decumates* and the valley of the Main, and by Trajan's great conquest of Dacia. Hence the frontier against the Germans became for long distances a land frontier, which required to be well policed and guarded. This gave occasion to the extensive system of the so-called *Limes*, which, especially in Germany, has been the subject of a thorough and illuminating investigation.

A river boundary can be protected by a series of forts along its banks. This was done on the Rhine before the conquests on its right bank, and this method was again resorted to after these had been lost in the middle of the third century.

For a land boundary the primary condition is to delimit

it and provide for its supervision. *Limes* means a narrow
zone of clearing in the forest adjoining the frontier which
increases the opportunities for observation and gives facilities
for the guard-houses along the frontier. From early times it
was provided with wooden " block-houses " provided with
towers from which a distant view could be obtained, and in
which the guard could find shelter when on duty. Later on
the towers were rebuilt in stone. Strange as it may seem, the
frontier in Germany was once for long stretches protected by
railings or hurdles. In Hadrian's time stout palisades were
erected, from which circumstance a boundary fence is still
called in German dialect, *der Pfahl*. A palisade is a somewhat
stronger protection than a hedge, but it is scarcely a fortification. Its object was not military : it was simply a barrier
which made it possible to watch and regulate the traffic over
the frontier. At intervals the frontier was provided with a
row of forts, which usually housed a *centuria* of infantry apiece.
In certain localities there were more elaborate forts which
held a larger detachment. These troops were the real frontier-
guard, but in the case of a serious raid help had to be sent from
the large legionary camps. Later on, after the time of the
Antonines, the barrier was strengthened and became of real
military importance. Then it consisted of a ditch and rampart
with towers of stone in Germany, and of a wall with towers in
Rhaetia.

Defences of a similar nature are found on all the land
frontiers. The two ramparts in Britain are well preserved.
Hadrian's wall was rebuilt in stone by Septimius Severus. It
has sixteen forts, numerous mile-castles—so-called from being
a mile apart—and towers separated by lesser distances.
Antoninus Pius' rampart was built of turves on a stone foundation with forts and watch-towers, and behind it ran a military
road. The Dacian frontier is not so well known. Two lines,
an earth rampart and a wall, cut off the Northern Dobrudja
near the present line of the railway from Czernavoda to
Constanza. Unfortunately we do not know when the Romans
determined to cut this territory off from their immediate jurisdiction. In Africa we can trace the repeated advancements of

the frontier line to the south under the Empire. The defensive arrangements are insufficiently known, but must have consisted here, as elsewhere, of a wall with towers. Even the frontier towards the Syrian desert was defended by forts and watch-towers, connected by a military road. Later on we hear of an outer and an inner frontier. The inner was the sphere immediately under Roman government ; the outer was steppe-land merging into the desert, occupied by tribes under Roman control and protection.

The Roman Empire was thus closed against the outside world, if not by an absolute Wall of China, yet, particularly later on under the Empire, by a scheme of defences strongly suggestive of it. The closing of the frontier was most effective on the Rhine, where the Romans borrowed the German method of protecting the frontier by leaving in front of it a zone of devastated territory. This is psychologically explicable by the severe defeats the Romans incurred in fighting the adjacent German tribes, the remembrance of which was never forgotten. As a matter of course, no aliens were permitted to cross the frontier with arms in their hands and the usual customs were levied. The frontier stood not merely for a sharp division of civilisation, but as a positive obstacle to traffic. This is proved by archaeological discoveries. Imperial coins of early date are found in independent Germany only where the Roman army passed. At the end of the first, and still more in the second, century they are more numerous ; but the distribution of the finds shows that they did not pass over the frontier, but followed the trade-routes. One of these went along the coast of the North Sea and up the Weser and Elbe or northwards to Jutland. In North German finds we come across a sort of bronze bucket manufactured in Belgica, probably at Aachen, along with *terra sigillata* from the Rhine factories, and glass from the great factories at Cologne. These must have been imported from the Roman province, but the distribution of the finds shows that they were not brought in by the nearest route over the frontier, but by sea and up the rivers. The coast of the North Sea was therefore an important link in the communications, and the tribes living there, the Batavi and Frisii,

Q

had been long under the Roman sway. There were Roman merchants in those countries ; for the Batavians began their rising in A.D. 70 with a massacre of the pioneers of Roman trade.

Trade was the forerunner of Roman culture among the Germans. Its influence was so great that a period of the Iron Age in the North is called the Roman Iron Age (A.D. 100–400). Finds of the products of Roman industry are not infrequent in Sweden, consisting of bronze vessels, cut glass and even statuettes. As an example of the wide circulation of Roman factory products, goods made by the Italian manufacturer, P. Cipius Polybius, may be cited. In Italy many bronze vases with his trade-mark have been found, nine in Pompeii, six in Denmark, and several in countries ranging from Scotland to Hungary. Again, the manufacturer, Ansius Epaphroditus, is represented by finds in Italy, Central Europe, Denmark, and even Halsingland in Sweden, more than 150 miles north of Stockholm. The numerous imperial coins of a still later date found in Sweden bear witness to trade relations with the Roman Empire, and the locality of the finds shows plainly by which route they arrived. Of 6400 examples, 4200 occur in Gothland ; 850 on the other two great islands of the Baltic, Öland and Bornholm ; 650 in the southernmost province of Sweden, Scania ; in the rest of Sweden only 100 ; in Denmark 600. Gothland was already the great centre of Baltic trade, and from it the chief route was to the mouth of the Vistula. In this direction the Goths migrated and descended into the region of the Black Sea ; while during the third and fourth centuries a stream of culture, and perhaps a stream of people also, took the same road in the opposite direction northwards.

In the first century of the Empire, another route, also ending at the mouth of the Vistula, was most important for the spread of Roman civilisation and Roman goods among the Germans. This was the old amber-route along the Vistula, Elbe, and through the Eastern Alps down to the Adriatic at Aquileia, along which we read that a Roman knight, during the reign of Nero, travelled from Carnuntum on the Danube. Everywhere this route is marked by finds, in East Prussia,

Posen, and Silesia. Thus the facilities for commerce between the Germans and the Roman Empire were more numerous and easy in these parts. Tacitus states that the Hermunduri were not, like other tribes, merely permitted to trade on the bank of the Danube which here formed the frontier, but also to enter Rhaetia and even its capital, Augsburg, without any supervision or interference. The kingdom of Maroboduus in Bohemia had established trade connections with the Romans ; for we know that when the capital was surprised by the Goths in A.D. 19, Roman merchants and sutlers were settled there. A considerable import trade existed with Noricum, celebrated for its metal industry, and also with Italy. Thus developed a native industry, in which Roman, Celtic, and German elements were mixed. Its products were distributed over independent Germany and stimulated further development elsewhere.

The closing of the frontier produced, or at least hastened, a profound internal change among the Germans. The first description of them in Caesar shows them pressing westwards as a still semi-nomadic people, who subsisted by hunting, on the milk of their herds, cheese and flesh. Agriculture meant little to them. They had no property in land, but from year to year moved on to new places, and the land which was cultivated was divided every year among the families. The tribes lived in mutual hostility, and purposely surrounded themselves with waste land as the best protection against their enemies. In important campaigns they obeyed a leader to whom each individual warrior was bound by an oath of fidelity.

The West Germans were divided from the East Germans by the uninhabitable tract between the Erzgebirge and the Lower Oder, which was mountainous and covered with forests and morasses, and lay between them and the Roman frontier. The population continued to increase ; but as they had no outlet, the frontier being closed, the West Germans had, perforce, to utilise more intensively the native resources of the country. The result can be read in the description of Tacitus, written a century and a half later. By then the Germans had fixed dwelling-places, and agriculture was of more importance, for it had to supply a far greater part of the food required. Julian, two and a half centuries later, in his campaign against the Alamannians, found country houses built in the Roman fashion, was able to provision his army from the German cornfields, and compelled them to supply timber and iron for the rebuilding of frontier fortresses.

GERMANY

At this point, researches into the early conditions of life in Germany add to our knowledge. We find that the tribe was built up out of families, which were closely bound together by the obligatory blood-feud and common labour. Villages were tribal villages, and each family and village had land of its own. Part of this was common land, used for common pasturage, and supplied timber and firewood for all. The arable land was also family property, in which each member had a right to a share, but not to any particular piece as his own property. According to Tacitus the arable land was shifted annually. Out of this primitive arrangement came the so-called *Haufendörfer*, which are characteristic of the districts inhabited by Germanic tribes from immemorial ages. The houses were built in a group, but were detached, each being surrounded by a garden plot. The arable land was divided into *Gewanne* in which each peasant had an equal share. The law of property has altered, but it is still possible to trace how each head of a household retained an interest in the common property of the village.

The East Germans had more elbow-room, and more political cohesion ; for their occupation of foreign soil forced them to adopt a more centralised form of organisation. They were therefore generally governed by a king. They were more exposed to Roman influences and came earlier and more widely in contact with them. Though their civilisation was therefore more advanced than that of the West Germans, who remained on their lands, their national vigour was not, for that very reason, so great. The East Germans were the tribes that undertook the great migrations during the transition period of the Middle Ages, and founded German kingdoms in the provinces of the Roman Empire. But here the ruling German caste was small and was soon swallowed up by the native population, and so the kingdoms disappeared in Italy, Spain, and Africa. From among the West German tribes were evolved the permanent kingdoms on Roman territory, the Frankish and later the German, for it was always possible for them to obtain reinforcements from their Germanic homeland, with which they never lost touch.

It was, indeed, this lack of organisation that gave to the Germans their greatest protection against the Romans and the Roman civilisation, which otherwise might have paved the way to a complete Roman Conquest. There never arose any centralised power among them, against which a decisive blow could be dealt, as was the case in Dacia, where, after various attempts at the formation of a kingdom, the overlordship of Decebalus provoked and made possible the Roman Conquest. Every combination was accidental—such as Maroboduus' kingdom in Bohemia, and the league under the headship of the Cheruscan prince Arminius, which, in the Teutoburg forest, drove the Romans out of the Germanic homeland. Arminius himself was killed in a family feud by his own people, who thought he wanted to make himself king, that is, to create a German State with a more centralised organisation. It was Tacitus who expressed the hope that the internecine conflicts of the Germans might keep them in check and save the Romans. He overestimated the importance of internal conflicts. Their divisions were more than outweighed by the growth in national strength. When there were no outlets, internal feuds occurred sometimes, as it were, by accident, but the pressure, nevertheless, was all the time becoming greater upon the closed frontier. Rome's policy of closing the frontier may be compared to closing the safety valves of a steam-engine. If there is no outlet the pressure of the pent-up steam increases, until there is an explosion.

PERSIA

In the East, Rome was flanked by the only great organised state, and, one must add, the only truly civilised state, which faced it in the world, Persia. The generally accepted opinion is that the Persian Empire was the Oriental, despotically governed world monarchy, which was repelled by the Greeks and crushed by Alexander ; but this conception does not do justice to Persia. It is true that it received a deep impress from Babylonian civilisation, but it had also contributed something new to the Oriental world—a respect for law and humanity—for the Persia of the Achaemenids was a state governed by law and not a despotism, and possessed a religion and a code of morals hallowed by religion, which had the deepest influence. Persia left its mark both on Judaism and Christianity, not to speak of pagan and half-Christian sects like Mithraism and Manicheism.

After a few generations Persia, under the leadership of the princely family of the Arsacidae, who belonged to the Parthian tribe on the northern bounds of the country, freed itself from Greek supremacy. This Parthian, or Arsacid, kingdom comprised, besides Persia, the homelands of Babylonian civilisation, Mesopotamia and Babylonia. Its capital was Ktesiphon on the Tigris, the successor of Seleucia and Babylon. As the outcome of their conquest of Syria the Romans became neighbours of the Parthians. The result of their first contact —the great defeat of Crassus at Carrhae by the Parthian cavalry—was not promising, and Antonius' campaign a little later, in spite of a brilliant display of generalship, ended in a strategic defeat which undermined his position. But the Parthian kingdom was a feudal state loosely knit together. By taking advantage of the domestic feuds in the royal family, Augustus succeeded in wiping out the disgrace of this defeat by inducing Phraates IV. to restore the captured standards and prisoners. At the end of his life, he could even send the Parthians a king, Vonones, the son of Phraates, who had lived as a hostage in Rome. The bone of contention was Armenia, where Roman and Parthian interests clashed. The greatest successes were won by Trajan, who, at the close of his life, incorporated Mesopotamia and Babylonia in the Empire. His successor, Hadrian, however, immediately gave up the newly acquired provinces, being convinced that in the long run it would be impossible to defend them. Septimius Severus, reconquered the northern part and constituted it a Roman province.

Soon afterwards (A.D. 226) there ensued a fateful revolution. The Arsacids were succeeded by the princely family of the Sassanids, and the neo-Persian Empire replaced the Parthian. A similar cycle of events occurred as when the Median Empire gave place to the Persian. The controlling power was forcibly removed from the northern tribes of Iran and seized by the southern Persian stock and its princely house, accompanied by a consolidation of the Empire and a great accession of strength. There is nothing which expresses more forcibly the newly awakened might of Persia than the rock-relief, on which is depicted the captive Roman Emperor, Valerian, coming as a suppliant and asking pardon from Sapor I., the King of Kings. This event created an unparalleled sensation. It impressed on the minds of all that the Persian and Roman Empires were on an equal footing—a thing undreamed of in the days of the Parthians.

In the Parthian Empire a good deal of Greek influence had remained. The kings called themselves philhellenes, and coins were struck with Greek inscriptions. When Crassus' head was brought to the King, he was just witnessing a performance of Greek actors, and one of them put the head on a spear, and sang an aria from the *Bacchae* of Euripides : " From the mountains we bring it, the spoil of our hunting." But the Sassanids based their strength on the fact that they were at once supported by, and were also consciously furthering, a national movement and national unity. Their coins always bear on one side a smoking altar, the appropriate symbol of their Empire. It was significant that the doctrines of Zarathustra, which had been put in the background by the Parthians, were restored and a sort of State Church organised, typifying fresh Persian impulses with far-reaching consequences. For here we have the first State Church, the first union between two independent powers, the throne and the altar.

The Persian king reigned by virtue of the favour of the Most High, Ahura Mazda, which hovered over the head of the lawful king like a halo, *hvarêno*, but departed from the usurper. It was a limitation of the King's omnipotence, which did not rest on written ordinances, but on the moral and religious conception of royalty. It was the most sacred duty of the king to maintain justice and religion. By the favour of the Most High, which overshadowed his head, he was raised above other mortals. He attained a position which made it possible for a vigorous ruler to make his will prevail even over the great feudal lords, whose selfish interests had brought the Parthian Empire to ruin. The nobility were brought to court, and made to do court service in a manner that reminds us of the age of Louis XIV. Ranks and titles were defined with exactitude, and scheduled in a kind of state calendar. The rank of the highest magnates was fixed by the number of ells which divided them from the king at high ceremonies. Only on these occasions did the king appear, in the full splendour of robes embroidered with gold and pearls, and with a richly jewelled tiara upon his head ; usually he was inaccessible, and some-times gave audiences concealed by a curtain. Those who approached him had to tie a cloth over their mouths in order not to pollute him with their breath, as was the case when they approached the sacred fire.

A vigorous monarchy was needed to rally the forces of a country cut up into feudal demesnes, and with it came into existence a strong centralised and bureaucratic despotism. This was the method employed to bridle feudalism—the anti-thesis of real despotism. The king's representative was the Grand Vizier, an office known to us from the Mohammedan world, but originally a Persian institution. Beneath him in rank were four dignitaries representing the four classes of society, forming a kind of ministry—the chief-priest, the commander-in-chief, the chancellor and a representative of the working classes. To them were added other high officials, such as the director of taxes, another priestly dignitary of doubtful functions, a host of lesser officials, provincial governors, generals, etc. The administration was divided among offices (*divans*) in which the course of affairs was regulated with the greatest precision. We know with certainty

of a secret chancery, a chancery for correspondence, one
for criminal jurisdiction, one for honourable appointments
and patronage, one for finance. The Persians were great
formalists, and the royal edicts were drawn up in the artificial
language of the official style before their final publication, after
they had been carefully revised. High offices were as a rule
reserved for the nobility, among whom seven great families
took the highest place ; one of these seven was that from
which the king was selected, though there was no regulated
succession. Thus feudalism was compensated for the loss of
its independence, which, in the last days of the Empire, led to
a fresh break up.

There was a clear distinction between the classes, which
could not be surmounted without special royal favour. The
four distinct classes were the clergy, the warriors, the bureaucracy and the workers, and in these classes there were sub-
divisions. At the beginning of the period of the Sassanids,
we hear of princes of the blood, the chief nobles, the principal
State officials and the inferior nobility. Those who followed
trades and special callings enjoyed little respect, and the
peasants seem to have been bound to the soil. In war they
had to follow on foot without pay, and cut a wretched figure
as soldiers.

The real strength of the kingdom was vested in the numerous
petty landed nobility, who, in time of peace, lived on their
estates and superintended the work on the land, and in time
of war supplied those mobile mounted archers and mail-clad
cavalry, whose irresistible attack overthrew so many Roman
armies. Certain of these petty nobles dealt with local administration and taxation. In contrast to the great nobles, the
lesser nobility was always faithful to the king, and as soldiers
and administrators formed the solid basis of the Sassanids'
power. Taxes consisted partly of a poll-tax, the amount of
which was fixed once for all, partly of tithes of the produce of
the land, which, after the total amount of the harvest had
been estimated, was paid on a sliding scale basis, varying from
a seventh to a third in different districts, according to the
fertility of the soil. In the seventh century the greatest of

the Sassanids, Chosroes I., when he drew up a land register,
altered and revised the system of taxation. A certain tax
in money was laid on cultivated land according to the way in
which it was sown and planted, and the poll-tax was graduated
according to property qualifications.

The priesthood consisted of a well-developed hierarchy.
At the head was the Priest of Priests, a Zarathustrian Pope.
In each village was a fire-temple with at least two priests,
and in provincial capitals there was a larger temple served by
a numerous priesthood. Religion influenced every branch of
life. The priests blessed and gave religious sanction to marriage
and the birth of children. They prescribed and took part in
sacrifices and purifications : in connection with the ritual
which distinguished restored Mazdaism, purifications were
constantly needed. But Zarathustra's doctrine was not
merely a ritual but also a severe and strict moral code. It
was the task of the priests to teach this moral code and the
duty of the people to obey it. The Mazdaic theology was
developed and studied. One of the first works of the Sassanids
was to collect the sacred books, and from that collection what
is still extant of Mazdaism has its origin. There were schools
in which priests were educated and instructed in the doctrine
of Zarathustra, and theological preceptors, who were consulted
on religious matters and disputed with Christians and other
unbelievers. Zeal for the true religion was succeeded by
fanaticism. The Christian heretics had to undergo many
persecutions, and the founder of Manicheism was crucified.
The administration of justice was closely connected with
religion ; the judges belonged to the priestly caste. As in
Mohammedan countries, God's law was also man's law. Legal
procedure was fully developed ; law and justice were maintained and respected ; but punishments were cruel and torture
universal.

The Church received tithes and gifts, and had extensive
possessions, so that it was economically independent and
practically formed a State within the State. Unfortunately
history has preserved no information about the Mazdaic pre-
lates, but it is not improbable that the chief-priest, who was

one of the great dignitaries of the Empire and played the chief part in the elections to the throne, tended to exercise the privileges of his position to an ever-increasing degree. There are numerous traces of conflicts between king and priesthood. For the king could assert that he, who ruled by the special favour of the Most High, was also Supreme Head of the Church. The combination of Caesar and Pope, also, has its roots in Persia.

In the religion of the Persians their national self-consciousness found its expression. The restored doctrine of Zarathustra was the ideal force that kept the nation together, and the Mazdaic Church was the instrument employed. The influences of religious ritual and bureaucratic organisation, even in their decadence, were so powerful that they were able to transform the victorious Mohammedan religion and state. The fanatical and mystical Shiah is the spiritual offshoot of Mazdaism, and the administration of the Caliphate is a legacy of the Sassanid State—probably also that of the Tartars—and thus Persia has sent a branch into the Russian Empire. Not without justification it has been said that the Caliphate of Bagdad was a continuation of the Sassanid Empire.

Socially the Persian State was founded upon class privilege, and the aristocracy, proud of its pure Aryan blood, was supreme. This aristocracy was haughty, imperious, high-spirited and often did not shrink from acts of violence ; but it possessed a strong sense of justice and—what is a specially aristocratic virtue—chivalry, a virtue of which Roman history and the Romans are devoid. Chivalry had already characterised the Achaemenids—how many persecuted Greeks found a refuge and an honourable reception with the hereditary foe from the days of Themistocles !—and equally it was a characteristic of the Persians under the Sassanids. With all their defects and their merits the Persian aristocracy was the flower of the nation and the backbone of the country. The reason of the decay into which Persia fell after the Mohammedan conquest, was the democratisation introduced by Islam, in which the Persian nobility perished.

Striking resemblances may be found between the Sassanid

and the later Roman Empire, with its continuation, the Byzantine Empire, resemblances which will, later, be made the object of a special study. They are to be found not merely in details, like the transformation of the cavalry into a great and independent branch of the army, the introduction of mailed cavalry, the imitation of Persian court-ceremonial and the Persian dress of state, but also in the leading ideas of the age. The Roman Emperor, too, became a despot, set apart, by God's grace, from his subjects. The Roman Empire became a class-State, and in its latest period feudalism raised its head. Bureaucracy and a State church became the final means of welding the Empire together.

It was not only a converging process on both sides, nor was the Greco-Roman world the giver only, as was at one time supposed; indeed, in the religious sphere the Persian influence on the Empire is as clear as daylight. In spite of superficial differences, Persia and the Hellenistic-Roman world since the days of Alexander were on the same cultural plane. The expansion of Hellenism over the East was promptly followed by the counterstroke—the expansion of Orientalism in the Greco-Roman world ; and after the unabated national vigour of the Persians and the powerful religious forces of Mazdaism in the Sassanid kingdom had been welded into a harmonious unity, this worked powerfully on the neighbouring Empire, already subject to Oriental influence and in a ferment of internal changes. The threads cross and re-cross. In social and cultural development the resemblance between the two States became ever greater ; the political and national contrasts —one may speak of a national contrast, because Persia was a national State—were embodied in the religious sphere ; here Christ, there Ahura Mazda.

ARABIA

In comparison with Persia, the other states with which the Roman Empire came into contact, have but little importance ; moreover, they were too distant to have any real influence. South-Western Arabia—the Yemen—was called Arabia Felix.

There a vigorous trade flourished ; from it came the frankincense, so highly esteemed by the ancient world. Here the Sabaeans or Himyarites had founded a kingdom, to whose advanced civilisation the native inscriptions and imposing ruins of fortresses and water systems bear witness. Their coinage shows connections with the ancient Empire ; the Sabaeans imitating the coin most current, first the Attic, then Alexander's and finally Augustus', but they provided it with inscriptions in their own alphabet.

Intercourse with Africa across the narrow strait of Bab-el-Mandeb was frequent. Trade went by way of the port Adulis to the kingdom of Axum (Abyssinia), the population of which had a strong infusion of Semitic blood. Even here Greek influences are to be traced. An inscription, from which we learn the extent of the power of Axum, which even controlled parts of Southern Arabia, is drawn up in the language of the country, in Sabaean characters, and in Greek. This connection was long maintained. In the fourth century Christianity was introduced and has lasted to the present day.

At the beginning of his reign Augustus sent an expedition to conquer Arabia Felix. The report of its fabulous wealth was alluring to the Romans, and in their ignorance of geography they under-estimated the difficulties. Owing to disease and lack of water the army had to return before it had reached the frontier of the Sabaean kingdom. From these districts there proceeded a great national movement, which has directed the history of the world into new paths. Here, too, Rome stretched out her hand, but in vain. No one knows what would have happened had Rome fastened her chains upon Western Arabia, an achievement which might have been accomplished by a fleet on the Red Sea. In that case Mohammedanism would not have become what it was and is. An expedition undertaken shortly afterwards against Ethiopia was of purely local significance. It was only a question of giving a lesson to the Nubians, who had invaded Egypt at a time when it was denuded of troops. The capital, Napata, was taken and plundered and the southern frontier secured.

THE FAR EAST

In the great account of his life and deeds Augustus mentions that he often received embassies from Indian kings, who had never before appeared in Rome. Probably he cultivated relations with India as a set-off against the Parthians, and to further a commercial policy : for we know that an ever-increasing trade was conducted with India. The Punjab had formed part of Alexander's Empire, and Greek cultural influences had won a footing in India. In the third century B.C. the great King Asoka, a zealous Buddhist, who sent embassies to the Hellenistic courts, was on the throne. To his time we ascribe the period of the so-called Gandhara art, which is related to Greek art. Later, Indian art seems to have been influenced by the Roman, but it rapidly coarsened and deteriorated and finally lost contact with the ancient world.

On the west coast of India and in Ceylon, Roman coins, brought there by trade, have frequently been found. After the conquest of Egypt by the Romans this trade began to develop greatly. The route was, as stated above, to the port of Berenice or Myos Hormos on the west coast of the Red Sea, and thence through the desert to the Nile. The geographer, Strabo, writes in the time of Augustus, that while under the Ptolemies scarcely twenty ships a year ventured beyond the Red Sea, now 120 merchant ships ply every year to India from Myos Hormos alone. In the pursuit of a selfish commercial policy the Romans seem to have monopolised for themselves the traffic to Arabia and India ; one never hears of any foreign merchants and vessels in their harbours. The traffic to India received a fresh impetus in the time of Nero, when an Egyptian captain, Hippalos, discovered a more direct route over the open sea by availing himself of the south-west monsoon. It then became possible to travel to and from India in little more than six months.

On one occasion only do we hear that a bold merchant ventured beyond Ceylon. Chinese annals have preserved the account of an embassy from the Emperor Marcus Antoninus, which went by sea by way of Tonkin to the Chinese Emperor

Huan-ti, who resided in Lo-yang on the Middle Hoang-ho. Probably, as often happened, a merchant acted as an envoy. The Chinese were called the Seres, the silk-people ; for silk was the chief and most costly product obtained by the ancient world from China. The trade-route went sometimes *via* India, but usually by the land road through Persia. The trade was thus controlled by the Persians, who got great gain thereby, and the Persian Empire was the barrier which prevented any considerable exchange of culture between the ancient world and the further East.

Yet the old impulses, which India received in the Hellenistic Age, continued to operate. The last offshoots of the influence of Greek on Buddhist art are found in the newly discovered wall-paintings in the deserts of Eastern Turkestan. From here the current flowed still further east and invigorated the art of Japan and China. Ancient astrology found eager devotees in India and in China, where the emperors, down to our own day, could not undertake any important action without consulting the court astrologers.

Of the close connection between the ancient world and the distant East the best witness is the remarkable expansion of Christianity eastwards across the Persian Empire. The East Syrian Nestorian Church, which in the Christological controversies of the fifth century was divorced from the rest of the Church, carried out a great missionary crusade in the end of the ancient world and beginning of the Middle Ages. Thanks to the schism with the Church of the Empire, it was generally tolerated in Persia. It won many supporters in India, the so-called Christians of St. Thomas—legends relate that the Apostle Thomas preached Christ to the Indians—it built monasteries in East Turkestan ; it played an important part in China, as we gather from an inscription of A.D. 781 from Si-ngan-fu in Syriac and Chinese characters. Of the Nestorian Church, which once covered all Asia, there are now only a few scattered survivals in Northern Persia and in India.

Manicheism, which once was a dangerous rival of Christianity and Mazdaism, and flourished in Asia as a rival to Nestorianism, has disappeared. It inspired the Persian miniature painters. Some remnants of its sacred books, destroyed by its opponents in the West, have reappeared among the finds of East Turkestan. East Turkestan was at this time not merely the country through which trade passed between China and the West, but was, also, the focal point where peoples and streams of civilisation from the West, India and China met and crossed each other. Its ruined cities, covered for centuries by the desert sands, have preserved memorials of Greco-Buddhistic art, Nestorian and Manichean buildings, and cart-loads of manuscripts in all languages, spoken and written in Asia, known and unknown. From the eighth century the flourishing cities of East Turkestan seem to have been abandoned and engulfed by the drifting sands of the desert. A change for the worse in the climate must have occurred with a consequent drought, and this contributed greatly to the interruption of communications between the West and the Far East. For the investigation of civilisation East Turkestan is an important area, from which many surprising and novel discoveries may still be made. The material has been for the most part collected, but it will be long before it has been fully investigated and utilised.

II

ROME AND THE PROVINCES

Tu regere imperio populos, Romane, memento! These words
put by Vergil in the mouth of Anchises, when, in the under-
world, he dilates on the long line of Rome's great men, express
the proud feeling which, at the beginning of the Empire, filled
the heart of the Roman citizen, particularly if he was of Italian
descent and could boast of his connection with the great
traditions of Rome. Then, indeed, Roman citizenship was a
magic formula before which princes and subjects bowed the
knee. We can realise its value to some extent from incidents
in the life of St. Paul. Its actual value was soon destined to
be lessened as the privilege of citizenship was extended to
peoples who had had no share in building up the power of
Rome. The very foundation of the Empire removed the
Roman citizen from the pedestal on which he had been raised
above the subject peoples, though this consequence was not
immediately noticed. After that, it was no longer the Roman
citizen, but the Emperor, who was lord of the Empire. Both
citizens and provincials were the subjects of the Emperor,
though the citizen was on a higher plane than the provincial.
Previously the Roman citizens were the rulers, the provincials
the ruled—the subjects; but now both were equally subjects
of the Emperor. This is the beginning of that levelling process,
the equalising of their varying legal statuses, which the inhabitants of the Empire underwent. The process was continually
speeded up, as the Empire grew older. Equalisation was the
chief characteristic of the Empire.

As a matter of fact, the city of Rome occupied a preferential
position, not merely as compared with the provinces, but also in

Italy itself. The mistress of the world was not to be dethroned easily, although it was no longer her citizens, but the Emperor, who ruled the destinies of the world. Her position as the capital city of the world was a proud one, although a step lower than that of mistress of the world. Rome was the Emperor's city and the seat of government, and that, together with her ancient traditions, was sufficient to invest the city with a kind of glamour, which has not yet totally disappeared, and enabled her to become in the Middle Ages the capital of Christendom.

The popular Assembly had ceased to function : without regret it, and its sovereignty, had sunk into oblivion. But the power and influence of the inhabitants of Rome were not, on that account, at an end. Rome had about a million inhabitants, and how much a capital of that size, which is also the centre of intellectual life, means to a country, the history of later ages affords striking examples. It is the capital which makes revolutions, and gives a lead to the hesitating or indifferent country. The intrinsically dominant position of Rome as the capital was strengthened by her historical traditions.

The Emperor did not shrink from the exercise of his authority to ensure order in the city. In the time of Augustus only three of the nine praetorian cohorts were in Rome, the others being stationed at various places in Italy ; it was Sejanus who united them all in a camp outside Rome. To them were added three cohorts of the city watch (*vigiles*) ; and even the fire-brigade, seven cohorts strong, was organised on a military basis and was reckoned as forming a part of the army. The employment of force is a mistake in dealing with the excitable and pampered population of a capital ; moreover the Roman populace was, to a large extent, without occupation and all the more difficult to manage. It had to be kept in a good temper, and the imperial policy of placation was comprised in the famous phrase, *panis et circenses*—bread and circus-games—both of which were supplied to the population of Rome at the public expense. The most obvious expression of Rome's preferential position was that she existed and amused herself at the expense of the Empire. These advantages have been represented as a compensation for the loss of universal suffrage, and there is some truth in that view. When public opinion could no longer express itself in the popular assembly, it made itself vocal in the theatre and the circus. Here the audiences must have afforded an excellent field for the study of mass-psychology. In the mass the individual disappeared and found a convenient shelter for the expression of his discontents, which in other circumstances would have infallibly brought him to ruin. From the purely physical standpoint this thousand-headed multitude was an alarming and imposing spectacle, flourishing its handkerchiefs and crying out as boisterously and violently as the sea lashed by a hurricane. Everybody could be influenced by the power of suggestion, and a single thought could be so deeply impressed on the masses that, on some occasions, they would repeat a phrase in unison, rhythmically, and to some definite tune. This gigantic chorus must have daunted the strongest will.

CIRCUS GAMES

The Emperors were able to gauge their popularity in the circus and theatre, where the demonstrations were usually loyal in character—but they could also gauge the measure of their unpopularity and that of their favourites. Whatever impulse excited the Roman people could be vented in the circus—questions relating to war and peace, the pressure of taxation and legal enactments, the popularity of poets, society scandals, gratitude to generous and popular Emperors, scorn, opprobrium and curses against the unpopular and their favourites. The expression of opinion in the circus could be regarded as an omen which boded the fall of the world-ruler. As rulers the Emperors often found it advisable to submit to the desires of the multitude even if these directly conflicted with their own. Thus Commodus' all-powerful favourite, Cleander, was overthrown after a prearranged and organised demonstration in the circus. Rarely indeed did the Emperor venture to oppose the multitude : only Caligula, just before his death, dared to arrest and punish the worst brawlers, after the mob in the circus had made a demonstration against the increased taxation. Sometimes an Emperor endeavoured to create a hostile feeling against individuals by introducing his agents among the audience.

Usually these expressions of opinion concerned matters of trifling importance connected with the games, such as a demand for the liberation of favourite actors or popular gladiators and condemned criminals who had fought bravely against the wild beasts. At the gladiatorial games the spectators could exercise the old privilege of indicating whether a beaten gladiator should be spared or receive the *coup-de-grâce*. A mob is cruel, and the sanguinary gladiatorial games, the power of life and death over the vanquished, excited their bloodthirsty instincts. On the other hand it was an interesting phenomenon that public opinion, deprived of its natural rights of expression, found a substitute in the old established right of demonstration by the circus-crowd.

Under Augustus there lived a very famous pantomimus and dancer, Pylades. A rival arose in the person of his pupil, Hylas, and the people took sides vehemently in the rivalry between them. When Augustus expressed his displeasure at this, Pylades replied : " You are ungrateful, Caesar ; it is to your advantage that the people should occupy themselves with us." He hit the nail on the head. Men have a certain instinct for grouping themselves into parties, and a liking for the excitement and stimulus of agitations and party strife. When the formation of the Empire brought the disputes of political parties to a close, party spirit transferred itself, instead, to the pursuits dearest to the people—the theatre and the circus. The charioteers, who competed in races in the circus, were even more popular than modern jockeys of European reputation, and amassed greater wealth than their modern counterparts. In competitions they were retained by and wore the colours of the various racing stables, or rather, companies, for companies with large capital had taken over the purchase and running of horses, owing to the heavy outlay required for racing. As usual the interests of the capitalist were blended with those of party. The oldest colours were the whites and the reds, to which at the beginning of the Empire, the greens and blues were added. Everybody was a partisan of one or other of the factions, and followed its victories and defeats with intense excitement. It was a more universal passion than is horse-racing in our time. The philosopher Marcus Aurelius actually felt it incumbent on him to thank his teacher for having saved him from slavery to the parties in the circus. Many Emperors openly took sides for one or another colour, and, what was still worse, sought by the means which were always at the disposal of the imperial power, to suppress the opposite party. Here was a door through which politics crept in. One could side with or against the Emperor's colour, and so either with or against the Emperor. This peculiar connection of the turf with politics only came into full prominence after the great conflict between paganism and Christianity had been finally decided in Constantinople, where it led to sanguinary conflicts, nominally over some race-horse or other, really over the imperial succession. The feuds of the circus-parties outweighed in importance all other matters and defied Christianity. They were an artificial and unhealthy substitute, in which political passions glowed like the underground fires in a coalpit ; they obscured realities and excited party passions.

Both games and distributions of free corn were an inheritance from the Republic. Provision of games was the method by which the entrant on an official career sought for popularity and the popular vote. The great expenses they entailed were defrayed later by the provinces, when the successful official had obtained a provincial governorship, as praetor or proconsul. During the Republic it was the aediles who gave games : Augustus transferred the burden to the praetors. The Emperor himself, however, was the greatest benefactor. Augustus staged eight gladiatorial combats, in which 10,000 men fought in the arena: twenty-six wild-beast shows, in which 3500 African animals were slaughtered : three athletic exhibitions, and twenty-seven other games. These were the extraordinary entertainments he gave in his own name or in that of others. It was by reason of the profusion and splendour of his games that Nero was so popular with the mob, and that several disturbers of the peace after his death took his name in order to win popular favour. The chief performances were those with which the first pair of consuls of the year celebrated their entry upon office. The organisation of games eventually became the only function of the old Senatorial officials—a sort of impost laid upon the wealthiest individuals.

FREE CORN

The distribution of bread in Rome is a striking example of what regulation of the provision market, in the first instance a useful and necessary precaution, may lead to, when it is pressed into the service of party politics. The Greek trading and industrial cities, which could not feed their population, were obliged to devote considerable forethought to the purchase of corn and the regulation of its price. The still undeveloped international trade could not, with present-day infallibility, supply the deficit in one place by transporting thither the surplus of another. These circumstances rendered the provisioning of the people extremely precarious, and greatly encouraged bold and reckless speculation in the most important articles of food. Translations from ancient authors do not always indicate the resemblance to modern conditions or the existence, then as now, of such things as " ramps " and such a process as the cornering of the wheat market. To prevent this some ancient States, including Rome, enacted severe laws. When Rome became a great city, and Italy's production of corn, thanks to the effects of world-politics, dwindled, Rome was confronted with this problem. She learned what the Greeks had to teach, but she had far greater opportunities than they for arranging conditions in her own interests. Thus, conquered Sicily was forbidden to export its surplus to any other country but Italy. The aediles placed this corn on the market at a price which regulated private trade as well, but only in exceptional cases can this price have been less than the cost-price, and so have involved the treasury in a loss. In time of famine and distress it was natural that the State, in order to avoid too high prices, should make up the differenec out of its own pocket.

This was the state of things when Gaius Gracchus intervened. This man, the greatest party tactician of antiquity, desired to build up a coalition against the Senate, in order to carry the democratic programme which had been the cause of the fall of his less able and more ideally-minded brother, Tiberius. This programme was meant to save the farmers of Italy and to improve the position of the agricultural class. Gaius did not escape the usual fate of the party tactician who fights for an ideal. He only succeeded in pulling down with one hand what he was building up with the other. He did succeed in effecting a cleavage between the owners of liquid capital, the knights, and the owners of capital invested in land, the Senators, but at the price of handing over the provincials, defenceless, to the profiteering of the knights. The age saw nothing remarkable in that; for the provinces were regarded as Rome's lawful prey. The method by which he won over the electoral mob of Rome to his schemes, was by lowering the price of corn to about half the price paid in Sicily, where it was produced. Thus he removed all possibility of a livelihood for the small farmers, with whom his policy aimed at covering Italy. To this we shall return later.

Towards the end of the Republic the extreme step was taken of distributing corn *gratis*, since it was essential to win the votes of the mob by any and every means. Attempts were made, with little success, to limit the number of recipients. They numbered 320,000 in Caesar's time, and cost the treasury an outlay of almost 77,000,000 sesterces annually—bread being, of course, the staple article of food. People liberated their slaves that they might share in the State's generosity, which applied only to free adult male citizens—but enjoyment of civil rights was no condition. The impoverished and idle population of Italy crowded to the place where the most important of the necessities for the support of life was to be obtained *gratis*, and this did not tend to improve the quality of Rome's population and popular assembly. This state of things could not be allowed to continue and Caesar lowered the number of the recipients to 150,000. But it increased again as time went on, and Augustus fixed it at 200,000, at which number it seems to have remained in the future. He realised the ruinous effect of the system on Italian agriculture, and entertained the idea of abolishing the free distribution altogether. But an idea it remained : for there were certain limits even to the power of the Roman Emperor. The existence of the Roman population depended on free corn ; it was out of the question to withdraw from it its only means of subsistence. The applicant for free corn had only to give in his name ; if there was a vacancy in the quota his application was granted, otherwise he was put on the waiting-list. Lists were posted up in public places, and each man received a ticket which entitled him to receive the dole. This obligation of giving in the names had the effect that only the poor who really needed support did so, and received their corn free.

The original political character of the distribution is shown by the fact that only citizens with a vote could participate in it, whereas slaves, women, and children were excluded. It was to further Trajan's policy of increasing the population that he allowed children a share. Thus it was only a minority of the population of Rome which was eligible for free corn, but the State did not escape having to look after the rest. The quantity of corn supplied to Rome by Egypt, Africa, and other provinces considerably exceeded the quantity required for free distribution, although it did not cover all requirements. But these quantities of corn were thrown on the market at a price fixed by the State, a policy which stabilised prices, and made profiteering by speculators at a time of scarcity impossible. The State price was a minimum, and sometimes involved loss : importation was encouraged by privileges granted to shipmasters and corn dealers. This cheap corn was issued from the State granaries on the presentation of tickets— bread-cards we might call them—bought at a fixed price. This regulation of prices also cost the State great sums. Of the extent of the arrangements required for this gigantic business, the extensive portion of Ostia covered by the depôts, in which corn was stored after being unloaded, gives the clearest impression.

It was a vast, wasteful, and costly machine which had to be

kept going, in order to provide Rome's population with corn, as is always the case when the State undertakes the responsibility of feeding the people ; and what was more, it became an important factor in politics. On it depended, as we shall see later, the Emperor's firm hold on the population of Rome. He held the key to the people's larder. Things were made still more convenient in the third century by the distribution of bread ready baked.

The gratuitous provisioning of the population of Rome continued until after the time of Constantine ; and in order that the new capital, Constantinople, should be placed on a level with the old, it was introduced there also. Its cessation was due to the decadence of Rome, the decline in the population, and the disturbances coincident with the period of national migrations. To the finances of the desperately straitened State the distribution of corn was like an ever-running sore, and it completed the ruin of the Italian yeomen, who had formed the core of the Republican State and army. Far-sighted men like Augustus realised its ruinous nature, and the impossibility of abolishing it. But even to Rome's inhabitants free maintenance was a gift of doubtful value. It lured the loafers to the city, and in course of time the working man became incapable of work owing to idleness, and thus the population was demoralised. For the people only asked for bread and games, and when they got them they were content. They sold their political birthright for a mess of pottage, but it must be admitted that a population which lived in idleness on the produce of the labour of the provinces was not fit to exercise political rights.

ADDITIONAL DOLES

Corn was the most important, but not the only article of food. A man required to flavour his bread with salt and to wash it down with a draught of wine ; olive oil satisfied the need for fats. Sometimes on festal occasions he wanted also a taste of roast meat. Even under the Republic there were, on special occasions, distributions of all these articles of food to the inhabitants of Rome. Measures were taken that oil, which in the south is an extremely important article of food, should be at the disposal of the population at a low price. It was good policy among the Greeks and other ancient States sometimes to provide a feast for the citizens at the State's expense. At the great festivals, in which the State sacrificed to the gods, Athens had an opportunity of setting before its citizens a feast of roast meat. The Republic adopted the same policy, though not on so great a scale as democratic Athens, and the Emperors continued it and sometimes gave meals to the Roman people. Under the later Emperors the gifts became a regular institution. Oil was distributed *gratis* from the time of Septimius Severus, and bacon from the time of Aurelian. The latter, we hear, also wanted to distribute wine *gratis*, but his praetorian prefect drily observed that the only thing wanting was for the State to make chickens and geese fly into the mouths of the Romans. However, wine was sold from the imperial cellars at a low price. A free distribution of clothing was occasionally made. Italy south of the Rubicon was charged with the duty of providing Rome with beasts for slaughtering, wine, and building materials. Even after Rome had lost a great deal of her importance, and the Emperors seldom visited her, and then only for short periods, the old tradition was so strong that free distributions steadily increased in frequency.

The Roman poor received not only food, but now and then money also, though they could not reckon upon it as a regular income, and probably considered it a gift of all too rare an occurrence. A precedent for this also dates back to the Republic, when victorious generals and officials sometimes added a gift of money to the free food, and candidates for office tried to win votes in the same way. Caesar was the first to make a disbursement of money on a grand scale, when in 46 B.C. he distributed to 320,000 people 400 sesterces apiece. It is well known how Antony roused the people to fury against Caesar's murderers by reading to them his will, in which he made a present of 300 sesterces to every man in Rome. Octavian discharged the legacy when making his début before the people, though Antonius had confiscated his inheritance. On

five other occasions Augustus made money gifts, one being out
of the booty of the battle of Actium, and another when his
grandsons assumed the robe of manhood (*toga virilis*). The
amount varied from 240 to 400 sesterces, and the recipients
numbered from 200,000 to 320,000 persons—more than those
who got corn free. It has been calculated that during the
century after Caesar's first distribution an average of more
than 8,500,000 sesterces per annum was distributed to the
inhabitants of Rome. Later the sums increased very considerably, owing to the fall in the value of money. The great
esteem in which this distribution was held is shown by a
Roman calendar of A.D. 354 containing a list of all such distributions. In it can be found the names of all the Emperors,
with the exception of a few who had very short reigns in the
troubled times of the third century.

Rome was a veritable land of Cockaigne. If roast sparrows
did not exactly fly into the mouths of the inhabitants, the poor
got their main subsistence for nothing. In modern times the
view has been put forward that man, who has been brought into
this vile world without his own volition, possesses a natural
right to be supplied *gratis* with the essentials of life. Never
has this demand been so near its realisation as in imperial
Rome, and probably will never come so near realisation again.
The only question is, who is to pay the bill, since it is undeniable
that no one prearranges his birth and so all have the same rights.
But the essentials required cannot be obtained without work.
Rome had solved the question by arms. That she lived at the
expense of the provinces was the final and most permanent
result of her conquest of the world by force. But when Rome
was no longer the mistress of the world, but only its capital,
the position was an anachronism. Rome too, in the long run,
had to suffer for it. Her population did not justify its existence
with productive labour. The stern law which says that if
a man will not work, neither shall he eat, can be made inopera-
tive, for a time, by force, but in the long run asserts itself. When
decay and disaster came, Rome had not that strength to resist
which is given by productive labour. When, during the
merciless pressure of the Great Migrations and the distress

caused by them, her privileges wilted away, she soon diminished in size, and at the beginning of the Middle Ages presented a pitiable spectacle of desolation. The catacombs were disused, for there was plenty of space for burying the dead within the city. Wild animals and highwaymen lodged in the ruins of magnificent buildings. The Sibyl's prophecy of the fall of Rome was almost literally fulfilled.

Public Buildings

We are still far from the end of our enumeration of the gifts showered on Rome. There still remains a very important instance, and one which still remains in visible form, namely, the buildings. In this respect the Republic had accomplished very little. In comparison with the splendid and well-planned cities of the Hellenistic kings, Rome, the mistress of the world, presented a shabby appearance. Caesar was the first to set to work on a grand scale, and Augustus could boast that he had inherited a city of brick and left one of marble. He enumerates a number of temples he had built himself, and adds that, in addition, he had restored eighty-two. But here we are only dealing with the buildings which served for the use or enjoyment of the people.

Among utility buildings, first and foremost were the aqueducts. It is significant of the strong hand of the Empire in works of public usefulness that, while the Republic could not boast of more than three aqueducts, Augustus added two, and by A.D. 100 four others had been added. How many aqueducts Rome finally possessed is not known ; when Vitiges besieged Rome the number is given as fourteen. An idea of what gigantic labours were involved in their erection is best obtained, when one views the ruined arches stretching in a long line over the Campagna ; but some figures might also be helpful. The total length of the first nine mentioned above was 267 miles, and in twenty-four hours they supplied over 330,000,000 gallons of water. At the present day four of the ancient aqueducts have been restored, and supply only one-seventh of the quantity of water, and yet Rome is the best-supplied city in the world, where it never occurs to any one to stop a fountain from flowing, even at night. There were almost 110 gallons per inhabitant in the twenty-four hours. This exceptional supply of water in antiquity was due to the predilection of the Romans for baths and fountains and drinking-places. Augustus built 105 fountains and 700 reservoirs. Somewhat later, splendid façades were added of the type of the Fontana di Trevi and others of more recent date. The Septizonium, the remnants of which were pulled down during the Renaissance, was probably something of the kind. The lavish use made of water is best explained by the requirements of the great thermae or bathing-establishments. Private persons received an exactly regulated supply of water on payment, so that the aqueducts furnished the treasury with a considerable income. An extensive staff was required for repairs and maintenance. The general director, *Curator aquarum*, was one of the principal civil servants of the Empire. One of these trusted officials, Frontinus, wrote, in the time of Nerva, a treatise on Rome's aqueducts, which is still extant.

In Rome, the Emperors built for themselves, for public purposes, and for the people. Augustus, Caligula, and Domitian transformed the Palatine into a maze of palaces, the magnificence of which befitted the dignity of the Roman Emperors. It became a show place, which later was not regularly occupied by the Emperors, who, in fact, from the end of the third century scarcely ever resided in Rome. Caesar began the rebuilding of the Forum, and as it was not extensive enough for the motley crowds which thronged this focus of public life, he laid out a new one close by. The earlier Emperors followed his example ; Augustus, Vespasian, Nerva, and Trajan each gave their names to a Forum. It is significant that after them, buildings for such public purposes were no longer erected, though one great exception was Constantine's great basilica. The largest and most magnificent buildings of the later Empire were planned solely for the people's enjoyment, which had not been neglected in the earlier Empire.

Pompey gave Rome its first stone theatre ; before that temporary wooden structures had been put up every time plays were exhibited. Augustus added a new theatre, named after his son-in-law, Marcellus. Caesar and Augustus rebuilt the great race-course (*Circus maximus*) below the Palatine, and many Emperors made additions and embellishments to it. Vespasian built and Titus inaugurated what is still, in spite of all the ravages of time, the most imposing memorial of ancient Rome, the Colosseum, or Flavian Amphitheatre, which is remarkable both for its architectural beauty and for its practical arrangement. It held 40,000–45,000 spectators, but the corridors and staircases are so well designed, that the building could be emptied in a few minutes without confusion. The spectators' seats were approached by 160 entrances. The oval arena is 94 yards in length and 59 in breadth.

During Augustus' reign, 66 days of the year were occupied by games ; and this number was gradually increased. Under Tiberius there were 87, and in the middle of the fourth century 175 days were set apart for them. This was exclusive of great festivals on special occasions. Titus celebrated the opening of the amphitheatre with a festival of 100 days, and Trajan commemorated his victory over the Dacians with one of 123. The games began early in the morning, and lasted till towards evening, so that the Roman's whole day was occupied. But what was he to do when no games were being given ? Then he could spend his day in the thermae, which were far more than an ordinary warm bath. In particular they were places where one could kill time, meet friends, converse and gossip. They were a substitute for the cafés of to-day, and every traveller knows how crowded the great cafés are in the South. Southerners crave society and conversation, and stay at home as little as possible. Things have not altered, in this respect, since the days of antiquity. In the thermae, moreover, they were surrounded by all the luxury which only the Emperor could afford—great halls of state with columns and walls of costly marbles, while numerous statues and famous works of art were erected within the building and in the surrounding gardens. After the bath they had, if they wished, an opportunity of devoting themselves to athletics. In thermae there were usually two or three palaestrae, or exercise-grounds. Nor was opportunity for mental relaxation wanting, if desired. There were lecture rooms and sometimes libraries. The thermae were veritable palaces of physical culture, nor was the craving of the intellect for cultivation neglected there; but they must generally have been used to kill, in comfortable indolence, time which people would or could not apply to useful work. Agrippa, Augustus' coadjutor, was the first to build thermae, and was followed by Nero and Titus. The greatest were those of Caracalla and Diocletian, the mighty ruins of which still remain. The ruins of Caracalla's thermae are impressive from their great size; Diocletian's are better preserved, the great hall being transformed into the church of St. Maria degli Angeli. If the imagination can obliterate later alterations and additions, nowhere can such a profound impression of the pomp and grandeur of imperial Rome be obtained as in her public buildings.

On the other hand, the Roman poor had to put up with very miserable private accommodation in great barracks with narrow frontages and dizzy staircases. The rents were not as moderate as the accommodation. Houses were carelessly run up, so that they often collapsed on the heads of the inmates. Destructive fires frequently devastated the city. The notorious fire in the time of Nero was but the best known of many. As a protection against fire Augustus surrounded his Forum with colossal walls, which still stand. There was a strong fire brigade and water in plenty, but against huge conflagrations they were completely powerless. The luxury of the public buildings compensated in some measure for the terrible squalor of the dwellings in imperial Rome. All that the people really wanted of the miserable little holes, for which they had to pay so dear, was to sleep in them. A glance at the map of ancient Rome is enough to show that public buildings occupied an enormously greater part of the town than in any modern city. When the population shrank into insignificance, the buildings remained and decayed. At the beginning of the Middle Ages Rome was a wilderness of stone, in which the few inhabitants could scarcely pick their way between palaces and houses which were continually collapsing and blocking up the streets.

We have now mentioned the chief privileges which fell to
the lot of the population of Rome. They are the more conspicuous because they have no parallel in our own time, and
this is due to historical circumstances. All our capitals have
developed as centres of kingdoms ; Rome was a city which
conquered the world and enjoyed the profits thereof.

POLITICS AND FINANCE

A capital is usually called the heart and brain of the
country. It is the centre of intellectual life, and from it
radiate sentiments, opinions and fashions over the countryside.
It unites all the threads of official and of private life, of politics
and administration, of finance and of economics. Politics
and finance can never be entirely divorced from each other.
Politics have to be financed, and finance must inevitably
influence politics in a manner which is most favourable to
its own ends. Both enter into a genuine alliance, which
may have its quarrels but is never in danger of complete
rupture, because the parties require each other's mutual
assistance. Outwardly the politician is the master of the house,
who desires to pose as sovereign and supreme, but, as in some
other marriages, the real facts of the case do not correspond to
the outward and visible signs, and in the secret councils of the
family it is often the other partner that decides the matter at
issue. But when suing for the suffrages of the electors it is
not good policy to ask them bluntly to give their votes to one
or other of the financial groups. It is then that the political
catchwords are bandied about.

Hence we realise that the world still makes use of very
much the same methods as the Roman Republic. But whereas
the alliance between politics and finance was then much more
undisguised, in our time the party which makes a cash profit
out of the transaction takes care not to appear. It was the
great party-tactician, Gaius Gracchus, who revealed the facts
of the case, when he made a division in the capitalists' interests,
and tried to win over liquid capital to the side of democracy
in order to vanquish, with its aid, capital invested in land. The
latter is fixed and bound to the soil ; but it is the liquid capital

which creates the greatness of a metropolis. It needs concentration to exercise its power to the fullest extent, and it needs acquaintance with politics to be able to calculate and enhance its possibilities for profit. The metropolis, therefore, becomes a pump, which sucks up capital from all parts of the kingdom.

In Republican Rome circumstances were, however, different from those of a modern State, in which trade and industry are the mainstays of finance. Roman high finance rested on Rome's paramount position of power. She did not trade in productive commodities, but sucked the conquered provinces dry. The great companies which farmed the provincial taxes and customs were the chief controllers of the supply of liquid capital. They directed the foreign policy of the State into fields where new sources for exploitation could be tapped, and so guided the internal policy that the State put as little obstacle as possible in the way of their greed of gain ; in short, it abandoned the provinces to their machinations. The result is notorious ; publicans and sinners came to mean much the same thing.

The provinces also required capital. The cities had to raise loans for their needs, and money could only be got from the Roman capitalists. The cities were not exactly distinguished for a wise financial policy, and a Roman capitalist had very different means of enforcing payment to those open to an ordinary creditor. In case of need he imitated Caesar's friend and assassin, Marcus Brutus, and borrowed soldiers from the proconsul, to send against the defaulting city. By such methods as these the cities were compelled to find the money.

For Rome the result was that the riches of the world flowed into the chests of the knights and Senators. The Senators indeed were technically forbidden by law to occupy themselves with such affairs, but they looked after them vigorously enough through their agents. Representatives of the great families, from which came the high officials, had many opportunities to feather their nests as governors of provinces.

The Empire effected a thorough alteration in the economic sphere, which in modern terms may be described as a socialisation of the State's revenues and their separation from private

s

interests.   The Emperors saw to it that the provinces were
governed with at least some measure of justice.   It was no
longer so easy for provincial governors to feather their nests
and to amass riches at the expense of the provinces.   The
State became its own tax-collector, and thus put an end to the
knights' most lucrative source of revenue.   They were allowed,
however, to retain the collection of customs some time longer,
because the State, at first, possessed neither the machinery nor
the departments necessary to take it over itself ; but the
margin of profits was cut down and carefully regulated.

So the most important financial interests, which had
their centre in Rome, were transferred from private control
to the State : they were socialised, that is they became a part
of the administration.   In consequence, Rome's dominant
position in the money-market suffered a severe shock.   The
network of private economic interests was replaced by the
stereotyped organisation of the State.   The socialisation of
the revenues was very necessary, and was a blessing for the
Empire as a whole, that is for the provinces which had been
bled.   But all such changes have usually more effects than one,
and even this fine medal had a reverse from Rome's point of
view.   It seems strange to us that there were not other
financial interests that could replace what was lost, *e.g.* those
connected with industry and commerce which are so prominent
in our days.   Trade and industry also played an important
part in antiquity, though not nearly so important as to-day.
But their foci were not in Rome, but far away in Syria, in
Asia Minor, or Gaul.   It was also a legacy of the world-conquest
that Rome was merely a consuming, not a producing member
of the Empire.   She was the seat of administration, the
dwelling-place of the Emperor and the high officials.   Industry
was scarcely known, nor trade either, except in so far as it
was a matter of providing the city with its requirements.   It
did exist to some extent, but did not suffice to make Rome the
economic centre of the Empire.

During the last two centuries of the Republic a multitude
of Italians are found in the East.   Mithridates' war against
Rome in 88 B.C. began with a massacre of Italians in Asia

Minor, in which 70,000 are said to have lost their lives. It was a sample of the bitter hatred stored up against them by the native population, which at last seized the opportunity for vengeance on its tormentors. These Italians were not only tax-farmers and collectors but also merchants. The Roman trade in the East was based on Roman arms. At Delos, the clearing house of the Italian merchants, all the slaves who were captured during the numerous wars in the East, and those whom the *publicani* caught in the provinces, were exhibited and sold. It is equally significant that Roman men of business occupied themselves exclusively with banking and the corn trade. The obvious centre of the money-market was Rome, into which the capital of the whole world flowed in the shape of taxes and exactions, while the Roman State controlled the corn trade to provide the capital with food. On the other hand the actual trade in commodities was altogether in the hands of the native population. After Asia Minor it became the turn for Africa, Spain, and Gaul to be exploited successively by the Romans.

The economic exploitation of the world reached its culmination in the last age of the Republic. Respect for Rome's name and arms and the Roman or Latin citizenship put the Italian merchant beyond fear of competition. In the days of the Empire this preferential position was modified, the provincials being placed on a position of equality, while the State itself took over the collection of taxes. During the first century A.D. the Italian men of business in the provinces became fewer in number, and by its close they were supplanted by Greeks in Greece and Asia Minor ; if any Romans remained they had been grecised. In the West the majority of business men were certainly Roman citizens, but no longer Italians by birth but romanised provincials. The Italians, supported by the arms of Rome and by the negligence or corruption of the provincial administration, practised economic robbery in the conquered countries during the decay of the Republic. When this was no longer possible, because the Empire stamped out the worst abuses, they disappeared and were replaced by provincials ; for they had never been genuine merchants.

The world-conquest then, which gave Rome her privileged position, had also its drawbacks. It hindered, or at least hampered, Rome from becoming the productive and commercial centre of the world she had vanquished. For it accustomed Romans and Italians to rely on force in exploiting the world's production in their own interests, instead of conquering the world in the interests of production and trade. Rome followed in the footsteps of the old conquering states. In contrast to her, the Empire of Athens had had quite a modern aspect. Its power had rested on the trade and industry of Athens, and of set purpose the Athenians strove to concentrate all trade and all economic life within the capital of their Empire. Rome let slip from her grasp the best method of fastening her domination on the Empire and welding it into a unity. For the right of conquest lapses if it rests only on force, and the widespread net of economic interests is incomparably stronger and more tenacious than the administrative.

Meanwhile the capital was no longer the sole ruler of the world. The Social War, the only great and decisive defeat suffered by the Roman Republic, had given Roman citizenship to all old Italy south of the Rubicon, and to Cisalpine Gaul south of the Po, and Caesar, forty years later, extended it to the foot of the Alps. For some few years the Po country was still governed by a proconsul, but this too ceased in 42 B.C. Italy thus included the whole peninsula. Italy, and not merely the city of Rome and its environs, was the land of Roman citizens. The old dialects disappeared ; the whole country adopted the Latin language. Italy as a whole thus assumed the dominant position. It was governed, not like the provincials by governors, but directly by the Assembly and Senate. Under the Empire, when the popular Assembly had only a semblance of life and was soon to die out, the Senate became the highest authority, at least for a time.

Before the Social War, Rome had been a state of the usual ancient type—a city-state in which all public life was concentrated in the city. The extension of citizenship to all Italy was bound to lead to a break with the old state tradition.

Italy could not be governed like a city. It contained considerable towns and cities of its own, and these were bound to put forward demands for looking after their own affairs, a model for which was to be found among the Roman colonies that were spread over Italy and were springing up in the provinces as well. Legally, however, the cities were subordinate to Rome ; a sign of this being the official designation, *municipium*. But they received self-government, and the right to administer justice, which the great Caesar laid down in his *lex Julia municipalis*. Municipal government was a copy in miniature of Rome's government, with a similar distribution of powers between council, magistrates, and people, and the same offices, only under other names.

Local self-government was thus provided for, but it was another matter with the full exercise of the Roman citizenship, which the inhabitants of Italy received. This could only be effectively exercised in Rome, where the popular assembly met. The vast majority was thus actually excluded from recording its vote in the decision of state affairs. Here we find clearly demonstrated the antithesis between the ancient state adapted to the narrow limits of a city, and the modern state embracing a whole country which has come into existence by the force of circumstances. We have the phrase, " representative system," on our lips, but the idea that a man could exercise his citizenship by deputy was so foreign to the ancient world that it would not have been able to comprehend it.

Only very rarely was there a great concourse of voters from the country districts ; the Roman assembly was usually composed of the populace of Rome. This abuse had already been evident in early days before the citizenship was extended to al the free inhabitants of Italy. Tiberius Gracchus fell because the country electors who supported his reforms could not attend the assembly. During the disorderly years at the close of the Republic, it was the city mob which dominated the popular assembly at Rome with its votes, and, if necessary, with its cudgels. It had its organisation in the *collegia compitalicia*— associations of inhabitants of the quarter, which were originally formed in connection with religious observances. Their conversion into electoral clubs was the work of Clodius, Cicero's notorious enemy and the agent of Caesar.

The popular assembly, so turbulent a few decades before, became dormant under Augustus, and was abolished by Tiberius, who transferred elections to the Senate, without the step exciting the slightest attention or protest. The rapid decline and painless death of the sovereign Roman assembly strikes us as an almost inconceivable occurrence. It cannot be explained by the magic formula—*panis et circenses*. The assembly could vote themselves bread, and they could squeeze games out of the rival candidates for office. It did not need to receive them as gifts of favour from the monarch's hand in exchange for the franchise. It had learnt that from past experience. It has been said that the Roman assembly, owing to scandals in the Forum, became morally bankrupt and lost its prestige. But in spite of all scandals, all openly advertised dislike of Parliament, and the deep contempt which some individuals feel for the standard of morals in parliamentary life, Parliamentarianism is still secure and has a future before it—of some centuries, at least—before it shares the lot of all human phenomena, and dies a natural death.

The explanation is to be sought in another quarter. The Roman assembly no longer expressed the will of the Roman citizens, but merely the current opinions and petty needs of a congeries of disconnected and ambiguous units, which played at being a national assembly, because the Roman State had outgrown the ancient state organisation. Rome's destiny, for weal or woe, depended on those citizens in Italy and the provinces, who never could attend an assembly, but could form public opinion. To them the popular assembly meant less than nothing. Whether it met or not was a matter of indifference, since it could do nothing useful, and had been antagonistic, as they knew well, to Italy's vital needs. Rome's mob of electors did not understand politics as anything but as a speedy way of filling the belly and the purse, and a means of spending idle hours in sensational scenes and interesting intrigues. Provided it got these elementary needs satisfied in other ways, it had no more use for the popular assembly.

Public opinion, too, which longed for peace and rest, was directly hostile to the violent behaviour which had marked the Roman popular assembly in the last days of the Republic.

In fact, the Roman popular assembly had lived too long and perished from want of any justification for its existence. The prerogatives of the population of Rome seemed to be a compensation for the franchise, but were, in truth, the result of Rome's world-conquest. But Roman arms had been largely borne by Italians, and it was a simple measure of justice that all Italy, and not Rome alone, should succeed to the position of ruler. Augustus tried to preserve this position. The chief expression of it was the army system, the recruiting of the Roman legions, and particularly the spear-head of the army—the praetorian guard—in Italy. If Italy was mistress, it was incumbent on her to defend her supremacy. It was a symbol of the position of the governed, the provincials, that they were not allowed to bear arms except in the auxiliary troops.

THE POSITION OF ITALY

The dominant position brought in its train economic advantages which Rome enjoyed in a high degree. It was only just that Italy should have her share. Corn-growing in Italy had been sacrificed to the welfare of the city of Rome ; consequently agriculture had been transformed. This found outward expression in the two methods of employing capital, the one extensive, the other intensive. The former was exemplified by the great pasture-lands and ranches, the latter by the gardens, vineyards, and olive plantations, which required much labour and time to give a return on the capital invested in them. Once, during the last years of the Republic, the exportation of oil to the provinces is recorded ; but far more important was viticulture, the products of which were especially acceptable to northern peoples. It seemed only fair that the Italian soil should be protected in respect of that article of produce which remained to it, and for which it was specially adapted. Even a century before the Empire (129 B.C.) there was a prohibition against making fresh vineyards and olive yards in the provinces. The Emperor Domitian, who, in spite of his bad reputation, inherited the financial acumen of his family, and was one of the Emperors who paid the greatest attention to his administration, intended to have half the vineyards in the provinces destroyed. At the same time he wanted to prohibit the making of fresh vineyards in Italy, in order to remedy the scarcity of corn. It was not strange that the crop which paid best was preferred, or that viticulture paid better than corn-growing, since the prices of corn destined for the chief centre of consumption, Rome, were lowered artificially for reasons of State. Italian agriculture was one-sided ; its prosperity depended on protective measures against the provinces. The situation was unnatural, and in the long run untenable. Some provinces, *e.g.* large parts of Gaul, were also excellently adapted for the production of wine and oil, and one may assume that the ordinances were often disobeyed. But it was not until the end of the third century, that the prohibition was abolished by the Emperor Probus, who introduced viticulture into Germany and Pannonia, *i.e.* the Rhine district and South-West Hungary.

Greater prosperity was only found in the country which had quite recently been incorporated into Italy, the fruitful plain of the Po. Central Italy stagnated, and Southern Italy —once Magna Graecia—and Sicily, recently Rome's granary, were in decay. In the plain of the Po there was not only a flourishing agriculture but also a number of other industries. At the beginning of the imperial age a revival of industry seems to have occurred in Italy ; it was conducted by imported labour, Oriental slaves, and thus was bound to suffer from the diminishing supply of slaves which was the result of imperial peace. Here, too, the situation was doubtful and insecure. In one special case we can follow the sequence of events. It is a knowledge of " the science of broken jars " that has contributed to the elucidation of questions of political economy. We are all familiar with the bright red pottery with figures in relief, produced at Arretium in Etruria, and therefore called Arretine or Samian ware. The former name must not be misapplied to similar pottery fabricated elsewhere than at Arretium, all of which products fall under the term *terra sigillata.* Arretine vases occur frequently in German military camps from the time of Augustus onwards, but are not found within the provincial civilisations. Thus in the camp of Haltern in the interior of Westphalia which the Romans occupied during their attempt to make the land between the Rhine and Elbe a Roman province, far more Arretine ware is found than, for example, in the city of Trèves, the chief city of North-Eastern Gaul. Thus the Italian wares accompany the soldiers ; they had been accustomed to them in Italy, and so they were exported to them, even when they were on the frontier or in the enemy's land. Later, under Caligula and Claudius, not a scrap of Italian pottery is found, but merely *terra sigillata* from Southern Gaul. By then Gaul had learned the art, and supplanted Italian manufacturers. A few decades later the Gallic wares also disappear, and are replaced by the manufactures nearer to hand at Trèves, in the Vosges, and the Rhine district. The frontier provinces provided themselves with the finer potteries. It is the same with glass. In the second century there was a great glass factory in Cologne, where a great technical step forward had been taken, the glass-makers mastering the chemical secret of making pure white glass. Its wares spread over the province and were imported into independent Germany. Italian industry was even less capable than Italian agriculture of maintaining the preferential position of the country.

Neither economically nor intellectually could Rome and Italy dominate the world which they had conquered. After a brilliant revival in the earlier Empire, when Rome was, for a while, the centre of Greek as well as Latin literature and science, the lead passed again to the Greek-speaking part of the Empire. But both of them were required if Rome and Italy, in peaceful rivalry with the conquered provinces, were to retain the position they had obtained by force. The victories were forgotten, and a grasp of realities and a know-ledge of what was requisite for empire were not acquired. The privileged position became an anachronism which was constantly and increasingly being undermined, and finally disappeared altogether owing to the levelling tendency of the

Empire. Only the population of Rome were allowed, from the force of tradition, to retain its ancestral privileges, which, as time went on, provincial cities imitated as well as they could. To understand the process of levelling, one must understand the original inequalities.

The Roman Empire was a confused medley of countries and peoples with different rights, to which, in our day, there is scarcely any parallel, except possibly in India. Here, below the dominant race, the British, are the natives, and their relations to the ruling power are different ; there are direct subjects and vassal-states, owing allegiance more or less closely to the British.

COLONIES AND PROVINCES

In the Roman Empire relations were still more complicated. From very early days there was citizenship of various grades ; and this circumstance had played an extremely important part in all extensions of Roman citizenship, and was to do so still more in the early Empire when it was extended to the provinces. When Rome conquered Italy she procured elbow room for her growing population and, at the same time, ensured quiet in the conquered districts by founding colonies of Roman citizens. From the time of Gaius Gracchus onwards these colonies were established in the provinces also. The object of the colonies was both military and agrarian—the Gracchi, for example, founding colonies in the interests of their policy of land reform. During the civil war the development took another direction. The colonies became a convenient means of rewarding and providing for discharged soldiers. These had to be settled in Italy, where the population in consequence received a very alien addition. For during the civil wars few questions were asked about the citizenship of the recruits ; they were taken from every quarter, and the provinces furnished strong contingents. Still greater was the revolution in the conditions of property-holding, caused by these colonies of veterans. In many cases the former owners were deprived of their whole estate by confiscation. Often a veteran colony was quartered on an already existing town,

which had to resign to it part of its territory. Thus two
communities with different status were formed in the same
town. This colonisation contributed to the latinising of Italy.
An example of that is Pompeii, where, after Sulla had imported
a colony of veterans, the Oscan language was driven out by
Latin.

Caesar founded some colonies in the provinces, and his
policy was imitated after his death. There was a distinction
between the colonies in the provinces and those in Italy. The
former were not, like the latter, exempt from land-tax, since
according to Roman conceptions, they had not full ownership
of their land, but it could be granted them. When eventually
the colony obtained Italian status, it erected in its Forum, in
commemoration of the fact, a statue of Marsyas, a custom the
origin of which is obscure. The model was the statue of Marsyas
in the Forum at Rome. Like Rome, the colony also erected
a Capitol with a Temple of Jupiter Optimus Maximus, and it
has been supposed that there was a Capitol in all colonies with
Italian status. The colony was, it was said, a copy on a small
scale of the Roman people, and its government and administration was copied from that of Rome. It thus had self-government and its own tribunals, but in certain respects was subject
to the provincial governor, and did not possess the right of
coining money. Roman civic rights in the provinces might
also be limited in other ways. In Gaul, conquered by Caesar,
and possibly also elsewhere, no one was eligible to hold any of
the old Roman offices of state, an ancient privilege of Roman
citizens.

Latin rights at this time were simply a more restricted form
of Roman civic rights. Originally they were incompatible
with Roman citizenship, and consisted in the privileges
which Latin cities allied to Rome possessed, *viz.* equality
under civil law with the Romans : the vote, though only in
one of the thirty-five tribes : and the possibility that a man,
who in his native town had held an office and had settled in
Rome, might aspire to full citizenship. Latin rights were an
effective means of binding the Latin cities to Rome and
attracting thither their best citizens. When, by the Social

War, the inhabitants of Latium received full citizenship, Latin rights did not lapse altogether, but were used elsewhere with the same object as previously in Latium. An example was found in the colonies with Latin rights. For the Latins, who had helped the Romans to win their victories, justly received a part of the booty also, and the colonies assigned to them were endowed with their legal position.

The Latin rights served to unite closely to Rome the more advanced cities, and were a preparation for full Roman citizenship. Thus the country between the Po and the Alps received Latin rights after the Social War, but did not acquire full citizenship until forty years later. The same policy was adopted under the Empire. Under Hadrian a still more advantageous form of Latin rights was created, full citizenship being granted not only to all who had held an office in a city with Latin rights, but also to the *decuriones*. Probably this was an attempt to encourage a willingness to undertake the duties of a *decurio*, which it was already difficult to get any one to accept.

There were great inequalities of rights and status among those of the inhabitants of the Empire who did not possess Roman citizenship. Foremost among these were the free and allied states, who had joined Rome under a collateral treaty. Theoretically this was an agreement between two states of equal rights, but, in reality, Rome's power was so preponderant that the other state concluding the treaty became a part of the Empire. This relation was expressed in the treaty by the state renouncing the right to an independent foreign policy and, in that respect, identifying itself with Rome. It kept its army, but this no longer served its own purposes, but was placed at the disposal of Rome as an allied contingent. What remained of the old sovereignty, was, however, valuable enough. The free and allied state was not under the provincial governor, and in token of this he laid aside his *fasces* when he entered its territory. It had its jurisdiction according to its own laws, and the right of coinage ; it paid no tax to Rome, but imposed and collected taxes and customs on its own account. It had its own full right of property in its soil. Thus, within the limits of its territory it was its own master in all cases in which it was not bound to have regard to powerful Rome. There were also free and allied states which received this right not by treaty, but as a gift from the Roman people. As Rome bestowed the gift so also she could take it away. Otherwise the position was identical, and the difference did not mean much, for the Roman Government usually had power enough to reduce to obedience a city allied by treaty, and, in case of need, to degrade it.

The other inhabitants of the provinces were tributary subjects, who, either by treaty or by unconditional surrender, had submitted to Rome. In law and in principle the position of the subjects was fundamentally different to that of the free cities. They were entirely subject to Rome, and their soil belonged theoretically to the Roman State, the token of this being the land-tax, which Rome collected. They were governed by a Roman official, who conducted the administration and the jurisdiction. But in practice their position was not very different. When Rome established a province in a country she was obliged, in the details of administration, to adhere closely to the old traditions and methods of government. An edict of the governor or of a special commission usually directed that the city organisation, where it existed, and the rights of property and the laws, should remain in force for the present. Life continued in the old ways though under Roman supervision. The cities retained their council, their popular assembly, and their officials, who ruled them in the old manner and administered justice according to native laws. Often they also had the right of issuing an independent currency. But of course the provincial governor could intervene, when he thought fit so to do.

Egypt had a unique position. It was no part of the domain of the Roman Senate and people, but Augustus' private conquest, and the Emperor's private property. So strictly did he retain this right, that Senators and even members of the imperial family were forbidden to enter Egypt without special permission. While all other high imperial offices were reserved to Senators, Egypt was governed by a prefect who was of equestrian rank. It was strictly a personal union which joined Egypt to the Roman Empire. It has been said that it is as correct to speak of the Pharaoh of Egypt reigning as Emperor on the banks of the Tiber, as of the *princeps* of the Roman people governing the land of the Nile valley.

Finally there were in the East a great number of vassal-states, whose kings were allied or subject to Rome. Little is known of their legal position, but the Emperor made decisions as to countries and princes in a very arbitrary way, as it seemed best to him from the point of view of the Empire as a whole. For instance, we know that the Emperor modified and even abolished principalities belonging to the family of Herod in Palestine.

To all these differences of status the Empire added another, which, however, did not affect the legal position of the inhabitants, but only the administration. Augustus divided the provinces between himself and the Senate. The Emperor took over the provinces in which there was an army, whereas the Senate kept the peaceful and civilised provinces in which armed force was unnecessary. The list of the Senatorial provinces varied from time to time. It included Sicily, Sardinia, Baetica (Southern Spain), Gallia Narbonensis (the Mediterranean districts of France), Macedonia, Achaia, Crete, Cyrene, Asia Minor, Bithynia and Pontus (the south coast of the Black Sea).

The Roman Empire, then, consisted of a collection of peoples and countries with very different rights, and in many cases races with varying privileges and legal status existed in close proximity to each other. This encouraged a free and independent spirit, and preserved old traditions and old forms of civilisation, but it made the administration of the Empire a complicated and difficult task. The death-struggles of the Republic had dissolved the administration, and it was the first great task of the Empire to recreate order. Bureaucracy always detests varieties and complexities. It insists on working by numbers and to schedule, for only then can facts and statistics be arranged, filed in office drawers and docketed so as to be accessible. The increasingly bureaucratic methods of the Government produced results similar to those which followed the creation of the imperial power, and in consequence the distinction between citizens and subjects of Rome was effaced by both becoming the subjects of the Emperor.

During the first century and a half of the Empire, the vassal-states were abolished and either converted into, or made part of provinces. Details are of no interest, but the following list with the year of annexation is suggestive : Galatia 25 B.C., the kingdom of Deiotarus in Pontus and Paphlagonia 7 B.C., Judaea A.D. 6, Cappadocia A.D. 17, Mauretania A.D. 40, Thrace A.D. 46, Commagene A.D. 72, and finally, Arabia, *i.e.* the country east and south of Palestine, A.D. 105, Galilee and Peraea, the district east of the Jordan, under Trajan. After that the Greek principality in the Crimea, and Great Armenia were the only vassal-states. Rome found herself unable to take over and administer directly either of these, for the Crimea was too distant and isolated and Armenia was always to remain an apple of discord between Rome and Persia. After Trajan there were no large territories not directly subject to Rome. The inhabitants of free and allied cities had been in theory only indirectly dependent on Rome, but at the beginning of the Empire the theory began to be forgotten. It is obvious that no one can be at the same time the subject of two states ; so one could not be a citizen of a free state, *e.g.* Athens, and at the same time a Roman citizen. The Republic adhered to this rule, but under Augustus it was already broken, so that one could be, simultaneously, an Athenian and a Roman citizen. Thus the theory of the existence of free and allied cities within the Empire was given up ; they had become cities of the Roman Empire, whose franchise was superior to theirs. In the second century the process which deprived free cities of their special rights went on rapidly. It was the decline and fall of self-government (which will be described in a later chapter) that subordinated both free cities, *municipia*, and provincial cities to the central government in equal measure, and wiped out the old distinction between them.

The really important thing was the extension of Roman citizenship. In this respect Rome had always pursued a liberal policy, and had thus laid the foundation of her own greatness. The number of citizens had increased in proportion to her power. This had been possible, because Rome was not a democratic State. Ancient democracies had always been careful to preserve the citizenship and its privileges. Athens, for example, in contrast to Rome, jealously excluded her allies, and thus prepared her own doom, because she omitted to build up her Empire with the only cement that could keep it permanently together, and to create the broader basis for her power which was needed to maintain it. Roman citizenship could be granted, not only by the assembly of the people, as in Greek states, but also by a general—that being one of the prerogatives of his office—and this was often done on a grand scale, *e.g.* in the foundation of a military colony. Service in the army brought a constant stream of new citizens, which had more effect than the manumission of slaves. The provincials who served in the auxiliary troops received the citizenship along with their children after their discharge, and those who were enlisted in the legions, which had to consist of Roman citizens, were granted this right on their entry into the service.

We still possess the extremely interesting and instructive figures from a census return, by which adult males were counted and taxed. The last pair of censors did their work in 69 B.C., and there were then enumerated just under a million adult Roman citizens. In 28 B.C. Augustus had a census made, which gave a total of 4,063,000. Thus in these forty years the number of Roman citizens had more than quadrupled. This was the result of the lavish grants of the citizenship made by Caesar and the triumvirs, but especially by Caesar. To him the preferential position of the Roman citizen was an anomaly and an impediment to the radical reform of the Empire which he contemplated. It was he who gave the citizenship to the inhabitants of the country between the Po and the Alps and to thousands of Gauls. Gaul was full of " Julii," whose name betrays the man whom they had to thank for their promotion to be citizens of the city that was mistress of the world.

Augustus had more census lists made in 8 B.C., and again, three months before his death, in A.D. 14. In the first the number was 4,233,000—an increase of 170,000 ; in the latter the number was 4,937,000—an increase of 704,000. The total increase was 874,000. In these forty-one years the number of citizens, which had quadrupled in the previous period, was increased by less than 25 per cent. Besides the natural increase of the population, we know that new citizens were constantly being added from the ranks of the provincials. A study of these figures demonstrates clearly the complete divergence of Augustus' policy from that of Caesar, *i.e.* his effort to maintain the dominant position of Rome and Roman citizens. This could only be done by preserving the dignity of Roman citizenship, and a necessary condition of that was that it should not be squandered on provincials who had not grown up in the Roman traditions.

Caesar's ideas had been far in advance of his age, and were destined to influence later developments. Successive Emperors followed his path rather than that of Augustus. First we have Claudius, whose reign ushered in a new epoch, in striking contrast to that of Tiberius, who had been the faithful executor of his adoptive father's will. Claudius was an antiquarian, and therefore made himself censor, but executed the functions of the old office in the spirit of the new age. In a speech to the Senate, which has been preserved, he strongly recommended that Roman citizens in *Gallia comata* should be made eligible for Roman offices of state, a right which, as already noted (p. 199), they did not yet possess. The Senate hesitated before acquiescing in so great an extension, and limited the grant to the old allies and friends of Rome, the Aedui. Claudius held similar views with regard to the grant of the citizenship to individuals. In Seneca's lampoon on the dead Emperor, Clotho wants to grant him a little respite, while he gives Roman citizenship to the few that are still left without it ; for he had already enabled all Greeks, Gauls, Spaniards, and Britons to swagger about in the *toga*. His rescript about the citizenship of the Anauni (near Trent) was characteristic. He regarded it as of doubtful validity ; but as they had assumed it for a long time, he preferred to confirm it rather than hold to the letter of the law.

During the next period we have no such certain information ;

T

but the tendency was for a similar policy to be followed. This is shown by the many Flavii, Ulpii, Aelii, Aurelii, whose names occur in provincial inscriptions, the Roman name designating from what Emperor they had obtained Roman citizenship. Military service, the royal road to citizenship, continued to provide more and more new burghers, as the provincial element became increasingly dominant in the army.

The most striking example of the extension of Roman franchise was, however, that by which the populations of whole cities received Roman citizenship. The foundation of a colony originally implied that a large number of Roman citizens, while preserving their citizenship, settled outside the territory of Rome, but under the Empire a colony was formed by Roman citizenship being granted to a provincial town and its inhabitants. It was thus not colonisation in the strict sense of the word, but a legal fiction, by which provincials were made Romans. The condition was that the inhabitants of the city could be regarded as being on the same level of culture as the Romans, a preparation and a preliminary stage of this being the grant of Latin rights.

Whereas Caesar had made great use of this method, Augustus, according to his habit, was much more chary. He granted Roman or Latin rights to a few towns in the Alpine districts, Gallia Narbonensis and the Spanish province of Baetica ; in other words, to the countries which had been most permanently and deeply affected by Latin culture. Only in the civil war after the death of Nero did the grants become more frequent. Tacitus blames Vitellius for having lavished the Latin rights on provincials : Vespasian gave Latin rights to all Spanish cities that were still without them. Somewhat later the same process developed in Africa. The distribution of Roman rights and the preliminary granting of Latin rights was a sign of the constantly growing culture and latinisation of the Western provinces under the early Empire. It presupposed that a provincial town had progressed so far in culture that it was worthy to be put on an equality with the ruling people. Figures here speak more plainly than words. Under the early Empire, Spain was the province which had attained the highest degree of civilisation. A statement of the elder Pliny (which must have been made just before Vespasian gave Latin rights to all the Spanish towns) mentions that Southern Spain (Baetica) had 115 cities, 17 of them with Roman and 29 with Latin rights; Western Spain (Tarraconensis) had 179, 25 with Roman and 18 with Latin rights.

The division and organisation of the country into city-spheres was significant. It was an attempt to divide the whole Empire into a number of cities with the territories belonging to them. The distinction between a city and a country district, or canton, was the distinction between culture and its absence. City organisation was the means applied by the imperial administration to raise the level of culture in the Empire. There were certain exceptions, *viz.* territories which were not under a city, more especially the great imperial domains which were constantly being added to. The social importance of these will be referred to later. Provinces which had not shared in the general culture or were not sufficiently advanced, were divided into cantons. Here, also, Egypt had a special position, due to its ancient traditions. It was an indication of the levelling up of the Empire that in A.D. 202 Septimius Severus introduced *curiae* (town councils) into Egyptian towns, whereas, in other matters, the old administrative system was retained.

Augustus divided Gaul into cantons and the Roman colonies were few in number. In fact, for some time, Lugudunum was the only one with Roman rights, though Pliny mentions Augusta Rauracorum (near Basel) and Noviodunum Col Equestris (Nyon by the Lake of Geneva)—and their numbers increased slowly. Those named in inscriptions must have had Latin rights, and date, at the earliest, from the reigns of Claudius or Vespasian. It is noteworthy that, as the complete subjugation of Gaul was of a late date, so Roman culture was late in taking firm root, and penetrated the whole country slowly. Still more noticeable is this in the case of the poorer and most recently conquered countries—Britain, Germany, Pannonia, Moesia. Cantons were divided into villages, and even if the village superficially looked like a town it lacked its organisation. But even here there existed a certain amount of self-government, and there were officials similar to those in the towns. Here too it was presumable that there would be, in due course, a similar progress, developing into city organisation and a position of equal status with the ruling people.

The story of the modification of provincial towns into Latin and Roman colonies is important, because, more clearly than anything else, this process is significant of the general raising of the level of civilisation. It certainly was a means of equalising different legal positions in the Empire, and it also implied a rise in the level of culture, since provincial towns must have attained to the same degree of general culture and the same aptitude for self-government as the old cities, before they were admitted to the same status as the civilian population of the Empire, and dignified with the name of colonies of Roman citizens. The ideal aimed at in the far distant future was the obliteration of the areas of barbarism within the Empire, when it should have indeed become an Empire containing Roman citizens only and no subjects of Rome. To attain this ideal, patient and laborious work was necessary and great care exercised to preserve the purity and dignity of Roman citizenship. But this, unfortunately, was already compromised by the numerous barbarians who, through manumission or service in the army, obtained the citizenship, and degraded owing to the fact that all inhabitants of the Empire became subjects of the Emperor. The value of the citizenship was not upheld either by the government or public opinion. The decline of culture in the second century had its effect on the progress of the work of civilisation. Everything contributed to make the acquisition of Roman citizenship easier and the qualifications less strict. When the age of the military Emperors began, and Syrian superstition and brute force were elevated to the seat of honour, the tradition of the importance of Roman citizenship was lost, and it created little excitement when Caracalla, in A.D. 212, extended it to all free inhabitants of the Empire. But the extension was not so unconditional as has sometimes been assumed. In the first place it was confined to individuals;

it involved no alteration in the different legal positions of the cities. Secondly, the *dediticii* were excluded, a phrase which properly means those who capitulated to armed force, but under the Empire all were counted as *dediticii* who did not belong to any city organisation and were liable to personal taxation, which was the characteristic mark of subjection, *e.g.* the inhabitants of Egypt, also those barbarians who had been permitted to cross the frontier and settle in the Empire, and finally, former slaves who had not been manumitted in legal form or who, before manumission, had incurred degrading punishments. Not all the gates were, as yet, opened for the equalisation of the foreign and barbarian element with the old citizens of the Empire, but the position was dangerously impaired. The process was completed during the violent revolutions of the third century, when brute force and ignorance prevailed. Then all formal distinctions between Roman and provincial citizenship came to an end, and the new régime no longer considered citizens as belonging to various grades, but only as subjects, who were all equally subordinated to the Emperor. The Empire was organised on an equalitarian basis by Diocletian. Differences in citizenship founded on geographical divisions had disappeared, and in place of them appear classes with different rights. The process was not complete in his day, but his legislation forms a definite epoch. The Empire was divided among four Emperors, each with his vice-emperor, or praetorian prefect, who was at the head of civil administration and jurisdiction in each of the four districts, Gallia, Italia, Illyria, and the Orient. Under them were twelve *vicarii* and 116 provinces, whose governors had different titles, but exercised the same functions. The provinces had become much smaller, characteristic and expressive of the powerful position of the new bureaucratic state and central government.

Italy no longer enjoyed a preferential position, but was itself split up into provinces. Augustus had previously divided Italy into eleven regions. The object of this little-known measure is obscure ; he certainly did not intend to limit self-government. With Diocletian the old privilege of freedom from taxation, which world-conquest had won for

Italy, came to an end. Financial straits and the collapse of self-government depressed Italy to the level of the conquered provinces during the third century, that age of ferment and reorganisation when all the ancient traditions were wiped out. Diocletian's colleague, Maximian, who resided at Milan, levied a tax on the territory north of the Rubicon, with which he defrayed the expenses of his court ; thus this region was called *Italia annonaria*. The land south of the Rubicon had to render certain supplies in kind for the maintenance of the population of Rome (p. 250), and from this obligatory tribute to the city of Rome it became known as *Italia suburbicaria*. Of the old citizen privileges, that which lasted most tenaciously was the privilege of the city of Rome to live and amuse itself at the expense of others. Rome was the seat of the Senate. The Senate had indeed sunk to the position of a municipal council for Rome under the supervision of the imperial prefect of the city, but it still possessed importance as the assembly of the most influential and wealthiest men in the Empire. But Rome was no longer the residence of the Emperor or the seat of the imperial government. During the disturbances of the third century the Emperors were constantly forced to take the field and seldom visited Rome. When, under Diocletian, a period of reorganisation set in, and the Emperors had greater opportunities for remaining in one place, the Empire was divided. Diocletian himself took the East for his share, and most frequently resided at Nikomedia in Asia Minor, not far from Constantinople. Maximian, who had Italy for his portion, held his court at Milan. Rome was dispossessed and seldom saw an Emperor within its walls. The usurpation of Maxentius, which occurred during the disturbances after the abdication of Diocletian, and was brought to an end by Constantine's victory at the Ponte Molle outside Rome, is partially explained by Rome's discontent at her humiliation. But this was only a transitory episode. By the foundation of the new Rome—Constantinople—the death-blow was dealt to the old capital, once the mistress of the world. The nightmare, which tormented the contemporaries of Caesar and Augustus, became a reality when the imperial capital was transferred to the East. Rivalry between the two capitals was quickly terminated by the separation of the Empire into two distinct halves ; but this was of no advantage to Rome, since during the disorders of the great migrations, the West-Roman Emperor resided in the well-fortified and inaccessible Ravenna.

But a great name, and the prestige of a great name, dies hard. When the Emperors abandoned the often unmanageable city, and spurned the splendour and traditions which the name of Rome still had to give, their place was filled by Rome's highest spiritual dignitary, the bishop of the Christian Church. It was the name of Rome and the absence of the Emperor from Rome which made the Bishop of Rome Pope, the supreme head of the Christian world.

Legally and actually the conquered world had been subordinated to the Rome of the Republic. In both these aspects we have followed the modifications which Rome's position underwent as a result of the general levelling tendency of the Empire. Some of the actual advantages remained and were even increased. But they were a factor in the economic decay, especially in connection with the financial and food difficulties with which the Empire had to deal, and it was not of paramount importance that the State continued to pay for corn and other foods for Rome's poor inhabitants, and to cater for their amusement. But the legal aspect of the case, on the other hand, the conversion of Rome's subjects into Roman citizens, was of great importance in connection with the problem of civilising the Empire. In itself this change was necessary and inevitable. The older the conquest, the more antiquated became the rights founded on it. Sooner or later a time must come when the rights of conquest expire and the conqueror must fuse the conquered with himself or abdicate his position. The equalisation of citizen rights was the legal expression of this process. The essential point was whether the form corresponded to the fact, *i.e.* whether those who were, in theory, received as Roman citizens, had also become Romans through and through and partakers of Roman culture. As was said above, this may have been the case in the second century.

During this century culture began to decline, and communal self-government and city-organisation to decay. There was little probability that the old culture and the city-organisation indissolubly bound up with it would continue to grow and flourish. The homage paid to the power of the sword by the first military Emperors was the prelude to the catastrophe of the third century. Equalisation of citizen rights went on, not in the sense that Rome raised the conquered peoples to her level but rather that she depressed the Romans to their level.

Rome did not succeed in fulfilling her mission of civilising the world she had conquered. But the strength of her influence must not be under-estimated. The whole of South-West Europe still speaks Romance languages ; only Britain and the frontier regions immediately west of the Rhine and south of the Danube were lost to that linguistic sphere of influence. Africa indeed was lost, but that was due to a fresh migration of peoples some centuries after the fall of the West-Roman Empire. In the East circumstances were different. The eastern half was not latinised, and the Greek language prevailed over the Latin. But the Greeks had not, like the Romans, to deal with barbarians, rude indeed and uncivilised, but still capable of imbibing education and culture. In the East lived peoples with strongly marked individuality, immemorial traditions of culture (lasting over a thousand years), and profound variations of blood and race. The ease with which the Arabs conquered the provinces of the Byzantine Empire south of the Taurus is only intelligible if one remembers the dividing line of religions which cut the Empire in twain. Here in the East also, the native languages had a new birth, when ancient civilisation weakened and drew near its end. It is significant that this renaissance is connected with the spread of Christianity. In the West, on the other hand, the Church retains Latin as its language to this day. This is a fitting symbol of the fact that the Roman Church continued the work which the Roman State began, though under other standards and by other methods—the Cross in place of the altar of the Caesars— the hierarchy and the sword of the Spirit instead of civil bureaucracy and military domination.

III

THE ARMY

In any description of the inhabitants and culture of the Roman Empire a chapter must be devoted to the army. The Roman army was more than the bond which held the imperial system together; it was, to start with, a civilising factor of the first importance, which became, later, an equally important factor in the destruction of civilisation. In the motley mixture of peoples and languages in the Roman Empire the army served as a bond of union. Latin was the language of command even in the East, and the language which the soldiers, drawn from all corners of the Empire, used to communicate with each other. During the time when the army was chiefly composed of Italians and lived up to a high standard, it contributed, more than anything else, to the spread of the Latin language and Roman civilisation. Whatever foreign elements there were in the army were romanised and obtained Roman citizenship.

It is difficult for us to realise fully the influence of the Roman army as a cultural force, especially as its numbers in relation to the population of the Empire were much less than one is inclined to imagine. We must realise the enormous difference between the army in any modern state and the army in the Roman Empire, in its relation to state and society. The typical modern army is that of a Continental power, such as France, recruited by universal service. The citizen who puts on uniform does not thereby become different from what he was, but remains attached to his old ideas and his old life, to which he returns when he puts off his uniform. The Roman army was a professional army; and the professional soldier takes a professional view of life which differentiates him from other citizens. Every profession tries to look after its own interests, but none has such means of securing them as a professional army. For the minority which bears arms is the real master of the great unarmed majority of the citizens. This is a lesson which history confirms, which to-day can be studied in the Bolshevist ascendancy in Russia, and the demand of the more extreme socialists for the arming of the proletariat and the disarming of the *bourgeoisie* in other countries. Universal compulsory service is society's only protection against a military dictatorship, whether in the reactionary or the Bolshevist sense : for such an army does not form a class group or a special profession, but includes all citizens in uniform. It is therefore indissolubly bound up with democracy. Ancient states were like all republics, in that they had a system of universal compulsory service. The men who introduced compulsory service in the Continental European states are the real originators of their democratic development. Democracy can exist only while universal compulsory service prevails, or when the sheltered position of the country frees it from the necessity of maintaining large armies, as is the case in the Anglo-Saxon countries. The abolition of compulsory service is the first step to the abolition of democracy. At present this truth is exemplified only in the ancient states, but it is none the less a truism. The transition of the Roman army from an army based on compulsory service to a professional army, a few generations before the appearance of Augustus, was the prelude to the transition of the Roman constitution from a republic to a monarchy. In Rome, as in other ancient states, the obligation of service rested on the man who owned some property ; for the soldier had to provide his own equipment, and the man who was too poor to provide himself with arms was exempt from military service. The expression, " excluded from the right of service," would, perhaps, better describe the actual position, for the obligation to service was accompanied by political rights. The citizen's rank in the army and his vote in the assembly were graded in exact proportion to the completeness of the equipment with which he was in a position to provide himself. The best equipped, *i.e.* those who could furnish a horse, were therefore the wealthy class. In this lay the origin of the timocratic principle, the graduation of civic rights according to property and income. But this soon lost its proper basis, and then became an arbitrary limitation which could not be maintained.

The Roman army was originally a citizen army, composed of owners of landed property, *i.e.* of farmers, who employed the time not occupied in agriculture, in fighting to secure for themselves and their children more land and new homes. As the State grew, wars were waged in ever more distant regions and countries, and became more prolonged. The farmers were taken away from their work, and their farms decayed or were sold. The Italian farmer paid for the imperialistic policy for which he fought with his ruin. We shall come back to this in another connection. In time, the supply of compulsory recruits fell off, since the inhabitants of towns and those who had moveable property were exempted. Marius, realising this, enrolled the proletariat in the army, risking the consequences. In reality he merely carried out and completed a development which had long been in progress. From his time the army of Rome was a professional recruited army, and was no longer, even in theory, an army based on obligatory service. The natural consequences immediately followed. The army no longer had any sentiment for the State and its citizens, but only for the profession and its profits, and the commander who knew how to exert his personal influence over it. The army became the instrument of its commanding officer and not of the State. Under Sulla it captured Rome, overthrew the democracy and installed the régime of the Senate ; under Pompey it overthrew the institutions of Sulla ; under Caesar it introduced monarchy ; under the triumvirs it brought about the proscriptions, and divided the Empire into two warring parts.

The problem of the Empire, which was at the same time the *raison d'être* and foundation of the imperial power, was, how to bring back the army once again under the authority of the State to serve its interests. The point was solved by the control of the State being entrusted to the hands of the commander of the army. His interest and that of the State being identical, the leader of the army, therefore, placed the army at the service of the State. The supreme war-lord, as *princeps*, became the leader of the State. This was the solution of the problem, artfully conceived by Augustus, on which he built up his own power. The danger for the future lay in the possibility that the individual who formed the uniting and reconciling link, might take the side of one party and consider himself to be the representative of the military profession rather than, primarily, the defender of the State. This was what actually happened, and the system of Augustus collapsed during the age of the military Emperors.

The problem of the army was one of the most intricate which faced the founder of the Empire. He had to demobilise the great forces which had been enlisted during the civil war, and, following the custom of the age, to provide the soldiers with money and land in Italy for a provision in their old age. In addition, the necessities of imperial defence forced him to create a standing army, which, in theory, the Republic did not recognise, and this raised yet another problem—how to provide means for the maintenance of the army, and for the time-expired men in civil life. Never had Rome beheld such an enormous army as during the civil war. Soon after the battle of Mutina there were 64 legions ; in 36 B.C. Augustus had 44 and Antonius 30 legions ; and, after the battle of Actium, Augustus had at his disposal at least 50 legions. After the conclusion of peace such numbers were not required, and many legions were disbanded. Military colonies were founded, and the soldiers were provided with land and money, a difficult undertaking, which could not be solved without violent measures. Land was confiscated, and money obtained from the plunder of vanquished opponents. The necessity for doing this, which could not be met by ordinary means, fully explains the striking contrast between Augustus' high-handed policy in his early days and his mild government, in time of peace, when he was older—a contrast which impressed his contemporaries.

Only a small number of the soldiers who fought in the civil war were retained with the colours. Augustus, at his death, left behind him 25 legions. Three had perished in the Teutoburg Forest, and two new ones were formed in their stead. Claudius formed two more legions ; at the accession of Vespasian the number was 30, increased by Septimius Severus to 33. The strength of a legion varied from 5000 to 6000 men. After the time of Augustus every legion had four squadrons of cavalry, each 120 strong, attached to it. Then there was the praetorian guard, whose strength varied from 9 to 10 cohorts, each 1000 strong, with 10 squadrons of cavalry. The citizen army thus amounted to about 150,000 men.

The legionaries were Roman citizens, at least nominally, but they formed only half of the armed force of the Empire, the other half consisting of auxiliary troops (*auxilia*), a minority of which were veteran detachments and citizen cohorts, the majority being provincials, who were without the citizenship. These *auxilia* included all the cavalry, a strong body of infantry, and special troops such as slingers and archers. After completing their service they received, on discharge, Roman citizenship, which was inherited by their children.

Thus the entire army numbered from 300,000 to 350,000 men. The cost of maintenance can be calculated only as regards the regular pay of the citizen troops, but it amounted to almost 200,000,000 sesterces per annum in the first century. This was the whole of Rome's much-vaunted army, insignificant in comparison with modern conditions for a population estimated to have been of 70,000,000–100,000,000. But it was as much as the Empire could support, and during the first two centuries it was sufficient for its work. The Roman Empire had no rival of equal strength ; the army was needed mainly for frontier defence and had no great tasks. The wars waged were not imperial but local frontier skirmishes. The provinces, which were administered by the Senate, with the exception of Africa, had no military force. The troops were not stationed in the interior of imperial provinces, save where an exception was made to meet special conditions, such as in cases of popular unrest or brigandage, but on the frontiers, as has been already implied in the description of the frontier defence of Syria and Africa, the Rhine and the Danube. We have seen how the defence of the frontier was rendered effective by the system of a *limes*, and by detachments posted along the frontier (p. 223). The legionary base camps were situated rather further back from the frontier, and, as a rule, the legions quartered in a province could, without assistance, deal with any ordinary situation and ward off hostile attacks. If they were not strong enough, legions had to be drawn from other parts of the Empire which, at the moment, were undisturbed by enemies.

This army of the early Empire was hardly ever, or at least only in emergencies, used as a striking force. It was, in some respects, not unlike the *gendarmerie*, which even pacificists still consider necessary to restrain savage races, who do not understand the blessings of peace, from encroaching on more civilised areas. This characteristic comes out in the fact that the army, to an extent inconceivable to us, was used for general labour purposes—the auxiliaries as a rule, but in some cases the legionaries as well. From earliest times the Roman army, at the conclusion of every day's march, constructed a fortified camp. The consequence was that even camps intended for a permanent garrison were built by the soldiers themselves. The mere idea that modern European troops should build their own barracks seems absurd. But then they are an army of compulsory service, not a standing army, whose spare time can be utilised. Military objects were served also by the long ramparts, or walls with numerous forts, which protected the land frontiers, and the roads which crossed the provinces in all directions.

In many places considerable remains of solid permanent camps built of brick are to be found. In the centre were the headquarters, with the sanctuary in which were preserved the standards and the imperial portraits, the offices, the Forum, and the dwellings of the *legatus* (commandant) and the officers. The barracks of the men were arranged in regular rows. In process of time comforts increased. Every camp, even for small detachments, had warm baths. At Novaesium (Neuss) on the Rhine the chief streets were provided with colonnades, the *quaestorium* (orderly-room) was converted into a private dwelling for the *legatus*, and the quarters of the superior officers were adorned with wall-paintings representing gardens. The soldiers themselves made the bricks for these buildings. Every legion had a brick-yard, and the custom by which legions affixed their own device on the bricks, still bears witness to all the work done, and has provided important evidence for the historian, inasmuch as he can trace the movements of the legions by a study of the stamped bricks.

The soldiers' labour was utilised for other purposes besides those which were purely military. It is probable that the legions sold the bricks they made to private individuals. Augustus had to issue a prohibition forbidding the employment of soldiers in the erection of private buildings, while permitting them to be employed on public works. Soldiers built temples and other public buildings, constructed aqueducts, dredged harbours and dug canals, *e.g.* that between the Meuse and the Rhine. This canal chiefly served military purposes, but the canal which connected the Bitter Lakes with the Nile, which was repeatedly dredged by soldiers, was the important waterway between the Red Sea and the Mediterranean. Sometimes soldiers were employed in quarries and mines—a form of labour usually regarded as suitable for convicts sentenced for serious crimes. Augustus employed soldiers to put in order the irrigation-system of Egypt and to revive the decayed agriculture of the country. To us it is more intelligible to read of the calling up of soldiers in Syria to fight locusts : even to-day, soldiers are now and then employed in cases of great emergency such as forest-fires or an earthquake. The Emperor Probus ordered the army to drain swamps and plant vineyards, but the order cost him his life. He had no longer to deal with the disciplined soldiers of the earlier Empire, but with semi-barbarians who loved fighting and loathed work. In Julian's time it is recorded as something remarkable that he succeeded in inducing the German auxiliaries to assist in the work of fortification.

An incident which may be said to symbolise the whole army system is the following. The Emperor Hadrian passed a criticism on the operations of the 3rd legion quartered at Lambaesis, which afterwards was inscribed on stone, of which the longest and best preserved passage deals with the work of fortification. In it he says, " What others take several days to do, you executed in one. A toilsome piece of walling, of the sort usually executed for permanent winter camps, you executed in not much longer time than it takes to build a wall of turves, which when cut into equal pieces are easily transported and dealt with and put up without excessive labour because they are soft and easy to handle. You, however, had to deal with big heavy stones of different shapes and sizes, which can neither be transported, nor lifted, nor put in position without inequalities appearing. You dug a straight ditch in hard and stony ground and cemented the sides. When the work was finished you returned in haste to the camp, took provisions and arms and followed the cavalry which moved out . . ."

All these works made it necessary to attach permanently to the legion a staff of mechanics, architects, and engineers to plan roads and waterworks. Both these and a whole army of artisans, smiths, lead-workers, stone-cutters, tilers, lime burners, wood-cutters, colliers, armourers, wheelwrights, and saddlers, are mentioned in later authorities when, by reason of the system by which wages were paid in kind, the legions were forced to provide for all their own needs.

If the Roman State found its soldiers expensive, at the same time it knew how to make use of their labour power. The army did not simply, as with us, drill, march, and when necessary, fight, but it had also, by the work of its hands, to advance material culture and serve as an example to distant regions and the uncivilised populations amongst whom it was quartered. It is a fascinating task to classify the finds in a garrison town, *e.g.* the Saalburg. We find that tools are almost more numerous than weapons, and, among them, tools of a perfection reached only in very recent times, *e.g.* planes with an iron handle. It is obvious that the Roman army was a factor of civilisation of the greatest importance, since an army corps acts like a magnet on a multitude of people. Sutlers, dealers, artisans, and women, who are excluded from the camp, settle outside its gates.

Wherever a legion or a detachment had its permanent base a civilian community grew up, dwelling in hutments which went by the name of *cannabae*. Even outside the camp of Haltern in Westphalia, which cannot have housed Roman troops for more than twenty years, traces of such a community have been found. Outside the lesser camps, like Saalburg, the civil community was small, but outside the large camps it was more important. A camp built for two legions had to hold 10,000–12,000 men, approximately the same number of auxiliaries, and considerable numbers of mechanics, etc. A permanent camp for about 25,000 men necessitated a civil community of corresponding size. Moreover, discharged soldiers often settled down to spend the remainder of their days near the camp in which they had lived and the comrades with whom they had served. The community outside the camp settled on land belonging to the legion : it was indispensable, and soon created an organisation of its own with *decuriones* and officials resembling those of towns. Officially it is described as " the Roman citizens " or " the assembly of Roman citizens who live in the camp huts." Most of the camp-communities were villages both in size and legal status. The larger ones became centres of trade and communication in the region. Factories sprang up, which provided both army and civilians with certain articles, *e.g.* pottery at Xanten and Neuss, and glass at Cologne. The fine Jupiter column at Mainz, which has been restored from numerous fragments, was set up by the *cannabarii*, the inhabitants of the camp community, in Nero's reign, and bears witness both to wealth and artistic taste. In the frontier districts these great camp-communities developed into cities, *e.g.* Mainz, Cologne, Xanten, Nimwegen on the Rhine, York in Britain, and Lambaesis in Africa. Their ground plan shows the same regularity as that of a camp—the headquarters in the camp being replaced in the city by the Forum with its temples and public buildings—and this regular plan set a fixed pattern for other newly founded cities.

The culture of the camp-city had a definitely Roman stamp. There was a significant difference between Roman culture on the Rhine frontier with its pronounced military character, and the culture of Central Gaul, where no soldiers were quartered, with its strong provincial character. The veterans who lived in the camp-community were, and called themselves, Roman citizens. The quondam provincials had, during their twenty years of service, undergone a thorough process of romanisation. Celibacy was imposed on them. They had no strong family ties which would have resisted the influence of comrades and superiors and kept the provincial true to his nationality. Latin was not merely the language of command, but was used on all official and public occasions. Divisions were sometimes formed exclusively from one people—thus auxiliary forces are often named after a people, *e.g. ala Thracum* (the Thracian *ala* or company),etc.,but in spite of the name they usually included soldiers of other nationalities. In a good-sized camp there was a strange mixture of tongues and races, even though, in some cases, one particular nationality might have been predominant. Moreover, especially at the beginning of the imperial age, the Italian element was strong, and during the first two centuries, the centurions, the under-officers and instructors of the rank and file, continued to be of Italian birth. Latin had also to be the means of communication between the soldiers themselves.

The chief method of converting the soldier drawn from the semi-barbaric tribes of the provinces into a Roman was hard work and strict discipline. Drill and fencing were learned and practised under specialist instructors ; three times a month there were route marches, in complete field equipment, of ten Roman miles (a little more than nine English miles), partly at a walk, partly at the double. The equipment carried consisted of provisions for seventeen days,fencing poles,and possibly tools. Vegetius estimates the weight of the pack at sixty Roman, or about forty-five English pounds. To this must be added the weight of the armour, shield, spear, and harness, which were considerably heavier and took up more room than the arms a soldier now carries. The superiority of the Roman army depended on its discipline, skill in manœuvring, and, above all, in its capacity for marching. We shall see that the more the army was barbarised, the more the discipline was relaxed, the drill lightened and the resultant superiority lost. It is no wonder that *Disciplina* was made a goddess which adorns the imperial coinage, for she it was that created the Roman army. But Hadrian made a very bad miscalculation when he believed that she was competent to make good Romans out of his barbarian recruits.

Just as in modern states, there was a graded system of decorations for bravery in the field and for good and faithful service. During the Empire these were graded according to rank. The higher officers received wreaths, a standard, and the so-called *hasta pura*, a kind of spear, whose real nature is uncertain, while the soldiers and non-commissioned officers, including centurions, received medals (*phalerae*), necklets and bracelets. The medals were comparatively large round plates, sometimes smooth, sometimes with emblems in repoussé, representations of gods and the like. They were fastened by leather thongs, which the infantryman attached to his armour, and the cavalryman to his horse. If an entire division was decorated, wreaths or medals were affixed to the pole of the regimental standard, just as the flag of a regiment is decorated to-day.

There were also other means by which the soldier was looked after and trained to respect and feel allegiance towards Emperor and Empire. From early days the individual soldier had the right to dispose of all that he earned on war-service, unimpeded by any legal decrees or by the usual rights of a father over his sons. But the State also saw to it that the soldiers did not squander their hard-earned pay and occasional presents. Every legion had a savings-bank, in which the pay and half of the donations received on special occasions had to be deposited. This was a complete parallel to the deposits in a post office savings-bank book of a part of the daily pay of a modern Swede during his period of army service. The difference is that the Roman legionaries had, out of this, to pay for their food, equipment, arms, tent, and clothing.

Clubs were as flourishing in the army as in civil life, but the clubs which united soldiers of the same grade in the service seem to have sprung up, first, under the soldier-emperor, Septimius Severus. The numerous co-operative societies, however,

may have been older.   Every legion had a burial-fund, just as
a fund to provide for burial is the object of many Friendly
Societies in civil life.   We can see the scope of these co-operative
societies from the record of a club of thirty-six persons in the
camp of Lambaesis.   A very high entrance fee of 3000 sesterces
was paid ; the members received, in case of a journey overseas,
travelling money ; in case of retirement from the service, an
allowance ;   an equipment-allowance on promotion ;   a compensation if they lost their post ; when they died, a sum was
paid to their heirs.   So it appears that this was an insurance
agency, which covered all those eventualities in military service
that were accompanied by any financial demands.   Besides
their obvious and primary economic importance these clubs
were also useful socially in educating and introducing soldiers
to the forms of Roman social life.

Religion had a powerful influence in the same direction.
The army or, more correctly, each independent division of the
army had its cult, the objects of which were the gods, the
standards, and the Emperors.   Of these the standards were
really the most important.   First came the legionary eagle,
next the Emperors' portraits, but every cohort and maniple,
every division and detachment, had its standard : the detachment was called *vexillatio* from the *vexillum* or flag which it
followed.   The standard consisted of a short cross-piece with
fillets at the ends, fastened to a pole, on which wreaths were
slung and to which medals and, in the case of the praetorian
guard, the Emperors' portraits were attached ; the *vexillum*
was a banner on a cross-pole.   In the field the standards were
carried ; in camp they were set up at headquarters, the eagle
in a chapel, the flags of the cohorts and maniples in side-niches.
The standards were the objects of a cult, which reminds us
strongly of the French cult of the tricolour, except that it was
religious in form, and not merely sentimental.

The gods which were worshipped in the army varied greatly.
Their images were fixed on the poles of the standards when the
commander-in-chief took the field.   Often we find the three
Capitoline gods, Jupiter Optimus Maximus, Juno Regina and
Minerva, the old tutelary divinities of Rome, and very often

others as well. The auxiliary troops, consisting of provincials, enjoyed also the privilege of taking with them the gods of their country. A particularly prominent part was played by the special protecting divinities of the different divisions, *genius legionis, genius alae, genius cohortis*, etc., and by pure personifications of soldierly virtues, Victoria, Fortuna, Honos, Virtus, Disciplina, etc. These were educational divinities, calculated to fortify and elevate the spirit of the soldiers.

The cult of the Emperor was the religious expression of the realisation of the power and unity of the Roman Empire. In accordance with Augustus' prohibition the most repulsive form of the Emperor cult, the worship of the living Emperor as a god, was not performed in Italy, but was confined to the provinces. It was the *genius* of the Emperor that was worshipped by the army, just as a household worshipped the *genius* of the master. Only after the Emperor died was he elevated to the gods. The distinction was subtle,—too subtle for the majority,—and the direct cult of the Emperor conquered in the end, and in the time of Gordian became the rule in the army. In the chapel at headquarters the statues of the Emperors were set up, together with the standards and statues of the gods. The chapel was not large and soon became so overcrowded that the statues of the apotheosised Emperors were removed to the colonnade outside. These statues were set up by centurions or tribunes or by a division of troops which wished to display its loyalty. The army was induced to co-operate in the cult of the Emperor, and so the spirit of loyalty was inculcated with still greater force.

All the details of military life had a single aim, *viz.* the education of the soldiers so that they should be loyal to Emperor and realm. That the desired effect was, in fact, attained, must not be overlooked in view of the well-known phenomena which suggest the contrary, such as the unbridled licence of the praetorian guard, isolated mutinies and attempted mutinies under the early Empire, and the military despotism of the third century. Then the self-interests of the professional soldiery and the progressive barbarisation of the army played their fatal part. Fidelity to the Emperor survived these temptations, and the sentiment for the Empire even outlived its fall.

For a clearer understanding of the influence for good and evil which the army exercised on culture and the movements of population within the Empire, it is necessary to inquire into its organisation ; for every army, and not least that of the Roman Empire, is an organism.

The army consisted of the Emperor's body-guard quartered in Rome, the specially favoured praetorians, the legionaries, and the auxiliaries.   In addition there was a provincial militia, which did not possess the same tactical units as the regular troops.   It was a *Landwehr*, employed only in its home, not reckoned in the army ; and ranking even below the *personnel* of the fleet.   The different classes of imperial troops were recruited by different methods, and had different privileges. The periods of service were alternatively 16, 20 and 25 years, but discharge was often postponed for lack of recruits and money.   The severe fighting in Pannonia and Germany in the later years of Augustus caused irregularities of this kind.   On the death of the old Emperor the complaint was made that toothless old men were retained in the legions.

The pay is either known, or can be reckoned with probability, over different periods.   Augustus gave the praetorians 2000 and the legionaries 600 sesterces per annum, but during his last years he had to raise the amounts to 3000 and 900. After Nero, the praetorians, in addition, received corn *gratis*. Domitian made an increase to 4000 and 1200 sesterces.   At the end of the second and beginning of the third centuries the military Emperors raised the pay repeatedly.   Commodus paid 5000 and 1500, Septimius Severus 6800 and 2000, Caracalla 10,000 and 3000.   The figures are eloquent, for they betray, not only the growing power and claims of the army and especially of the praetorian guard, but also the drop in the value of money.   But Caracalla was wildly extravagant.   To defray the immoderately increased outlay on the army, he extended Roman citizenship to all the inhabitants of the Empire, thus making them all liable to legacy duty, which, simultaneously, was doubled.   Unfortunately we have little knowledge of the rate of pay of the auxiliaries. By reckoning on rather scanty information it has been assumed that in the later days of Augustus it reached 300 sesterces.

We must also reckon the sums paid to soldiers on their discharge after serving their time. These are usually described by the Latin word *praemia*, an expression which conceals the real fact that these sums served an object which no State with a fixed military system can dispense with, *viz.* the civil provision for its discharged soldiers. In A.D. 6 Augustus created a special fund, the *aerarium militare*, in an attempt to put this urgent part of financial administration on a sound basis, assigning to it a capital of 170,000,000 sesterces, and the profits of new taxation. In these *praemia* at discharge we find a similar gradation between the different troops : the praetorians receiving 20,000, the legionaries 12,000 sesterces, the auxiliaries nothing but the still valuable Roman citizenship and the right to contract lawful marriage, by which their children obtained the same privilege, any children born previously being legitimised.

With these liabilities one can understand that the army weighed heavily on the financial resources of the Empire ; but if the Empire was to exist the burden had to be borne. Crushing, too, was another great item of expense, which also had its origin in republican times, when the people and the soldiers of the victorious general received in gifts their share of the booty won. Augustus followed Caesar's example, and at his death bequeathed to the praetorians 1000 sesterces apiece, and to the legionaries 300. But still more dangerous was the custom introduced by Claudius, of giving, on his accession, a donation to the soldiers, particularly the praetorians. This directly incited them to play the part of kingmakers, which, to the detriment of the Empire, they played with the zeal of amateurs, who speedily realised that the Emperor could be set up by their favour and depended on their good will. In comparison with this direct challenge to the soldiers to trample on the neck of the State, the actual expenditure of money was of small account. In the case of Claudius and Nero the amount is known. It was equivalent to five years' pay—in other words, 15,000 sesterces. Hadrian doubled the amount since, at first, his throne was insecure, whereas Marcus Aurelius returned to the usual scale (*i.e.* allowing for the increase in pay). The legionaries mattered less as the Emperor was not so dependent on them, and Marcus Aurelius gave them 900 apiece. Their time came, when Septimius Severus won the throne with the help of the Illyrian and Pannonian legions against the praetorians, who sold the throne by regular auction. As a reward for their services they demanded 20,000 per head. The money was procured by proscriptions and confiscations in the provinces. When Septimius Severus felt himself secure he diminished the expenses. On the occasion of his ten years' jubilee he gave his new praetorian guard no more than Augustus did in his will, 1000 sesterces apiece. It must be added that the donations were paid in gold, and consequently were independent of the rapidly diminishing value of the silver currency.

These dry figures illustrate better than words the reverse of the medal, the growing caste spirit of the soldiers, who plundered State and citizens as their lawful booty. As the arrogance and licence of the soldiery became more unbridled, so much the more did they become unsuited to act as a civilising agency. The most unmanageable element in the army was the Italian, which soon was limited to the praetorians and the officers; yet, on it depended the romanisation of the army, and, through the army, of important sections of the provincial population. The strength of the army depended on recruiting, which, in the long run, determined its character as a military force and a civilising agency.

As has been stated, Roman citizenship was required for admission to the legions. During the civil war, when great armies were being raised, necessity compelled the admission of provincials to whom the general, by virtue of his *imperium*, granted citizenship on their enlistment. Augustus could not entirely avoid this, though he brought it within strict limits. The Empire was already on the slope which led to the barbarisation of the army, the old conditions being evaded by a fiction. Recruiting took place, partly by voluntary enlistment, partly, when enlistment failed, by conscription. Conscription was unpopular and used only in case of necessity. In both cases Italy was privileged, and, next to Italy, the citizen colonies in the provinces. The privilege in the two cases had opposite effects. In voluntary enlistment the Italians had the preference ; in compulsory conscription Italy was spared. In this lay the germ of later developments brought about by the ever-growing dislike to military service.

The same geographically distributed privileges carried with them preferential right of entry into the better paid *corps d'élite*, the praetorians in particular. For their recruiting area Augustus prescribed a narrower circle in Italy—Latium, Etruria, Umbria, and the oldest citizen-colonies, which preserved the purest Roman blood. There also the three cohorts that served as gendarmes in Rome were recruited. The rest of the Italians found a place in the legions, and the citizens from the provinces in special cohorts, which were not attached to the legions. The auxiliary troops consisted of provincials who had the status of provincial citizenship. Here too a certain measure of civilisation was required, *viz.* the organisation of a city.

This was the system of the earlier Empire. In it the dominant position of Italy was obvious enough. As the Italians had conquered and dominated the world by force of arms, a duty was devolved on them of maintaining and preserving their *imperium* by arms. But this duty they refused to fulfil. The principle broke down with the admission of provincials into the army with the grant of citizenship and domicile in a city. The question arises, in what manner and at what rate this change, which led to the exclusion from the army of the once dominant people, was effected.

Augustus attempted to maintain the principle. The numerous exceptions at the beginning of his reign were made in the special interests of the armies of the civil war and occur in the provinces in which Antonius' legions were quartered. The desperate situation after the loss of the three legions in the Teutoburg Forest compelled him to raise a legion of non-citizens from Italy, and another from the warlike Galatians

—Celts, who formed the army of King Deiotarus. Under
Claudius and Nero the provincial citizens thronged into the
legions. The inscriptions supply interesting statistics in spite
of their scantiness and fortuitous character. Of the soldiers
whose native place is recorded, from the time of Augustus to
the accession of Vespasian, 67 per cent. came from Italy, and
17 per cent. from the largely romanised Gallia Narbonensis,
whereas for the other provinces the proportions are small,
Macedonia 6 per cent., Baetica 4 per cent., Galatia 4 per cent.,
Noricum 2 per cent., Gallia Lugdunensis 2 per cent., Hispania
Tarraconensis, Germany, Asia each 1 per cent. But Tacitus
states that at the battle of Cremona, which gave the Empire
to Vespasian, the soldiers of the 3rd legion greeted the rising
sun after the Syrian fashion. The 3rd legion had its headquarters in Syria, and if it did not chiefly consist of Syrians, it
had learned Syrian customs.

The disturbances after Nero's death produced fresh irregularities. The German legions, which began the rising, consisted of Italians. Vespasian disbanded three legions, and
formed two new ones of marines, thus introducing freed men
to the legions. Dated inscriptions from Vespasian to Trajan
give for every 15 Italians, 6 inhabitants of Gallia Narbonensis,
and 6 from other provinces. From Hadrian's time come
instructive lists of soldiers from the camp at Lambaesis.
The oldest class—those who entered the service under Trajan
—has 78 names: from Africa and Numidia 15, Cyrene 1,
Egypt 6, Syria 32, Bithynia 22; Italy is not represented.
Later lists give names chiefly from Africa and Numidia.
This clearly shows the change which had taken place. With
the second century Italians disappeared from the legions.
Hadrian recruited the legion at its local headquarters, and
after Antoninus Pius no notice was taken any longer of citizen
birth. A similar but more gradual modification took place in
the praetorian guard. After Caligula's death we find in the
legions hardly a single soldier from their recruiting districts :
the supply had begun to dry up. Under Claudius people from
the northern frontier of Italy appear in the guard, since the old
recruiting area no longer sufficed. In lists of the time of Hadrian

and Antoninus Pius, Italians without distinction and some provincials appear. The process may be summed up thus— at first the legions were chiefly recruited from Italy, now the supply was not even sufficient for the favoured praetorian guard.

What was it that caused the change ? The requisite quota of recruits was not large—for the guard 600–700, for the legions about 7000 men annually. The period of service had been extended so that the efficiency of the army was endangered. At Augustus' death there were toothless old men in the legions. Tiberius retained soldiers beyond their time owing to the difficulty he experienced in keeping the cadres up to strength by enlistment, and under Claudius we find soldiers with thirty three years of service. The necessary number of recruits was really not so great but that Italy might have supplied them.

The solution is to be found, not in the decline of the population in the civilised areas, though that had some effect, but in the spirit of pacifism which spread through the Roman world. Men shrank from military service and its hardships in spite of the advantages it offered. Men cut off their thumbs to avoid military service. Pacifism is one of those deep revulsions of sentiment which, when it attacks a people, overrides every obstacle, defies all reason, and requires a century or more to lose its effects. The longing for peace spread widely during the tedious and disastrous time of the civil war : it was fostered by Augustus, who built on it his reorganisation of the Empire and his imperial power : it became a powerful factor in the new religious movement. This overwhelming desire was acceded to to a great extent, and for two centuries there was profound peace all over the Empire. The army became no more than a frontier-guard against the barbarians, and wars, with few exceptions, were confined to frontier-wars to restrain the barbarians from the confines of civilisation. In the interior an enemy was never seen except as a captive, nor a soldier except on the march.

Pacifism permeated all classes of the civilised population, and exemption from military service became a privilege of culture. The privilege consisted simply in the fact that no recruits came forward voluntarily. Forced conscription was hateful and was only applied in the provinces, and even in these, the most advanced, Baetica, Gallia Narbonensis, Greece, and Asia Minor, were exempted. There was also a domestic and social reason. Italy was again becoming a land of small cultivators, but these were now tenant-farmers. The peasant makes a good soldier, but loathes the military profession, unless, as in the days of old Rome, he is compelled to follow the path of conquest by land-hunger. Another factor, too, was the turbulence and want of discipline which the Italian troops often showed, *e.g.* the Rhine army in the year of the three Emperors. The Emperor had occasion to beware of such dangerous servants and turned to the provincials, who, outwardly at least, were more submissive.

It is a dangerous privilege to be able to lay aside your weapons and let your comfort and culture be defended by others—by uncultivated provincials of different blood and race. It did not take long for the barbarous or semi-barbarous soldiers to realise the position, and to set their feet upon the neck of the peaceful and pacifist population. The Emperor, Septimius Severus, learned the old lesson that a small resolute force which bears weapons is master of the great unarmed multitude. On his death-bed he advised his sons to neglect everything else but to enrich the soldiers. Caracalla followed his precept to an extreme degree : it was his pride to be a ranker. As a consequence of its ingrained pacifism the civilised population of the Roman Empire handed over its defence and the custody of its culture to the uncivilised. By so doing it placed on its back a master who ruled it with a rod of iron.

The turning point in the composition of the army was the introduction of recruiting at the headquarters of the various legions, which was done under Hadrian. This was convenient, since the necessity for collecting contingents of recruits and marching them long distances was avoided. There was a productive source of recruits among the children born in the camp-towns, who had no objection to following the profession of their fathers. Their growing number can be demonstrated by the help of inscriptions. Egyptian lists under Tiberius show 2 soldiers' children out of 36 recruits, those of A.D. 168 20 out of 37 ; the oldest list of Trajan's time from Lambaesis shows 4 soldiers' children out of 78 recruits, whereas, in the later ones of Hadrian's time they form a third to a half of all the recruits. The children of a soldier were Roman citizens, but they were often bastards and only legitimated on the father's discharge. A high standard of education could not be expected of them. There ensued a kind of hereditary succession in the military profession, which intensified the caste spirit and the separation of its interests from the civil population.

There was imminent danger of the army losing its uniform Roman stamp when the Italian element disappeared, and the provincials crowded to fill the legions. Hadrian, who introduced local recruiting, clearly realised this danger, and tried to obviate it by introducing stringent methods of training into the army. His strict notions of discipline and drill are known from the memorandum already quoted (p. 288) after one of his inspections. The instructors who were to train and romanise the army were Italian officers, and especially the non-commissioned officers, who in daily routine were in immediate contact with the soldiers and maintained their Italian character longer. The recruiting of officers and non-commissioned officers was of vital importance for the problem of civilising and romanising the army, and it leads us deep into its organisation.

In the Roman, as in every modern army, there were different careers open to officers and non-commissioned officers—in the Roman no less than four. In this connection the real reason for the arrangement so often objected to by the lovers of democracy, namely the effort to inculcate the value of culture in and over the army, can clearly be seen. In the Roman Empire culture coincided, on the whole, with Roman citizenship and Italian birth or origin from a provincial city of equal rank with the Italian. The exceptions—especially those applying to the Greek world—were not of great importance. This circumstance makes it possible to follow the process and to view its results in a clear light.

The four careers were : one for men of Senatorial rank, one for knights, one for the senior non-commissioned officers, the centurions, and one for the junior non-commissioned officers. The organisation of the army in outline was as follows. An army was commanded by an imperial *legatus*, who was usually a provincial governor as well. Every legion, with the auxiliaries attached to it, was commanded by a legionary *legatus*, and next under him ranked the legionary tribunes. The permanent quarters of the army made a camp commandant (*praefectus castrorum*) necessary. The tactical units within the legion were the ten cohorts, the first of 1000, the remaining nine of 600 men. As to the subordinate commands, the old division of the cohort into three maniples, and the maniple into two centuries was retained. There were two centurions for each maniple, which made sixty in all for the legion. The centurions were non-commissioned officers, but their position was far more important than that of non-commissioned officers in a modern army. About 100 men were under each of them ; they were appointed by the Emperor, and the chief centurions regularly took part in the councils of war of the legion. All other non-commissioned officers were appointed by the officers, and were called collectively *principales*. Each centurion had by his side an *optio*. Moreover, the service necessitated *principales* of very different kinds, ensigns and standard bearers, quarter-masters, orderlies, clerks, etc. The various grades of rank in the cavalry and auxiliaries are less important and may be passed over. It need only be observed that meritorious centurions were promoted to be prefects of a cohort of auxiliaries or an *ala* of cavalry. The junior non-commissioned officers were taken from the ranks.

The supreme command was entrusted to men of senatorial rank. By a year's service as legionary tribunes they acquired a certain military training. If they continued in the military career, they became legionary legates or provincial governors, and as such, army commanders. The military experience of legionary legates must often have been insufficient ; so for the details of the service they relied upon the camp commandants who had been promoted from among the centurions.

If the highest career was reserved for the senatorial nobility, the next highest was reserved for the municipal nobility, which belonged to the equestrian order. Originally the knights entered the service as legionary tribunes. Later on in the imperial age we find they were eligible for three or four definite posts, usually the command of the cavalry squadron attached to the legion, of a cohort of auxiliaries, the position of legionary tribune, and the command of an *ala* of cavalry. After that the knight could return to his native place with a reputable military title, or he might remain in the imperial service and aspire to high positions, *e.g.* as *procurator* in various branches of the administration, or even as governor of one of the smaller provinces. Two of the highest officials of the Empire were knights, the praetorian prefect and the prefect of Egypt.

Privates, called *caligati* from their shoes, might be promoted to *principales* and could reach the rank of centurion, but usually the latter were selected from the praetorian guard or were volunteers, sometimes of equestrian rank, which for the time being they were allowed to discard. The qualification of Italian birth or descent from Roman military colonies was strictly maintained, even in the second century. Augustus created a peculiar institution, which was often drawn upon for the recruiting of centurions. Soldiers who had served their sixteen years with distinction in the praetorian guard, or even, though less frequently, in the city cohorts, and had been promoted to *principales*, were retained in military service and called *evocati*. They received various posts, and often entered the clerical departments of the legions or became centurions.

A centurion's promotion depended upon circumstances. In theory he began as the junior centurion in the 10th cohort and had to pass through all the sixty grades till he became *primus pilus*, the chief centurion, who, as chief of the permanent staff of the legion, occupied a very important position. Promotion was often accelerated by passing over several steps, but in that case it was always combined with a transfer to another legion. By this arrangement, care was taken for the uniformity of the army in training and character. The centurions travelled throughout the Empire and served now in one army and province, now in another. They had no time to vegetate and develop any provincial peculiarity : they retained their Roman stamp and impressed it on the troops, whose proper teachers and trainers they were. Their symbol of office was a vine-staff, which they well understood how to use on the soldiers' backs. The centurion's pay was high, being 10,000 sesterces under Augustus (doubled in the case of the *primi ordines*), and the amount was gradually raised as the pay of the army increased.

Usually, after his discharge, the centurion went back into private life, and in country towns belonged to the cream of society ; but some were promoted to be legionary tribunes, prefects of a cohort, or procurators. There are several examples of a centurion rising to the highest office in the Empire, *i.e.* that of Emperor's deputy, which was the position of the praetorian prefect. Promotion of this kind was given to those especially who had started on their centurion's career as volunteers. In spite of the existence of the four careers, difference in position and birth was no absolute hindrance for competence to assert itself and rise to the highest and most important posts. The barriers could be surmounted, and in normal circumstances culture and training were duly rewarded.

Augustus had contemplated an army composed of the ruling people and supported by provincial auxiliaries—the latter only becoming Roman citizens when, by service in the army, they had acquired Roman discipline and the Roman spirit. But even he had been forced, by circumstances, to depart from this principle, and under Hadrian it came to an end. The army was recruited from the region where the legion was quartered, and to a great extent from soldiers' children. The inculcation of Roman discipline and Roman spirit was put into the hands of the centurions in reliance on the power of training over human nature. They were to form the element which held the army together and made it a Roman army. Therefore the centurions had to be of Italian birth.

Italian birth became a privilege in the service, but such a privilege was dangerous, with its natural tendency to create caste spirit and an arrogant and licentious class, which pervaded the army and particularly manifested itself in the praetorian guard, which was eventually to sell the throne to the highest bidder. The inevitable vengeance followed at once on the accession of Septimius Severus, who, with the aid of the Illyrian legions, seized the throne the same year in which the auction took place. He has been accused of purposely extirpating the Italian element from the army. The alteration—for an alteration undoubtedly took place—was not so sudden as that. The Italians' dislike for military service resulted in a process which prepared the way for it ; and it was finally brought about by the circumstances under which Septimius Severus gained power, and the inclinations he acquired from his African origin and his Syrian marriage. His rule forms an epoch in the Orientalisation of the Empire and the barbarisation of the army, and is the first instance of military despotism, though under the strong hand of Severus this had no opportunity to display itself openly.

Septimius had won the throne by the arms of the Illyrian and Pannonian legions in conflict with the praetorian guard. By the new system these troops were recruited where they were stationed, chiefly among the fierce and stubborn Illyrian tribes, whose descendants have not greatly changed in character even to-day. The old Italian praetorian guard was disbanded, and replaced by a new and stronger one, selected from the legions, particularly those of Pannonia. As a reward for efficiency and faithful service, legionaries were now promoted to the guard, as we find from the records of their birthplace in inscriptions. Thus the guard became a *corps d'élite* of tried soldiers from all parts of the Empire, but it became also a corps of semi-barbarians. The old qualification of Roman citizenship lost its importance after Caracalla had granted citizenship to all the inhabitants of the Empire, and the army became as motley and barbaric as the Empire.

This transformation of the guard marks an epoch in the history of the army. Its privileges continued, and from it constantly proceeded a great proportion of the officers, though now most of them rose from the ranks. In every case the centurions came directly or indirectly from the rank and file of the legions.

x

The guard was no longer Italian. Septimius Severus brought to an end the preponderance and privileges of the Italian element. The reform would seem to have paved the way for efficiency, but it is certain that it made the way broad and easy for unlettered ignorance. Previously a *principalis* had undertaken various duties which introduced him to all the minuter details of the service before he was promoted to the rank of centurion. Now all *optiones*—the assistants of the centurions—were qualified for the rank of centurion, and were advanced directly. A centurion of this class was a fighting man and nothing more; but, for the officers of the army of a civilised people, education is as important as the art of fighting.

Septimius Severus' reform of the army may be called democratic, in so far as promotion from the ranks was made the normal procedure and the distinction between Italy and the provinces was abolished. It was an important stage in the process of levelling. But it did not check, but rather promoted the caste feeling of the soldiers, which was encouraged by semi-barbarian provincials instead of by the Italians, who, despite all their bad habits, were more highly civilised. Septimius Severus exerted himself to make popular reforms. Previously, centurions, *evocati*, and *optiones* who expected promotion to centurionship, wore the gold ring of the knight : this privilege was now granted to all *principales*. He and his son raised the rate of pay to such a degree that it threatened to give the finances of the Empire the *coup-de-grâce*. Thus the self-consciousness and arrogance of the soldiery was increased, education reduced to a minimum, provincial idiosyncrasies emphasised, and the natural rivalry of the various armies increased ; loyalty to the State and fidelity to the Emperor disappeared, the bonds of discipline were loosened, and respect for authority undermined. The iron will of Severus had been able to keep the army in subjection, but when Caracalla, who was a monomaniac on the subject of soldiering, and the insignificant Emperors of the house of Emesa came to the throne, military despotism was complete. When the weak tie of legitimacy through the female line, which brought Alexander Severus to the throne, was severed—he was murdered by the soldiers like his cousin and predecessor, Heliogabalus—the army proclaimed an Emperor who had risen from the ranks. What followed has been described already. Emperors were removed as fast as they were set up, a claimant to the throne arose in every army, and when, simultaneously, external foes made an attack, the Empire came near to falling to pieces. Only one Emperor fell fighting against the enemies of the Empire, but dozens fell victims to their own soldiers.

During this period events followed the line of least resistance. Senators dropped out of the army of their own wish, from lack of military efficiency or from mistrust of the Emperor. Any man with the reputation that the rank of Senator and an active public life afforded, and the power that a devoted army and the governorship of a province brought with it, was a dangerous rival to the Emperor. This danger, of which there were so many examples, caused Gallienus to exclude Senators from service in the army. The command of the legion was transferred to the camp-commandant. After that time generals were regularly taken from the non-commissioned grades, which were no longer Italian.

The rank of knight lost its old importance for military service, and the same was the case with the *evocati*, who represented the sum of the soldiers' military experience and training. The soldiers were approximated to equestrian rank, and Gallienus granted all soldiers an old privilege of the knights, *viz.* white parade uniform. The same Emperor conferred the equestrian rank on all sons of centurions and *principales* at birth. In place of the old equestrian order, which had lost its importance, he tried to create a new one on a military basis. No better illustration can be given of the dominant position of the soldiery than this grant of equestrian rank to the children of non-commissioned officers and the permission for privates to wear equestrian dress. At the same time the mobility and fighting strength of the army were diminished.

Another of Septimius Severus' popular reforms was to permit soldiers "to cohabit with women." The Greek expression is ambiguous. It is generally interpreted to mean that he permitted the soldiers to marry, but it should rather be taken literally. The soldiers' connection with women who dwelt in the camp-town had probably, even before his time, not been entirely without legal sanction ; now they received permission to reside with their wives in the camp-town. The camp was no longer their barracks, but the place to which they repaired for their daily exercise. Previously if a soldier had a wife and children, it was an affair which did not concern the State. If he was transferred he had to manage as best he could for his family. Now the State could no longer disregard the wives and children of soldiers. When a legion was ordered off to new quarters it was followed by a long train of ox-waggons, which conveyed wives and children and furniture. The pay had increased, but the value of money had gone down. It was difficult for a soldier to maintain a family on his pay. The legion had extensive lands around it and from these he was allotted a portion to till at a moderate rent, and this applied to auxiliaries also. The land passed to the children together with the obligation of service, and they became peasants with a military organisation—not unlike " Territorials." But this was the surest way to diminish the army's readiness to fight, which, apart from more modern instances, is proved by the history of Egypt under the Ptolemies, and Babylon after Hammurabi. For example, Charles XI. of Sweden introduced, about 1680, a system which lasted till within living memory, of making both large and small grants of farm-land to officers and other ranks respectively. The effect of this on Swedish military efficiency was anything but satisfactory. Here was the germ of the decadence of the legions in Diocletian's army system. The phenomenon is illustrated best by the results on the German frontier. There, almost all the auxiliary troops vanished from the Army List. When the frontier districts were lost, the soldier-peasants remained on their lands and were automatically cut off from the Empire.

Decay in military efficiency set in as a consequence of the disappearance of culture from the army and its officers. The centurions—the hard-handed trainers of the soldiers— who did not wield their staffs lightly, were not in touch with the professional feeling and self-consciousness of the new army, and were always the first victims of mutinies. They gradually disappeared, the last being mentioned in Africa under Constantine. It can easily be conceived what their disappearance meant for military training. Everything united to break down the old organisation. The distinction between the legion and the auxiliaries was abolished, its *raison d'être* ceasing to exist when Roman citizenship was extended to the whole Empire, and the legions had adopted the more primitive methods of warfare of the provincials. The provincial militia, although its tactics differed, and it was often ignorant of the Latin language, had been employed several times by Antoninus Pius for extra-provincial warfare, and was utilised to a still greater extent by Marcus Aurelius in the crisis of the war with the Marcomanni. In the following century it was incorporated in the Imperial Army. On the roll of any army in the second half of this century, Gaesatae, Dacians, Britons, Cantabrians, Palmyrenes are conspicuous.

These were the problems which confronted Diocletian when he had to carry out reorganisation. The army provided him with two tasks,—one to bring back the soldiers to obedience and to secure the Emperor against their aggressions—in this he succeeded—the other to strengthen the army and make it competent to drive back the foes of the Empire,—and this was the harder task. The increased pressure on the frontiers, since the Germans had grown strong and the powerful neo-Persian Empire had been founded, required much greater efficiency than had been necessary in the two first centuries. The quality of the army had declined. The decay in efficiency had to be compensated for by an increase in numbers. It is said that Diocletian quadrupled the army. We shall come back later to the way in which he extorted the means required for this great increase in spite of economic exhaustion.

The leading idea in Diocletian's military system was the division of the army into frontier troops and field army. The frontier troops were to receive the first shock. The field army was quartered in the interior, to move when an attack on the frontier took place. It followed the Emperor, who travelled about widely, and so was called *comitatenses* : its commander-in-chief had the title of *magister militum*. The frontier troops were composed of the old legions, which, in the manner described above, were stationed permanently on the frontier, and had to surrender their best men to the field army. They were divided into staff and garrisons of frontier forts, and were partly composed of peasants with land free from taxation, which passed to their sons along with the obligation of service. They thus became second-line troops, for which men of weaker physique and a lower standard of height were eligible. Only on the Danube these troops had a better status, a significant fact, showing the military importance of this frontier. The frontier exits and entrances and the frontier fortifications were strengthened. An attempt was made to replace by material defence what was lacking in the quality of the army. The praetorian guard was a source of danger even after its remodelling, so it was diminished in number and lost its importance by being left in Rome and no longer attending on the person of the ruler. In its place a new and stronger guard (*palatini*) was formed, composed of the élite of the army.

Constantine further developed Diocletian's reforms. He strengthened the field army at the expense of the frontier troops. In the battle of Ponte Molle he overcame the praetorian guard which fought for Maxentius. Thus its fate was sealed : it was dissolved, and Constantine created a body-guard (*scholae*) which consisted of picked men, barbarians of course, and chiefly Germans. They were all mounted, received higher pay, and were distinguished by more splendid equipment. Very great importance attached to the auxiliaries, who must not be confounded with the auxiliaries of the old régime. They ranked before the field army and immediately after the guard. They were composed chiefly of Gauls and of tribesmen from the right bank of the Rhine, who were therefore either freely enlisted Germans or prisoners of war. The best troops of the Empire were thus entirely barbarian. In war they had an importance which surpassed their rank. They played the chief part in the decisive battles after the age of Diocletian. These barbarian troops were, from a military point of view, superior to the troops of the Empire. The German mode of fighting had superseded the Roman, and the Emperor's army went into battle with the German war-cry. The Roman art of war, the superiority of which had laid the world at Rome's feet, was a thing of the past.

The recruiting of the army took place as before, to a great extent, by means of voluntary enlistment, but the recruits came chiefly from the barbarian tribes—Illyrians and others—and from beyond the frontiers. In addition, many who, from their position, were exempt from military service often tried to escape their duties by enlisting. The better elements in the Empire had no desire to offer themselves as soldiers ; they preferred to become subordinate officials in some of the innumerable departments of the civil service. A new phenomenon was the obligation to supply recruits by a kind of taxation, which was imposed on landed property in certain provinces. A landowner had to select a recruit among his retainers ; if the property was not large enough, several landowners had to combine to supply a recruit. Naturally the landowners selected the worst possible specimens whom they could hope to get taken, for the State could reject only the undersized. By this method of recruiting the poorest material was obtained, and this may well have been the reason for the human tribute being commuted for a money-tax. From the proceeds of the sum paid the State bought other recruits. The regulations give an alarming picture of the severity with which the recalcitrants were pressed into military service. Even those who cut off their thumbs were not exempted, but were used in various ways in the service of the State, or were condemned to the stake, penalties being inflicted on their employers. Nevertheless two mutilated persons were counted as one recruit. Any one who sheltered a deserter was condemned to penal servitude in the mines, or rendered liable to the seizure of half his property if he was of a superior station. An estate manager, by whom a man liable to service was concealed, was sentenced to be burned alive, and the landowner's property confiscated. Scourging, forced labour in mines, deportation for life, heavy fines in recruits or money according to a man's position, make up the list of penalties. By such means recruits had to be squeezed out of the Romans! The authorities were no longer confronted with pacifism only : severe economic pressure was also playing a part. It is not to be wondered at that the native troops were the worst in the Empire.

The germ of an hereditary obligation to serve existed already in the fact that the legions were largely recruited from soldiers' children. After the frontier-soldiers had become peasants, bound to furnish recruits, the obligation was legally recognised. The great privileges which Constantine granted to the veterans and their sons were counterbalanced by a stricter obligation of service. Special lists of soldiers' children were drawn up. A man who, on reaching adult age, did not enter the service, was treated as a deserter. In the East this practice was so universal that pay was given even to the children of soldiers. This is the first instance that we find of a system which eventually permeated the whole Roman community—the inheritance of position and profession.

Finally there were barbarians who were allowed to settle down in the Empire under a Roman prefect and had land assigned to them, such as the Alamannians, Suebi, Sarmatians, Franks. In Gaul they are called *laeti* ; probably the *gentiles* who were found even in Italy were somewhat similar. On them lay the obligation to furnish a comparatively large number of recruits.

The praetorian prefect was deprived by Constantine of his purely military command, and thereafter stood at the head of the administration and jurisdiction. The supreme command was committed to two *magistri*, one for the infantry and one for the cavalry ; but both commands could be held by one individual. Under them were the troops of the guard and the field army. The frontier troops had, in each province, a special commander with the title of *dux*. Thus this word, in Romance languages, has become identical with the German *Herzog*, or army leader.

Promotion went through an unbroken series of grades throughout the whole army, from the frontier troops to the field army, and, after that, to the Emperor's personal body-guard, or *protectores*. As a rule it was slow, and the majority usually never rose very far in the scale, but promotion could be accelerated by a man being transferred into a higher troop. The highest of all was the body-guard. In this were enrolled not only soldiers who especially distinguished themselves, but also young nobles who took to a martial career. The body-guard became a nursery for the training of officers under the eyes of the Emperor. It was very necessary. Any one who knows the importance of the staff of non-commissioned officers for the training of an army, can understand what it meant when a proper supply of these men was lacking in the Roman army of the time. But even this age felt the need of some practical education for officers of respectable birth and upbringing. There arose a new nobility of officers' sons, again an instance of a hereditary calling. But the road to the highest commands was open to any barbarian whatsoever, and they did not fail to use it. Soon the high posts of command were full of German names. During the period of the Great Migrations the German *magistri militum*, Arbogast, Stilicho, Aspar, Ricimer, were the real masters of the Empire and emperor-makers.

There was a still more dangerous method by which Rome procured the help of the barbarians. It was awkward and difficult to enlist them individually, but easy and simple to take into the service a whole tribe under its native leaders. Rome always had had allies, who placed themselves under the protection of the Empire, and, in return, placed their military forces at her disposal. But the character of an alliance of this description depended upon the relative strength of the allies. The allies of the Roman Republic became its subjects ; the allies of the Roman Empire became, in the end, its masters. Allies formed the frontier guard of the Empire, such as certain tribes in the Caucasus, the Saracens on the Euphrates, and the Ethiopians on the southern frontier of Egypt. The most important were Germans, especially the Goths who had crossed the Danube and settled on its southern bank. The Empire, in theory, existed to protect the allies, but the allies had to guard the Empire ; and the latter had, in common with all its soldiers, the right of maintenance from the Empire. But Rome's performance of this duty was practically non-existent. The maintenance was commuted for money paid yearly, irrespective of whether the Empire used the services of its allies or not. If the money was not paid, the allies knew how to extract it by force of arms. It was in fact a tribute, which the Empire paid to the barbarians in order to be at peace.

When the alien German army was in the Empire under its own captains it formed a State within the State and, to all intents and purposes it was the dominant State. The Germans were masters of the Empire long before it fell. What we call the fall of the West Roman Empire consisted merely in the fact that these hordes of Germans extorted, or seized by force, the lands under the authority of their own kings. This was done by the tribes who, during Honorius' reign, broke into Gaul, and it was the desire for land which caused the German troops in Italy, in A.D. 476, to overthrow Romulus Augustulus and proclaim Odoakar king. By so doing they did not intend to abolish the Emperor's authority, though it was only of a formal character. That passed to the Emperor in Constantinople. Odoakar regarded himself as his ally, and, as his ally, Theodoric moved against Odoakar and defeated him, just as Alaric, scarcely a century earlier, marched against Honorius and Italy in the character of Arcadius' general. The dissolution of the Empire was complete when the army had, in fact, become a foreign people under its native king.

It remains only to mention a peculiar phenomenon in the fifth century, which clearly shows how far the dissolution had advanced. The German hordes knew only one bond, that of personal fidelity to their selected master. It was the German reverence for this obligation of fidelity which caused the Roman Emperors even in the first century to fill their personal body-guard with Germans. In the disturbed years of the fifth century, when the bonds of the State power were relaxed, other highly placed and wealthy men also began to provide themselves with a body-guard (*bucellarii*) who would defend their master in battle and serve him in peace. No officer was without such a following, which was pledged to him personally, and even civil officials had a similiar entourage. Later on this developed into a veritable *condottieri* system : the chief condottiere was Justinian's well-known general, Belisarius. That was in the East. In the West this pheno- menon foreshadowed the coming of feudalism. Another cause of disruption is to be found in the agrarian conditions which will be examined later.

The above-mentioned developments may be briefly summed up thus. Before Diocletian there was not the slightest trace of enlistment from beyond the frontiers. With him was intro- duced the diametrically opposite principle. The purer bar- barian a soldier was, the more highly he was esteemed. From a military point of view the old peaceful and highly civilised provinces no longer existed, least of all the mother lands of ancient civilisation, Italy and Greece. Among the provincials the least civilised were rated most highly—in the East the Galatians and Isaurians, in the West the Batavians, Tungrians, and other German tribes. Units named after barbarians, both within and without the Empire, were found in great number and of all kinds. They were knit together according to the different types of peoples. Value was attached to their varying and individual military tactics. The most esteemed, the body- guard, were barbarians, and bore barbaric names. The cavalry became more important than ever, and the special weapons of the barbarians were borrowed. The Roman art of war, a creation based on the traditions and practice of centuries, intensive training and discipline, had disappeared, and with it its methods and tactics. The last battles which were won by tactical manoevres were fought under Con- stantine ; after that brute force prevailed. When the Romans had fallen back to the level of the barbarians, what was lost in quality had to be replaced by increased numbers. Thus an extra burden was laid on the sinking Empire. The army was necessary. There could be no talk of anti-militarism when every year smoking ruins and bloodshed signalised the advance of the barbarians into some devastated corner of the Empire, but pacifism had done its work. That the Empire imposed on itself a crushing economic burden was the least of its calamities.   It betrayed civilisation by providing weapons, first to the barbarians within the Empire, and afterwards to the barbarians without.   First it was barbarized by its own people, and in the end was overrun by aliens and subjected to their domination.

IV

THE POPULATION PROBLEM

In the previous chapters an attempt has been made to describe the peoples and civilisations comprised within the Roman Empire. In so far as this has been successful, it has thrown light upon the great distinctions which existed—old civilisations with diverse origins and differing essentially in form and composition like the Greco-Roman and the Semitic, and cultures ranging from the most aesthetic and refined to the primitive barbarism and squalor of the Ligurian cave-dwellers. Parallel with these differences ran differences in the legal position of the citizens. All these manifold and varying grades of culture existed alongside of each other in the same Empire, subjected to the same administration and protected by the same peace, traversed by the same roads and encompassed by the same civilisation. A levelling up or down was bound to follow, as certainly as different solutions kept in the same jar combine. The very existence of a strong and purposeful administration produced a stabilising tendency. Parallel with the equalisation in culture went the equalisation of civic rights.

In the earlier Empire the civilisation of backward peoples and districts was levelled up. Generally speaking, the level of culture in the Empire rose, and though, perhaps, one must admit that the highest intellectual culture did not retain its creative force, this was chiefly due to the gradual but powerful influence of Orientalism. In the third century the catastrophic revolution occurred. The leaven was too small to leaven the whole lump. This was most marked in the army, which, by reason of the position it occupied as master of the peaceful

317

population by right of arms, exercised a paramount influence for evil and good.

But we have not yet touched on the greatest problem. That depended not on the equalisation of rights, nor on the growth or decay of culture, however important one may regard those factors, but on the equalisation of races and the mixture of blood among all the different peoples of the Empire. It was one thing that the subject peoples should be placed on an equality with the Roman and acquire their culture ; it was a far more important thing if the Romans and the subject tribes and races were to be fused into one. Ancient culture is a creation of the Greeks and Romans, and it is a fact of fundamental importance that culture rests on racial character. The question was whether the Romans would be able to absorb the provincials or would be absorbed by them. This process must not be confused with the outward extension of the Latin language which secured a hold in all Western Europe, nor with the extension of a superficial veneer of Roman culture. It was a question of race and blood.

Profound and decisive as these factors are in the development of humanity, it is difficult to comprehend them fully and to define clearly their operation. They have been greatly misunderstood. In no sphere do trivial hypotheses and ingenious but unsupported theories thrive more than in this ; but if one rejects the whole field because of the abundant weeds, one commits the greatest mistake of all. Only in reaction against the neglect of the importance of race, can one understand the assertion that a people with all its peculiarities and all its culture is a product of the country and environment. But nature lavishes her gifts in vain on a people that does not know how to use them. Compare the position of the North American continent during the period when it was occupied by Indians only, to that which it has attained since its development by Europeans. The territory adjoining the Hebros is not different from or worse than that which adjoins the Axios. But whereas the Macedonians created a World-Empire, the Thracians—according to Herodotus, the largest nation next to the Indians—never succeeded in building up a state. In

Southern Italy and Sicily the Greeks found an environment similar to that of their native land ; but the Sicels, Oenotrians, and Messapians had never been able to develop any higher culture there ; the Greeks had to bring it with them. It was the Greek race and not the country which created that culture upon which ancient and modern times have built.

The question whether the Romans would be able to assimilate the provincial population and raise it to a high level of culture, or would themselves be assimilated and absorbed by it, depended on the vitality and power of expansion inherent in the Roman people. Once before something of the sort had been achieved, when Roman colonies were scattered all over conquered Italy, and when, after the Social War, the Oscan and Umbrian tribes and eventually the Celts of the Po valley had been merged in and invigorated the Roman nation. But even this brilliant picture of national expansion had its blemishes. In Southern Italy and Sicily it was the impoverishment of the country which led to latinisation : the free yeoman population of Italy, which formed the backbone of the Roman State and the Roman army, steadily declined under the capitalistic system of agriculture, and was driven out by the crowds of slaves who tilled the lands of the great proprietors. The slave was cheaper than the free labourer ; he could not allow himself the luxury of a family and useless mouths to feed. When he died, a new one was bought. But along with imperial peace came a scarcity of slaves. The old slaves had died without leaving offspring ; but before that, they, or more correctly the capitalistic system, had, at least to a great extent, driven out the free yeoman population.

To this and to the efforts made to save the small cultivators we shall return in another connection ; here we have only to point out their importance in connection with the remarkable alteration effected in the national stock in Italy. That foreign elements poured in to fill the gaps may be assumed and in some cases can be proved. The importation of slaves left its traces on the population, as will be shown later. During the civil war, at the close of the Republic, a great part of the lands belonging to Italian cities was assigned to the soldiers as their reward.

All possessors of power from Sulla to Augustus founded a
number of military colonies. But in most cases these soldiers
were not Romans. During the civil war recruits were obtained
wherever they could be found, and on account of this, also,
foreign blood in Italy received a large accession.

The population of Italy, the core of the Empire, was, then,
at the beginning of the Empire not so homogeneously Roman as
language and culture would make one suppose, but none the
less, the Romans had, on the whole, succeeded in assimilating
the alien elements. Now they were confronted by a similar but
prodigiously greater task. Success in this depended on whether
the Roman race had preserved and increased its vital force,
its capacity to expand and to assimilate. This question was
intimately connected with certain moral and social conditions.
It is quite correct, as has been observed, that our knowledge
on this point is chiefly based on information concerning
the upper classes, but for our purpose this is, on the
whole, sufficient. The upper classes set the example, the
middle and lower classes followed them, as far as their more
limited circumstances permitted, then, as in our own day. It
is true not merely of morals and customs but of all national
culture, that they originate from the higher classes to a much
greater degree than one is inclined to believe, unless one has
devoted special attention to the phenomenon.

People often condemn unjustly the immorality of the
Empire—unjustly, that is, when they have in mind only the
most flagrant instances and the spicy descriptions of certain
authors. There is a special collection of scandalous stories
of this kind belonging to the earlier Empire—one may instance
Augustus' daughter Julia, Messalina, or Juvenal's famous sixth
satire—but one could make as choice a collection of scandals out
of our own *beau monde* and upper ten, and scandals which have
obtained a place in world literature under Juvenal's name
are very similar to those that appear in our yellow press.
Besides, one must not forget that the moral standard of
antiquity was different from that of to-day, and every age
must be measured by its own and not an alien standard.

In any case, it is necessary to investigate the question of

female emancipation. It certainly was not emancipation in our sense of the word. There was no question of votes for women or their employment in State or private service, though the bluestocking had appeared and the sportswoman won laurels at the public games, but it was exclusively a question of personal independence and rights over property, of a woman's right to act as she pleased and, if married, to dispose of her property as she thought fit. The old Roman law gave the father unlimited authority over his family, and a woman, by marrying, passed into the power of her husband or of his father, if he was alive, with all her property. Beside the ceremonial forms of contracting a marriage, there was from early days another, the legal effect of which rested on custom. If a woman for a whole year lived in a man's house, she became his lawful wife and passed into his power, together with her property. This form of marriage contained the possibility for the emancipation of women as regards the right of property. If custom was broken by the woman spending three nights in succession during the year outside the man's house, the effect of marriage on her rights of ownership did not ensue. This form of marriage was invented quite early under the Republic and made great use of. As an unmarried woman could not legally manage her property herself, this was evaded either by a fictitious marriage or some other legal fiction. Who the man was did not matter ; after the performance of the marriage ceremony he disappeared from view, but the result, the economic independence of the woman, was permanent.

Thus the economic independence of woman had been completely attained, though by a circuitous path. The old form of marriage disappeared under the Empire. Woman retained her property, and, legally, the man had not even the right to enjoy the income of it. The law regulated the limits within which spouses were allowed to give each other presents. The relation of a husband to a rich wife, conscious of her position, was not enviable and must often have been humiliating, but there are many instances on record of women who helped their husbands by financial sacrifices. It is significant, however, that these were regarded as especially praiseworthy and remarkable, and not of common occurrence. The management of a woman's property, in cases when she did not permit her husband to control it, was often entrusted to some *procurator* with legal knowledge, who frequently played the part of protecting cavalier and lover, and is a stock figure in jokes about outwitted married men.

The old Roman definition of matrimony was, " a lawful union to produce offspring." Such an outspoken description may perhaps be somewhat repellent to a later age, which has composed and written elegant poetry celebrating marriage as the union between twin souls, with love as its sole foundation, and has produced so many novels dealing with the problems of married life, conceived as the conflict between two individualities, in which the one party threatens to predominate and the other rises and maintains his or her personality against the usurper. The usual conception of marriage in poetry and in the literature devoted to the art of living and the contemplation of life, is that of a bilateral problem. But the natural consequence of married love is children. If two souls have made a mistake as to their compatibility, the only means of correcting the mistake is to give up a joint life which leads to disagreement. But what is to become of the third factor ? Modern legislation, which has found itself increasingly obliged to respect the individualistic view of marriage, has discovered no better expedient than that employed by the imperial legislators in connection with the children of retainers who belonged to the estates of two different masters ; these were divided between the parents according to circumstances. The individualistic view of marriage disregards its social importance. A past age thought that marriage and parentage existed for the sake of the coming generation, and regulated legislation accordingly, whereas our age thinks that they exist for the benefit of the married couple, children being an accidental though inevitable consequence. In real life it is different. Two individuals embark upon the voyage of life, and then, if they are reasonable beings, nature asserts its rights. Marriage becomes an economic life-partnership with a division of labour between man and wife, its object being to bring up the new generation as members of the community. But the powerful effect of literature and the discussion of problems must not be under-estimated. They have left their mark upon the legislation of certain modern European peoples concerning marriage and its rights.

In our age the semi-philosophic individualism of *belles-lettres* combines with economic individualism to undermine the social foundations of marriage and to overthrow the barriers of convention. In antiquity we can trace the emergence of this theory of economic individualism. Individualism as a mode of life came into existence, and the whole spiritual history of the later ancient world is full of it, but its effect on the problem of marriage escapes our judgment. The red rose of love, with which the marriage bed is now planted, so that its ethereal blossoming conceals its earthy foundation, is the offspring of the blue flower of romance ; the family tree can be traced further back to Christian avoidance of the world and asceticism. It is well known that in the eighteenth century people discussed without shame, and with a frankness surprising to us, matters which we hardly venture to mention. Conventions of what is decent have changed. In ancient times they were still further removed from the delicate sensibility which now prevails. The Latin authors who are banished from the school programme, because in them boys may read of things which otherwise they only learn in prurient conversations, bear witness to this.

A different standard of decency and an open discussion of natural things do not necessarily imply a lower morality and a lower ethical standard. If these really existed in antiquity, we must search for proof in other directions, and no doubt they are to be found. The standard of marital fidelity was not lower than now, but it was confined to the woman. There is no trace of a demand for a similar standard for the man. The primitive view, in some ways reasonable enough, was held that the fidelity of the man is not necessary, because his infidelity does not bring bastards into the family. The extra-marital connections of the man, whether casual or permanent, were regarded as natural. It is significant that a religious inscription from Asia Minor, which otherwise inculcates a morality with which any one may be satisfied, expressly permits connections with women who have already lost their chastity. Against such connections there was not the moral ostracism which, in spite of changing conditions, still constitutes a powerful deterrent, and slavery gave every facility for keeping women for the satisfaction of lust.

The evil went deeper than merely prostitution for the poor, and mistresses for the rich. The dissolution of the legal forms of marriage, which was brought about by women's demand for economic independence, supported by their fathers and relations, obliterated the sharp distinction between the married and the unmarried state, which, in spite of everything, is maintained by modern peoples. In the second century of the Empire even the forms of marriage, whose legal basis was custom, had become antiquated. Marriage consisted in the mutual consent of the parties, whether formally expressed in writing or not, and the fact of their living under the same roof. What was legally called concubinage was not based on any form of marriage, but on the position or special agreement of the contracting parties. Lawful marriage could not be contracted between a man of Senatorial rank and a woman who belonged to the freed-man class, nor between a free-born Roman citizen and a woman who was without full citizenship. Soldiers, who were long forbidden to marry, found a compensation in concubinage. From a legal point of view the evil effects of concubinage were felt by the children, who were excluded from inheriting their father's position and property. Concubinage was not a loose connection. It was unlawful to have a concubine together with a wife; but whether it was forbidden to have more than one concubine is doubtful. Augustus regulated concubinage by law, and recognised it as a species of marriage, thus relieving men from the disabilities which other legislation had imposed on celibacy. The importance of concubinage was greatest in the upper circles of society. Some of the most distinguished Emperors, like Vespasian, Antoninus Pius and Marcus Aurelius, lived in concubinage. In the lower grades of society the distinction between marriage and concubinage must have been negligible.

In concubinage the man had evolved a sort of economic emancipation from the family. He could have a home and wife and bring children into the world without bringing on himself the economic consequences which conventional marriage entailed. Many, like Marcus Aurelius, lived in concubinage instead of marrying a second time, so as not to introduce divisions into the family and diminish the inheritance of the children by the first marriage. It is difficult to say whether the emancipation of men or of women produced the greater consequences. But it was undoubtedly the emancipation of women which undermined the established forms of marriage and introduced those facilities for its dissolution, which, more than anything else, destroyed the old conception of a union between man and woman to bring children into the world and train them for the good of the community.

We may read many accounts of men and women who contracted five, six, or seven marriages, and of the case of a man who, being a candidate for one of the offices of state, for which celibates were ineligible, married when he came forward as a candidate, and divorced his wife the day after he had received the office.

We have, not without reason, been warned against drawing general conclusions from scandalous stories applying only to the higher classes ; but it is significant that on the gravestone of a deceased wife it is often mentioned as an honourable circumstance that she had had only one husband. However much one may discount scandalous literary ancedotes, yet this much remains, that the stimulus to raise a family which is encouraged by a conventional disapproval of loose and irregular connections, was lacking. Casual connections were regarded as natural and a matter of course, and if permanent ᴠ ɔre recognised in law. Any one could live with a woman without incurring those responsibilities which a regular marriage entails and the burden of the bringing up of children. Any one could satisfy his desires *ad nauseam*, without incurring the disapproval of public opinion, or those economic consequences which usually result from the working of nature's laws.

For economic individualism children are a costly appendage.

To what extent the instinct of natural tenderness for off-spring is retained depends on the morals of the age. In antiquity there was never any great tenderness displayed towards infants. Custom and law permitted their exposure to perish or to be taken up by the first man-hunter who was looking for potential slaves. The exposed daughter, rediscovered when grown up, is one of the commonest themes in ancient comedy. Roman legislation recognised the father's right to dispose of an infant, though with certain reservations. However cruel and unnatural this custom seems to us, there may have been some excuse for it under primitive conditions, when food was scarce and difficult to obtain, or in respect of deformed children, in which case antiquity regarded exposure as a duty. But when this right remains and its arbitrary exercise is not liable to the censure of public opinion in a community in which economic individualism has superseded the responsibilities of marriage, then it becomes little better than legalised child-murder, enabling a parent to avoid the expense of bringing up his offspring. Instances of this are numerous in literature, and the frequent appearance of native Italians among the slaves confirms the evidence of literature.

The exposure of infants is the worst blot on ancient culture. Philosophers inveighed against it, but it was only Christianity which put an end to it. One must not, however, imagine that the practice had any considerable effect on the numbers of the population. The number of children exposed was limited, and most of them did not perish but survived as foundlings, as is the case still in Southern Italy. More serious was the fact that it was the educated classes which were decimated by the diminution in the birth-rate, since the children who were saved sank to the level of slaves. In antiquity, too, other and less revolting means of preventing the production of children were known which certainly had a much greater effect than the exposure of children, in whose case natural feelings could not entirely be stifled. These are often mentioned in medical literature. Doctors would only sanction them in case of necessity, but there are indications that they were regarded in much the same light as they are by certain sections of society to-day.

The increase of celibacy and childlessness in the upper classes is thrown into prominence by one of the most peculiar and most often mentioned phenomena in the social life of the early Empire, *viz.* legacy-hunting. None of its characteristics is described so often as this vice, which defied the wrath of moralists and the prick of satire until economic decay and altered social conditions put an end to it. It originated in the Roman custom by which people in their wills remembered friends and acquaintances by a present, this being a point of honour of binding character for the rich and highly placed. To what an extent it had grown can be realised by quoting instances. A man like Cicero received more than 20,000,000 sesterces in legacies from his friends and relatives. Augustus himself states that during the last twenty years of his life he received in testamentary bequests no less than 1,400,000,000 sesterces, but no doubt the Emperor had greater opportunities for getting himself remembered in wills than lesser individuals.

From the childless rich, above all, large sums might be expected as legacies and gifts. They were therefore surrounded by a swarm of men who endeavoured by every conceivable means to become their confidants, pandered to their needs and whims, relieved them of their worries and business, applauded what they said and wrote, and gave them presents in the hope of ultimately getting more in return. The objects of all this flattery and cringing knew how to utilise their position to the uttermost. They excited hopes, they alluded to the will which they constantly altered, they pretended to be weak and sickly, so that the legacy-sharks might believe that the end was near and redouble their exertions. There were clever rascals who pretended to own large estates in the provinces and armies of slaves and merchant ships, who lived in luxury at the expense of the legacy-hunters, and, significantly enough, were not discountenanced by public opinion. The evil took the most repulsive forms when it was a case of some old maid who had plenty of money.

Things went so far that respectable people did not dare to make a present to a childless man for fear of being suspected of legacy-hunting. When Juvenal orders a sacrifice to celebrate

the escape of a dear friend from shipwreck, he adds that the
rescued man had three children, and that it would not occur to
any one to waste a sick hen or a crow on him. Things had come
to a pretty pass when the legislature had to devote attention to
the scandal and prescribe that legacies made with the object of
getting larger ones in return should be invalid. We find a
still stronger witness to the moral degradation in the words
which the philosopher, Seneca, could seriously write in a con-
solatory address to a mother who had lost her only and promising son : " To apply a ground of consolation which sounds very
strange, but is none the less true—in our society, if one is
childless, one gains much more in influence than one loses, and
the solitude which seems to deprive old age of its support, gives
it, instead, such a power, that many feign to hate their sons and
renounce them, in order, by artificial means, to make themselves childless." The amazing thing is that a Stoic philosopher
could imagine that he was comforting a sorrowing mother by
these sentiments ! The moral standards of the upper classes
must have been very debased, and the contagion spread to all
classes. Nowhere else does the premium which society placed on
childlessness appear in a clearer light. Legacy-hunting would
be comical if the matter were not really so terribly serious.

The lowering of the birth-rate as a result of economic
individualism seems to be a phenomenon which accompanies
all the higher civilisations. It is easy to explain this, for
children prevent the individual from enjoying the pleasures of
culture to the extent that he otherwise might. At the zenith
of their power and culture ancient nations were attacked by the
same phenomenon. We have here an instance and a proof of
the widespread theory which postulates that the more mouths
there are to feed, the fewer of nature's gifts will fall to the share
of the individual, and therefore the increase of the nation must
be limited. The calculation seems so simple and incontro-
vertible—the fewer there are to share, the more each will have.
But the theory forgets that for a cultured man there are other
things besides the gifts of nature. He has also to undertake
his share of the work and the responsibility that his place as a
cultured man gives him. In the ancient world the upholders

of culture became too few, and they faltered and broke down under their burden.

A nation which deliberately limits its birth-rate automatically diminishes its culture and its capacity for expansion. The Romans deprived themselves of the only means of absorbing the population of their extensive Empire, the means by which they had succeeded in making Italy, on the whole, a Roman country, though, in the case of Italy, close relationship to the Italian peoples had been a great assistance to them.

In our day, it can be proved by statistics that the decrease in the birth-rate begins in the upper classes, and spreads in ever wider circles down to the bottom of society. This was the case in antiquity, but with this difference, that then such drastic remedies were proposed, that even those who, in our day, talk most vociferously of race-suicide and put forward measures to force people to bring children into the world, would never have dared to talk or even to think of anything so comprehensive.

In his youth Augustus had been a child of his age. His third marriage to Livia had caused some scandal, but he atoned for it by a happy married life till his death. In his riper years he, as a statesman, realised the danger with which the decay of morality and the marriage-tie and the spread of childlessness threatened the Roman people, especially its ruling and leading classes. The measures he took caused him the bitterest pain of his life, as he did not spare his own flesh and blood. His daughter, Julia, was a handsome and elegant, temperamental and highly-educated woman, who gave herself up entirely to the pleasures of the age. She was probably not worse than many others, but she had the misfortune to be the Emperor's daughter. An example had to be made of her. When Augustus discovered her frailties, he banished her to a lonely island, where she lived in poverty under strict surveillance. Some years later the same fate overtook his granddaughter. Stern and irreconcilable to the last, he put in his will a clause forbidding the unfortunate women to be buried in the imperial sepulchre.

Augustus' moral legislation aimed at the limitation of

luxury, the prevention of separations, the punishment of adultery and the protection of chastity, with special reference to the upper classes. Only three years after the battle of Actium he issued a decree which ordained severe penalties on celibacy and on marriages between men of senatorial rank and freedwomen. The law was so unpopular and the resistance so universal, that Augustus had to abandon it. But he did not abandon his conviction of its necessity or his intentions. Ten years later he issued his famous law dealing with marriage among the upper classes, which required that every noble Roman between the ages of twenty-five and sixty should be married, or at least betrothed. Since many tried to evade the law by betrothing themselves to children or by delaying and finally breaking off the betrothal, he had to make an additional ordinance that betrothal might not last for more than two years and was not valid if the girl was under ten.

Rights of precedence in the offices of State, were given to the married man with children; the unmarried were excluded from the games, of which all were passionately fond. This was as if unmarried people to-day were forbidden to go to the cinema! Opposition to this continued, and the Emperor found himself obliged to grant a transitional period, to mitigate the penalties and increase the privileges. In A.D. 9 came the final ordinance. Parents of three or more children received special distinctions, preference in competition for official positions and relief from such offices as entailed special burdens. The unmarried were excluded from the right to receive testamentary legacies, and the childless inherited only half. The irony of fate determined that the consuls, who had given their name to the law, Papius and Poppaeus, were both unmarried. Again the resistance was violent. In the theatre the knights presented a strongly-worded petition to the Emperor, but this time he was adamant. He called up Germanicus' six fine children and bade the knights go and do likewise.

Augustus tried to strike at the root of the evil and work against it by using the same methods as produced it. He limited the rights of property of the unmarried and childless, and their social honours and worldly enjoyments—the very things for which people deliberately chose celibacy and child-lessness—with a severity which no social reformer in our day has even ventured to imitate in his draft of measures against the threat of depopulation. If any legislation with this view could be effective, this was bound to be so. But the result was less than one might have expected. A race that is deter-mined to commit suicide is not hindered by any external means. Moral legislation which endeavours to thwart the spirit and public opinion of the age is doomed to failure, though it em-ploys the most drastic methods. However, the laws of Augustus remained in force. Incidentally they created many oppor-tunities for extortion and chicanery. Tiberius took measures against informers and Nero reduced their perquisites by half. The Emperors defeated their object by bestowing on individuals as a personal favour the legal rights given by the possession of three children (*ius trium liberorum*).

One of the most remarkable inconsistencies in human society, which is so rich in inconsistencies, is that the State, by its legislation, represents marriage as the only permissible, or, at least, normal means for the production of children, but at the same time puts a premium on celibacy and childlessness. The feeble efforts made to increase the rewards and to lessen the burden of taxation of the father of a family are so unim-portant and ineffectual that they may fairly be ignored. It is intelligible that the private employer who purchases a man's labour, pays by results without considering whether the workman has only his own or several mouths to feed. The State as an employer of labour must stand on the same plane as other employers, but as representative of the community and thus raised above private interests it might be expected to recognise another point of view besides that of private enterprise. But in the matter of the family it does not do so. The burden involved in bringing up children it leaves to the individual to bear, and is itself content with enjoying the fruits. The rising generation is, to a greater degree than anything else, of general social interest, and the State is there to protect and insure it against the interests of individuals, when they pull a different way. Yet the State has never found it to be its duty to combat economic individualism in the interest of the family and the children.

It is possible to build up a community on another basis than the family. It has actually been done, to some extent at least, by certain primitive peoples, among whom the social group takes the place of the family. The development goes in a circle. Society gives way more and more to economic individualism and individualism as a mode of life, but will not realise that the obvious consequence is free love, and State-supported orphanages. No more to-day than in antiquity are people capable of thinking out a question which is, after all, fundamental for all human life. All peoples with a cultural mission have founded their social system on the family, and the principle seems, to most people, so self-evident that they will not even take the trouble to reflect that opposing tendencies may end in dissolving it. But they are blind indeed if they do not realise what is likely to happen when the State, founded on that system, pursues a course which is bound to contribute to its dissolution. A society which is dependent upon the rising generations for its continued existence, relies blindly on the hope that natural impulses will overcome economic considerations. But it is the essence of all culture that, as it rises higher in the scale, it should exercise an increasing control over man's natural impulses, and it should not occasion wonder or complaint if that control affects, also, the impulse on which the continued existence of the race depends.

The Roman was the only state which realised that, from the economic point of view, the rising generation was an interest of the community and not merely of the individual, and, therefore, sought to relieve the individual from the burden of caring for children and to place it upon the community. Stress and danger made it realise this—the imminent danger that the Roman element might die out. As usual in social questions the realisation of the truth came so late that the disaster could no longer be averted.

Augustus, by legal procedure, took steps to prevent the loosening of the marriage tie and to check the increasing fall in the birth-rate among the upper classes, but his eyes were open to the fact that the phenomenon went further down, right to the bottom of society. Conscious that the upper classes in this aspect of social life set the example to the rest, he probably hoped that if he succeeded in bringing about a change above, the example would spread downwards. He did not altogether refrain from doing something for the lower classes as well. When he found a poor family with a large number of children, he gave it money presents—1000 sesterces for each child. The fixed sum indicates that this liberality must have been practised on a generous scale. It was noted in the official gazette that he had Gaius Crispinus Hilarus of Faesulae escorted in solemn procession up to the Capitol with his eight children, thirty-five grandchildren, and eighteen great-grandchildren, and had sacrifices offered there. The man was plainly a marvel for the age, but his name is suggestive of a Greek freedman.

THE ALIMENTARY INSTITUTIONS

In the age of Augustus we hear of the first instance of an institution, which, supported systematically by State assistance and the patriotic liberality of individuals, was to become the chief method whereby the Roman civilised population was to be saved from extinction, viz. alimentary institutions. An inscription in the little town of Atina in Latium states that a certain Titus Helvius Basila gave the town a capital sum of 400,000 sesterces, the interest of which was to be applied to the provision of corn for the children of the inhabitants, and to provide a lump sum of 1000 sesterces apiece for each of them when they had grown up and were about to find occupation. Helvius was proconsul and imperial *legatus*, and, therefore, was one of Augustus' trusted servants, though not one of the most important. He cannot have done what he did without the Emperor's knowledge, and it is so entirely on the lines of his policy, that one is inclined to think that it must be referred to his initiative. Sheer chance has determined that the inscription of Atina has been preserved to our day, but the institution was certainly not unique of its kind. What happened in the first century has been forgotten, but the decline of the birth-rate among all classes of the Roman population must have increased and given occasion to growing anxiety ; for during the last years of the century the Emperor Nerva was responsible for a stringent measure of far-reaching consequences, inasmuch as it is reported of him that he ordered that the sons and daughters of poor parents in the cities of Italy should be maintained at the public expense. It was the habit of the imperial age to commemorate important events and acts of government by symbolic representations on the coinage ; what was thought of the measure in question may be seen from the fact that there are coins of the year A.D. 97 referring to it. How Nerva carried out the details of the scheme is uncertain—the information is extremely scanty—but he certainly made an appeal to voluntary generosity, as was the case in the great extension of the scheme set on foot by his successor, Trajan.

Two important inscriptions give us full information about this later institution—one from Veleia in the country north of the Po, the other from the region of Beneventum. In Veleia a certain Cornelius Gallicanus, at the Emperor's command, first of all set aside a certain sum, and some years later Trajan funded a capital of 1,044,000 sesterces. Out of the revenue, 254 boys were to receive 16 sesterces apiece per month, and thirty-four girls 12 sesterces. The boys were the favourites ; for in antiquity, as in the East to this day, the State relied on them, whereas the birth of a girl was not greeted with joy. The tie of marriage was to be upheld, illegitimate children being excluded from the bounty : only one of either sex was entitled to it. The inscription of Beneventum is not in such good preservation. The amount of the fund is unknown, but it appears that the Emperor made assignments of capital on no less than ten different occasions. Trajan provided for children in the city of Rome by allowing them, to the number of 5000, to share in the free distribution of corn.

The solution of the population question was, however, not the only object the Emperor had in dispensing these funds. Equally acute was the land problem, and the Emperor determined to encourage Italy's agriculture in the same way by giving it cheap credit. The funds of alimentary institutions were invested as mortgages on landed property—the inscriptions mentioned are lists of such mortgages—in safe investments, below a twelfth of their value, bearing interest at 5 per cent., a rate which was low for the time. These institutions were so numerous that it was a large capital which, by this means and on moderate terms, was made available for agriculture. It appears that the small cultivator was favoured, for most of the mortgages were invested in quite small properties.

These are fortuitously preserved instances which give us a valuable insight into details, especially the information that the alimentary institutions were closely connected with the land question. The widespread character of the measures is confirmed in another way. In the Forum at Rome two marble balustrades with reliefs, which Trajan had executed to decorate the historically famous Rostra of the Forum, are still standing. The insides represent the two acts of State by which the Emperor thought he had the strongest claim on the gratitude of the people. One is the burning of the records of arrears of taxation ; the other is the institution of alimentary institutions. The importance of these is still more clearly demonstrated by the intricate organisation created for their supervision. The funds were administered by the respective cities, but a general supervision was necessary, co-ordinated with other contemporary measures, for bringing order into the administration of cities. The momentous and urgent task was entrusted by Trajan to two respected men, the above-mentioned Cornelius Gallicanus and Pomponius Bassus. When the scheme had been got into regular working order, prefects of alimentary institutions appear. From the time of Hadrian at least, this office was combined with that of director of the great roads of Italy. The directors of the roads were bound to be well acquainted with the rural districts of Italy, and, therefore, had special qualifications for the supervision of the alimentary funds of the towns. Later, after Marcus Aurelius, we hear of special prefects of alimentary institutions, who were taken from among the most eminent men of the Empire, such as the ex-consuls. The administration seems to have been centralised in Rome.

Trajan's successors, Hadrian, Antoninus Pius, and Marcus Aurelius continued the work. The personal interest of the Emperors induced rich people, who wanted to win praise and renown by making donations, to apply their wealth in this way, and the institutions spread outside the bounds of Italy. Pliny the Younger gave his ancestral city of Comum a present of 500,000 sesterces with this end in view. An inscription from Sicca Veneria (in Tunis) was erected in honour of Publius Licinus Papirianus, imperial procurator under Marcus Antoninus, who gave the town 1,300,000 sesterces, from the interest of which 300 boys and 300 girls were to be maintained from their third year till the boys reached the age of fifteen and the girls thirteen. Boys received 10 sesterces, girls 8 a month. The amount is lower than at Veleia, probably because the cost of living was less in the province. In regard to numbers, both sexes were placed on an equality. The alimentary institutions were a great innovation, perhaps the greatest measure of social reform known in history, if one takes into account the economic resources of the day and the purchasing power of money. We should be glad to know the exact amount of the capital that was allotted. We can only get a general and approximate idea from the fact that a little place like Veleia received more than 1,000,000 sesterces from the Emperor, and that the private institutions handled sums amounting to almost 500,000. If one generalises from the known examples to all the cities of Italy, one reaches such fabulous sums that one can hardly conceive the feasibility of the scheme. Nothing shows more clearly how urgent the matter was in the opinion of the age than the amount of these sums. The outlay was probably justifiable and necessary. On the success or failure of this experiment the preservation of the national stock depended, that stock which had conquered the world, and created and maintained the Roman character of ancient civilisation.

The funding of capital is a doubtful means of assuring it for any length of time. The craze for converting lands and properties assigned to institutions into money for the sake of convenience may well have been cured from the experiences of recent years, if there is any sense of responsibility left among administrators. The real value of capital falls with the fall in the value of money—slowly under normal conditions, suddenly in the case of catastrophes like that which we have lived through recently, or the still worse calamity which befell the third century. When the State has the supervision of the funds a further complication is added, since in times of acute financial crises the State confiscates all accessible revenues. Owing to this the fate of alimentary institutions was inevitable. Pertinax could not pay the arrears for the last nine years of the reign of Commodus. In spite of every difficulty, a great effort was made to retain them. Alexander Severus inaugurated a new fund, and officials who managed such institutions are still found at the end of the third century. But, by then, the funds must have dwindled into insignificance, amounting to a mere nothing, a twentieth or less of their former value, and how much disappeared altogether during the unrest of the third century cannot be estimated. Owing to this colossal depreciation, the alimentary institutions became bankrupt, and conditions were such that, to be made effective again, they would have had to be carried out on such a scale as to include the whole original Roman population. Under Constantine we find that they have come to an end. They were, in fact, no longer needed ; the fate of the national Roman element was sealed, and no one attached value to it any longer.

For a fuller knowledge of the problem, one ought to have more information regarding the numbers and the ebb and flow of the population, but concerning this nothing is more uncertain. Our calculations are based on scanty and dubious records, and the figures arrived at vary very greatly. Beloch, whose treatment of the question is the latest and most critical, reckons the population of the Roman Empire at the beginning of the Christian era at 70,000,000–80,000,000, and at the beginning of the third century at 100,000,000. The population of Italy is considered to have been stationary as regards the free element ; if slaves are included, it is thought to have increased. But the latter hypothesis is not very credible, as we know that slaves were becoming scarce at the beginning of the Empire and became ever scarcer, so that there was an agricultural

z

crisis caused by the failing supply of labour and slaves had to be replaced largely by small tenants. Beloch's view that the population grew in the first two centuries may be correct, but the growth was due to an increase in the provinces, not in the old centres of culture, Italy and Greece. The alimentary institutions confirm this for Italy ; and we have contemporary descriptions of the desolation of Greece (cf. p. 181). At the same time prosperous cities were growing up in the provinces, in which the standard of comfort rose and, with it, the population. The proportion was shifted to the advantage of the provinces.

PROBLEMS OF POPULATION

Moreover, absolute growth is not the decisive factor. A population should not be counted merely, but also weighed. The homogeneous European national states do not afford a parallel with the Roman Empire, though a few states show somewhat similar characteristics. Their problems are national problems. Only the United States of America, with their motley and mixed population of different races, assist us towards an understanding of the population of the Roman Empire, though there the dominant English element is considerably stronger than was the Roman in their Empire, and moreover has received a valuable addition from the numerous immigrants of the closely allied Germanic stocks. In spite of the very great absolute growth in population, the United States suffer from a baffling population problem. The birth-rate of native Americans is low, especially in the oldest and most cultivated districts of New England. Public morality is certainly stricter than in Europe, but this is more than outweighed by an advanced economic individualism, examples of which are the far greater economic independence of women, and their recklessness in entering into and dissolving marriages. Methods of keeping down the birth-rate are in vogue, though of a different character to those employed by Europeans. The two great sources of anxiety are the growth in the so-called " undesirable " immigrants and the high birth-rate of the negroes. To avoid being swamped by Russian Jews, certain

South-European peoples, Asiatics, and other less valuable elements, they try to protect themselves by strict immigration laws. The negroes are established in the country, and cannot be got rid of or prevented from multiplying. The white Americans have to be content with repressing them politically and socially, and relegating the question to a solution by future generations.

The problem is, then, the relatively greater growth of the less valuable element. The inevitable result of that is the suffocation or absorption of the cultured population. Even if this picture of the future is painted in too dark a shade, still the anxiety is great ; there is a risk of the stable character of the country being lost. The problem was the same in the Roman Empire. It possessed a motley population of different races and degrees of civilisation, which, owing to political exigencies and the growth of communications, had been intermingled. Culture and the State system rested on the old dominant civilised population, especially the Roman part ; for the Greek had already become so diluted and tainted that it did not play a great rôle in this respect, and the Greeks who counted were for the most part Grecised natives of Asia Minor and the East. The problem was whether this population could assimilate to itself the less civilised population and the Orientals. The situation became more desperate as the one diminished and the other grew. The Roman statesmen realised this and therefore devoted their efforts to stimulating the growth of population in Italy. Apart from the race question, the fate of the Empire and civilisation depended on whether the rate at which the provincials imbibed Roman culture kept pace with the rate with which they obtained Roman citizenship, and the answer to that question has already been given. In other words, it depended on the degree in which the new citizens were of a definitely lower culture and on the quality of the alien cultures they brought with them. The problem of race was decisive inasmuch as upon it depended the culture and composition of the Empire. As long as the alien races were depressed and in the position of subjects, the Empire held together, but when they were raised to equal rights with the ruling people they asserted themselves, and burst the frame in which they had been enclosed.

The next step in our analysis is to examine the recruiting of classes of the citizens, and the movements which took place within the population of the Empire, in so far as these questions have not been already treated. Towards this, the description of the broadening of the basis of Roman citizenship and of the army has already been a valuable contribution. In addition to this we have to take into consideration the manumission of slaves, by which masses of aliens were made citizens, and the wholesale incursions of races from beyond the frontier, which certainly did not create new citizens, but added still more to the varieties of the population and the barbaric element. Readjustments and alterations in the composition of the free population have already been alluded to in respect of an important and typical example, the army. In two other cases it is also possible to form some idea of the alteration in society, namely its connection with the Senators and high officials, and with the mercantile class. Freedmen had also great importance in the composition of the population because their descendants were on the same footing as other citizens.

The proscriptions did the same service for Augustus, as the Stockholm massacre did for Gustavus Vasa—they removed the heads of the old aristocracy, who would not submit to the new order. But Augustus tried in every way to save the remnants of the old families. He sincerely desired to preserve the ruling and leading classes of Rome, and to make them competent, working with the Emperor, to bear their part in the government and administration of the Empire. But like every other close caste, like the full citizens of Sparta, and the nobility of Sweden, the Roman nobility showed a tendency to dwindle. Its extinction, well on in the second century, has been laid at the door of the suspiciousness of the Emperors, which decimated its numbers, but this is not a strictly accurate diagnosis. Apart from natural decay, there were other causes of an economic character. The great family estates which the nobility required to maintain their position must, as a rule, have been acquired under the Republic. They

were radically modified in the civil war, especially by the proscriptions. By no means all of them were seized by the State ;
most passed into fresh hands. The Empire removed the
opportunity for provincial governors to amass properties by
concealed or open exactions ; but a brilliant entourage and a
great house were necessary for the position of a *grand seigneur*.
Properties were wasted by the pomp and splendour which, for
the honour of their class, the members of the old nobility were
obliged to maintain, and so they fell below the Senatorial qualification. Tacitus describes them as a pitiable and impoverished
body, idle and no longer warlike. Even if, by a gift of favour,
the Emperor now and then saved a famous old family, it did
not help in the long run. The old nobility was replaced by
the vigorous nobility from the country towns of Italy and the
provinces.

Over the Julio-Claudian house and its age rests something
of the glamour of the great Roman families of the period of the
Republic, which, in status and mode of life, might justly have
been described as princely. In the person of Vespasian a
representative of the middle class who preferred an old-
fashioned simplicity, came to the throne. Trajan loved to
retire to the circle of his friends in his villa at *Centumcellae*
(Cività Vecchia), where he enjoyed a frugal meal and intimate
conversation. Antoninus Pius abhorred court etiquette and
preferred to work in the vineyards on his estate in company
with his friends. The heir to the throne, Marcus Aurelius,
was brought up with Spartan rigour. In winter he shivered in
his room, and one fine day he found a scorpion in his bed. His
life in no way belied his upbringing. The middle class, having
been raised to power, set the fashion, we are told, but it is more
probable that the upper classes acquired bourgeois habits, the
old traditions of the magnates dying out and being replaced by
provincial simplicity. Vespasian sprang from a middle-class
family in an Italian country town. With Trajan the first provincial came to the throne. He and his successor, Hadrian,
were Spaniards. Antoninus Pius came from Southern Gaul,
and Marcus Aurelius was of a Spanish family.

The change was remarked by contemporaries. Tacitus

says that the old wealthy and renowned noble families fell owing to their love of luxury and display ; their prestige rested solely on the magnificence of their palaces and entourage, on a great name and a numerous train of clients. But after the Emperors had removed many of them, and greatness and dignity only paved the way to ruin, the survivors became more wary. Moreover, many new Senators were received from the *municipia*, colonies and provinces, and brought with them habits of a simple life which they retained in spite of their high position and their wealth. The Emperors, who themselves lived a life of bourgeois simplicity, promoted simpler habits, and example from above is more effective than the fear of laws and punishments. The letters of Pliny the Younger introduce us to the circle of the new nobility. His correspondents do not bear the old names familiar in Roman history, but come from Italian *municipia*, from Gaul or Spain. This nobility lived a more frugal and respectable life than the old. The great vices had disappeared, and, apparently, the great abilities also. The conditions which put a check on the birth-rate applied also to the new nobility, just as in our day they also affect the *bourgeoisie*. Three of the Emperors mentioned above were childless.

These outlines have been confirmed and fixed by investigations into the origins of the Senators. It is certain that relatively fewer citizens from the provinces than from Italy attained to the highest rank in the Empire. It was more difficult for a Roman citizen from a provincial town than from an Italian town to win entry into the Senate, and in certain cases, *e.g. Gallia comata*, and Egypt, there were also certain legal restrictions. Thus, when we find an ever-increasing stream of provincials attaining Senatorial rank, it demonstrates, even more than the extension of the citizenship, the growing importance of the provincials. The first provinces from which a large number of Senators proceeded, were the most strongly romanised—Baetica and Gallia Narbonensis (Southern Spain and South-Eastern France), and later the province of Africa and Asia Minor, where, at the beginning of the Empire, there were comparatively few Roman citizens. To become a

Senator and to hold the high offices of State, it was necessary to master the Latin language and have some knowledge of Roman law. Educated men in the East were without these necessary qualifications, by reason of the respect for, and self-sufficiency of, Greek culture, and the old national traditions of government and administration, which Rome allowed to persist. This was a serious obstacle in the way of great men of the Greek-speaking countries becoming great men of the Empire. That Greece itself was poorly represented was due not merely to its depopulation, but to its intellectual independence, which prevented it from falling to Roman culture like Gaul and Spain. Spain was able to boast the first two consuls who came from the provinces, as early as the last years of the Republic. By the first century A.D., many Spaniards had won the highest honours in the Empire. The first consul from Gallia Narbonensis was appointed by Tiberius, from Africa by Vespasian, from Syria by Domitian. The Orientals who attained high posts served, at first, principally in the East, *e.g.* the Jew, Tiberius Alexander, procurator of Judaea and prefect of Egypt, and the Syrian, Avidius Cassius, who, when governor of Syria, owing to a premature report of the death of Marcus Aurelius, had himself proclaimed Emperor. This was a concession to the national peculiarities of the East, which foreboded the division of the Empire. With Hadrian the restrictions disappear, and after that it seems almost as if Orientals were in the majority ; the West appeared to be used up. It has been asserted that Septimius Severus led the Orientals to victory by a sudden revolution in the upper classes as well as in the army, but this is an exaggeration. The change did not come suddenly, but by a steady and gradual development due to natural causes. When the obstacles caused by language, by peculiar or local traditions, were removed, the Orientals' talents and their upbringing in the environment of an old civilisation asserted themselves. This alone must have sufficed to give them an important, almost a dominant position ; but it is true that their infiltration into the ruling classes of the Empire reached its height under Septimius Severus, coincidently with the general victory of Oriental religious ideas.

Thanks to the exalted position of the Senators, owing to which records of their origin have been preserved, we can trace the rearrangement of peoples and the entry of provincials in large numbers into the highest class of the Empire. But we have much less knowledge of the similar process among the lower strata of the population. The actual composition of the senatorial class, however, proves that the same movement, and to an even greater extent, affected the lower classes. We can give one or two cases in point which enable us to show this.

Of greater variety than elsewhere was the medley of races in the capital, where individuals congregated from all quarters, either on business with the rulers and the government or as fortune seekers in the great city, where great possibilities were open to all. It is almost impossible for us to realise the extraordinarily motley character of the Roman mob. The only city in our own day which can rival it is Constantinople, the most cosmopolitan town in the world. Numerous passages in the works of classical authors refer to it, from Cicero, who calls Rome a city formed by the confluence of nations, to Constantius, who, when he visited Rome, marvelled at the haste with which all the human beings of the world flocked there. Expressions such as " the city common to all," " the world's assembly," " the world's hostelry," " a compendium of the world " are common.

There were Romans who viewed the population of the capital with deep pessimism. In Nero's time Lucan said that Rome was not peopled by its own citizens but filled with the scourings of the world. The Oriental element seems to have been especially strong. Juvenal's well-known words :

> "Sirs, I cannot bear
> This Rome made Grecian; yet of all her dregs
> How much is Greek ? Long since, Orontes' stream
> Hath fouled our Tiber with his Syrian waters,
> Bearing upon his bosom foreign speech
> And foreign manners . . ."

are confirmed by other circumstances. The language of the first Christians was Greek, *i.e.* they were Grecised Orientals. The Jewish element was strong, as the Jewish catacombs testify. In 4 B.C. 8000 Jews are said to have accompanied a deputation which came from Palestine to wait on the Emperor. The figure is perhaps exaggerated, as in the case when twenty-three years later Tiberius deported all the Jews from Rome, and is said to have had 4000 sent to Sardinia. After the fall of Sejanus he revoked the prohibition which forbad Jews to live in Rome, and they once more became so numerous that Claudius, when he renewed the deportation order, found it impossible to execute it.

Mixture of peoples in the provinces was not as great as in Rome, where the Roman blood must have been diluted almost past recognition. But Rome was the heart and centre of the Empire, and therefore set an example for the provinces also. Her own culture was bound to be affected by the mixture, and this reacted on the provinces. In the provinces, also, the *Pax Romana* and the facility of communications helped to bring about the mingling of types, and we have accounts of the remarkable spread of the Jews throughout the provinces. Since the days of the Ptolemies they were most numerous in Egypt, where they seem to have formed between one-seventh and one-eighth of the population ; next in Cyrenaica (Tripolis) and Cyprus, where, in a Jewish insurrection, it is said that hundreds of thousands of them were slain. In Asia Minor and South Italy they were numerous, also on the coast of Africa and in Southern France, and in Spain about A.D. 300 they were many and powerful. On the ground of their religion and the inflexible attitude they took up towards all other religions, the Jews occupied a special position, which does not make them a good example for judging the mixture of peoples. In antiquity they were not, as now, a race of financiers and small traders : they became especially distinguished in this connection at the beginning of the Middle Ages.

Trading operations played an important part in the movement of races, and in this connection we can trace the squeezing out of the Italian element by the provincials.

The part of Italians as men of business in the last days of the Republic, when they exploited economically the conquered provinces, has already been described, and also how they disappeared when robbery was no longer possible under the

ordered administration of the Empire. In Greece and the
Grecised lands, the Italian merchants disappeared in the first
century A.D., after which time trade was in the hands of the
native population. In Syria the Italians never played any
important part as men of business, but, on the other hand,
there is no doubt they did do so in Egypt, where, in Alexandria,
they had one of their greatest factories. Italians handled the
export trade with Rome, but in the interior of the country
trade was conducted by citizens of Alexandria. In the West,
under the Empire, the traders were certainly Roman citizens,
but they were probably romanised Celts.

The Italians never understood the real art of trade and
productive investment. As soon as circumstances had brought
about the cessation of exploitation based on force, they
generally disappeared from the provinces ; all who remained
were swallowed up in the native population. The only real
nation of merchants in the ancient world was the Syrian, which
occupied the position which the Jews do now. Salvian mentions crowds of merchants and Syrians, who had flocked into
all the large towns and thought only of lying and deceit. As
early as the third century B.C. Syrian merchants appeared
in numbers in the islands of the Aegean. The famous old
mercantile city of Tyre had great depôts in Rome and at
Puteoli, which was an important harbour for Rome. In Puteoli
we also find a depôt from Berytos and one from Heliopolis. In
Rome there were depôts from Tiberias in Galilee, from Gaza
and Palmyra. Syrian merchants were found in all the provinces of the Empire from Africa to Dacia. In Spain there was
in the first century A.D. a Syrian guild at Malaga, and in Gaul
they were numerous. As late as the sixth century many of
them were organised in special Christian congregations, especially at Paris and Orléans.

In Rome and Italy domestic trade was certainly in the
hands of the inhabitants of the country. But in Rome there
were a number of Greek retailers and chandlers, who, towards
the end of the Empire, were banished by an imperial edict, but
in A.D. 440 were permitted to return, plainly because they
could not be dispensed with. But the Italian business men

were no longer Italians and Romans by birth. Their names betray them, and show that they came from the East or the Grecised countries. The manner in which they received their Roman citizenship was by manumission. In antiquity merchants, even retailers, were freedmen. The only exception occurred in Italy, where the great men of business employed slaves in their offices and in the management of their concerns. Many of these were manumitted, and continued to manage their masters' business as freedmen, or founded a business of their own, which, from the practical experience they possessed, they could easily make profitable and flourishing.

Here we have arrived at an obviously important source for the recruiting of citizenship and the alteration of the national stock, *viz.* the manumission of slaves ; and this was no small matter. In Rome it was a point of honour to manumit slaves, by will, if not before. The manumitted slaves followed the funeral cortège, and the magnificence of the funeral was estimated by their number. Sometimes a man liberated his slaves so as to snap his fingers at his creditors. In Cicero's time it was regarded as an exception if a slave had to wait longer than six years for his manumission. Augustus, in consequence, found it advisable to set up legal barriers against too liberal manumission. The number of manumissions was regulated in proportion to the number of slaves owned by the liberator, and in no case was to exceed a hundred. Manumission by insolvent debtors was declared illegal, and minors and soldiers were only permitted to free their slaves according to a prescribed form and after legal investigation. If slaves who had committed gross offences and had undergone degrading punishments were freed, they were denied citizen rights ; they became free, but a special legal status was created for them under the title of *dediticii* (*cf.* p. 277).

In some respects the great period of the freedmen was at the beginning of the Empire when the imperial administration was in their hands. Under Augustus, the director of tax collecting in Gaul, Licinus, reigned for many years as a king in Lyons, and amassed untold wealth. Augustus let him stay, but squeezed the sponge when it became too full. To a simple cashier of the imperial provincial treasury in the same province, when he died in Rome, a monument was erected by his slaves, who accompanied their master thither. They were sixteen, among them an *homme d'affaires*, and a doctor. The Emperor Claudius' notorious freed-men, Pallas, Narcissus, and Polybius, ruled the Empire as real imperial ministers. It was, however, a scandalous state of things when the most powerful men in the Empire next the Emperor were freedmen. This was due to the fact that the imperial administration could only be carried on under the forms of private administration, and this was exercised by the sole experts, slaves and freedmen, since the State officials, at the end of the Republic, had been mere ignorant dilettanti. Such a state of things could not be endured for long. The knights, the representatives of liquid capital, whose sphere of economic activity was ever more limited since the State had begun to collect its own revenues, drifted into the position of imperial officials. Private financiers sank in importance ; everything gradually fell more and more into the hands of the freedmen. In his *Cena Trimalchionis*, Petronius has left an immortal description of the freedman type, with its blatant luxury and conceit, its total lack of education and leanings toward the grossest superstition. But Trimalchio was not the worst of his class, and in spite of his grotesque manners he is to some extent likeable. He was not ashamed of having stood up for sale with chalked feet, in the slave-market, and of having raised himself up to freedom and riches. But it was a great danger to culture that liquid capital was in the hands of such people.

The great handicap of the freedmen was their social inferiority, which even the possession of wealth could not alter. They could never hold municipal offices, never swagger in the purple-edged toga, nor take a place on the *sella curulis* at the public games. Augustus, however, did something to satisfy their honourable ambitions. The cult of the Emperor in the *municipia* was given over to colleges named *Augustales*, whose members were drawn from among the wealthy freedmen. At the head of the college were six men, who plainly were copied from the six officers who formed the magistracy of the *municipia*.

Like them, they had to pay for the honour with a certain sum of money, and like them they had to give games. At the games they had to preside in the place of honour on the *curule* chair clad in the purple-edged toga, and in the processions were preceded by lictors with *fasces*. The Augustales had a seat on a *bisellium*, which, as a place of honour, was also given to *decuriones*. It was a stroke of genius of Augustus, by which he made the influential and wealthy freedmen loyal servants of the Empire, and utilised their wealth for the benefit and enjoyment of the cities.

Positions to which the freedmen could not themselves aspire were open to their descendants. Their sons could hold the rank of knights and their grandsons were put on a level with citizens of free-born stock. In the first year of Nero's reign a proposal was discussed in the Senate for taking stronger measures against worthless and deceitful freedmen—the question being whether manumission could be made revocable. The difficulty of exposing the freedmen to the arbitrariness which such an arrangement would entail was recognised. Their class was widespread—they filled the tribes and the subordinate posts in the State service, and it was said that most of the knights and many Senators sprang from freedmen. If the freedmen were expelled, there would be a deficiency of free-born. The proposal was therefore rejected ; but the discussion is instructive in showing the importance of freedmen in the rearrangement of the people in professions and classes.

The freedmen were one of the most important elements of the population in the earlier Empire. It is of importance to examine what was their origin. In the first place, what classes of slaves were manumitted ? Generally they were domestic slaves, who formed the personal retainers of the master and were personally known to him. Their loyalty and good services were liberally rewarded. On the estates there were probably a far greater number of slaves, but these never saw their master, only the overseer ; the master at best knew them as an entry in the ledgers. They had no greater prospect of becoming free than beasts of burden, nor had they the opportunity to scrape together the little personal property (*peculium*) which was permitted to slaves, and thus purchase their freedom. Tips and other extras were to be had in cities ; but it was next to impossible to save out of the scanty provision for subsistence.

Domestic slaves and those who ministered to luxury, who attended the master and managed his affairs, came chiefly from the Semitic Orient and the Grecised countries of the East. The rude barbarian never secured those positions in which a certain training and polish were necessary. The moral standards of the freedmen bore ineradicable signs of their previous position. By flattery, sycophancy and lip-service they won the favour of their master ; by petty cheating and other and worse villainies they amassed their wealth. They had learned to cringe to power and to abuse it recklessly when they possessed it. To their account is to be set a considerable part of the moral decay under the early Empire and a still more considerable part of the orientalisation of religion and views of life which broke down the ancient faiths. It was from these people that the upper classes were largely recruited.

A proof of the correctness of these general statements is supplied by an investigation of the inscriptions and their information as to the nationality of slaves. They confirm the proverb that the Syrians were a nation of born slaves. Next to the Syrians, the Grecised inhabitants of Asia Minor and the Jews are most numerously represented. More than half the workmen in the Italian potters' workshops in the earlier Empire bear Greek or Oriental names, and this is confirmed by a comparison of the names of Italian handworkers in other callings. Next come the Egyptians and Ethiopians, but among these the physical traits were so striking that they could never be as dangerous as the Semites and natives of Asia Minor. In Europe there were no peoples naturally predestined to slavery, but Thrace, Dacia, Germany, Gaul, Spain, and Sardinia supplied a proportion of the slaves, though a comparatively small one. Instead, they supplied their human material to the army. For if Orientals were excellent slaves, they were correspondingly incompetent soldiers. We find mention of only two domestic Pannonian slaves, but what a multitude of them were to be found in the army ! It is remarkable how great a number of slaves have Italy for their native place. This is explained by various causes. During the Empire slaves were encouraged to marry, and the resulting slave children were born in Italy. Home-born slaves (*vernae*) are often mentioned. Exposure of infants and kidnapping of children also contributed a supply to the slave-market, and it also occasionally happened that people who could not prosper—failures in life—sold themselves as slaves, a sad illustration of the decadence of the Italian population.

The importation of slaves and their manumission contributed largely to the mixture of peoples, especially in Italy, and the effects of this, in a few generations, were felt even by the upper classes. It was one of the chief causes of the orientalisation of the Roman people and the still stronger orientalisation of the mind and intellect which distinguishes the later Empire.

There was another reason for the mixture of racial stocks, which did not work so quickly or extensively as the manumission of slaves, but in the long run was bound to be of importance, *viz.* the immigration of barbarians from the North. Of these, some, though comparatively few, came in as slaves ; considerably more entered the army, in which their numbers steadily increased, till the Germans became masters of the Empire before it formally broke up, as has already been described. Here we may confine our investigation to the immigrations of tribes from the other side of the Rhine and Danube. These were of frequent occurrence in the earlier Empire. During Augustus' earlier years Agrippa transferred the German Ubii to the left bank of the Rhine. The step was successful, for they proved to be a German tribe which remained faithful to Rome. Their chief town, *Ara Ubiorum*, was intended to become the centre of the contemplated province of Germany. The province remained embryonic, but the place grew into the most important town of Roman Germany, *Colonia Agrippina, i.e.* Cologne. Later 40,000 Sugambri and Suebi were allowed to settle in Gaul, and 50,000 Dacians were taken from the country north of the Danube over to Thrace. Under Claudius, Vannius, the king of the Suebi, was driven out by a rival and took refuge with his supporters in the Roman

Empire, where they received land and dwelling-places in Pannonia. Under Nero, again, masses of people were brought over the frontier from the north bank of the Danube, together with their wives and children, their number being said to be at 100,000 persons.

After this, reports of such mass movements cease for a century. The next occasion they are mentioned was in the time of Marcus Aurelius, when the barbarians were knocking impatiently at the gates of the Empire, and the plague was decimating the already diminished population. Within the Empire there was room in abundance, and, without it, people in abundance. When Marcus Aurelius succeeded in conquering the Marcomanni and Quadi by arms, he found a means of relieving the pressure on the frontiers by allowing these peoples to settle in large numbers in the Empire, in Dacia, Pannonia, Moesia, Germany, even in Italy, *e.g.* in the neighbourhood of Ravenna. The legal position of the immigrants seems to have varied, according as they had joined the Romans in the war, or had capitulated when conquered. The Cotini, who lived in the towns of Mursa and Cibalae in Pannonia, and formed a community of their own which received Roman citizenship, seem to have been an instance of the former class. From the beginning they probably had the status of Roman allies. The great majority were, however, put in the lower legal position of *dediticii*. Their freedom of movement was limited ; they were not allowed to leave the land they tilled, and thus, to some extent, they became serfs. Immigrations under similar conditions occurred in later times, though we have no historical information as to the precise dates. But under the names *laeti* and *gentiles*, we have already met with those immigrants who played an important part in the recruiting of the army (p. 312).

To a modern historian, describing the downfall of the ancient world, this invasion of barbarians at the close of the second century is an epoch-making event. The Western half of the Empire was filled with Germanic blood, and the birth-rate began to rise again. In the many foreign and domestic wars of the third century there was never any complaint of the inability to raise fresh recruits, whereas Marcus Aurelius could only recruit his army with the greatest difficulty, says Seeck, quoting Ammianus Marcellinus' description of the blue-eyed, blonde, tall, pugnacious Gauls as a proof of the germanisation of the population of Gaul. On the contrary, another historian has asserted that the population of the Empire increased till the close of the second century, but declined during the misery and confusion of the third. For this assertion there is no proof but the hard times, and that is not convincing enough. It is possible that the losses incurred by the population from incessant wars were more than compensated by a rise in the birth-rate. In spite of all the confusion of the third century one must, nevertheless, remember that the ancient armies were small in comparison with the number of the population, and that great stretches of the country in which social life pursued the even tenor of its way were left at peace.

On the other hand, Seeck's proof of a sudden change in the composition and birth-rate of the population is not satisfactory. That it was extremely difficult to fill up the *cadres* in Marcus Aurelius' army for the war against the Marcomanni during the ravages of the plague which carried off his soldiers by thousands, is intelligible enough from the circumstances of the time. That under ordinary conditions it was possible to raise the not very excessive number of recruits for the Roman army is not strange, as soon as the policy of recruiting from among the barbarian inhabitants of the Empire had been initiated. The complaint of the scarcity of recruits continued only so long as they were raised from among the civilised inhabitants of the Empire ; it ceased when a levy was made on the martial barbaric peoples, the Pannonians, Illyrians, and others. They were sufficient to convulse the Empire during the third century. But, on the other hand, the raising of the minimum height for recruits is significant. It shows that there was a greater choice. In old days the standard was 5 Roman feet or about 4 feet 11 inches, whereas in A.D. 367 approximately 5 feet 5 inches was prescribed. The latter is more than the minimum height for the Swedish army (5 feet 4·2 inches) and yet the Swedes are one of the tallest nations in the world. In 1893

2 A

the minimum height in the German army was lowered to the same as the French (5 feet 0·8 inch). But if any definite conclusions are to be drawn from these figures, it must be remembered that if the first, somewhat doubtful, figure applies to earlier times, it referred to volunteers of whom there was not a great supply. The standard of A.D. 367 applies to conscripts, at a time when it was desired to select the best specimens from among the *coloni*, while the proprietors were as anxious to provide the worst. A racial change cannot have occurred so suddenly even in the provinces which bordered on Germany, nor does Ammianus Marcellinus' description prove that the population of Gaul was Germanised; for the Celts are described in ancient literature, and represented by ancient artists, in a manner which strikingly reminds us of the Germans—the same bright red hair and blue eyes, tall stature and defiant temper. But neither must the importance of the immigrant Germanic element be under-estimated. They provided a strong admixture from a vigorous and uncivilised population, and paved the way for the occupation of the Empire by Germans at the beginning of the Middle Ages, and it is highly probable that they brought about a change in the birth-rate, by which conditions were altered still more to the disadvantage of the old population.

What has been stated here must be completed by what was previously said of the army and its recruiting. During the earlier Empire the old Roman families were replaced in the higher posts by men who rose from the ranks of the freed-men or came from the civilised and, at first, principally from the romanised provinces. During the third century, when government was by the sword, the road to the top of society went through the army, and the army consisted of civilised and vigorous provincials, chiefly drawn from the northern provinces of the Empire. One may conjecture that after the bureaucracy was organised, a good part of the cultured population sought refuge in the service of the administration and in its departments.

In the rearrangement of peoples we find two great currents. One came from the East and was represented by slaves, freedmen and merchants, and was composed mainly of people of Semitic birth and Grecised peoples of Asia Minor. The other came from the northern provinces and the further side of the Rhine and Danube, supplying an agricultural population which was bound to the soil, and, in ever-increasing numbers, the recruits for the army. But the problem is not so simple that we only have to consider two currents which influenced the stock of the Empire's population. It lay, in a greater degree than has hitherto been implied, within the Empire itself. For while it has been pointed out that the population contained many samples of different peoples, races and languages, to what extent this was the case and how deep and strong the distinctions were, is what we must now try to understand clearly if we seek to judge of the mixture of peoples within the Empire.

The true state of things is concealed to some extent, in the West, by the fact that the racial languages were so completely driven out by Latin as to leave scarcely a trace. But the races persisted, though they had adopted a new language, and contributed their share to race-mixture. Even Italy was inhabited by many different peoples, besides the Romans and their kinsfolk—Illyrian tribes, Greeks, and a primitive native population of uncertain race, a whole series of tribes, *e.g.* Oenotrians, Sicels, Sicanians, etc., of whose connection or absence of connection with each other we know nothing. Levelling and romanisation took place even under the Republic, so that Italy under the Empire had, except in the north, outwardly at least, an homogeneous population. The mysterious Etruscan nation had disappeared. Its language, which cannot successfully be classified with any other known language, died out at the beginning of the Empire. In the district of the Po the Celtic element was dominant, though it adopted the Latin language. In a poet like Catullus, who came from Sirmio on Lago Garda, is found a definitely non-Roman trait, and his passionate temperament is rightly ascribed to his Celtic origin. In North-West Italy and South-East France lived the great people of the Ligurians, who, at the beginning of the imperial age, retained, in certain districts, their poverty and independence. Their language has disappeared ; of its affinities we know, in fact, nothing, in spite of the attempts of some scholars to show that they belonged to the Aryan stock. It seems certain that this was not the case and that they were a primitive population conquered by Italians and Celts. Certain scholars have tried to show that the national type and language in the territory which was once Ligurian, show traces which are a survival of their ethnologically peculiar position.

Cisalpine Gaul (the Po district) and Transalpine Gaul (France) were named after the ruling people, the Gauls, who are generally called Celts. As already stated, their language survived. In the time of Irenaeus sermons had to be delivered in Celtic at Lyons, and in Ulpian's time it was permissible to use Celtic or any other surviving country dialect in wills. Celtic continued as the popular speech into the fifth century and was even spoken in families of high rank. The Gauls had painfully to acquire Latin. And even in France the Celts were themselves an immigrant conquering people. They dwelt principally north of the Cevennes ; in the south-east lived the already mentioned Ligurians, in the south-west the Iberian tribes. The Iberians also occupied the Spanish Peninsula, where only a few small Celtic tribes had pressed in and combined with Iberians into the Celtiberian people. Among the Iberians we find, again, a mysterious, non-Aryan people, which, like the Ligurians, seems to have been aboriginal. In North-West Spain some hundred thousand people still speak the Basque language, which, in structure and vocabulary, is totally different from the Aryan languages, and has no known affinities. It is the only fragment of the pre-Aryan speech of Europe that has persisted to our time, and it is natural to connect it with the Iberians. But the Iberian inscriptions which, like the Etruscan, have not been deciphered, do not seem to confirm this view. It has therefore been proposed to refer Basque to the Ligurians, who also dwelt in Spain, or to seek a connection with the Berber language, but no great degree of probability attaches to either view. Ligurian is an unknown quantity, and kinship with Berber speech is at least, not obvious.

In the British Isles, too, the Celts were immigrants. Consequently we have to expect there, also, considerable remains of a native population. To these belong, especially, the wild, never subdued Picts of Scotland. The marked difference which exist to-day between all three of the Celtic-speaking populations cannot escape notice. One cannot despise the suggestion that they are, to a certain extent, Celts only in language, and that they, by race, belong to an older population which adopted Celtic speech. Certainly the Celtic type is popularly represented as undersized and dark, but this conflicts directly with all the evidence of ancient literature and art and is a fancy picture drawn from the modern French, in whom are seen descendants of the Celts. If we keep to facts, we must recognise that the Celtic type, which was much more like the German, disappeared. It is rather the racial type of the primitive population which survives on in the present-day French, and this is not strange. As with the Celts, the Germans, and other conquering peoples, the not very numerous immigrants were absorbed racially by the homogeneous native population, even if they succeeded in teaching their language to the conquered. Celtic tribes had also migrated to Pannonia and the Balkan Peninsula, but they were too few to have been of any great importance. The population of Pannonia seems to have been principally Illyrian, *i.e.* Albanian. In Dacia and the Eastern Balkan peninsula lived the people called Getae or Daci, who belonged to the great Thracian stock. Both peoples belong to the Aryan race, though they never combined to have any historical importance. Unfortunately our information is more than usually meagre, and permits no conclusions concerning the older population which possibly may have existed in these countries.

We are better informed about the remaining province of the Latin half of the Empire, Africa. It has already (p. 192) been observed that the Punic tongue lingered on during the Empire, and that further inland dwelt the Berber tribes, which even to-day preserve their language and their peculiar racial type. Most of St. Augustine's audiences, but not all, understood Punic, which was the language of the peasants in the neighbourhood. Many Christian congregations did not understand Latin, a circumstance which was the cause of many

difficulties in the Church.   A sister of the Emperor Septimius
Severus often embarrassed her brother by her scanty knowledge of Latin.   It was so inconvenient in Roman society, that
he had to send her back to Leptis.   If the Latin polish was so
thin in imperial circles, one can understand that the romanisation of the Empire was much more superficial than has sometimes been stated, even after the country dialects had disappeared and Latin was employed for all monuments and in
literature.

In the Eastern half of the Empire the situation is clear,
except in Asia Minor.   In Egypt and the Semitic East, Greek
culture had never been more than a superficial veneer which
soon wore off.   In Asia Minor the ethnological conditions
were very varied.   In no part of the Empire was there such a
melting-pot of migrating peoples as there.   The political power
of the Hittites had long been crushed, but the race lived on and
probably was merged into the Armenians.   Lydians, Carians,
and Lycians have left inscriptions behind them ; the speech of
the last has been with doubtful success connected with the
Aryan family, whereas Lydian is unique.   Aryan tribes,
Thracians and Celts, came in from outside.   In spite of the
spread of hellenisation, the popular languages survived into
Christian times more persistently than has usually been
imagined ; this, in itself, is a sign of the continued existence of
the races.   Mysian was not yet extinct at the beginning of the
fifth century, and this people seems to have been a mixture of
the Thracians and Lydians.   The famous Isaurian robber
tribes spoke their own language even at the end of the sixth
century.   Similar conditions prevailed in Lycaonia, and
Phrygian survived at least to the fifth century.   Under the
cover of a veneer of Greek civilisation there existed great
differences of speech and nationality, which are mirrored in the
division into those numberless sects, whose chief strength lay
in the native lower classes, which maintained themselves
tenaciously in the heart of Asia Minor.

Apart from Asia Minor, the conditions in the East were
totally different from those in the West.   Although the clergy
had to preach in Punic or Celtic, there never was a Punic or

Celtic translation of the Bible. In the East the Bible was translated into Syrian, Coptic, and Armenian, and a literature, chiefly, it is true, of a religious kind, grew up in the local dialects. Armenians and Copts formed their own alphabets on the basis of the Greek. The higher cultural standpoint and independence of the Oriental were expressed in the fact that the local languages were elevated into the position of literary languages, and the Church fell in with this, though at first it did not encourage it. In the West, local languages were doomed to be the despised speech of the lower classes which the Church did not recognise more than was absolutely necessary. Herein she contributed to romanisation more powerfully than any other factor.

We are moving in an obscure and little-explored region, but even these few scattered instances should be enough to give some idea, not only of the vast number of peoples and races included under the rule of the Roman Emperor, but also of the many variations existing among them. Modern Europe affords us no similar picture. Apart from some few comparatively unimportant intrusive peoples of different race, it presents the picture of an Aryan population, divided certainly into different peoples, but sprung from the same root. The study of European languages is a better test. Kindred languages cover, as we have good reason to assume, great differences of race, though, on the other hand, new races have grown out of the old mixture of peoples.

The great discussion about the origin and division of the Aryan stock has had the effect of obscuring the true character of race-relations in early Europe. We have been influenced, subconsciously and involuntarily, by the preconception of an original unity, which has since been split up. We now realise that as regards the primitive population of Europe we have to start with a multiplicity of different races and languages, which died out or were merged in the intrusive dominant Aryan people. The victorious extension of Aryan speech removed the primitive variants, *e.g.* Etruscan, Ligurian, Iberian, etc., and substituted languages sprung from one original root. This movement was proceeding during the Empire, when the extension of Latin gave it a great impetus

and the hitherto non-Aryan South-Western Europe was assimilated. The process was not completed till the beginning of
the Middle Ages—and not completely then, since Basque still
survives as a reminder of the past.

It is against the background of these relations that we must
view the race-problems of the Roman Empire. As long as the
people of Western Europe remained in their old independence
and primitive condition, the relations were comparatively
stable. The Greek colonists were few in number, and were
antagonistic to, and often in open hostility with, the people in
whose territory they had settled. In Italy, the Latin and
Oscan-Umbrian races expanded at the expense of the older
population. Connections with the Greco-Oriental world were
frail and scanty. Stability was certainly threatened by the
immigrating Celtic tribes, but these kept together in large bodies
which occupied certain districts. In all South-West France
and the greater part of the Spanish Peninsula the primitive
population generally remained in undisturbed occupation. In
some degree immigration was bound to lead to race mixture ;
of this the Celtiberians bear witness by their very name. But
civilisation was undeveloped, communications poor, and the
pressure incurred by the old races was transient ; it might lead
to a limitation of their territory, but it did not threaten their
actual existence. The natural boundaries between the independent and often hostile tribes usually prevented fusion to
any considerable degree, even if the conditions for it were
favourable.

The Roman Empire altered all this. The *Pax Romana* and
the Roman administration effaced the old frontiers. The
different tribes came under one administration, and the same
culture was open to all. The Roman roads facilitated communications, culture, and trade, and the Empire's needs
developed them. Race fusion came about and was promoted
by all those circumstances which tend to draw the citizens of a
civilised state from one place to another within its frontiers.
Men who previously lived and died and reproduced themselves
within the territory of their own people, were jostled against
each other in the great melting-pot which coincided with the

bounds of the Empire, and even people from the outside were drawn into it. This is the fundamental fact the effects of which we have to consider.

The Romans were the bearers of culture and the connecting element in the Empire. Their task was to assimilate to themselves the Empire's many barbarians, to impart to them their culture and raise them up to their own level. If this was to happen, a decided increase in the birth-rate was required, just as when Italy was latinised ; for the world was large and the barbarians numerous. Instead, the numbers of the Roman population constantly declined, and the gaps were filled by provincials. Certainly the outward and visible signs of Roman culture spread widely ; municipal organisation and the Latin language covered large portions of the Empire, but the Roman race could not penetrate it and assimilate its population. Instead, the Roman blood became more and more diluted, and the stock which replaced it had not sufficiently imbibed the Greco-Roman culture. The salt of ancient culture lost its savour. The great crisis came in the third century, when, owing to the incessant wars and economic stress, the old cultural standard declined, and the semi-cultured were raised to the highest positions of society. When some sort of order was restored, the West had been barbarized, and the way opened to that collapse of the Empire which was ultimately brought about by the great migrations of the Germanic peoples. The Germans had no culture to give. Thus the Empire became orientalised, while the growing self-consciousness of the East was expressed in the fact that its native tongues rose to be literary languages.

A race mixture produces not merely a problem of culture, but also one of biology. At the time when a crude, popular Darwinism dominated thought, the theory was seriously maintained that the suspiciousness of emperors and rulers, which removed every one distinguished for independence and originality, and got rid of all those who were above the average, had, by an artificial selection, created a people of slavish soul and intellectual sterility. It is an untenable theory that a selection, whether natural or artificial, can produce such an effect in a few generations. If the whole of the educated class in Sweden were removed, the peasants of Sweden, from whom nine-tenths of them come, could immediately make up the loss, provided that an environment of culture existed in which the new generation could grow up. For culture is tradition. The annihilation of the civilised environment during the economic misery of the third century worked far more destructively than all the judicial murders of the Emperors and the violent acts of the soldiers.

The biological problem is that of race fusion itself, and the study of heredity has taught us to understand its workings, at least in general outline. The human species is in a high degree variable, being surpassed by few other species in that respect. Every race is the product of an historical development, even if the development took place in that primitive period, the history of which has long since been forgotten and was never recorded. The condition of the formation of a race is, that a group of men, whether reckoned in millions or in hundreds, during a long period of time exists in comparative isolation, so that alien and disturbing elements do not affect it. If we assume that this group from the first contained a mixture of mental and physical qualities, the natural conditions under which the group lives tend to favour some of these characteristics and to be unfavourable to others. Natural conditions, though more slowly and not to the same extent, have the same effect as when the breeder consciously interferes to produce and maintain a breed of animals. These conditions work with a strength proportionate to the sphere of action, and the smaller the number of the group the greater is the inbreeding. The final result depends more on the qualities which are latent in the race and which develop in the course of time than on the outward environment. Why it is that certain races may be very suited to the conditions of life in the land they inhabit, but are incapable of rising higher, and why other races form states and create culture, is a riddle, concealed in that darkest of all darknesses— the human soul and the qualities of the soul, the variability of intelligence and will, and other race qualities.

Primitive conditions are favourable to the formation of a

multiplicity of races. The population is sparse and divided into small groups, and communications play a very unimportant part. The tribes either live in constant enmity or as strangers to each other, without much intercourse, each in their own territories. A fact of fundamental importance for the development of society and race is the claim of the tribe to the possession of its territory, which seems to be instinctive in the nature of man, as in that of certain animals. Strangers who intrude into the territory of the tribe are driven away or killed. The primitive tribe keeps itself free of alien blood till, with growing culture, slavery appears and is first applied to women. But in the most primitive conditions even this form of race mixture is not very effective or important, since neighbouring tribes are often already closely related.

What we are entitled to expect in primitive conditions is a multiplicity of races with slightly differing characteristics. In certain cases, the possession of some special quality may result in a particular race asserting itself in the struggle for existence with other races, and obtaining a pre-eminent position over wide territories. Again, migrations, caused by over-population or restlessness, may bring a foreign race into a country. If we take the two last-mentioned possibilities into account, the state of things in Europe and Africa before the Roman domination is exactly what we might expect to find. In Africa the Berbers dwelt alongside of the immigrant Carthaginians; in West Europe the Iberians and Ligurians alongside of the immigrant Celts and a number of tribes of whose racial affinities we know nothing. Most varied of all is the race-map of Italy, because our information about the older tribes there is more plentiful. Besides the primitive population and the immigrant Aryan tribes, we have the Etruscan people, whose language shows that it cannot have had affinities with any other people, and whose other racial characteristics were peculiar. The Balkan Peninsula and the countries south of the Danube have an Aryan population, but possibly, also, remains of an older one, suppressed by the immigrants. Asia Minor had been from time immemorial a wrestling ground of different races. Syria had a Semitic population, whose tribes were mixed with

each other mainly owing to the policy of the Assyrians towards
their subject population. In Egypt the old stable race was
preserved without being greatly influenced by the foreign
masters of the country.

When, under the protection of the Roman Empire, all these
races—and these are only the most important of those about
which we know something—were blended together, there arose
an unchecked " mongrelising." But that process involved
dangers, the reality of which cosmopolitanism will not recognise,
but which are confirmed by the study of heredity.

The race is a group of men with specific hereditary
characteristics, defined and developed by natural selection.
There are inferior races and superior races. A cross between
two races, which differ from one another beyond a certain
degree, involves a racial deterioration, at least from the point of
view of the superior stock. The dislike of mixed marriages
(*e.g.* between negroes and whites in America) is therefore fully
justified from the standpoint of biology. The situation becomes
even more dangerous, when the races differ so widely that a
crossing brings with it the risk of race-deterioration, yet not
widely enough for a natural repulsion for mixed marriages to
assert itself. And, moreover, this repulsion, as is well known,
is an extremely frail defence against race-mixture.

The intermingling, by which a higher race is swamped by a
lower, is, however, not the only, nor even the greatest danger.
Physically and mentally a normal pure stock forms a definite
type, which, from the homogeneity and unity of its characteristics, asserts itself in the direction in which those characteristics point. If these characteristics tend to evolve a state or
to develop culture, as was the case with the Greeks and Romans,
they create standards for the culture and life of the state, and
are regulated by fixed custom and law. But the result of
crossing is a mosaic of the hereditary characteristics of the
races in question, in which pure chance unites different hereditary characteristics from different quarters in different ways.
Nor is this all. Characteristics which previously were latent in
one or other of the races that are crossed, may become dominant
and affect the products of the crossing in ways that are manifold

and unaccountable. The uniformity and harmony of the race and the individual are abolished, and even personality becomes unbalanced. The individuals who are born of this crossing are without a fixed type ; from the psychological point of view they lack stability, and oscillate precariously between antagonistic and varying hereditary characteristics. They may often possess brilliant intellectual endowments unsupported by moral strength. This biological condition is endangered still more when, as in the Roman Empire, the firm frame of culture is loosened and when even spiritual life is affected by ferment and revolution.

Mongrels have a poor reputation. One need only point to the Levantines, Eurasians, Mestizos, and Mulattos as a proof of this. It is customary to refer the lack of stamina and the bad name of cross-breeds to the unhappy conditions under which they grow up—neglected, unstable, an object of repulsion to both their paternal and maternal stocks. But this is but a superficial, and not the full, explanation. Deep down we recognise the destructive effect of mixed breeding on personality. The Roman Empire became increasingly a realm of mongrels, most notably in the mother-country, Italy, into which people gathered from every quarter, and to a greater degree in the higher and refined classes of the population than in the lower, which could not travel or leave their birthplace with such facility. Through the medium of the army, through trade and general communications, cross-breeding spread to all corners of the provinces which were under the rule of the Roman Emperor. The rapidity with which the process went on cannot be wondered at. In contrast to race formation, hybridisation works immediately in the first generation, and is naturally accelerated by cross-breeding from the hybrids. The rapidity with which it sets its marks on a nation depends only on the extent to which it takes place, and we know that it went on on a very large scale in the Roman Empire.

Hybridisation on a considerable scale involves the break up of superior races into a heterogeneous and loose mass lacking stable spiritual and moral standards. This is, of itself, a sufficient explanation for the collapse of ancient culture and the

Roman Empire. But even if mixture of peoples in its immediate results produces chaos, it is not the final result. Out of
chaos a new race may arise with valuable hereditary characteristics, which render it capable of building up anew what has
been destroyed. We know the conditions necessary for this.
They are, that cross-breeding should cease and the nation be
isolated, so that the mixture gets time to settle, and a new
race has a chance to be definitely characterised by the given
conditions. This had happened once already at the beginning
of antiquity. The ancient cultural nations, the Italians and
Greeks, entered the land that became theirs during the second
millennium and settled among a population of different race.
The Italians and Greeks of historic times were, in consequence,
the products of a race mixture. The course of this development is better known in Greece than Italy, and in it we can
follow the process in its broad outlines. The time between
the Mycenaean Age and the beginning of historical times is a
dark period. Culture declined prodigiously. Localities were
isolated from each other. The proof is to be found in the
sharply marked differentiations of the geometric style of design
which was characteristic of each district and each island, whereas
the Mycenaean style was constantly uniform over all Greece,
and even over the whole Mediterranean basin. Every little
ancient city shut itself off from its neighbours as a sovereign
state. Within the narrow limits of the city state, inbreeding
regularly prevailed, and was intensified by the smallness of the
cities. The cities did not recognise a connection with a woman
of another city as a lawful marriage. It is significant that
in Attica, even after the reforms of Cleisthenes, domicile did
not change with change of actual residence, but was inherited
from generation to generation. This separation and isolation
stamped and stabilised the race, as did the separation of villages
and neighbourhoods in the north. In this way arose the
peoples who created ancient culture and state life.

A similar process was repeated, only on a much greater
scale, after the fall of the Roman Empire. Intellectual culture
was confined to a small number and to a small compass. Communications ceased ; the Roman roads were disused ; society

was broken up into small self-sufficient districts—we usually call this phenomenon feudalism—and the population became tied to the soil. Hence, once again, primitive conditions came into being, in which men sought their wives from their own kin. The peoples and races of modern Europe grew up in the Middle Ages, and found political expression in the modern national states, whose frontiers, even to-day, place an effective obstacle in the way of an unchecked mixture of people of that harmful kind which actually was the cause of the fall of the Roman Empire. As is so often the case in history, Nemesis ordained that the consequences of victory should be destructive to the victors, who were first engulfed and finally disappeared in the mass of the vanquished.

INDEX

369

2 B

THE END

PLATE 1

AUGUSTUS AS " IMPERATOR " OR COMMANDER-IN-CHIEF
From the Villa of Livia at Prima Porta near Rome

PLATE 2

THE FAMILY OF AUGUSTUS

Relief from the "Altar of Peace," dedicated in the year 9 B.C.

N.B.—*The identity of the persons is uncertain. In the upper panel the lady en face may be Julia, the daughter of Augustus, and the man next her, Tiberius, her husband. In the lower panel, the lady on the left may be Antonia Minor, niece of the Emperor, with her husband Drusus, in military costume. The lady behind him may be Antonia, the grandmother of Nero.*

PLATE 3

THE TRIUMPH AFTER THE VICTORY OVER THE JEWS

*From the Triumphal Arch of Titus, showing the Seven-branched Candlestick
and the Table of Shewbread*

MAIL-CLAD ROMAN CAVALRY AND DACIANS

From the Column of Trajan

PLATE 4

NERO (A.D. 54–68)

CLAUDIUS (A.D. 41–54)

PLATE 5

ROMAN LADY

Illustrating coiffure of the age of Trajan

PLOTINA, WIFE OF TRAJAN

PLATE 6

MARCUS AURELIUS RECEIVING THE SUBMISSION OF THE GERMANS
Relief from a Triumphal Arch (restored)

PLATE 7

CARACALLA (A.D. 211–217)

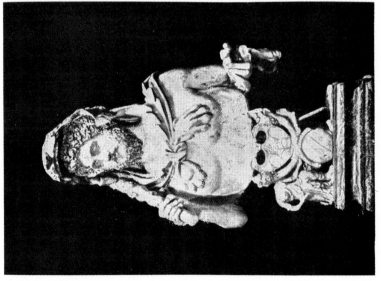

COMMODUS WEARING THE ATTRIBUTES OF HERCULES

PLATE 8

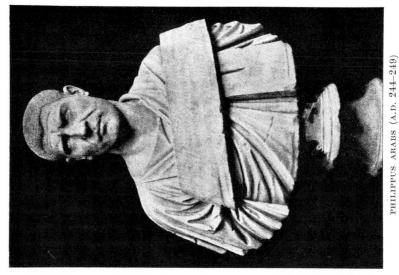

PHILIPPUS ARABS (A.D. 244–249)

MAXIMINUS THRAX (A.D. 235–238)

PLATE 9

GALLIENUS (A.D. 253–268)

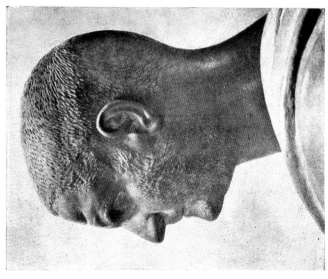

TREBONIANUS GALLUS (A.D. 251–253)

PLATE 10

CONSTANTINE AS DEFENDER OF THE FAITH
(Ivory Diptych)

ANTONINUS PIUS
(A.D. 138–161)

DIOCLETIAN (A.D. 284–305)

PLATE 11

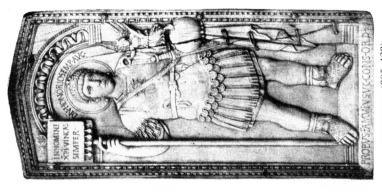

HONORIUS (395–423)

HOLDING THE SYMBOLS OF VICTORY

VALENTINIAN I (A.D. 364–375)

JULIAN THE APOSTATE

(A.D. 360–363)

PLATE 12

TRIUMPH OF TIBERIUS

From a Cameo. Upper register shows Augustus enthroned with attributes of Jupiter : beside him the goddess Roma. Tiberius descends from a chariot to do him homage.

Lower register shows Roman soldiers with German prisoners, erecting a trophy.

INSCRIPTION OF LA TURBIE (restored) COMMEMORATING AUGUSTUS' VICTORY
OVER THE ALPINE TRIBES

PLATE 13

THE THEATRE OF MILETUS

THE TEMPLE OF THE SUN AT GERASA

PLATE 14

REMAINS OF THE GREAT TEMPLE AT BAALBEK

PLATE 15

VIEW OF TIMGAD

PLATE 16

MAIN STREET OF TIMGAD, SHOWING TRIUMPHAL ARCH OF HADRIAN

PLATE 17

THE " PORTA NIGRA " AT TRÈVES

ROMAN GATE AT AUGUSTODUNUM (AUTUN)

PLATE 18

RELIEF SHOWING THE HARBOUR AT OSTIA

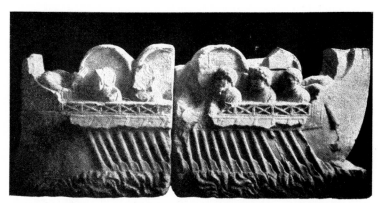

RIVER BOAT ON THE MOSELLE LADEN WITH WINE CASKS
From a Sepulchral Monument at Neumagen near Trèves

PLATE 19

THE " PONT DU GARD " AQUEDUCT AT NÎMES

REMAINS OF ROMAN BRIDGE AT NARNI

PLATE 20

RESTORATION OF ROMAN FORT AT SAALBURG

PALISADE AND WATCH-HOUSES OF THE "LIMES"
From the Column of Marcus Aurelius

PLATE 21

THE EMPEROR VALERIAN BEFORE SAPOR I
Rock Carving at Naksh-i-Rustam

AHURA MAZDA GIVING THE RING, THE SYMBOL OF POWER, TO SAPOR I
Rock Carving at Naksh-i-Rustam

PLATE 22

PORTA MAGGIORE, BUILT BY CLAUDIUS AND RESTORED BY VESPASIAN AND TITUS

AQUEDUCT (AQUA CLAUDIA) IN THE CAMPAGNA NEAR ROME

PLATE 23

BRICKS INSCRIBED WITH THE STAMPS OF THE LEGIONS

INSTITUTION OF THE ALIMENTARY FOUNDATION

Relief from the rostra of Trajan's Forum. On the left the Emperor pro-mulgates the edict, on the right a woman holding child in her arms stands before the Emperor.

PLATE 24

A GERMAN WOMAN

The so-called Thusnelda

PLATE 25

IMPERIAL COIN PORTRAITS.

1. The Emperor Augustus (31 B.C.–A.D. 14).
2. The Emperor Claudius (A.D. 41–54).
3. The Emperor Trajan (A.D. 98–117).
4. Hadrian's wife, Sabina.

PLATE 26

IMPERIAL COIN PORTRAITS.

1. The Emperor Hadrian (A.D. 117–138).

2. The reverse, showing the figure of Britannia (the prototype of Britannia on our pennies), commemorates his activities in Britain. (S.C. = *Senatus Consulto*, " by decree of the Senate " indicates a bronze issue; the other coins figured in these plates are gold.)

3. The Emperor Antoninus Pius (A.D. 138–161).

4. The reverse shows the figure of Jupiter Stator, holding a thunderbolt.

PLATE 27

RELIEF FROM THE ARA PACIS, ROME.

The scene is of a public sacrifice on a State occasion. The central figure is probably that of the Pontifex Maximus (Lepidus):
the young matron on the right is probably Julia, daughter of Augustus, the little boy her son Lucius Caesar; on her right is her
husband Tiberius, the future Emperor. The stately figures convey a strong sense of Roman formal dignity.

PLATE 28

VERULAMIUM · THE ROMAN THEATRE

PLATE 29

A ROMAN PROVINCIAL CITY.

The Forum at Timgad in Roman Africa.

PLATE 30

PUBLIC BUILDINGS IN A PROVINCIAL TOWN.

Arles in Roman France (see p. 234): the theatre is seen in the left foreground.

PLATE 31

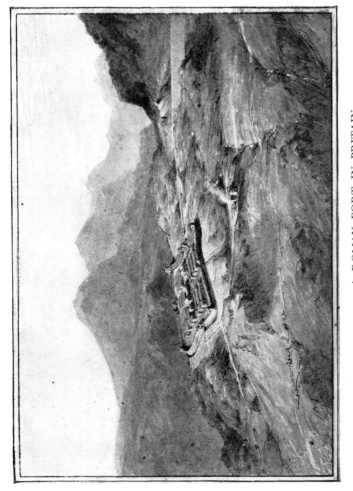

A ROMAN FORT IN BRITAIN.

Hardknot Castle, a commanding site in Cumberland: an imaginary reconstruction. Below the fort is the bath-house; to the right is the parade ground.

PLATE 32

ROMAN LETTERING.

An inscription, very finely cut (the letters are eight inches high), from Uroconium (Wroxeter), a Roman city near Shrewsbury. The full text runs IMP(ERATORI) CAES(ARI) DIVI TRAIANI PARTHICI FIL(IO) DIVI NERVAE NEPOTI TRAIANO HADRIANO AUG(USTO) PONTIFICI MAXIMO TRIB(UNICIAE) POT(ESTATI) XIIII CO(N)S(ULI) III P(ATRI) P(ATRIAE) CIVITAS CORNOVIORUM ("To the Emperor, Caesar, son of the deified Trajanus Parthicus, grandson of the deified Nerva, Trajanus Hadrianus Augustus, Pontifex Maximus, in the fourteenth year of his reign, thrice Consul, Father of his Country, the community of the Cornovii (erected this)").